THE LIBRARY OF CHRISTIAN CLASSICS

THE LIBRARY OF CHRISTIAN CLASSICS

VOLUME VIII

AUGUSTINE: LATER WORKS

THE LIBRARY OF CHRISTIAN CLASSICS

Volume VIII

AUGUSTINE: LATER WORKS

*Selected and translated
with Introductions by*

JOHN BURNABY
Regius Professor of Divinity,
University of Cambridge

PHILADELPHIA

THE WESTMINSTER PRESS

Published simultaneously in Great Britain and the United States of America
by the S.C.M. Press, Ltd., London, and The Westminster Press, Philadelphia.

First published MCMLV

Library of Congress Catalog Card Number . . 55–5022

Printed in the United States of America

GENERAL EDITORS' PREFACE

The Christian Church possesses in its literature an abundant and incomparable treasure. But it is an inheritance that must be reclaimed by each generation. THE LIBRARY OF CHRISTIAN CLASSICS is designed to present in the English language, and in twenty-six volumes of convenient size, a selection of the most indispensable Christian treatises written prior to the end of the sixteenth century.

The practice of giving circulation to writings selected for superior worth or special interest was adopted at the beginning of Christian history. The canonical Scriptures were themselves a selection from a much wider literature. In the Patristic era there began to appear a class of works of compilation (often designed for ready reference in controversy) of the opinions of well-reputed predecessors, and in the Middle Ages many such works were produced. These medieval anthologies actually preserve some noteworthy materials from works otherwise lost.

In modern times, with the increasing inability even of those trained in universities and theological colleges to read Latin and Greek texts with ease and familiarity, the translation of selected portions of earlier Christian literature into modern languages has become more necessary than ever; while the wide range of distinguished books written in vernaculars such as English makes selection there also needful. The efforts that have been made to meet this need are too numerous to be noted here, but none of these collections serves the purpose of the reader who desires a library of representative treatises spanning the Christian centuries as a whole. Most of them embrace only the age of the Church Fathers, and some of them have long been out of print. A fresh translation of a work already translated may shed much new light upon its meaning. This is true even of Bible translations despite the work of many experts through the centuries. In some instances old translations have been adopted in this series, but wherever necessary or desirable, new ones have been made. Notes have been supplied where these were needed to explain the author's meaning. The introductions provided for the several treatises and extracts will, we believe, furnish welcome guidance.

JOHN BAILLIE
JOHN T. McNEILL
HENRY P. VAN DUSEN

CONTENTS

THE SPIRIT AND THE LETTER

TEN HOMILIES ON THE FIRST EPISTLE
GENERAL OF ST. JOHN

PREFACE

The three works of St. Augustine translated in this volume, in whole or in part, were all published in the years between 410 and 420, when Augustine was in his late fifties or early sixties, still at the height of his powers, and not yet wholly absorbed by the Pelagian controversy, which forced him to imprison his doctrine of Grace in a system of rigid logic—the "Augustinianism" whose authority has weighed so heavily and so unhappily upon Christian thought, though it has never been accepted by the *consensus fidelium*.

The title, *Augustine: Later Works*, might more properly be applied to the writings in which this system was worked out after the condemnation of Pelagianism in 418. It has been chosen as the simplest general description of a group of works nearly contemporaneous with one another, and separated by an interval of some twenty-five years from most of those included in the volume of his *Earlier Writings* in the present series.

The *De Trinitate*, though begun perhaps as early as 400, was not finished before 417. Augustine's own words in the dedicatory letter to Aurelius, Bishop of Carthage, are "I was young when I began it, an old man when I published it"—which suggests an even longer period of composition, though in Roman usage a man of forty was still a *juvenis*. We may take the year 410 as an approximate *terminus a quo* for the writing of the second half of the treatise, which begins with Book VIII, and contains much the most original and interesting part of Augustine's thought on the subject. There has been room for a complete translation only of Books VIII, IX, X, XIV, and XV; but the Introduction attempts to survey the whole work, and summaries are given of the argument of Books XI-XIII.

The *De Spiritu et Littera* was written in 412, soon after the Pelagian doctrines had gained notoriety in Africa by the condemnation of Caelestius, but before Augustine had been led to study the writings of Pelagius and embark upon their refutation in detail. Thus it has the advantage of offering a positive statement of the writer's understanding of St. Paul, rather than a controversial argument against Pelagianism. It is translated in full.

The *Tractatus in Epistolam Iohannis* were almost certainly delivered at Eastertide in the year 415, when Augustine's most pressing concern was the final elimination of Donatism in his own diocese. Although direct references to the Donatists are not more than occasional, the *Homilies* can only be appreciated against the background of the schism; and this background is sketched in the Introduction. The *Homilies* have been considerably abbreviated in translation, but it is hoped that this has been done without serious loss.

The selection has been made in order to provide examples of the finest works of Augustine, as speculative and mystical theologian, as *Doctor Gratiae*, and as preacher of Charity. The translator's aim has been to reproduce three acknowledged masterpieces of "the greatest man who ever wrote Latin,"[1] in an English which will not be intolerably irksome to read. This can only be achieved by a fairly liberal though not unscrupulous use of paraphrase, and (in the *Homilies* especially) by a fairly severe pruning of the preacher's luxuriance in rhetorical question and repetition. Reference to previous translations has been deliberately avoided: there is very seldom any difficulty in seeing what Augustine's Latin means.

In the translation of Augustine's Biblical quotations, his own text has been carefully followed. It must be remembered that he used one or other of the Old Latin versions current in Africa when he became Bishop. Jerome's revised version (the Vulgate) became available by the year 400. In the New Testament it was not conspicuously different from the Old Latin, and Augustine regularly used it for the Gospels. But he was most reluctant to substitute Jerome's version of the Old Testament, made direct from the Hebrew, for the Old Latin based on the Septuagint which for Augustine was an inspired text. Thus his Old Testament quotations often differ widely from the versions with which we are familiar.

[1] The judgement of Professor Alexander Souter of Aberdeen in *J.T.S.*, Vol. XI, p. 150.

There has not been space for more than a minimum of explanatory notes, but the separate Introductions to each work are designed to make them reasonably intelligible to the ordinary reader—who must not be unduly discouraged, in the case of the *De Trinitate*, by its author's gloomy prophecy, in a letter to his brother-Bishop Evodius (Ep. 169), that "few people would be able to understand it."

The text used is the Benedictine, in its second Paris edition of 1836–8, except for the *De Spiritu et Littera*, which is the only work of the three to have been issued in a critical modern text in the Vienna *Corpus Scriptorum Ecclesiasticorum Latinorum*. For convenience of reference to the original, the numeration of sections follows that of the Benedictine edition.

J. B.

Cambridge
  St. Augustine's Day, 1953

The Trinity

INTRODUCTION

AT THE BEGINNING OF THE FOURTH CENTURY, THE
Christian religion, which had for so long been regarded
as a menace to the unity and stability of the Roman
Empire, was adopted by a sudden *volte-face* of its persecutor as
the religion of the State, to serve the very purpose which it had
been deemed to threaten. That purpose could only be served by
a Church at unity in itself, possessed of a clearly defined and
universally accepted system of belief. The Church was therefore
compelled to think out and formulate the doctrine of God
involved in the Christian gospel. This was indeed a process
which had been going on in the Church from the first. Throughout the second and third centuries, the Apostolic tradition had
had to meet the challenge of rational thought. The first great
essay in systematic theology had been made by Origen at
Alexandria, the intellectual centre of the Empire. But the
speculative system of Origen had not claimed the status of
"orthodoxy," and had encouraged rather than restricted the
independent activity of Christian thinkers. So it was an attempt
to rationalize the Christian doctrine of God, made by "heretics"
who could claim to be followers of the great Alexandrian, that
demanded from the Church, at the critical moment of her
summons to give a religion to the Empire, a sustained effort of
her common mind.

The Arians believed themselves to be contending for Biblical
and rational monotheism. The Church had always preached the
one God against the polytheistic cults of Greece and Rome; yet
its own faith and worship had been given to Three. When
reason faced the apparent inconsistency, it was natural that
some should take for their starting-point the axiom of divine

unity, while others began with the traditional expressions of Christian religious experience. The former approach led in the direction of the Sabellian solution—representing the one God as successively revealed in three temporal forms of activity: God is three "for us," as we learn to know him in time, but eternally one "in himself." The latter would try to preserve the "monarchy," the unitary divine rule, by subordinating the Son to the Father and the Spirit to the Son, while maintaining the real and eternal distinction of the Three. In Arianism, this subordination was carried to the point of asserting a difference not only of status but of essential nature between Father and Son: absolute Godhead was reserved to the Father alone as Creator; Son and Spirit are his creatures. The purpose of the momentous decision of the Council of Nicaea, making the confession of the Son's "consubstantiality" with the Father a test of orthodoxy for office in the Church, was to insist that there can be no such degrees of divinity: if Christ be God, he must be God *in the same sense* as the Father. But the test word itself was so ambiguous as to arouse suspicion of a Sabellian intention; and it took half a century of controversy to reach a common consent on the two fundamentals of Trinitarian doctrine: that Son and Spirit must be confessed as alike truly God, God without reservation, and yet that Father, Son, and Spirit are not mere names of one divine Being or "Person." It was the work of the great Cappadocian Fathers, Basil of Caesarea and the two Gregories of Nyssa and Nazianzus, to incorporate these two principles in a Christian doctrine of the one God which could be held without self-contradiction. They distinguished between the substance or essence of Godhead, one and indivisible, and the three forms of existence or objective embodiments of the one divine essence which constitute the "Persons." They were well aware that this looked like a doctrine of three Gods—three particular "subsistences" (hypostases), each possessing the common "essence" or nature of Godhead; and they endeavoured to defend themselves against the charge of tritheism by maintaining (*a*) that the Godhead is one *in operation*, without any division or separation of functions, not as a harmony but as a single agency, and (*b*) that the "Persons" are one *in being*, inasmuch as Son and Spirit are both derived, both spring eternally from one divine origin which is the Father.

This was as far as Trinitarian theology had advanced at the end of the fourth century. The Cappadocians were constructive theologians; but their writings no less than those of Athanasius

were the product of controversy and controversial in form. Of
Augustine's Latin predecessors, Hilary of Pictavium called his
treatise *De Trinitate*, but devoted it entirely to establishing by
anti-Arian argument the true Godhead of the Son; and the
same may be said of the *De Fide* of Ambrose. In Augustine's *De
Trinitate* there is scarcely any element of controversy. He begins
by taking the Catholic doctrine of God for granted: observing
(Bk. I, 7 (iv)) that his predecessors have taught that "Father,
Son, and Holy Ghost mean a divine unity in an inseparable
equality of one and the same substance, and therefore are not
three Gods but one God: though the Father has begotten the
Son, and therefore he who is Father is not Son; the Son is begotten from the Father, and therefore he who is Son is not
Father; the Holy Spirit is neither Father nor Son, but only
Spirit of Father and Son, himself co-equal with both and belonging to the unity of the Trinity." And he goes on to say that
not the Trinity but the Son alone was incarnate, crucified,
risen, and ascended; not the Trinity but the Spirit alone descended upon Christ at the baptism and upon the apostles at
Pentecost; and not the Trinity but the Father pronounced the
words "Thou art my Son" at baptism and transfiguration. Yet
Father, Son, and Holy Spirit are inseparable in their *working* as
well as in their *being*.

The first half of the *De Trinitate* deals with the problems raised
by the Catholic doctrines (*a*) that God is one, and that the whole
Trinity is active in all divine operations, and (*b*) that the three
"Persons" are distinct from one another not only for our apprehension but in their eternal being.

Books I–IV are concerned with the interpretation of Scripture on the assumption of the equal Godhead of all three "Persons." When Scripture texts referring to Christ imply subordination of the Son to the Father, this is generally to be
explained on the lines which Athanasius had laid down: the
Son as incarnate has the "form of a servant" as well as the "form
of God," and when Scripture speaks of him as inferior to the
Father the reference is to his human nature only (Bk. I).
Augustine allows, however, that in some cases the reference may
be to the "form of God," inasmuch as the Son's Godhead is
itself derived from the Father: here Augustine follows the lead
of the Cappadocians. But Scripture tells us of "missions" of Son
and Spirit in temporal history. These signify visible manifestations of the second and third "Persons," and are not to be
limited to incarnation and Pentecost, for the Word and the

Spirit have been active in the world since its creation. Before Augustine, the Old Testament theophanies were almost universally interpreted by the Fathers as appearances of the Son—on the ground that the Father is essentially invisible. Augustine believes that we have no reason so to limit their significance: the whole Trinity is essentially invisible to the eye of flesh, but as God became visible to men in the incarnate Word through his human body, so (we may believe) for the manifestations of himself recorded in the Old Testament, whether as Trinity or as one or other of the several "Persons," he used angelic agencies, whose instruments were the natural and material potentialities implanted by God himself in the world of his creation (Bks. II and III). The supreme mission of the Son is of course the incarnation (Bk. IV). Augustine states its purpose in three aspects: (i) to remedy men's pride and men's despair by displaying at once the depth of their unworthiness and the greatness of God's love; (ii) to win for them a restoration of life both spiritual and bodily by the sacrifice of the Saviour's death; (iii) to restore them from division and dispersion into unity, through incorporation in the one Mediator. For this purpose the Son was manifested in the temporal and visible form of a creature—which is what his "mission" means. Similarly the Holy Spirit is manifested at Pentecost and in the Church's life. And it was "fitting," both that the first mission should be of that divine "Person" who is eternally begotten or derived from the Father, and that the second should be of the "Person" who proceeds eternally from both Father and Son. But no inequality in the Trinity is thereby implied.

In Books V–VII, Augustine passes from the interpretation of Scripture, the supreme authority on which the Catholic faith is based, to the formulation of the faith in terms of the logical and metaphysical categories which he shares like the Greek Fathers with contemporary philosophy—especially the Neo-Platonism of Plotinus. The metaphysics of Plotinus distinguished within the eternal world of spiritual reality a "trinity" of the One, Mind, and Soul or Life, in which Soul forms the link between spirit and matter, eternal and temporal. Soul is both one and many, and is itself product of the activity of self-conscious Mind —mind thinking itself; whereas Mind in turn derives from the ultimate and absolute Unity in which there is no distinction of subject and object. The One is "beyond being," because to say that the One "is" would be to give it a second attribute in addition to its one-ness. "Being," therefore, for Plotinus, begins with

Mind. For Augustine as a Christian, the one eternal Being or "substance" is God himself—the God whose name is "I am." Of this divine substance the essential marks are unity and changelessness, which are but negations of the creaturely character that belongs to all else that exists. Creaturely substance as such is not "simple" but composite, and subject to change because of its composite nature. Change, in a man, means the loss of some attribute, physical, mental, or moral, which he formerly possessed, but the loss of which does not involve his ceasing to be a man. Such attributes are called "accidental." God cannot change without ceasing to be God; for the substance of God is not compounded of parts, but is absolutely one or "simple." This dogma of the divine "simplicity" as the logical ground both of unity and changelessness is common to Augustine and Greek theology in general. It is expressed in the formula "God is what he has," and corresponds to the assertion of the medieval scholastics that in God essence and existence coincide. The being of God is not like the being of a man separate from any of his attributes: in technical terms, God can have no accidental attributes. And since God's being is absolutely "simple," there is no real difference between one divine attribute and another: God's power, God's wisdom, God's goodness, are one and the same thing.

Book V introduces, on the background of this metaphysic of substance, Augustine's important distinction between substantive and relative terms in the theology of the Trinity. In the logic of substance, it is true that all "accidents" imply the possibility of change, and cannot therefore be predicated of the divine substance. Arians argued from this that the terms "unbegotten" and "begotten" in their application to what is divine must denote substance, and being contradictory must involve a difference in the substance of Father and Son. But (Augustine replies) it is not true that all predicates applicable to God denote substance: they may denote eternal and unchangeable relations. "Begotten" is the same as "Son," and Sonship is relative to Fatherhood: "unbegotten" simply negates the relation of Sonship. The third "Person" is related to the other two as gift to giver; and this relation denotes an eternal potentiality in the Godhead, of "giveableness" even before the existence of creatures to whom the Spirit might be given. Terms such as "Lord," which have no meaning apart from the created world, denote an "accident" not in God but in the creature's relation to him.

Books VI and VII discuss the application of substantive

terms to one or other of the "Persons" as such. Christ is called the Wisdom of God; but it cannot be maintained (as some of the orthodox opponents of Arianism had done) that wisdom belongs to the Father only by his generation of the Son. For wisdom is a term denoting substance, and all such terms belong to Godhead as Godhead: God "is what he has"; in him to be is to be wise. The Trinity is not a "triplicity," an organism of parts: the equality of the "Persons" means that each possesses the whole substance of Godhead. The Son is therefore Wisdom from Wisdom, just as he is God from God. Scripture applies the term especially to the Son, inasmuch as his incarnation provides the pattern of the divine wisdom which men are called to follow. Augustine discusses at length the theological terms used to denote the distinctions within the Godhead, and finds that these terms are inevitably unsatisfactory. Both the Greek *hypostasis* and the Latin *persona* in ordinary usage are terms of substance, not relation. In the proper sense, the Person of God is his essential being, his substance. We can only use the term "Person" in its Trinitarian application *faute de mieux*, and must always bear in mind that in the theology of the Trinity it does not bear its ordinary sense: its implication is negative—the Father is *not* the Son, etc.—rather than positive.

It is clear that in this sifting of the proper application of theological terms, Augustine has so far not advanced beyond the position of the Cappadocian Fathers. He has not maintained—what indeed would be meaningless—that the Persons of the Trinity *are* relations; for he knows that a relation is nothing but a logical term predicable of that which is or possesses substance. He has simply pointed out that what differentiates the divine substance as it exists in the several Persons of the Trinity is a specific form of relation which in no way affects the "substantial" equality of the Persons. But he has done no more than the Cappadocians to make the unity of the divine substance in three Persons intelligible. The substance of Godhead might still be conceived, not as a concrete reality, but as an abstract or general notion, realized only in three individual beings who are in fact three Gods.

The purpose of the second half of the *De Trinitate* (Bks. VIII–XV) is not to work out a speculative re-formulation of Trinitarian doctrine, but to seek for an "understanding of what has been believed." It must be noted that faith, the act of believing, throughout our treatise has the meaning of acceptance of the Christian gospel as proclaimed on the authority of the Church.

Augustine is aware that Christian faith involves the trustful commitment of the whole self to Christ; but it is plain to him that such personal commitment must be grounded on acceptance both of the historical facts of the gospel and of the authoritative interpretation of these facts by the Church. And this acceptance is necessarily the acceptance of a testimony which is deemed sufficient—whether it be the teaching of Scripture or that of tradition. At the beginning of Book VIII, Augustine announces his intention of endeavouring to present the content of faith to the grasp of the understanding "by a more inward way." This "more inward way" is that which (as he tells us in the VIIth Book of the *Confessions*) he had been taught to follow by his reading of the "books of the Platonists"—the way of "returning into himself" and looking for God "within." It is the method of introspection of which Augustine was so great a master. He believes himself fully justified in seeking in the nature of the human soul for a pointer towards the understanding of the Trinity. For it is a matter of *faith* that God is manifested in "the things that are made" (Rom.1:20), and that of all the things that are made it is man and man only that is made in the image of God. But just because Augustine is resolved, whether his search for understanding prove successful or not, to hold fast to the *data* which faith provides, the search itself cannot be free or unprejudiced. *He knows already what he is looking for*: his discoveries are in large measure predetermined. If there is indeed an image of God in the human soul, it *must* be a unity in trinity: it must, that is, disclose three realities which are "consubstantial" in the sense that one and the same substance is exhibited in all of them "without any difference or inequality"; and these three must be distinct from one another solely in virtue of their mutual relations. These relations, again, cannot be relations of parts to a whole; for in that case the one substance could not be present in each of them in its entirety. It is therefore not surprising that we find a tendency, in the course of the psychological discussions which occupy so much of the Books with which we are concerned, to leap to the desired conclusion and translate psychological into theological terms. But it says much for the honesty and integrity of Augustine's introspective research, that at the end of it he is careful (in Bk. XV) to emphasize and elaborate not the perfection of the image but its inadequacy. At the best, we see God in his image *per speculum in aenigmate*—"through a glass, darkly." To speak of Augustine's *doctrine* of the Trinity as "psychological" and therefore unitarian in tendency is seriously to misapprehend his purpose. As we have already seen, he will employ the term *persona* of the distinctions within the Godhead only with the reservation that it is no more than an indispensable label. But that is because "person" in normal usage denotes an independently existing substance and therefore can properly be predicated only of God as God, not of the divine being as differentiated in a system of relations. How far Augustine is in fact from conceiving the Godhead as uni-personal, is shown by the way in which he dwells (in Bk. XV) upon this very point of difference between image and original. The human trinity, he says, "belongs" to an Ego, to a single "person": the "Persons" of the divine Trinity are not one but three, although "the Trinity of three Persons is more inseparable than the imaged trinity of one" (XV, 43 (xxiii)). It is not necessary to suppose that here Augustine has forgotten his own caveat against the application of the word "person" in its ordinary sense to the members of the divine Trinity, and has slipped into employing it univocally of the human and the divine. He is insisting that whereas in the human individual the ultimate reality is one *and not three*, this is not to be said of God: in the divine being three-ness and one-ness are both equally ultimate. In Christian theology neither is unity prior to multiplicity (as in Neo-Platonism), nor is multiplicity prior to unity (as in any form of tritheism).

In the *Retractations*, Augustine says that his treatise *De Vera Religione*, the last work which he wrote as a layman (i.e., about the year 390) was designed to present "true religion" as the worship of "the one true God, that is, the Trinity of Father, Son, and Holy Spirit." In the last chapter of this work, of which the philosophy is still strongly Neo-Platonist, he had asserted his worship of "one God, the one beginning of all things, the wisdom by which every wise soul is wise, and the gift by which all things blessed are blessed . . . the Trinity of one substance . . . the beginning to which we return, the form (or pattern) we follow after, the grace by which we are reconciled . . . the one God whose creation gives us life, through whose re-forming we live wisely, by the love and enjoyment of whom we live blessedly."

This is the basic Trinitarian pattern which Augustine retained all through his theological development. There is a brief reference to it some ten years later in the *Confessions* (XIII, 12 (xi)), where he calls his readers to contemplate the triad of being, knowing, and willing *in themselves*—a triad which is indeed "far other" than the divine Trinity, but in which there is nevertheless "an inseparable life—*one life, one mind, one essence*" (this phrase recurs in *De Trin.*, X, 18 (xi))—"an inseparable distinction which is still a distinction." He plays on the same theme with elaborate variations in Book XI of the *De Civitate Dei*, which is probably later in composition than most of the *De Trinitate*. "The whole Trinity is made known to us in its works. Thence has the Holy City . . . its origin, its informing, and its beatitude. Ask what gives it being: we answer, God's creation. Ask what gives it wisdom: we answer, God's enlightening. Ask what gives it happiness: we answer, the enjoyment of God. In existence it is controlled, in contemplation it is illumined, in union it has delight. It is, it beholds, it loves. In God's eternity it is strong, in God's truth it shines, in God's goodness it rejoices" (XI, 24). To the same pattern corresponds the traditional division of secular philosophy into physics, logic, and ethics (XI, 25). Finally in *our own* being, knowledge, and love, we can recognize an image of the Trinity—"the Creator to whom belongs true eternity, eternal truth, eternal and true charity." "Contemplating that image in ourselves, we are moved like the younger son in the Gospel to *return to ourselves*, to arise and make our way back to him from whom our sins had drawn us away. There our being will meet no death, our knowing no mistaking, our loving no failure" (XI, 26–28). In the *De Trinitate*, the second and third members of this triadic pattern are retained throughout the search for the image of God in the soul. The first member, however, being, existence, or life, appears only when in Book X Augustine is enumerating the certainties of self-knowledge: we know for certain that we exist or live, that we think, that we will. But being, existence, figures in none of the psychological triads to which detailed study is given. The reason for this is evidently that Augustine needs three terms which imply relations, whereas being is not relative and cannot serve as distinctive analogue for any one Person in the Trinity. And it will have been partly for this reason that the first of his images of the Trinity, the triad of mind, knowledge, and love, is replaced by the second triad of memory, understanding, and will; for mind, as he is obliged to admit, is an absolute and not a relative term.

Augustine tells us in the *Retractations* that before he had finished Book XII of the *De Trinitate*, certain persons got hold of what he had already written and put it into circulation without his permission. We can understand his vexation. At first he was

inclined to drop the whole project, and publish only a statement
of what had taken place against his will. But he yielded (as he
generally did) to the entreaties of his friends: he revised and
completed his work, with its last three Books, and sent it to the
Bishop of Carthage, Aurelius, with a letter which he asked to
have prefixed to any published version. In this letter he explains that his annoyance at the premature circulation of the
unfinished work was not only because it needed a thorough re-
vision, but because it had been planned to be read as a whole—
"because each part was linked to what preceded in an advancing
enquiry." This insistence upon the order and connection of the
treatise has often been neglected, and the various "images of the
Trinity" in the last seven Books have been treated as though
they had little or no logical dependence upon one another. It is
true that Augustine's literary method is digressive (though even
his digressions are often no more than longish footnotes). But
his work is never shapeless. The last eight Books of the *De
Trinitate* do present an "advancing enquiry."

Book VIII prepares the way for what is to follow. After a
preliminary warning against the application of ordinary quantitative ideas of number and magnitude to Trinitarian theology,
Augustine endeavours to show that our natural make-up as
thinking and willing beings points us to God as the Truth which
is the ultimate object of knowledge and the Good which is the
ultimate satisfaction of desire. But the knowledge and the love
of God are inseparable: in order to know God we must love
him; and Scripture assures us that in love itself God is known to
us as a present reality. The nature of love, involving subject,
object, and relation, already indicates a "three in one." It is not,
however, Augustine's intention to dwell on this "trinity of
love." He passes immediately in Book IX to apply what he has
said of the inseparability of knowing and willing, cognition and
conation, to the discovery of a trinity in the mind that knows
and wills. At once the enquiry is determined by its purpose.
If there is an image of the Triune God in the human soul, it
must be a self-contained trinity of mutually related terms. The
mind's knowing and willing *must* therefore be regarded as reflexive, directed inwards upon itself and not outwards upon
other objects. So the image proposed in Book IX is mind, its
knowledge of itself, and its love of itself; and having shown that
this human trinity is in fact like the divine Trinity "of one substance," in which the three terms display both co-equality and
mutual relatedness, Augustine does not hesitate to apply to it

the traditional language of theology. The second Person of the Trinity is Son, Word, and Image of the first; the third is "not begotten, but proceeding." Similarly, the mind's self-knowledge, if it is a true knowledge, is an expression or "word" which can be described as "begotten" from the mind of which it is a kind of image or likeness; while the realization of this self-knowledge presumes a movement of will which "proceeds" from the mind as capable of self-knowledge, and finds its satisfaction in the self-knowledge realized in the "word."

Thus we are led, through this reference to the divine original, from a purely static account of the mental trinity to a dynamic one. The whole of Book X is occupied with the process by which the mind *comes to know* itself in its true "word" or expression. The process is a kind of search, of which the motive is love in the sense of desire or appetition. Augustine establishes at length the principle that there can be no love for what is unknown; from which it follows that the mind could not seek for a knowledge of itself unless it were already in some sense known to itself. The solution of the problem is found in the conception, which Augustine has acquired from Plotinus, of "self-recollection." All men possess a knowledge of their own real being as a spiritual activity of thought and will; but this knowledge has been obscured by an over-lay of false notions derived from the material world. So we have "forgotten" ourselves; but the "memory" of what we are persists (in modern phrase) below the level of consciousness, and only needs to be recalled. By reflection, the human mind can be certain that it possesses memory, understanding, and will—and this offers to our view what Augustine calls a "more evident" trinity, which like the first is understood reflexively, of the mind's remembering, understanding, and willing itself.

What makes this second trinity "more evident," clearer? and what is its relation to the previous triad of mind, its self-knowledge, and its self-love? Thomas Aquinas, approaching the question with the Aristotelian distinctions of "habit" and "act," the potential and the actual, in his mind, supposed that Augustine's first triad described the structure of the mind *in potentia*, as *capable* of self-knowledge and self-love; whereas the second presents these potencies as realized in conscious activity. And a modern follower of Thomas [1] has argued that the second and

[1] A. Gardeil, *La Structure de l'Âme et l'Expérience Mystique*, Vol. I, pp. 21–130. The important passages in Thomas are I *Sent. Dist.*, 3, qu. v, and *De Veritate*, qu. x, a. 3.

third terms of the first triad, knowledge and love, are to be understood in a passive sense, as equivalent to the mind itself in its two essential capacities for *being* known and *being* loved by itself; and further that these two terms, denoting capacities as yet unrealized, together compose the "memory" which appears as first term of the second triad, and thus link the two trinities to one another genetically: the second emerges from the first. Augustine certainly gives us no hint of his having envisaged his two trinities in this way; and it is very doubtful whether he can actually have done so. It must be remembered that the triad of mind, self-knowledge, and self-love was suggested by a consideration of the trinity of subject, object, and relation to be discerned in the nature of love. In the self-conscious mind, subject and object are the same, and can only form one term of the triad. The other two terms are relations which are *both* active *and* passive—active in the mind as subject and passive in the mind as object: the mind knows and loves itself as subject, is known and loved by itself as object. Moreover, it is in Book IX and still within the frame of the first trinity that Augustine develops his conception of the "birth" of the mental "word," which is of course (in Thomist terms) an "act" and not a "habit," and which at the end of the same Book is expressly identified with the mind's self-knowledge. This seems fatal to Thomas's distinction between the first triad as purely potential and the second as actual. The fact is rather, as Augustine says at the conclusion of his study of the first triad in Book IX (IX, 9 (vi)), that the human mind as thus analysed is *not* a "changeless being," but a life in the making; and what we need to know is not so much what it *is*, but what according to the everlasting law of God it *ought* to be. Henceforth, the true image of the divine Trinity must be sought in the mind as God means it to be, and as it cannot and will not be until its renewal by the grace of God is complete.

This renewal is the subject of Book XIV. The three intervening Books, XI, XII, and XIII, of which only brief summaries are given in this volume, have the appearance of successive *excursus* or digressions which break the continuity of the argument. But Augustine knows what he is about. "When he shall appear, we shall be like him, for we shall see him as he is." The divine likeness in the human soul will be perfectly realized only when God himself and not his created image becomes the object of the soul's loving contemplation. But the Christian life is a gradual ascent to this contemplation, in which the soul must use the things of its outward environment, things spatial and temporal, in order that it may rise above them. In particular, the significance of the time-factor has been brought out by the discussion in Book X of the mind's search for self-knowledge, and the introduction of the notions of memory and recollection. The thinking or reflection which is needed in order to realize in the mind its trinity of memory, understanding, and will is a conscious process occurring in time. In Book XI, Augustine seeks to illustrate this temporal process by a study of sense-perception. At first sight this is a retrograde step; for the field of sense-perception belongs to the "outward man," though the "inward" is involved in it. But it is *reculer pour mieux sauter*. For the examination of the "trinity of sense" leads to that of the "trinity of imagination," based upon sense-perception, in which the actual working of memory and recollection can be followed in its simplest form. Images of things seen are stored in the memory, and are re-presented to the inward vision (understanding) by the voluntary act of attention (will). This is still so far a trinity of the "outward man," inasmuch as it is dependent upon the deliveries of the bodily senses. But it reminds us that the "outward" and "inward" man are in this life linked together in a single organism. The nature of this union, what Augustine calls the "confine" or borderland of outward and inward, is studied in Book XII, in which the reasonable soul is shown to have a two-fold activity: the one, that of dealing by rational judgment with the objects and events of the external world and its temporal experiences, the other, that of contemplating the inward and eternal world of truth. Applying to this distinction the texts of I Cor. 12:8 and Job 28:28, together with Col. 2:3, Augustine gives to the two functions the names of Knowledge (*Scientia*) and Wisdom (*Sapientia*). "Knowledge" is the sphere of the "lower reason," which has its proper place and function as servant of the "higher"; but because it is concerned with the transient, the life we lead in time, it must never become the dominant partner but always be held in conscious subordination to the "higher"—to the growth and perfecting of the "Wisdom" which is worship, the "fear of the Lord." In other words, Augustine like Plotinus insists that the true end of man is not action but contemplation; and this means that the perfect image of God can only be found in the mind at worship. For Augustine, this relation of action to contemplation, of Knowledge to Wisdom, of the life of man in time to his worship in eternity, corresponds to the difference between faith and sight. Christian faith, no less than Christian conduct, is concerned with things temporal; for faith rests upon the history of our salvation, the things wrought in time by the incarnate Word on our behalf. And this *fides historica,* as the only sure ground on which man's natural desire for a well-being that is not destroyed by death can look for satisfaction, is the subject of Book XIII. The believing mind holds the content of this faith in memory, and realizes it in conscious thought by the act of loving attention; but this "trinity of faith" is itself transient, because its object belongs to the realm of time. The Christian life in time is a passage through Knowledge to Wisdom (XIII, 24 (xix)).

So Augustine returns to the point reached at the end of Book X. He has cleared the way for his final identification in Book XIV of the image of the Trinity in the human soul with that soul's perfecting in Wisdom, where God himself is the object of the mind's memory, understanding, and will: where the mind's knowledge of itself is the knowledge that it *is* God's image, enabling it so to fix its contemplation no longer upon itself but upon God (XIV, 15 (xii)). The soul of man is made for eternal life; and that means that the image of God in it cannot finally be identified with anything that is confined to its activity in time. The mind as God's creation is endowed with a natural capacity for the remembering, understanding, and willing of itself; and when these powers are rightly directed, the self will be recognized in its true order of being in relation to the God whose image it is. In our fallen condition, sin holds this natural capacity in abeyance, but can never destroy it: it is in fact what alone makes possible the work of grace. Grace awakens the dormant power of the mind to see God's image in itself, to see itself, that is, *as* God's image. Christian faith, the belief in the historic acts of incarnation and redemption, and the life of Christian practice issuing from that faith, are the means which grace employs in this re-fashioning of the soul. What Augustine is saying in effect is this: the Church teaches us to believe that God is Trinity—one eternal Being in three related Persons. But to "understand" what we have believed is only possible in the measure in which the *gratia Christi* enables us to recover in ourselves that image which the Triune God imprinted on us in our creation. The inspiration of the *De Trinitate* is as much devotional as theological.

To sum up: Augustine recognizes and distinguishes three phases of the divine image in man. There is, first, the ineradicable likeness to God in which man is created, belonging to his essential *nature*. There is, secondly, the temporal and progressive recovery of this likeness, obscured by sin, which takes effect in the Christian life under the influence of *grace*. And there will be, thirdly, the perfection and maturity of the likeness, in the life to come, when knowledge shall have given place to wisdom in that state of *glory* which is the vision of God.

In this life, it is impossible for us, just because we are travellers, *in via*, to anticipate the perfecting of the divine image. Nevertheless, Augustine will attempt in Book XV to lift our thoughts from the image to the original; and since the image in its perfection is beyond our present experience, he will make his comparison between the image as we know it in its fallen and disfigured state, and the original after which it was created (XV, 39 (xx)). He draws out the differences, both formal and material, both in respect of triunity and in respect of the correspondence between the several members of the human and divine Trinities respectively. The only criterion at his disposal is the authoritative dogma, based on Scripture and tradition, and accepted by faith. The Christian is bound to believe that what (for lack of a better word) he calls the "Persons" of the Trinity are one God, because they differ from one another only by the relations in which they stand to one another. But this is not the case with the human trinity of memory, understanding, and will: these are three specific functions which make up or constitute the spiritual being of a man, and they differ from one another essentially in themselves, and not merely in their mutual relations. Behind the three powers or faculties of the mind there is the human person, the Ego who is the ultimate subject of their exercise: it is I, not my memory, that understands and wills, I, not my understanding, that remembers and wills, I, not my will, that remembers and understands. Whereas in the divine Trinity full personality must belong to each "Person": the Persons are not faculties or functions of a divine Ego.

On the other hand, Augustine believes that the value of his analysis of the mental trinity goes further than to show how three things can at the same time be one: he discerns a real image of the Father in memory, of the Son in understanding, and of the Spirit in will (XV, 43 (xxiii)).

In the case of the first Person, the likeness consists simply in the character of "memory" as the source or fount both of understanding and of will. It is to be noted that while Augustine retains this conception of the divine Fatherhood as a relation within the Godhead, he does not follow the Cappadocians in treating it as constitutive of unity. For the second Person, the ground of the likeness is of course the Scriptural and traditional doctrine of the divine Word. In the Fathers before Augustine, the Logos-doctrine had displayed a continual wavering between the Biblical conception of the Word of God, as the revelation to men of his will and purpose, and the Greek philosophical idea of the divine reason immanent in the cosmos. Since human speech is the instrument of rational thought, the spoken Word of God could naturally be conceived as the expression of the reason which is eternally *in* God: his Word is also his Wisdom. The second century apologists, in their endeavour to take advantage in the Christian interest of the Stoic belief in reason as the formative cosmic principle, had attempted to interpret the Sonship of the Logos as God's begetting or bringing forth his rational purpose in the creation of the world. This proved a false step, which had to be corrected by Origen with his doctrine of the eternal generation of the Son. But neither Origen nor his followers made use of psychological analogy in their presentation of the doctrine. Indeed, Augustine's only important predecessor in this respect was Tertullian, who argued in his *Adversus Praxean* (c. 5) that both reason and Word must be conceived as existing in God before the world's creation, comparing the unspoken word or dialogue in the mind which is involved in the process of human thinking, and justifying his comparison on the ground of man's making in the image and likeness of God.

Augustine's treatment of the subject is plainly inspired by the Neo-Platonist theory of self-conscious Mind (*Nous*) which is both subject and object of thought and so contains a duality in itself. In Augustine's mental trinities, the mind's self-knowledge and self-understanding closely correspond to the self-contemplating activity which Plotinus ascribes to *Nous*. The human mind in the act of conscious recognition of itself "begets" an image of itself which is true when it fully corresponds to the self which it reproduces, in the utterance of its inward "word." So in the divine Trinity the Son is the eternal self-reproduction of the Father; and this is the primary significance of the "Word" as title of the second Person. In Book XV, however, Augustine does not confine his comparison of human and divine "words," as we might have expected, to this reflexive aspect of self-consciousness. He considers the "word" both in man and God as a cognizance taken not only of the cognizing self but of other things as well; and so draws his contrast between the scanty content of all human knowledge and the divine omniscience. He has been led to this extension by his treatment of the image as perfected in Wisdom: for the divine Wisdom is more than self-knowledge; it is the knowledge of all things. But, though Scripture speaks of Christ as the Wisdom of God, Wisdom is not, like Word, a distinctive title of the second Person of the Trinity, but an essential attribute of Godhead; and the Son is therefore Wisdom only as being "from Wisdom," as he is God "from God." Augustine has previously established this point in Book VII, where he explains the Scripture's appropriation of the name Wisdom to the second Person on the ground that the Word incarnate reveals to men the pattern of the divine wisdom in whose image they were made and must be re-made. In this way, as we can see, Augustine finds place for the revelational or declaratory function of the Word. The Son took flesh, as our inward word clothes itself in spoken language, for the purpose of communication (XV, 20 (xi)). It remains true, however, that the aim of the *De Trinitate*, in regard to the second Person of the Trinity, is to find within the human image an analogue of the Word that "was in the beginning with God," and to show the appropriateness of the idea of filiation to designate the "express image" of the Father's *hypostasis* (Heb. 1 : 3); and it is upon this eternal relation of Son to Father in the Godhead that in Augustine's view the work of the second Person in revelation and redemption depends.

In the application of the third member of his mental trinity to the Person of the Holy Spirit, the work of Augustine is much more original and determinative for the history of Trinitarian theology; and it is of course intimately involved in his own doctrine of grace. There is surprisingly little allusion to Pelagian errors even in the later Books of the *De Trinitate*. But the Pauline text—"the love of God is shed abroad in our hearts by the Holy Spirit which is given us"—which is the main theme of the refutation of Pelagianism in the *De Spiritu et Littera*, gives the key to the appropriation of charity to the Spirit in our treatise. The text of John—"God is *Agape*"—forbids the identification of any one Person of the Trinity with charity. Augustine will not go further than to claim justification for giving the name of charity "in a special sense" to the Spirit, exactly as the name of wisdom may be given "in a special sense" to the Son: in both cases the usage of Scripture is the sufficient authority. But charity (like wisdom) is properly a substantive term applicable to God "in himself," or to each and every Person of the Trinity *qua* possessed of Godhead. The relational term for the third Person is Gift. The difficulty here is that this term in Scripture plainly denotes the Spirit as given *to men*; and Augustine hesitates to transfer the notion directly to an inter-Personal relation within the eternal being of the Godhead. He says that the Spirit is eternally Gift as being eternally "giveable," whereas his "giving" is a temporal event (V, 16 (xv)). But it is abundantly clear, from the persistence with which the function of will or love in the human trinity is described as bringing together or uniting the other two members of the triad, that the guiding thought is of the Spirit as the *vinculum Trinitatis*, the bond or "communion" of Father and Son. Father and Son are alike and equally "holy," alike and equally "Spirit": "Holy Spirit" is "common to both," and may therefore most fittingly be spoken of as the "mutual charity whereby the Father and the Son love one another" (XV, 27 (xvii)). The conclusion lies very near—though Augustine does not draw it in so many words—that charity is communion *because* it is self-giving. As "Charity from Charity," the Spirit when given to men binds them in union to God, making "the whole Trinity have its habitation within us" (XV, 32 (xviii)). The love whereby we love God is God's gift of himself, and apart from him we can do nothing. Thus what was really at stake in the Pelagian controversy was the reality of the divine presence, through grace, in the soul of man.

Note on terminology

It is impossible in translation to convey the exact meaning of the keywords in Augustine's analysis of the image of the Trinity in man. The most important of these are *mens* ("mind"), *intelligentia* ("understanding"), *memoria* ("memory"), *amor* ("love"), and *charitas* ("charity").

(1) *Mens.*—"Mind" in Augustine's usage stands for the element in human nature by which it is distinguished from anything possessed in common with the lower animals. It connotes especially the power of reasoning, but it does not mean the "intellect" in our sense of the word. It is rather the "rational soul," which feels, desires, and wills as well as thinks.

(2) *Intelligentia.*—For this word, "understanding" is the only convenient equivalent, but it has the serious disadvantage of suggesting "comprehension," in the sense of appreciating the

significance of an idea or a proposition, and observing its logical connection with the rest of our knowledge. Augustine always thinks as a Platonist of the objects of knowledge as so many concrete realities "laid up in heaven"; and like Plato he can only describe the knowing mind's relation to these realities in terms of the "most noble" of our bodily senses, that of *sight*. The difference between faith and understanding is the difference between indirect acquaintance on the basis of another's testimony, and the immediacy of vision at first-hand. To "understand," therefore, is simply to "see with the mind," to "apprehend" rather than "comprehend," and the act of understanding is intuitive, not discursive.

(3) *Memoria.*—"Memory" is Augustine's word for the retention of experience in the human mind. As memory, the mind is a storehouse in which traces of the passing experience are preserved. But we only "remember" what is in the store-house by entering it (as it were) and looking in it for what we want, or (as in the case of involuntary recollection) by stumbling upon some particular item of its content. Thus the Augustinian "memory" corresponds roughly to the modern notion of the "sub-conscious" or the "unconscious." But Augustine believes that the content of the "unconscious" is not limited to the traces left by sense-perception; for the mind at birth is more than a *tabula rasa* dependent entirely upon impressions from the external world. Being the creation of God and bearing the image of God, the mind must always retain a knowledge of its own nature as God's created image; and thus it must possess a "memory of God" which is indelible, however deeply hidden away.

(4) *Amor* and *Charitas.*—The primary connotation of "love" in Augustine is "desire." It is the motive of all human action, the source of energy which compels a man to seek the satisfaction of his needs; and Augustine compares it to the force of gravity. "My weight is my love: by it I am carried whithersoever I move" (*Confessions*, XIII, 10 (ix)). The end which love pursues is "fruition," enjoyment, and the quality of love depends on that of the objects whose enjoyment is sought. It is therefore neither good nor bad in itself. When it is directed towards "lower things" in the scale of existence, it will be evil *unless* such things are desired only as means towards the attainment of man's true end—"the fruition of God and of one another in God" (*De Civitate*, XIX, 13). Thus love (*amor*) is a neutral term: if it seeks final satisfaction in "what is lower," it is "covetousness" (*concupiscentia*); if it is directed ultimately

upon God, or (in Augustine's phrase) "referred to God," it is "charity." But it is important to observe that both *amor* and *charitas* include feeling as well as striving or conation: indeed it is the affective element in love that supplies its dynamic. In virtue of this affective element, love does not cease to exist when it has attained its object. So Augustine can define love as "nothing else but the will, seeking after *or holding in possession* an object of enjoyment" (*De Trin.*, XIV, 8 (vi))—a definition which makes clear the difference in connotation between "will" and "love." The two words denote one and the same activity, but *voluntas* fixes attention upon the conative element in this activity, while *amor* always connotes feeling.

The Trinity

BOOK VIII

The Search for God by the Understanding

ARGUMENT

[Terms which distinguish the Persons of the Trinity from one another denote relations only. Terms applicable equally to each Person and to the whole Trinity denote substance or essence. How can we apprehend the divine essence? The first necessity is to dismiss the quantitative notions which we acquire from the world of sense-perception. The Persons of the Trinity are co-equal, simply because in absolute truth or reality there can be no degrees. We cannot grasp, otherwise than by momentary intuition, the conception of ultimate truth (reality) because our minds are weakened by sin and error (§§ 1–3).

It may be easier to reach the conception of God's essence as goodness—the universal Good which is implied by the existence of particular good things, and our ability to recognize them as good. The soul can win or lose goodness; and this implies a goodness that is independent of the soul, towards which or away from which the soul can move (§§ 4, 5). The soul can hold to the supreme Good only by love; and love, for its advance to the knowledge of vision, must be supported by the knowledge of faith (§ 6).

Our beliefs, with regard to matters with which we are not directly acquainted, e.g., the facts of the Gospel story, are grounded not on the mental picture which we form of them, and which is usually erroneous, but on general or abstract ideas (§ 7). But our belief in the Trinity, our belief in God, cannot be based on any "general idea" (§ 8). Our love, e.g., for Paul, is love of the "righteous soul"; and we know what "soul" is because we ourselves *are* souls. But if we are not righteous ourselves how can we know what "righteousness" is? and without knowing it, how can we love it? The knowledge must somehow be "in our-selves," though not derived from sense-perception. It can be based only on a form or pattern actually present to the soul, which can hold to it only by way of love (§ 9).

What is the nature of this love? Simply the "will to righteous-ness" for ourselves and for others. But the love of neighbour ultimately depends on the love of God; and the love of God is the love, not of power, but of love (§§ 10, 11). Because God is love, we can know him when we love our brother.

But how is the knowledge of love, charity, the knowledge of God as Trinity? All love must have an object; and John's Epistle teaches us that the love which has a brother for its object is not only "of God," but "God." But we cannot love a brother, without also loving love. In other words, the two great com-mandments are inseparable (§ 12). Paul's description of the character of God's ministers (II Cor., ch. 6) kindles our love through its correspondence with the pattern present to our inward vision (§ 13). And all love implies, besides itself, a loving subject and a loved object: three entities, one of which (love) is link between the other two.]

THE TEXT

1. We have already observed that the only terms which can strictly be applied to distinguish the several Persons of the Trinity are those which denote their mutal relations: Father, Son, and Holy Spirit, Gift of both. The Trinity is neither Father nor Son nor Gift. But the terms applicable to the several Persons, regarded in themselves, denote not three beings in the plural, but one, that is, the Trinity itself: thus the Father is God, the Son God, the Holy Spirit God; the Father is good, the Son good, the Holy Spirit good; the Father almighty, the Son almighty, the Holy Spirit almighty; yet there are not three Gods, or three good, or three almighty; but one God, good, almighty [1]—the Trinity itself; and so for every other term which denotes not a mutual relation, but the several Persons regarded in them-selves. We may describe such terms as "essential"; for the essence or being of God is the same as his being great, good, wise, and anything else which is true either of each several Person or of the Trinity itself. We use the expression three Persons, or three substances, not to suggest any difference in essence, but

[1] Phraseology adopted in the *Quicumque vult*.

to furnish ourselves with some one word by which to answer the question: *What* are these "three"? [2]

In this Trinity there is an absolute equality. In divinity the Father is not greater than the Son; nor are the Father and the Son together greater than the Holy Spirit; nor is any single Person of the three anything less than the Trinity itself. All this has been said before, and repetition may familiarize our minds with the idea. But there must be a limit to repetition. Let us now beseech God, with reverent devotion, that he will open our understandings, and remove from us all contentiousness of spirit, so that our mind may contemplate the essence of truth, free from all thought of physical mass or motion. It is now our purpose, so far as the Creator's own wonderful mercy may assist us, to address ourselves to the same theme as before, but by a more inward method of approach: still observing the same rule, that the truth which has not yet become luminous to our understanding be still held fast by faith.

2 (i). We say that in this Trinity two or three Persons are not any greater thing than one of them. Our material habit of thought fails to grasp this, simply because, while it is aware according to its capacity of those truly existing things which have been created, it cannot perceive the Truth itself which has created them.[3] If it could, the fact of which we have spoken would be as clear as the light of day. Only Truth itself has true being: in its substance there is nothing "greater" but that which more truly is. But in the realm of the spiritual and the changeless there cannot be degrees of truth; for all is equally changeless and eternal. What is called "great" is great only because it truly is. If then "greatness" is truth itself, to have more greatness must mean to have more truth: that which has not more truth cannot have more greatness. Whatever has more truth is the truer, just as whatever has more greatness is the greater. In this realm therefore the truer is the greater. But Father and Son together have no more true being than the Father alone or the Son alone. Both together, then, are no greater a thing than either of them singly. And since the Holy Spirit no less truly is, no more are

2 Augustine has examined the inadequacy of the Latin term *persona* and the Greek *hypostasis* in Book VII: see Introduction, p. 22.
3 Throughout this passage, "truth" stands for the Platonic "true being" or absolute reality, which belongs to nothing in the world of sense. Like Plato, Augustine holds that in this world things have no more than a "degree" of reality, varying according to their measure of likeness to, or participation in the absolute reality or "Truth" which is God himself.

Father and Son together anything greater than the Spirit, because they are nothing that more truly is. The Father and the Holy Spirit together, since they do not surpass the Son in truth (for they have no more true a being), do not surpass him in greatness. So the Son and the Holy Spirit together are as great a thing as the Father alone, because they no less truly are. And the Trinity itself has the same greatness as any one Person: the Person who is not truer is not greater, where truth itself is greatness. In the essential being of truth, to be true is to be: to be is to be great. To be great, therefore, is to be true. Here therefore what is equally true must be equally great.

3 (ii). In the case of material things, one piece of gold may be as true as another, and yet not as great, because here greatness is not the same thing as truth: it is one thing to be gold, another to be great. Similarly with the soul, we do not call a soul true in respect of the same quality which makes us call it great. A true soul belongs no less to him who is not great-souled. For the essence of body and soul is not the essence of truth itself, as the Trinity is God, one, sole, great, truly real, really true, true reality. If we would conceive of him, so far as he allows and vouchsafes, we must conceive of no spatial contact or connection, no conjoined structure like that of the three-bodied Geryon in the legend. Any image of that kind, greater in its three parts than in any one of them, less in one than in two, must be unhesitatingly rejected, even as we reject everything that is material. Even in the world of spirit, nothing that is changeable must be taken for God. When we rise from the deep submergence in which we live, and draw breath towards the heights of heaven, it will be matter of no small knowledge for us, before we are yet able to know what God is, if we can at least know what he is not. Certainly he is neither earth nor sky, nor of the nature of earth and sky or of anything that we see in the sky or that may perhaps exist there though we see it not. Multiply in your imagination the light of the sun, make it greater and brighter as you will, a thousand times or times out of number: God will not be there. Conceive the being of pure angelic spirits, animating celestial bodies,[4] changing and turning them at will for the service of God: not if all those thousand thousands were brought together and made one, will God be any such thing—not even if you could conceive those same spirits

---

[4] I.e., not the stars, but the "celestial bodies" of which Paul speaks in I Cor. ch. 15. But in *Enchirid.*, 15 (lviii), Augustine says it may be that sun, moon, etc., belong to the same "company" as the Angels.

as bodiless, difficult as that is for our materially determined thinking. Behold, if thou canst, thou soul heavily burdened by the body of corruption,[5] laden with earthy conceits many and diverse, behold if thou canst: God is Truth. It is written, "For God is light" [6]—not the light seen by these eyes of ours, but that which the heart sees upon hearing of the words "He is Truth." Ask not, What is Truth? At once will rise the fogs of material images, the thick clouds of phantasm, and darken that clear empyrean which shone forth for a single instant upon your sight at that word, "Truth." In that instant, that flash of vision that touches you with the word "Truth," hold fast—if you can. But you cannot: you fall back into this familiar world of earthly things. And what—I ask you— is the weight that pulls you down again, but the defilements contracted from the mire of passion and the delusions of your wanderings? [7]

4 (iii). Try once again, and consider the matter this way. Nothing draws your love but what is good. Good is earth with its lofty mountains, its gentle hills, its level plains. Good is the beauteous and fertile land, good the well-built house with its symmetry, its spaciousness and light. Good are the bodies of living things, good is the temperate and wholesome air, good is the pleasant and healthful food, good is health itself free from pain and weariness. Good is the human face with its regular features, its cheerful expression, its lively colouring; good is the heart of a friend whose comradeship is sweet and whose love is loyal; good is a righteous man, good is wealth for the things it can enable us to do, good is the sky with its sun, moon, and stars, good are the angels of holy obedience; good is the speech that instructs the hearer winningly and counsels him appropriately, good is the poem of musical rhythm and profound thought. But enough! This is good and that is good: take away "this" and "that," and look if you can upon Good itself: then you will see God, good not by the possession of any other good thing, but the goodness of every good. For among all these good things, those I have named and any others you may see or conceive, we could not pronounce with a true judgment any one better than another, were there not imprinted on our mind the

---

[5] The allusion is to Wisdom 9:15, which expresses the Greek view of the relation of body and soul.

[6] I John 1:5.

[7] Cf. *Conf.*, VII, 17: this "flash of vision" and the inevitable relapse, constantly described by Augustine, is what he had experienced in his own attempts to achieve the mystic elevation of the Neo-Platonist.

idea [8] of Good itself, as the standard by which we should either approve or prefer. So our love must rise to God, not as we love this or that good thing, but as the Good itself. The soul must needs seek that Good over which it will not range superior as judge but to which it will cleave in love. And what is that Good but God?—not the good soul, the good angel, the good heavens, but the good Good!

Perhaps this may make it easier to grasp what I mean. When I hear, for instance, the phrase "good soul," those two words convey two things to my mind: that there is a soul, and that it is good. It was no act of its own that made it a soul, for it was not there to bring itself into being. But for it to be a good soul, I can see that voluntary action of its own was needed: not that there is no good in its very existence as a soul, for then it could not be called, and truly called, better than a body. But it is not yet to be called a good soul, because there needs yet the activity of will to give it excellence. If that activity is neglected, it rightly incurs blame and is properly called no good soul. It differs from the soul that is so active, and since the latter deserves praise, clearly the former's failure so to act must deserve censure. But when a soul sets itself to this purpose and is becoming good, it cannot achieve its end unless it be directed towards something which is not itself. Yet to what may the soul turn so as to become good, but to *the* Good, loving, pursuing, attaining it? If it turn away again, and lose its goodness by the very act of turning away from good, there will be nothing to which it may return once more (if it desire to amend), unless that Good from which it is declining abides still in itself.

5. It follows that there could be no changeable goods, were there not a Good that is changeless. You hear the word "good" applied to this and that, things which at another time may be called not good. See then if you can pass beyond the things which are good by virtue of their share in goodness, and rise to the vision of that Good whose partial presence makes them good. You must know the meaning of Good itself, when you hear that this or that is good. If then you can set them aside and reach the sight of Good in itself, you will have reached the sight of God; and if you shall cleave to him in love, you will in that moment receive beatitude. [9] Other things are loved only because they are

---

[8] This *notio Boni* is not of course the Platonic "Idea of Good," but its reflection in the mind.

[9] Augustine here describes what for him is only a theoretical possibility. When he wrote the *De Trinitate*, he had long ceased to believe that the vision of God was attainable in this life.

good. It were shame to stay cleaving to them and not to love the Good itself which makes them good. A soul may not yet have the goodness of conversion to the changeless Good; but simply as a soul, we may give it a value (if we rightly apprehend) higher than that of any material luminary. Yet its value for us lies not in itself but in the creative art that made it: it is our seeing that it was worth the making that makes us approve it as made.

This is the Truth, the absolute Good—nothing else but Good itself, and therefore the highest good; for the only good that can be diminished or increased is that whose goodness is derived from another good. The soul's goodness, then, comes from its conversion to that same Source which has made it a soul. The soul's perfecting in goodness comes from the conforming of will to nature, when the will turns in love towards that Good from which is derived the existence that cannot be lost, even if the will turns away from its Source. When it turns away from the highest Good, the soul ceases to be a good soul, but not to be a soul—which is itself a good that is superior to body. The will loses what the will gains; for the soul already existed, with power to will its turning towards its Source, but it was not there to will to be a soul before it existed. The good for us is to see how it was or is right for that thing to be, the rightness of which we can understand; and if there is anything of which we cannot understand the rightness, to see that it could not have been unless it was right for it to be. And this Good is not far from each one of us: for "in him we live and move and have our being." [10]

6 (iv). But we have to stand fast by that Good in love, and cleave to it, that we may enjoy the presence of him from whom we have our being, and in whose absence we could not be at all. "We walk by faith as yet, and not by sight": [11] not yet do we see God, as the same apostle says, "face to face." [12] But unless we already love him, we shall never see him.

Yet how can we love what we do not know? A thing may be known and not loved; but we may question whether that which is not known can be loved: if it cannot, no-one can love God before he knows him. To know God means to perceive him with the assured grasp of the mind: he is not a body to be observed with the eye of flesh. But to see and apprehend God, as he may be seen and apprehended, is given to the pure in heart: they, we read, are "blessed, for they shall see God." [13] And before we

[10] Acts 17:27 f.   [11] II Cor. 5:7.
[12] I Cor. 13:12.   [13] Matt. 5:8.

have gained strength for that seeing, there can be no purifying
of the heart to make it fit to see him, unless he be loved by faith.
Faith, hope, and charity, those three virtues for whose building
up is mounted all the scaffolding of the Bible, are only in the
soul that believes what it sees not yet, and hopes and loves what
it believes. Therefore there can be love even of him who is not
known, if yet he is believed. Doubtless, we must beware lest the
soul, believing what it does not see, feign for itself an image of
that which is not, and put its hope and love upon a lie. Then
there will not be that "charity from a pure heart and a good
conscience and a faith unfeigned, which is the end of the commandment," [14] as Paul says.

7. When we acquire beliefs from the reading or hearing of
material things which we have not seen, the mind cannot but
form for itself some image in outline and shape such as may
present itself to thought. But it will not be a true image: or if it
is, as may very exceptionally happen, there will be no advantage
in retaining it for the maintenance of our belief, though it may
serve a purpose in suggesting to us something else. Most people
who read or hear the writings of Paul or his history will form
some picture of his appearance, and of that of all the other persons whose names occur in connection with his. Of all the many
people who know his letters, one will picture the forms and
features of these persons in one way, one in another: but none
can say whose picture is the nearest resemblance. Our belief is
not concerned with the outward appearance of the men, but
only with the fact that by the grace of God their lives and doings
were what the Scripture tells us. That is the belief which is both
profitable and attainable, and the belief we should seek for. The
bodily appearance of the Lord himself is represented by an innumerable variety of mental images; but whatever it actually
was, it was not more than one. In our faith concerning the Lord
Jesus Christ, the salutary element is not in the mental image,
which may be a long way from the facts, but in the idea of
Man: fixed in our knowledge is a definite standard of human
nature, by which we immediately recognize, upon seeing that
which conforms to it, that this is a man or a human form.
(v). By this knowledge our thought is shaped, when we believe
that God was made man for us, to be an example of humility,
and to prove God's love towards us. What is good for us to be-

---

[14] I Tim. 1:5—in what follows Augustine uses the expression "faith unfeigned" for a belief that is *not* grounded on baseless imaginings, and so
cannot deceive.

lieve and to keep firm and unshaken in our hearts, is that the humility whereby God was born of a woman and brought by mortal men that shameful way to death, is the supreme medicament for the healing of the cancer of our pride, and the profound mystery that can loose the fetters of sin. So also it is because we have the idea of omnipotence that we believe the power of his miracles and of his resurrection to have come from the omnipotent God; and we think of such facts in accordance with our systematic knowledge of general and specific notions, whether innate or acquired by experience, so that our faith be not feigned. We do not know the appearance of the virgin Mary, of whom Christ was marvellously born, so that both in conceiving and in giving birth her virginity was preserved. We do not know the figure of Lazarus: we have not seen Bethany, the grave or the stone which Christ made them take away when he raised him from the dead, nor that new tomb cut in the rock from which he himself rose, nor the mount of Olivet where he ascended into heaven. And if we have not seen them, we are wholly ignorant whether they are as we imagine them: indeed we suppose it the more likely that they are not. For if ever a place or a person or any physical object presents to our eyes the same appearance as it had in our imagination before we saw it, we are struck with astonishment—so rarely does it happen, if ever. Yet we have a most firm belief in the Gospel story, because we conceive it in accordance with our assured knowledge of general and specific notions. We believe that the Lord Jesus Christ was born of a virgin called Mary: but what is a virgin, what is to be born, what is a proper name, we do not believe but simply know. Whether Mary had that form which comes to our mind when we tell or remember the story, we neither know nor believe. And so without damage to faith we may say, "Perhaps she was like this, perhaps she was not." But "Perhaps Christ was born of a virgin" is what no-one can say without damage to his Christian faith.

8. Now it is our desire to gain such understanding as may be granted us of the Trinity, its eternity, its equality, its unity. But before we can understand, we have to believe, and we must take care that our faith be not feigned; for our happiness rests upon the fruition of the Trinity, and if our belief about it be false, our hope will be vain and our love not pure. How then can we love, through believing, the Trinity which we do not know? The love which we can have for Paul is based upon a knowledge of general and specific ideas. We may be entirely ignorant of his

appearance, which may have been quite different from our imagination of it. Yet we know what a man is, for we need go no further than what we are ourselves. Plainly, Paul was a man: his soul was linked to a body, and lived a mortal life. We believe of him what we find in ourselves according to the genus or species in which every human nature is equally contained. But knowledge of genus and species can tell us nothing of the transcendent Trinity: there are not a number of such trinities, experience of some of which could enable us to form a generalized notion, and believe that the divine Trinity is similar; and so, by analogy with what we know, love that which not yet knowing we believe. No: we can love our Lord Jesus Christ's resurrection from the dead, although we have never seen anyone so rise again; but we cannot in the same way love, through believing, the Trinity which we do not see and the like of which we have never seen. We know what death and life are, because we are alive and we have seen and experienced the death and the dying of others. To rise again, then, is simply to return to life. But when we say and believe that the Trinity exists, we know indeed what the word "Trinity" means, since we know the meaning of "three"; [15] but that is not what we love. We can have "three" whenever we like, by holding up three fingers. Is that which we love, then, not *any* Trinity but the Trinity which is God? Is it God in the Trinity that we love? But we neither have seen nor know any other God; for there is but one only God whom we have not yet seen, whom through believing we love. The question is, what likeness or comparability in things we know can form the belief by which we may love God, before he is known?

9 (vi). Let us go back, and consider why we love the apostle. Not, surely, because of that form of humanity which is familiar to us and which we believe he shared. If it were so, our love would now have no object, for his soul and body are divided and he exists no longer in human form.[16] That which we love in him, we believe is now living: for we love the righteous soul. But this implies reference to a pattern of genus or species— that we know what a soul is, and what "righteous" is. Now we may properly say that we know what a soul is, because we ourselves have a soul. We have never seen it with our eyes or formed a generic conception from a number of things seen; we know it

[15] The Latin *trinitas* means simply "triad," not "three-in-one-ness."
[16] Augustine defines "man" as "a reasonable soul having a body" (*In Jo. Ev. Tr.* XIX, 15).

because we have it. I know nothing more intimately than that which I am aware of being, that by which I am aware of all things else—the soul itself. The bodily movements by which we are aware of the life of others, we recognize from their likeness to our own: life makes us move our bodies as we observe other bodies moving. When a living body moves, our eyes do not find their way in to a vision of the soul, which eyes cannot see; but we are aware that in that bodily mass there is something of the same kind as we have in ourselves to move our own bodily mass —namely, life and soul. And this is not peculiar to human intelligence and reason: animals are aware of life not only in themselves but in one another and in us. They do not see our souls, but become aware of them from movements of the body with a simple and instinctive immediacy. From our own soul then we draw the knowledge of soul in anyone else and the belief of it when we do not know it. We are not only aware of the soul but are able to know what soul is by the consideration of our own; for we *have* a soul.

But how do we know what is "righteous"? We said that the only reason for our love of the apostle is that he is a "righteous soul": we must know then what "righteous" is, as well as what is "soul." What "soul" is, we know from ourselves as we have said; for there is soul in us. But how do we know what is "righteous," if *we* are not righteous? If none but he who is righteous knows what "righteous" is, none can love the righteous but the righteous. The mere belief that a man is righteous cannot make you love him, if you do not know what "righteous" is. As we have already shown, one can only love what one believes without seeing, on the basis of some standard conception of genus or species. If then none can love the righteous but the righteous, how can anyone who is not yet righteous desire to be so? For no-one desires to be what he does not love. Yet it is impossible to become righteous without willing it; and to will it one must love the righteous. It follows that a man not yet righteous himself can love the righteous; but this cannot be if he does not know what "righteous" is. We must allow that a man not yet righteous may know the meaning of the word; and we ask whence such knowledge comes. Clearly not by the visual sense: a body is not righteous, as it is white or black, square or round; and nothing but bodies are seen by the eyes. The righteous element in man is the soul, and a man is called righteous in virtue of his soul and not his body. Righteousness is a beauty of the soul which can exist in men whose bodies are deformed or ugly; and the

soul's beauty no more than the soul itself is visible to the outward eye. Whence then can a man not yet righteous learn the
meaning of the word, and through loving the righteous become
righteous himself? Bodily movements might give indications of
righteousness in this or that man; but if one were wholly ignorant of the meaning of "righteous," one could not recognize
that such were signs of a righteous soul. The problem remains.
Somehow or other we know what "righteous" means, before
we are righteous ourselves. If that knowledge comes from the
external world, it must be derived from some bodily source;
but its object does not belong to the bodily realm at all. It
must therefore be *in ourselves* that we learn the meaning of the
term "righteous." When I look for the proper way to describe
it, I can find the answer nowhere but in my own mind. If I ask
another man, he must look within for his answer; and no-one
can give a true answer unless he has found it in himself. When
I want to describe Carthage, I enquire of myself and I find an
image of Carthage in my own mind. But I have got it by way of
sense perception, having been in the town in bodily presence,
seen it and remembered it, so that the right word will be at my
disposal whenever I want to describe it. Its "word" is the
actual image in my memory—not the sound of two syllables
when I say "Carthage," nor the silent passing of the name
through the mind: it is the object of my inward vision, when I
pronounce, or before I pronounce, the two syllables "Carthage." Similarly, if I want to describe Alexandria which I
have never seen, an image of it is at my disposal. I have been
credibly informed that it is a great city, and have constructed a
picture of it as described to me to the best of my ability. And
that is the "word" of it in my mind, when I want to speak of it,
before I pronounce the five syllables of the well-known name.
But if I could display my mental picture to people who know
Alexandria, they would assuredly say "That is not it!"—or if
they said "It is," I should be greatly surprised, and when I
considered the picture in my mind I should still not *know* that
it was Alexandria: I should only believe those who had seen it.

But this is not how I enquire the meaning of "righteous": it
is not how I find it or contemplate it when I describe it, how my
description is accepted or how I accept another's description.
It is not as though I had seen anything of the kind or perceived
it, by any bodily sense, or heard of it from others who had their
knowledge in that way. When I say, and say with knowledge,
that "the righteous soul is that which by rational principle in

life and conduct assigns to each his own," [17] I am not thinking
of an absent object like Carthage, or imagining one like Alexandria correctly or incorrectly. I perceive something *present*,
perceive it in myself, though I am not myself what I perceive.
Many, on hearing me, may accept my description; but whoever
does so knowledgeably will himself be perceiving in himself the
same thing, though he be not himself what he perceives. When
a righteous man says it, he is perceiving and saying what he
himself is; but he too perceives it "in himself." That is natural
enough: where should he see himself but in himself? The surprising thing is that the mind or soul should see in itself what
it has seen nowhere else, that it should see truly, see the truly
righteous soul, being itself soul yet not the righteous soul which
it sees in itself. We can hardly suppose the presence of *another*
righteous soul in the soul which is not yet righteous. But then
what *is* present to the soul when it sees and defines the righteous
soul, and sees it entirely in itself though itself is not righteous?
Our answer is, that what it sees is an *inward truth* present to the
soul that has the power to contemplate it. Not all have the
power; and those that have are not all themselves what they
contemplate—not all themselves righteous souls, though they
can see and define the righteous soul. They can only become it
themselves, by cleaving to that same form or pattern which they
contemplate, being conformed to it and becoming righteous
souls: not only perceiving and declaring that the righteous soul
is "that which by rational principle in life and conduct assigns
to each his own," but by making righteous life and conduct
their own, assigning to each his own, "owing no man anything
but to love one another." [18] The only way of cleaving to that
pattern is by love. If we love another man whom we believe
righteous, we cannot but love the pattern itself which shows us
what the righteous soul is, in order that we too may become
righteous. Indeed, did we not love the pattern, we could have
no love for the man; for our love for him is based upon the
pattern: it is only that so long as we are not righteous our love
of it is insufficient to make us righteous.

Our conclusion is that love for the man who is believed
righteous is based upon that pattern and truth which the lover
perceives and apprehends in himself. But love for the pattern
and the truth itself cannot be based upon anything extraneous.

[17] The definition of *Justitia* given by Cicero in *De Fin.*, V, 33, and set at the
beginning of Justinian's *Institutes* as the basis of Roman law.
[18] Rom. 13:8.

We cannot find anything outside itself, so that our belief in it and our love for it, when it is still unknown, might be based on a previous knowledge of anything of the kind. It is itself the thing you behold wherever you behold anything of the kind: indeed there is nothing else "of the kind," for it alone is what it is. Accordingly our love for men must have their righteousness either as the cause or as the purpose of our love. In the same way a man's own righteousness must be either cause or purpose of his love for himself: only so can he safely love his neighbour as himself. If his self-love has any other ground, it is an unrighteous self-love, for he will be loving himself so as to be unrighteous—and therefore to be evil, so that it will be no real self-love; for "he who loves iniquity, hateth his own soul." [19]

10 (vii). It follows that in this enquiry concerning the Trinity and our knowledge of God, the first thing for us to learn is the nature of true love—or rather the nature of love; for only the love which is true deserves the name. All other is covetousness: it is a misuse of language when the covetous are said to love, as it is when those who love are said to covet. The aim of true love is the life of righteousness in cleaving to the truth; and this means that nothing in this world should have any weight for us beside the love of men, which means the will that they may live righteously.[20] That gives all the value to the readiness to die for our brethren, which the Lord Jesus Christ taught us by his example. There are two commandments on which hang all the Law and the Prophets: love of God and love of neighbour; but it is not without reason that the Scripture often puts one of them for both. Sometimes it is the love of God. "We know that all things work together for good to them that love God." [21] "Whosoever loveth God, he is known of God." [22] "The love of God is shed abroad in our hearts by the Holy Spirit which is given to us." [23] In such sayings it is implied that he who loves God must do what God has commanded, that his love depends upon his doing, and so he must love his neighbour also, because this is what God has commanded. Sometimes Scripture mentions only the love of neighbour. "Bear ye one another's burdens, and so shall ye fulfil the law of Christ." [24] "The whole law is fulfilled in one saying, namely, Thou shalt love thy neighbour

[19] Ps. 11:5.
[20] "The will that men live righteously" includes the approval of righteous living where it is present.
[21] Rom. 8:28.   [22] I Cor. 8:3.
[23] Rom. 5:5.   [24] Gal. 6:2.

as thyself." [25] Or as in the Gospel, "Whatsoever ye would that men should do unto you, even so do unto them; for this is the Law and the Prophets." [26] There are many other places in Holy Writ, where it seems that the love of neighbour is alone enjoined for our perfecting, and nothing is said of the love of God; though the Law and the Prophets hang upon both commandments. The reason for this is that he who loves his neighbour must necessarily have first the love for love itself.[27] But "God is love, and he who abideth in love, abideth in God" [28] It follows that he must have first the love of God.

11. Those who seek God by way of the spiritual powers [29] set over the world or its parts, drift far away from him—separated not by space but by difference of affection. They strive towards the external, and desert what lies within them, though God is more inward than the innermost. They may have heard or conceived of some holy celestial power; but what draws them is the admiration that human weakness feels for the works of such a power, rather than the model of reverent submission which attains to the rest of God. They choose rather the pride of angelic potency than the devotion of angelic being. No holy person rejoices in his own power, but in the power of him from whom is derived all potency for fitting action. He knows that it is a mightier thing to be united in willing worship to the omnipotent, than to display in his own power and will a potency which is fearful to those who have it not. So when the Lord Jesus Christ himself wrought miracles, he sought to convey to those who marvelled a fuller truth, to turn them from their absorption in temporal portents to things inward and eternal. "Come unto me, all ye that labour and are heavy laden, and I will refresh you: take my yoke upon you." He does not say "Learn of me, for I raise up them that have been dead four days"; but, "Learn of me, for I am meek and lowly of heart." The firm ground of humility is stronger and safer than any windy elevation. So he goes on, "And ye shall find rest for your souls." [30] For "Love is not puffed up": "God is love": "the faithful in love shall rest in him," [31] called back from the noisy outer world to the joyful silences.

---

[25] Gal. 5:14.　　　　　　[26] Matt. 7:12.
[27] That love in action implies the "love of love," i.e., the will to love, is axiomatic for Augustine.　　　[28] I John 4:16.
[29] Augustine is thinking of the "worshipping of angels" condemned by Paul in Col. 2:16, which he extends to cover heathenism generally.
[30] Matt. 11:28 f.　　　　　[31] I Cor. 13:4; I John 4:8; Wisdom 3:9.

"God is love." Why should we go speeding to the height of heaven and the nethermost parts of the earth, seeking for him who is with us, if we would but be with him? 12 (viii). Let none say: "I do not know what I am to love." Let him love his brother, and he will love that same love: he knows the love whereby he loves better than the brother whom he loves. God can be more known to him than his brother—really more known, because more present; more known because more inward; more known, because more sure. Embrace the love that is God: through love embrace God. He is the very love that links together in holy bond all good angels and all God's servants, and unites them and us to one another and in obedience to himself. The more we are clean from the cancer of pride, the more are we filled with love; and he who is filled with love is filled with God.

But now you will say: "Charity indeed I see; I fix my mind's eye upon it as best I may; I believe the word of Scripture, that God is charity, and he that abideth in charity abideth in God.[32] But my vision of charity is not a vision of the Trinity." Well, let me try to make you see that it is, trusting that Charity itself be present to move us to a good end. The charity that we love is a loving charity, and it is because it loves that we love it. What then is the object of charity's love, which makes charity itself lovable? If it loves nothing, it is not charity. If it loves itself, it cannot love itself *as charity*, unless itself have some object. A transitive word denotes itself as well as connotes its object, but it does not denote itself *as transitive word*, unless it denotes itself as connoting an object; similarly charity may love itself, but only if it love itself as having an object of its love will it be loving itself *as charity*. The object of charity's love must be something which charity makes us love; and that, if we are to start from what is nearest, is our brother. Remember the apostle John's commendation of brotherly love: "Whosoever loveth his brother, abideth in the light, and there is no cause of stumbling in him."[33] Evidently he has set the perfection of righteousness in the love of brother: he in whom there is no cause of stumbling is plainly perfect. Yet he seems to have said nothing of the love of God. The only explanation of that is that he means God to be comprehended in brotherly love itself. And a little later in the Epistle he says explicitly: "Beloved, let us love one another; for love is of God; and everyone that loveth is born of God and knoweth God. He that loveth not, hath not known God; for

[32] I John 4:16.   [33] I John 2:10.

God is love." ³⁴ The train of thought makes it clear enough, that this same brotherly love (the love wherewith we love another) is being proclaimed with apostolic authority to be not only "of God," but "God." It is God, then that causes us to love our brother, when love causes us to do so; and the first object of our love must needs be that very love wherewith we love our brother.

We infer from this that the Two Commandments cannot be separated. "God is love." He who loves love, assuredly loves God: he who loves his brother, must necessarily love love. So we read soon after: "He that loveth not his brother whom he sees, cannot love God whom he seeth not." ³⁵ The reason of his not seeing God is that he does not love his brother. He who does not love his brother is not in love, and he who is not in love is not in God, for God is love. Again, he who is not in God is not in the light; for "God is light, and there is no darkness in him." ³⁶ Naturally, then, he who is not in the light does not see the light, which means that he does not see God; because he is in darkness. He sees his brother with the outward human vision to which God is invisible. But if he loved with spiritual charity the brother whom his outward vision sees, he would see God, who is Charity itself, with the inward vision whereby God can be seen. Thus he who loves not the brother whom he sees cannot love God, whom he does not see just because God is the love which he lacks. We need not be disturbed by the question, How much charity ought we to give to our brother and how much to God? The answer is, To God incomparably more than to ourselves, and to our brother as much as to ourselves; ourselves we love the more, the more we love God. It is, then, out of one and the same charity that we love God and our neighbour: but we love God for God's sake, and for God's sake ourselves and our neighbour.

13 (ix). What is it, I would ask, that kindles the fire in our hearts, when we hear or read such words as these?—"Behold, now is the acceptable time, behold, now is the day of salvation: giving no occasion of stumbling in anything, that our ministration be not blamed, but in everything commending ourselves as God's ministers: in much patience, in afflictions, in necessities, in distresses, in stripes, in imprisonments, in tumults, in labours, in watchings, in fastings; in pureness, in knowledge, in long-suffering, in kindness, in the Holy Ghost, in charity unfeigned, in the word of truth, in the power of God; by the armour of

³⁴ I John 4:7 f.   ³⁵ I John 4:20.   ³⁶ I John 1:5.

righteousness on the right hand and on the left, by glory and
dishonour, by evil report and good report; as deceivers and yet
true, as unknown and yet well known, as dying, and behold, we
live; as chastened, and not killed, as sorrowful, yet always rejoicing, as poor, yet making many rich, as having nothing, and
yet possessing all things." [37]—If the love of Paul the apostle is
kindled in us at this reading, surely it is because we believe
that his life was like that. But that God's ministers *ought* so to
live, is not a thing we believe on hearsay: it is what we see
within ourselves, or rather above ourselves, in very truth. The
Paul whom we believe so to have lived, we love because of what
we *see*. And were it not that above all we loved that pattern
which we perceive in everlasting fixity and changelessness, we
should not love the apostle because we retain the faith that his
life in the flesh was correspondent and accordant to that pattern. Yet we find that we are somehow stirred more largely to
love of the pattern itself, through the faith by which we believe
that a man has lived in accord with it, and by the hope which
forbids us, since there have been men who so lived, to despair
of ourselves who are men like them being able to live like them;
so that we desire it more ardently and pray for it more confidently. What makes us love their life is the love of that pattern
according to which we believe they lived; and their life, when
we believe it, stirs in us towards the same pattern a more burning charity. So that the stronger burns our love for God, the
more sure and unclouded is our vision of him; because in God
we behold the changeless pattern of righteousness, in accord
with which we make our judgment that a man should live.

Faith then avails for the knowledge and the love of God, not
as though he were wholly unknown or wholly unloved before,
but that he may be known more clearly and loved more steadfastly. 14 (x). Now the charity praised and preached with such
energy by divine Scripture, what is it but love of the good?
Love is the activity of a lover, and it has a certain object. There,
then, we have three things: the lover, that which is loved, and
love.[38] Love itself is nothing but a kind of life which couples
together or seeks to couple some two entities, the lover and the

---

[37] II Cor. 6:2 ff.

[38] Augustine thus fulfils his undertaking (11 (vii) above) to display a trinity
in love, but immediately warns the reader that this trinity is not "what
we seek": the reason being that the loved object is something external
to the lover. It is worth noting how small a place this particular analogy
occupies in his thought.

loved. This is so in the carnal loves of the external world; but
let us leave the flesh beneath our feet and rise to the soul, where
we may drink of a purer and more limpid spring. What does
any friend love in his friend but the soul? There too are the
three: the lover, the loved, and love. A further ascent still remains for us, a higher realm in which our search is to be pursued, so far as men may. But here we may pause—not supposing
we have found what we seek, but having found (as seekers do)
the place in which to look. We have found, not the thing itself,
but where it is to be sought; and that will suffice to give us a
point from which a fresh start may be undertaken.

BOOK IX

The Trinity of Mind, Knowledge, and Love

ARGUMENT

[We begin by considering the triad of love, lover, and beloved on the human level; for man is at least an image of God. But the human mind loves itself. Then subject and object coincide, and we have two entities instead of three, the mind and its love: two as related to one another, but together one as a spiritual reality (§ 2).

So far there is no trinity. But self-love implies self-knowledge, and once more we have three entities: the mind, its love, and its knowledge, in their perfect or ideal condition corresponding to one another in an absolute co-equality (§§ 3, 4). Self-knowledge and self-love are not properties attributable to the mind as subject, but themselves substantive realities, though not independent since essentially relative to one another (§§ 5, 6). Nor are they parts of a whole, or elements in a mixture: they are of one and the same substance, reciprocally inherent (§§ 7, 8).

We must distinguish, however, between the individual human mind as self-known and self-loved, which is no immutable reality, and the ideal form or pattern of mind which we recognize and approve in the light of truth (§§ 9–11). True knowledge may be regarded as a "word," conceived from our vision of truth and as it were "begotten" by inward speech (§ 12).— All our judgments of value, true or false, involve the production of such a "word," which owes its "conception" to love, and its "bringing forth" to the conscious act of approval (§§ 13, 14).— "Word" may thus be defined as = knowledge + love (§ 15). Since all knowledge must exhibit a correspondence or likeness to its object, the mental "word" is also appropriately called an "image" (§ 16). Love, on the other hand, is not "begotten" of

56

the mind (§ 17), as is the mind's knowledge of itself; for this knowledge is a discovery which presumes a *search*, and love is the motive of the seeking (§ 18).]

THE TEXT

1 (i). The object of our present enquiry is Trinity—not *a* Trinity, but *the* Trinity which is God—the true, supreme, and only God. The reader then must be patient: we are still enquiring, and such enquiry deserves no censure, provided that our search for what must baffle knowledge and expression be made in unshaken faith. Affirmation indeed calls at once and rightly for censure from any who may see and instruct to better purpose. "Seek God, and your soul shall live" [1]; but we are warned against all premature conceit of apprehension: "Seek his face alway." [2] "If any man," says Paul, "thinketh that he knoweth anything, he knoweth not yet how he ought to know. But whosoever loveth God, he is known of him." [3] He does not say "hath known him," which would be dangerous presumption, but "is known of him." So elsewhere, after saying "now that ye have known God," he at once corrects himself: "rather, are known of God" [4]; and most emphatic is that other passage: "Brethren, I count not myself to have apprehended; only, forgetting that which is behind and reaching out to those things which are before, I am intent to follow after the prize of the high calling of God in Christ Jesus. Let us, therefore, as many as be perfect, be thus minded." [5] By perfection in this life he understands nothing but to forget the things which are behind, and to reach out intently after the things which are before. The safest intention is that of seeking continually until the goal of all our effort and our reaching out be attained. The intent is rightly directed only if it set out from faith. A sure faith is itself a beginning of knowledge; but sure knowledge will not be perfected till after this life when we shall see face to face. [6] Let us then be thus minded, convinced that the temper of the truth-seeker is safer than that of rashly taking the unknown for known. Let us seek as expecting to find, and let us find as expecting still to seek. For "when a man hath done, then he beginneth." [7] Let us shun all doubt concerning matters of faith, let us refuse all hasty affirmation concerning matters of understanding: in

1 Ps. 69:32.   2 Ps. 105:4.   3 I Cor. 8:2 f.   4 Gal. 4:9.
5 Phil. 3:13 ff.   6 I Cor. 13:12.   7 Ecclesiasticus 18:7.

the one, holding to authority, in the other, seeking out the truth.

As for our present enquiry, let us believe that Father, Son, and Holy Spirit are one God, maker and ruler of the whole creation: that Father is not Son, nor Holy Spirit Father or Son; but a Trinity of mutually related Persons, and a unity of equal essence. And let us seek to understand this truth, praying for the help of him whom we would understand, and desiring to set forth what we understand as he shall enable us, with such careful reverence as to speak nothing unworthily, even if we sometimes speak mistakenly. Let us endeavour, for example, that if we say of the Father what properly does not belong to him, it may belong to the Son or to the Holy Spirit, or to the whole Trinity; that if we say something of the Son which does not properly apply to the Son, it may at least apply to the Father, or to the Holy Spirit, or to the whole Trinity; that if we say of the Holy Spirit what does not in strict propriety befit him, yet it be not foreign to the Father or to the Son, or to the one God which is the Trinity itself. We may desire to see whether the Holy Spirit be properly that most excellent gift of charity.[8] If he is not, then either the Father is Charity, or the Son, or the whole Trinity; since we may not oppose the certainty of faith and most mighty authority of the Scripture which says "God is charity." But we must never let the error of impiety so lead us astray that we speak of the Trinity that which belongs not to Creator but creature, or else is a product of vain imagining.

2 (ii). In view of all this let us consider those three things to which our enquiry has brought us. We are not yet concerned with things in heaven, not yet with God, Father, Son, and Holy Spirit; but with this image, inferior but still an image, which is man—so much more familiar and less difficult for the infirmity of our mind to study. I, the enquirer, present in my love for anything three things: myself, what I love, and love itself. Love itself, if I love it, must have its object; for there is no love where nothing is loved. Lover, the loved, and love: these are three. But suppose my love's object be myself; then the three become two—the object of love, and love. For when the lover loves himself, subject and object are the same; just as loving and being loved are in the love of self the same thing: there is no difference between the statements "he loves himself," and "he is loved by himself." In that case, to love and to be loved are not two things,

---

[8] This question is not taken up for detailed consideration until Book XV, 27 (xvii).

any more than are the lover and the beloved two persons. But still the love and its object remain two. For self-love is not love, unless the love itself be loved; and to love oneself and to love one's love are not the same thing, since (as we have said) love which is loved must already have its object, else it is no love.[9] In self-love, then, there are two things present, love and what is loved: the lover and the loved being one. From which it appears that a triad is not necessarily implied in the existence of love.

Let us abstract from our present consideration all the other elements of which human nature is composed; and in order to find what we are looking for in as clear a form as the matter permits, let us take the mind in isolation. In the mind's love for itself, two things are displayed—mind and love. Self-love is the will to be at one's own disposal for self-enjoyment. If the mind wills to be no more and no less than what it is, then will corresponds to mind and love is equal to lover.[10] If love is a really existing thing, it is not body but spirit. The same is true of the mind; yet the mind and its love are not two spirits, or two essences, but one, though this one thing is somehow two— lover and love, or (if you prefer to put it so) love and love's object. And these two are mutually related terms; lover being related to love and love to lover; for it is by love that the lover loves, and love is the activity of a loving person. Mind and spirit, on the other hand, are not relative terms, but denote the essence in itself: the mind and spirit are not what they are because they belong to a particular man. The term "man" connotes body; but if we abstract the body, mind and spirit remain, whereas if we abstract the lover, there is no love, and if we abstract the love, there is no lover. Thus as mutually related terms, they are two: in themselves, each is spirit, and both together are one spirit; each is mind, and both together are one mind. Where then is there a trinity? Let us apply all our powers to the question, invoking the everlasting Light to illuminate our darkness, that we may see in ourselves as may be permitted to us the image of God.

3 (iii). The mind cannot love itself unless it also knows itself. That it should love what it does not know is impossible. It would be folly to allege that the mind forms a general concept from its experience of other minds, and believes itself to belong to the same class of being. How can a mind, not knowing

---

9 See VIII, 10 (vii) n. Love as a relation remains a distinguishable reality, even when the subject and object related coincide.

10 This point is developed in § 4 below.

itself, know any other mind? It cannot be compared with the body's eye which sees other eyes but not itself. We see bodies with the bodily eyes, because the rays which flash from them and touch the thing seen cannot be reflected back upon the eyes, unless we are looking at a mirror. This is a very delicate and obscure subject, which needs much research before it can be clearly proved to be so or otherwise.[11] But whatever be the truth about our power of vision, the power itself, whether it acts by rays or in some other way, is something that we cannot see with our eyes: we enquire about it with the mind, and comprehend it (if we can) with the mind. We may say then that the mind acquires knowledge of corporeal things by the bodily senses, and of things incorporeal by itself. Being itself incorporeal, it must know itself by itself: if it does not know itself, it cannot love itself.

4 (iv). Now just as we found a duality, of mind and its love, in the fact of self-love; so there is a duality of mind and its knowledge in the fact of self-knowledge. Accordingly, the mind, its love, and its knowledge, constitute a triad. These three are one, and if perfect they are equal. If the mind's love of itself does not reach the measure of its being—if (say) the human mind, which is greater than the body, loves itself only with the love due to the human body, then there is sin: the love is not perfect. Again, if the measure of its self-love exceeds that of its being—if it should love itself with the love due to God, to whom it is incomparably inferior—then also there is great sin, and no perfect self-love. The sin is yet more perverse and iniquitous, when the body is loved with love due to God. Similarly a knowledge which falls short of its object, where full knowledge is possible, is not perfect. A knowledge which is greater than its object implies a superiority in the nature of the knower to that of the known: the knowledge of a body is greater than the body which is the object of the knowledge. For knowledge is a mode of life in the knowing mind, whereas the body is not life; and any life is greater, not in extent but in power, than any body. But when the mind knows itself, the knowledge does not exceed the self, for the self is both subject and object of the knowledge. If it knows the whole of itself, without any alien importation,[12]

---

[11] The theory of vision propounded in Plato's *Timaeus*, according to which "rays" proceed from the eyes and "mingle" with light in the atmosphere, was rejected by Aristotle.

[12] The error resulting from "alien importation" is discussed in Book X, 7 (v) ff.

the knowing is correspondent to the mind; for it is no less apparent that in this self-knowledge the knowing is not dependent on any other source. And when this knowledge takes in the whole self and nothing more, it is neither lesser nor greater than the self. Thus it is true to say that when each member of our triad is perfect, it follows that all three are equal.

5. At the same time we find ourselves encouraged to conceive how this triad really exists in the soul, inseparable though distinct to consciousness as so many substantive or essential realities; not as properties of a subject, like colour or shape in a body, or any other quality or quantity. For nothing of that kind can pass outside the subject to which it belongs: the colour or shape of a particular body cannot belong also to another. But the love whereby the mind loves itself can be directed to an object outside itself; the mind knows not only itself but much else as well. Therefore love and knowledge do not belong to the mind as attributes to a subject: their existence is as substantive as that of the mind itself. They can be regarded as mutually related terms, but each exists in a substance of its own. As related terms they are not comparable to colour and the coloured subject, where the colour possesses no substance proper to itself: the substance is the coloured body, the colour is *in* the substance. The relation is to be compared rather to that of two friends who are also men, that is, substances. "Men" is not a relative term, "friends" is.

6. "Lover," "knower," "knowledge," "love" are all substances; but while "lover" and "love," "knower" and "knowledge" are at the same time, like "friends," related terms, "mind" and "spirit" are relative no more than are "men." Yet it is not the case with "lover" and "love," "knower" and "knowledge," as it is with men who are friends, that they can exist apart from one another. It may appear that friends, *quâ* friends, can be separated in body only and not in soul. But it is possible for a friend to begin to hate his friend and thereby cease to be his friend, though the other may not know it and continue to love him. On the other hand, if the love with which the mind loves itself ceases to exist, the mind will also cease to be lover; and so with the knowledge whereby the mind knows itself. A head is a head, and it and that which is "headed" are related terms, though also substances, both being bodies; and if there be no head, the thing will not be "headed." But in this case severance can separate the two from one another, which is not so with "love" and "lover," or "knowledge" and "knower."

7. If any bodies exist which cannot be cut or divided at all, they must still be composed of their own parts or they would not be bodies. Part and whole are related terms, since every part belongs to some whole, and the whole is whole by a totality of parts. But since both part and whole are bodies, they exist not only as related but as substances. May we say then that the mind is a whole, and that the love with which it loves itself and the knowledge with which it knows itself are like two parts composing the whole? Or, alternatively, that they and the mind itself are those equal parts making up the one whole? The difficulty here is that no part embraces the whole to which it belongs; whereas the mind's knowledge when it knows itself as a whole, that is perfectly, extends over the whole of it; and when it loves itself perfectly it loves itself as a whole, and its love extends over the whole of it. Take another possible comparison. A single drink may be composed of wine, water, and honey: each component will extend throughout the whole, and yet they remain three: there is no part of the drink which does not contain all three—not side by side as would be oil and water, but completely mixed: all are substances, and the whole fluid is one definite substance made out of the three. Can we suppose that mind, love and knowledge exist together in the same kind of way? Apparently not. Water, wine and honey are not themselves of one substance, though one single substance of drink results from that mixture. But it seems certain that our "mental" triad must be of one and the same substance; since the mind itself loves itself and knows itself, and its "threeness" does not involve its being loved or known by anything else. The three must then necessarily have one and the same essence; and if they were intermingled they would not be three, nor capable of mutual relation. Three similar rings, for example, might be made out of one piece of gold: they might be linked together, but would still be mutually related, as being alike, and all likeness being a relation. We should have a trinity of rings and all one gold. But if they were melted down and mixed with one another in a single lump, there would be an end to the trinity. We could still speak as with the three rings, of "one gold," but no longer of three golden objects.

8 (v). In our triad, on the other hand, in which the mind knows and loves itself, we have a permanent trinity of mind, love, and knowledge. There is no loss of identity in mixture; though severally each is in itself and mutually each as a whole is in the others as wholes, whether each singly in the other pair

or the pairs in each singly. In other words, all are in all. The mind is in itself, being a substantive term; though it is termed knowing, known, or knowable in relation to its knowledge, and loving, loved, or lovable in relation to the love with which it loves itself. Knowledge is indeed related to the mind knowing or known, but still it is properly termed known and knowing in itself, for the knowledge by which the mind knows itself is not unknown to the knowledge itself. Similarly love, though related to the loving mind to which it belongs, still remains of itself and in itself; for love is loved, and that can only be by the love which is itself. This shows that each of the three singly is in itself. Again, they are alternately in one another: the loving mind is in the love, love is in the lover's knowledge, knowledge in the knowing mind. They are severally in the remaining pairs: the mind which knows and loves itself is in its love and knowledge; the love of the loving and self-knowing mind is in the mind and its knowledge; the knowledge of the self-knowing and loving mind is in the mind and its love, because it loves its knowledge and knows its love. The three pairs are in each single member; for the mind which knows and loves itself is in the love together with its knowledge, and in the knowledge together with the love; and the love and the knowledge are together in the mind which loves and knows itself. And the manner in which wholes are in wholes we have already indicated: the mind loving and knowing the whole of itself, knowing the whole of its love, and loving the whole of its knowledge, whenever the three members are each in themselves perfect. In a wonderful way, the three are inseparable from one another, and yet each one of them is a substance, and all together are one substance or essence, though mutually related to one another.

9 (vi). But the object of the human mind's self-knowledge and self-love is not something changeless. Any individual man may upon introspection "speak his own mind" in one way, by observing what takes place in himself, but give a definition of the human mind according to genus or species in a different way. Thus, when he speaks of his own mind and tells me whether he understands something or not, whether he wishes something or not, I believe him. But when he gives a true definition of the human mind by species or genus, I recognize and confirm the truth. This shows that what the individual sees in himself, which his neighbour may believe, without seeing, upon his word, is not the same as what he sees in very truth, which his neighbour may contemplate also. The one changes in process

of time, while the other stands fast in a changeless eternity. It is not that we see many minds with the bodily eye, and so by comparison put together a knowledge of the human mind according to genus and species. No, we contemplate that imperishable truth, from which we derive our more or less adequate definition, not of that which the mind of any individual man *is*, but of that which in the everlasting order it *ought* to be.

10. Even with regard to the images of material things, acquired through the senses and imprinted in the memory, making it possible for the mind to form imaginary pictures of things not seen, which will either differ from the actual originals or display a chance correspondence with them—we must admit that our judgments of approval or disapproval of these images, if rightly made, are based upon quite other standards, which in their changeless existence transcend our own minds. Whether I recall the walls of Carthage which I have seen, or picture those of Alexandria which I have not, I distinguish between the different images which present themselves, and my preference of one to another is a rational preference: there is a higher judgment of truth, strong and clear, based in its own right on its inviolate standards. It may be partly covered by the cloud of material images, but it remains itself uninvolved and unconfounded.

11. But much will depend on whether I am shut off from the transparent heaven, beneath or within this fog of obscurity, or whether I stand as on a mountain top in the open air between, looking up to the unclouded light above me and down upon the thick mists below. Whence comes it that the warmth of brotherly love is kindled in me, when I hear of some man who has endured the sharpest torments in steady and undisfigured faith? Point out to me the man himself, and I am eager to meet him and know him, to be bound in friendship with him. If opportunity offers, I approach and greet him, I talk with him, I put my feeling for him into such words as I can, I want him in return to have and to express such a feeling towards me; and I strive for an embrace of spirit in faith and trust, since I cannot all at once find my way to a thorough discernment of his inmost heart. And so I love him as a brave and faithful man, with a love pure and true. But suppose that as we talk he admits, or shows by some unconsidered remark, that even his faith is not what it should be, that he seeks in God for some material benefit and has borne his sufferings in that false hope—whether in the desire of monetary reward or in the vain lust for human

praise. At once the love which carried me towards him falls back rebuffed: it removes itself from the man's unworthiness, and remains in the unchanging pattern which had made me love him when I believed him worthy. If I do still love him, it is that he may become such as I have found him not to be. In him nothing has changed; though change is possible, and he may yet become what I had believed him. In my mind there has been a change in my estimate of him, which is no longer what it was; and my love has been diverted at the bidding of supreme and changeless right, from a purpose of enjoyment to a purpose of amendment. But the pattern of truth, unshaken and stead-fast, by which in the belief of his goodness I might have enjoyed his friendship, and by which I now seek his amendment—this pattern still sheds the constant and eternal light of pure and incorruptible reason, upon my mind's gaze, and upon that cloud of imaginings to which I look down from the mountain when I reflect upon the man I saw.

In the same way, I may recall to my mind some finely pro-portioned arch which I have seen, say, at Carthage. Then, an object conveyed to the mind by ocular report and imparted to the memory, is the cause of my imaged vision. But my mind's eye sees something else, which is the ground of my approval for the work of art, and which would enable me if I disapproved to correct it. We pass judgment on this in accordance with that other, and that other pattern is object of the rational mind's contemplation. We may be in contact with things present through the senses, we may retain images of things absent in the memory; we may use such images to form pictures which we could realize in actual construction if we had the will or the ability. But it is in one way that we frame our mental images of bodies, or perceive bodies with the bodily sense: it is in another that we apprehend with the grasp of intuition the principles of art embodied in such forms, and transcending the mind's vision.

12 (vii). Thus, in that realm of eternal truth from which all things temporal were made, we behold with our mind's eye the pattern upon which our being is ordered, and which rules all to which we give effect with truth and reason, in ourselves or in the outer world. Thence we conceive a truthful knowledge of things, which we have within us as a kind of *word*, begotten by an inward speech, and remaining with us after its birth. When we speak to others, we apply the service of our voice or of some material sign to this indwelling "word," in order that by means

of a perceptible prompting there may take place in the hearer's mind something like what remains in the mind of the speaker. There is nothing that we effect through the body by act or speech involving judgments of ethical value, that is not preceded by the utterance of such an inner word. No-one does anything deliberately that he has not previously spoken in his heart. 13. And this word owes its conception to love, whether it be the love of the creature or of the Creator—of that which is by nature changeable, or of the changeless Truth. The word is conceived, that is, either by covetousness or by charity. I do not mean that the creature should not be loved; but a love of the creature, if it be referred to the Creator, becomes charity and not covetousness. It is covetousness when the creature is loved for its own sake; and then it serves not to aid our use but to corrupt our enjoyment. The creature is either equal or inferior to ourselves: the inferior is to be used in relation to God: the equal is to be enjoyed, but only in God. As you ought to enjoy yourself, not in yourself but in him who made you, so you should enjoy him whom you love as yourself. Thus we are to enjoy ourselves and our brothers in the Lord, not daring to let ourselves sink downwards into our own keeping.[13]

The word is born when we approve the product of our thought, either for sinning or for doing right. And this word of ours, and the mind of which it is begotten, are united by the middle term of love, which binds itself to them as a third member in a spiritual embrace without any confusion. 14 (ix). Conception and birth of the word coincide, when the will comes to rest in the knowledge itself—as happens in the love of things spiritual. The man, for example, whose knowledge and love of righteousness are perfect, *is* thereby righteous, even though there be no occasion for an outward and bodily act displaying it. In the love of things carnal and temporal, on the other hand, the conception of the word and its bringing forth, like the conception and bringing forth of animals, are two

13 This paragraph summarizes the central principle of Augustinian ethics, viz., the distinction between "use" and "enjoyment," which is worked out in the first Book of the De Doctrina Christiana. The final end of man's existence is the "enjoyment" of God, which consists in union with him through knowledge and love. Nevertheless, our love of one another is not merely a means to the love of God: the love of neighbour is a love of "enjoyment," not of "use," for in the love of God the love of neighbour is necessarily included or contained. The "peace of the Heavenly City" is a "fellowship of perfect order and harmony in the enjoyment of God and of one another in God" (De Civ., XIX, 13).

different things. Here, what is conceived by desire is born by acquisition. Avarice is not satisfied by the knowledge and love of gold without its possession: sensuality or ambition require not only the knowledge and love of eating and drinking and sexual intercourse, of dignities and powers, but their exercise. Yet all such things will fail to satisfy even when possessed. "He that drinketh of this water, shall thirst again"; [14] or as the Psalm has it: "He hath conceived sorrow, and brought forth iniquity" [15]: that is, sorrow or toil is conceived in the conception of that which it is not enough to know and love, so that the soul is sick and fevered with need until it attains them, "brings them forth." Our Latin words for "gains" (*parta*) or "finds" (*reperta, comperta*) appropriately suggest derivation from "bringing forth" (*partus*). "Covetousness when it hath conceived bringeth forth sin." [16] So the Lord cries aloud: "Come unto me, all that travail and are burdened," and again: "Woe unto them that are with child, or give suck in those days." [17] Every good deed or sin is related to this bringing forth of the word in the saying: "From thy mouth thou shalt be justified, and from thy mouth thou shalt be condemned" [18]; where "mouth" signifies, not the one we see, but the invisible inward "mouth" of thought and heart.

15 (x). The question properly arises, whether all knowledge is "word," or only the knowledge which is loved. We know also what we hate; but we should not speak of the mind's conceiving or bringing forth that in which we take no pleasure. Not all that affects us in any way is "conceived": some things which are known only, are not to be called "words"—and with these we are now concerned. We must distinguish three senses of "word." First, the word temporally extended in syllables, whether spoken aloud or only thought. Second, anything known and fixed in the mind, so long as memory retains it for production and definition, though the thing itself be displeasing. Third, that in the mental conception of which we take pleasure. In this last sense of "word" we understand the apostle's saying: "No man *saith* Jesus is Lord, but in the Holy Spirit" [19]; whereas we learn that others may say the same thing, but in another sense, from the Lord's own words: "Not every one that saith unto me, Lord, Lord, shall enter into the kingdom of heaven." [20] Yet we should note that when it is *right* for us to take no pleasure in anything that we hate and to disapprove it, our disapproval

14 John 4:13.   15 Ps. 7:14.   16 James 1:15.   17 Matt. 11:28; 24:19.
18 Matt. 12:37.   19 I Cor. 12:3.   20 Matt. 7:21.

itself is approved, pleases, and is a "word." It is not the knowledge of faults that displeases us but the faults themselves. It
pleases me that I know and can define the meaning of intemperance; and that constitutes its "word." So in any art or skill
there are known faults of which the knowledge is rightly
approved: the connoisseur discerns the appearance and the
lack of a particular excellence, and can affirm or deny its presence; but the lack of the excellence and the liability to the
fault are properly condemned. To define intemperance, to utter
its "word," belongs to the art of morals: to be intemperate,
belongs to that which the same art censures. Again, it belongs
to the art of speech to know and define a solecism; but to commit one is a fault to which the same art attaches blame.

The purpose of this discussion has been to suggest that what
makes a "word" is knowledge together with love. Thus when
the mind knows and loves itself, its "word" is united to it by
love. And since it loves the knowledge and knows the love, the
word is in the love and the love in the word, and both are in the
mind that loves and speaks. 16 (xi). Now all knowledge that
deals with a positive object is like the thing it knows. There is
another knowledge dealing with negations or defects which we
express in the form of disapproval. The disapproval of the
defect is commendation of the positive object, and therefore is
itself approved. The mind therefore will possess a certain likeness to the object known, whether this object pleases or its
absence displeases. And accordingly so far as we know God, we
are like him—though not of course to the degree of equality,
since our knowledge of him is not equal to his knowledge of
himself. When sense perception makes us acquainted with
bodies, a likeness of them appears in our mind, which is the
memory-image: it is not the bodies themselves which are in our
mind when we think of them, but their likenesses. If we accept
one for the other, we are mistaken: to take one thing for another
is precisely to "mistake"; and yet the imaging of a body in the
mind is of higher value than the bodily object itself, in so far
as the former exists in a higher being, namely, a vital substance
such as the mind. So it is with our knowledge of God. We are
indeed raised to a higher goodness than we had before we knew
him; when that knowledge is delighted in and loved as it deserves, it becomes a "word," and effects in us a certain likeness
to God. Yet it is an inferior likeness, as existing in an inferior
being: the soul is creature, God creator. We conclude that
when the mind knows and approves itself, the knowledge as the

mind's "word" is entirely and constantly correspondent and adequate to the mind; being knowledge neither of a lower essence like the body, nor of a higher, like God. And while all knowledge has a likeness to its object, that is to the thing known, the likeness in this knowledge, by which the knowing mind is known to itself, is perfect and adequate. Accordingly it is both image and word, being moulded upon the mind to which in the act of knowing it is equated; and the thing begotten is equal to the begetter.

17 (xii). We turn now to love, and ask whether it too is not image, word, or offspring. If the mind begets its knowledge in knowing itself, why should it not beget its love in loving itself? If, because it is knowable, it is the cause of its own knowing, it should be the cause of its own love because it is lovable. It becomes hard to say why it should not be the begetter of both. In our thought of the supreme Trinity, God the omnipotent Creator, in whose image man was made, this is a question apt to perplex men who are called to faith in God's truth by way of human modes of speech. Why may we not believe or understand the Holy Spirit also to be begotten of God the Father and to be nameable as his Son? What we are now endeavouring is to pursue this problem as best we may in the human mind. From the study of this inferior image, where we can look for answer to our questioning from the nature we know as our own, the mind's eye may acquire the keenness which it needs if we are to lift it from the illumined creature towards the changeless Light. It may be that truth itself will convince us that even as no Christian doubts the Word of God to be his Son, so the Spirit is charity. Let us then return to that creaturely image which is the rational mind, and address ourselves to it with a closer questioning. We find here arising in time a knowledge of certain things unknown before, and a love of some things which were not loved before; and this may put us in the way of a clearer account, since for a discourse which must move in time from point to point, a subject which belongs itself to the temporal order is the easier to expound.

18. And first it should be plain that a thing can well be knowable, a possible object of knowledge, and yet be unknown; while it is impossible for that which was not already knowable to be known. Clearly then we must hold that everything we come to know begets in us the knowledge of itself. The knowledge is offspring of both the knower and the thing known; so that in knowing itself, the mind is sole parent of its knowledge,

being itself both known and knower. Before it knew itself, it was knowable to itself; but the knowledge of self was not at that time contained in it. In coming to know itself, it begets a self-knowledge which is equal or adequate to itself; for the extent of its knowledge is not less than its being, and the knowledge is not other in essence, the mind itself constituting (as we have said) both subject and object of the knowledge. We come back, then, to our question about love. Why should not the mind, in loving itself, be said similarly to have begotten its self-love? Before loving itself, it was lovable to itself, having the capacity of self-love; just as before knowing itself it was knowable to itself, having the capacity of self-knowledge. Otherwise it could never have acquired either self-knowledge or self-love. Why then may we not say that by the act of self-love it has begotten its love, exactly as by the act of self-knowledge it has begotten its knowledge?

The answer may be that the *source* of the love must plainly be that from which it proceeds; and that is the mind itself, which is self-lovable before it is self-loving, and thus is source of the love by which it loves itself; but that there is good reason for not calling this love "begotten" of the mind, like the knowledge by which it knows itself, because knowledge is a thing discovered, and the discovery is often preceded by a search which aims at resting in its object. Search is a striving for discovery, which is the same thing as finding; and things found are as it were "brought forth"—we remember the connection between the Latin words *partus* and *repertus*—and so comparable with an offspring. The bringing forth can only be in the knowledge itself, where they are (as we may say) shaped and formed. The actual things we seek and find, already existed; but the knowledge did not, and the knowledge is the "offspring" which we count as being "born." On the other hand, the striving which appears in the search proceeds from the seeker, remaining in a kind of suspense, and only coming to rest in the desired end, when the object sought is found and coupled to the seeker. This striving or search may seem a different thing from the love by which the thing known is loved, inasmuch as the knowledge sought is yet to be realized. None the less, it is something of the same kind. It can really be described as "will": for everyone who seeks is willing to find; and if what is sought is matter of knowledge, then every one who seeks is willing to know. If the will is eager and earnest, we call it diligence—especially as applied to the pursuit and acquisition of the various branches of learning.

Accordingly we may say that the mind's "bringing forth" is preceded by a kind of striving, by which, in the seeking and finding of what we desire to know, knowledge is born as off-spring. It follows that this striving, whereby knowledge is conceived and brought forth, cannot properly be called "brought forth" or "offspring." This same striving, or eager pursuit of the thing yet to be known, becomes love of the thing known, when it holds in its embrace the offspring, the knowledge, in which it delights, and joins it to the begetter.

Here then, is a kind of image of the Trinity: the mind itself, its knowledge which is at once its offspring and self-derived "word," and thirdly love. These three are one, and one single substance. The mind is no greater than its offspring, when its self-knowledge is equal to its being; nor than its love, when its self-love is equal to its knowledge and to its being.

Book X

The Realization of Self-knowledge: *Memory, Understanding, Will*

ARGUMENT

[The notion of love as a "search" raises the question whether it is possible to love what is not known. In all pursuit of knowledge there is love (§ 1). The student, e.g., of languages, already knows the value of linguistic knowledge in general: his love is directed to an ideal present to his mind. He seeks to know the unknown for the sake of something that he knows already (§§ 2–4).

But though we can in this way understand the search for knowledge of other things, such explanation is not applicable to the mind's search for knowledge of itself. In desiring and seeking self-knowledge, the mind cannot be entirely ignorant of itself (§ 5). Yet there are serious objections to any idea that the mind can either know or be known "in part" (§ 6).

It is best to take the maxim "Know thyself" as an injunction to reflect upon our own nature, and to accept in practice our real status—under God, over the material world. We are unconsciously assimilated to what we love; and love of the material causes the mind to conceive itself as material (§§ 7, 8). Hence the various materialist theories of the mind's nature (§§ 9, 10). We can "know ourselves" only by freeing ourselves from all such theories, which have no immediate self-evidence (§§ 11, 12), and confining our beliefs to the immediate deliveries of consciousness—the indubitable facts of our mental and volitional life (§§ 13–16).

Among these, we find in memory, understanding, and will, a triad of certainties with regard to the nature of the mind (§ 17). They present a single substantial reality, in differing relations to itself; and they correspond co-equally and completely to one another (§ 18). In the following Book, we shall try to illustrate their relations by a study of the temporal processes of sense-perception (§ 19).]

THE TEXT

1 (i). We must now attempt a keener analysis in order to achieve a clear and connected view of the matter we have been discussing. In the first place, we note that it is quite impossible to love anything which is entirely unknown. This requires us to observe carefully the nature of the love involved in any diligent study: I mean the love of one who does not yet know, but desires to know, a particular subject. In matters to which we do not customarily apply the word study, a love will arise from what is heard: the report of a thing of beauty will arouse in the mind the desire to see and enjoy. We have a general knowledge of physical beauty drawn from a number of instances previously seen; and so we have in our mind a standard of valuation for the external object of our interest. In this case, the love aroused is not for something completely unknown, since we have a knowledge of the *kind* of thing. Again, our love of a good man whose face we have not seen is based on a knowledge of the virtues which truth itself has given us. In the pursuit of knowledge of the various branches of learning, it is generally the authority of some eulogizer or professor that sets us going: yet if we had not already in our mind a summary impression of the learning concerned, we could feel no ardour for its acquisition. No-one, for example, would devote care and trouble to the study of rhetoric, if he did not know that it was the science of speaking. Sometimes we may be struck with admiration of the achievements of a science, reported or experienced, and so be set on acquiring by study the ability to perform them. A man ignorant of letters might be told that there is a science by which anyone may be enabled to send words wrought by hand in silence to a recipient at any distance, which the latter will apprehend not through the ear but through the eye; and he may see the thing done. Naturally, in his desire to know how to do it, his zeal will be directed to the purpose which he already knows. It is in this way that the learner is stimulated to diligent study. For no-one can possibly love that of which he is wholly ignorant.

2. If you hear an unknown signal, such as the sound of a word of whose significance you are ignorant, you may want to know what it means, what is the object which the sound is used to indicate. You hear, say, the word *temetum*; and because you do not understand it, you enquire what it means. You must already be aware that it is a signal, that it is not a purposeless

noise but has a certain significance. Otherwise, knowing already
the three syllables uttered, and having an impression of them
formed in your mind by the sense of hearing, what further knowledge about it could you require, knowing as you do all its
letters and sound-quantities? You are not satisfied, because you
are simultaneously aware that it is a signal, and that arouses
your desire to know what it signifies. The fuller the knowledge
which yet falls short of completeness, the greater the mind's
desire for what remains to be known. If you were aware only
of the existence of the sound, but not of its being a signal of
some object, you would look for nothing more, sense perception
having already conveyed to you all that was perceptible. But
since you have learnt that it is not only a sound but a signal,
you want a complete knowledge of the signal; and no signal is
completely known without a knowledge of what it signifies. An
ardent seeker for such knowledge, who eagerly pursues his
study, can hardly be said to have no love.

What then does he love? It is certain that a thing cannot be
loved it if is not known. In the case supposed, what he loves is
not the three syllables of which he already has knowledge. He
may love the known fact that they have a meaning; but that is
not our present concern, for that is not what he seeks to know:
we are asking what it is that he loves in the object of his study,
which obviously he does not yet know; and the reason for this
love is a puzzle to us because we are assured that only things
known can be loved. The only possible explanation is that in the
universe of reason he knows and contemplates the beauty of
that learning which embraces the knowledge of all signs or
signals, and the usefulness of the technique which gives human
society the power of inter-communication: for the meetings of
men would be no better than absolute solitude if they could not
exchange their thoughts in converse. The beauty and the usefulness of this ideal is what the soul perceives, knows, and
loves; and to enquire about what is unknown in significant
sounds is to seek by study for the fuller realization of that ideal
in oneself. To behold it in the light of truth is not the same as to
covet its possession. One may behold in the light of truth the
greatness and goodness of a universal comprehension and
speaking of the languages of all nations, so that none would be
as the language of a foreigner to any man. The worth of such
knowledge may be perceived in thought, and loved as a thing
known. The view of it may so inspire the studies of learners that
it becomes the centre of their activity, and towards it is aimed

all their labour in pursuit of a possession by which they may realize in practice what they have recognized in idea. The possession that is hopefully approached is object of a love so much the more eager and ardent. We study with the more energy the sciences which we do not despair of understanding: that which a man has no hope of acquiring he will love either feebly or not at all, though he may see its beauty. Accordingly, the knowledge of all languages being beyond the hopes of most, everyone will give more particular study to that of his own people; and though one may feel that a complete knowledge even of that exceeds one's capacity, yet no one is so indolent in the matter as not, when he hears an unknown word, to want to know its meaning, and to enquire into it and learn it if he can. The enquiry implies a zeal for learning, and the enquirer appears to be loving a thing unknown to him. But it is not so. For what touches his soul is the ideal which he knows and meditates, from which shines forth the value of a union of minds through the hearing and returning of familiar sounds; and that kindles in him the zeal for study, in which he will seek for what he does not know, but contemplate and love the known ideal to which it appertains.

Let us return to our example. If you were asked, on your enquiring what the word *temetum* means, how that concerned you, you would reply: "Because I might hear someone use the word and not understand him, or come across it in reading and be ignorant of the writer's meaning." No-one would retort that you must not understand what you hear or know what you read about. Nearly every rational soul can immediately see the beauty of this acquirement whereby the thoughts of men are made known to one another by the utterance of significant sounds. Because you know the value of it, and love it because you know it, you enquire with the interest of a student about the unknown word. And when you have heard to your satisfaction that *temetum* was an ancient name for wine, but in our modern usage has become obsolete, you may still count it needful for you to know as a reader of ancient literature. Or if you have no use for such reading, you may think it not worth committing to memory; since you see that it has no relevance to the known ideal of learning which your mind contemplates and loves.

3. We may conclude that the love active in the student mind, which wants to know that of which it is ignorant, is not the love of something unknown but of something known, for the sake of

which it desires a knowledge not possessed. A man may indeed be moved not by anything already known but by mere curiosity, carried away simply by the love of getting to know the unknown. He ought to be distinguished from the student and called rather "curious." But not even he loves the unknown: indeed it would be more appropriate to say that he hates the unknown, which in his wish to know everything he would reduce to non-existence. If the problem be thrown back upon us with the objection that it is no more possible to hate than to love what one does not know, we may concede the point; but it should be understood that the statement "He loves [1] to know the unknown" is not equivalent to the statement "He loves the unknown." It is possible for anyone to love to know the unknown, but not to love the unknown. In the former phrase the words "to know" are not otiose; for it is not the unknown but knowledge itself that is loved by him who loves to know the unknown. And unless knowledge itself were known, one could not say with confidence either that one knew or that one did not. Not only does the statement "I know," if it is a true statement, involve the knowing what knowledge is; but the same is involved also in the statement "I do not know," if made confidently and truly, with knowledge of its truth; for the speaker must distinguish the ignorant from the knower, if looking into his own mind he says truly, "I do not know." And if he knows that he speaks the truth, how could that be if he does not know what knowledge is?

4 (ii). To sum up: neither the true student nor the curious enquirer loves the unknown, even in his most ardent pursuit of the knowledge of what he does not know. Either (1) the object of his love is already known to him in kind, and he is seeking to know it also in some particular case or cases, which he may hear commended though as yet unknown to him. His mind will form an image of the thing, and that will stir his love; but it can only have been formed from what he knew already. If he should find the example commended to him unlike the pictured mental image already made familiar by reflection, he may have no love for it: if he has, the love will arise from his acquaintance with it. Before that, what he had loved was something else to which the formative work of the mind had accustomed his imagination. If, on the other hand, he finds the thing spoken of to be like his

---

[1] It must be remembered that throughout this examination of the "love involved in diligent study" (*amor studentium*), "love" connotes "desire": it is love as yet unsatisfied. (See Introduction, *ad fin.*)

picture of it, so that he might truly say that "he loved it before he saw it," that love will still not have been for the unknown, for its object will have been known to him in the image. Or (2) we see something and love it under the ideal form of timeless reason: and when we find it expressed in terms of temporal reality, led by the testimony of another's experience, and so love it, we are not (as sufficiently argued above) loving the unknown. Or (3) we love something we know, for the sake of which we seek for something unknown; and then it is by no means love of the unknown that possesses us, but of the other known thing, to which we know that the knowledge of what we still seek in ignorance is relevant. This was illustrated above by the unfamiliar word. Or lastly (4) the love is for knowledge itself, which cannot be unknown to anyone desiring it.

For these reasons, when we wish to know what we are ignorant of, and the eager pursuit of our enquiry makes it impossible to deny the presence in it of love, it appears as though we were loving the unknown. But I think that a careful observation must be convinced by my argument that the matter stands otherwise, and that nothing at all is loved if it be unknown. The examples given, however, apply only in regard to persons wanting to know things other than themselves. We must be prepared for a new aspect of the problem, when we look at the mind's desire for knowledge of itself.

5 (iii). What then is the object of the mind's love, when, still unknown to itself, it eagerly seeks to know itself? There is the fact, of the mind's seeking to know itself, and devoting itself with ardour to the study. In this there must be love; but for what? Not, surely, for itself, since as yet it is ignorant of itself, and no-one can love what he does not know. Let us examine the possibilities. (1) Its form may have been described to it by report, in the way in which we are told about persons absent. In that case what it loves may be not itself, but an imaginary picture of itself which may be quite different from what it really is. Or the picture may be like itself, so that in loving the picture it is loving itself before knowing, since it contemplates a likeness of itself. It must then have known other minds from which the picture is drawn, and so be known to itself generically. But why should it have knowledge of other minds and not of itself, seeing that nothing can be more immediately present to it than itself? To the bodily eyes, it is true, other eyes are more known than themselves; but if the case of the mind is similar, it may as well abandon a hopeless quest. Eyes will never see themselves except

in mirrors; and we cannot conceive of any similar appliance for the contemplation of incorporeal things, by which the mind could know itself as in a mirror. (2) A second possibility is that it sees in the eternal truth of reason the excellence of self-knowledge, loves what it sees, and studies to realize it in itself. Though it is not known to itself, it knows how good it would be to know itself. Yet it seems strange indeed that the mind which does not yet know itself should know already the beauty of self-knowledge. (3) Or again, it may see a final good, its own safety and happiness, by means of some hidden memory which has remained with it in all its journeyings afield; and it may believe that it can never attain that end, unless it know itself. So the love of the end may cause it to seek for the means: it loves the known end and therefore seeks the unknown means. But why should the memory of its happiness have been able to remain with it, and not the memory of itself? Why should it not know the self that wishes to attain the end as well as the end it wishes to attain? (4) Lastly, in loving the knowledge of itself, its love may be not for the self which is still unknown but simply for the knowledge: it may naturally resent that its own place should be vacant among the objects of that knowledge which it would have to be all-embracing. It knows what knowledge is, and, loving what it knows, desires also the knowledge of itself. How then can it know its knowledge and not know itself? It knows that it knows other things and not itself: that is what enables it to know what knowledge is. But how, if it is ignorant of itself, can it know itself as having any knowledge? It is not some other mind that it knows as knowing, but itself: therefore it knows itself. Similarly, in its seeking to know itself, it knows itself as seeking: again therefore it must already have a knowledge of itself. It follows that the mind cannot be entirely ignorant of itself, since the knowledge of itself as ignorant is to that extent a knowledge of itself: if it were ignorant of its ignorance, it would not seek for self-knowledge. And therefore the fact of the seeking proves that it is more known to itself than unknown; for in seeking to know itself it knows itself as seeking and as ignorant.

6 (iv). Are we then to say that the mind partly knows and partly does not know itself? It would be absurd to maintain that the whole mind does not know what it knows. I am not saying that it must know the whole, but that whatever it knows, the whole of it knows. Accordingly, in any knowledge about itself, which must be possessed by the whole mind, it knows that the

whole mind is knowing.[2] Further, it knows itself as having some object of its knowledge; but any such object must be present to the whole mind. Therefore it knows the whole of itself. Again, nothing about the mind can be more certainly known to itself than the fact of its being alive: it cannot be mind and not be alive, though it has intellect over and above life, whereas the souls of beasts have life without intellect. Now just as the mind is the whole mind, so it is the whole of it that lives. But it knows that it is alive; therefore it knows the whole of itself. Finally, in seeking to know itself, the mind must know that it is a mind: otherwise it would not know whether it was really seeking itself, and the search might be wrongly directed; since, for all it knows, it may not be a mind, and then its search for knowledge of the mind would not be a search for itself. Thus, since it knows that its search for the nature of mind is a search for itself, it must necessarily know that it is itself a mind; and if it knows no more of itself than that it is a mind, and wholly a mind, it must know the whole of itself.

But let us suppose that it does not know that it is a mind, but in seeking itself knows only that this is what it is doing. If it is ignorant of its own nature, it may still mistake the object of its search: if such mistake is to be avoided, it must certainly know what the object is. And if it knows what it is seeking, and is in fact seeking itself, then it knows itself. Why then should the search go on? Suppose it knows itself in part, and in part is still seeking; then the object of the search is not itself—which means itself as a whole—but a part of it. In that case, knowing that the whole of itself is not yet found, it must know the extent of the whole: it will be seeking what is lacking to its knowledge, in the way that we try to recall to our mind what has escaped, but not altogether escaped our memory—since we can recognize when it comes back to us that this is what we were looking for. But here there are two difficulties: the notion of the mind's returning

2 The MSS. vary between *tota se scit* ("the whole of it knows itself"), and *totam se scit* ("it knows the whole of itself"). Augustine has just said that the idea of a knowledge possessed by only part of the mind is absurd: what he has to prove is that if the whole mind knows itself, it cannot be knowing only a part of itself. The first of the two MS. readings merely repeats what has already been said, while the second begs the question. The translation given assumes that the original text was *totam se scit scire*, which gives the required step in the argument. If the *whole* mind knows, it cannot be unaware of that fact; but if it knows itself as wholly possessing an object of knowledge, that is as much as to say that it knows itself as a whole.

into the mind seems to imply that the mind can be absent from itself; and also we have to say that it is not seeking for the whole of itself, having already found a part, and yet that the whole mind is seeking. It is present to itself as a whole, and then nothing remains to be sought; for what is lacking is the object not the subject of the seeking. Thus if the whole mind is seeking itself, no part of it can be lacking. Or if what seeks is not the whole mind, but the part already found, seeking the part not found, then the mind will not be seeking itself, since no part of it seeks the same part: the part found does not seek itself, nor does the part unfound seek itself, being the object of search to the part found. It would follow, since neither the whole mind nor any part of it seeks itself, that the mind is not seeking itself at all.

7 (v). What then can be the purport of the injunction, Know thyself?[3] I suppose it is that the mind should reflect upon itself, and live in accordance with its nature: that is to say, strive to be ordered according to its nature, under him whom it should be set under, and over all that it should stand over— under him by whom it ought to be ruled, over all that it ought to rule. For perverse desire makes it act often as though it had forgotten itself. It sees beauties of the inward realm, belonging to that transcendent reality which is God. Its duty is to stand fast for the enjoyment of them; but because it would ascribe them to itself, and instead of being a derived likeness of God, derive from itself the being that is his only, it turns away from him, loses its stability and sinks into something constantly diminishing, in the fancy that it is constantly increasing. For neither can it suffice itself, nor can aught else suffice it if it withdraw from him who alone suffices. Through poverty and distress it grows over-occupied with its own dealings and the restless pleasures gathered from them; and so, bent on the acquisition of knowledge from external things, the like of which it knows and loves and feels that it may lose unless it put forth all its energy to retain them, it loses its security, and reflects upon itself the less, the more secure it imagines itself against the loss of itself.

---

[3] The reference is to the famous maxim of Greek wisdom, attributed to Thales and inscribed in Apollo's temple at Delphi. Augustine may be thinking of Cicero, *Tusc. Quaest.*, I, 22: "When Apollo says, Know thyself, he means, Know thy soul." It was Augustine's own early ideal to "Know God and the soul" (*Solil.*, I, 7)—the ideal which he is now attempting to realize.

Not to know oneself is a different thing from not thinking of oneself. We do not say that a man proficient in many branches of learning is ignorant of grammar when he is not thinking of it, because at the moment he is thinking of the art of medicine. But though not knowing oneself and not thinking of oneself are different, the power of love is such that what the mind has long and lovingly thought over will stick to it like glue, and accompany it even when it comes back (as it were) to the thought of itself. Its love has been devoted to the material things with which the bodily senses have involved it in a persistent familiarity; and because it cannot take with it into the inward realm of immaterial being the material objects themselves, it collects and carries along images of them, formed in itself and of itself. It puts into their making something of its own substance, preserving a certain power of free judgment upon the form of such images—a power which is the peculiar property of mind or rational understanding, whose capacity for passing judgment is not lost; whereas those parts of the soul which receive impressions corresponding to material objects we are conscious of sharing with animals.

8 (vi). Now the mind goes astray through uniting itself to these images by a love so intense as to make it suppose its own nature to be like theirs. It becomes as it were conformed to them, not in reality but by supposition: supposing itself to be, not an image, but the actual thing of which it carries the image in itself. There remains active in it the power of distinguishing the material and external object from the interior image; except when these images so take shape as to give the effect of external impressions instead of internal, as happens in dream, or madness, or ecstatic experiences. 9 (vii). Thus the mind, supposing itself to resemble its own images, supposes itself to be a bodily thing. It is well aware of its own domination over the body; and this has caused men to ask what part of the body has most power in the body, and to consider this to be the mind, or even the whole soul. Some have found it in the blood, others in the brain, others in the heart. Here the "heart" is not that of which the Scripture speaks: "I will give thanks to thee, O Lord, with my whole heart" [4]; or "Thou shalt love the Lord thy God with thy whole heart" [5]: where the word is used in an altered sense, transferred from body to soul. This theory identifies the soul with an actual part of the bodily viscera which can be exposed

[4] Ps. 9:1.
[5] Matt. 22:37.

by anatomy. Some have thought that it is composed of minute
individual corpuscles, which they call atoms, colliding and
uniting with one another. Others would make its substance to be
air, or fire; others would not have it to be substantial at all,
since they could conceive no substance that is not bodily, and
found no evidence that the soul is a body: they imagined it to
be no more than the body's harmony or the resultant of that
compound of elements out of which the flesh is constructed.[6]
All these theories treat the soul as mortal, since what is either
body or a composition of body cannot endure everlastingly;
whereas those thinkers who have found its substance in a life
that is not corporeal at all—life being what animates and
vivifies every living body—have consistently endeavoured to
prove its immortality to the best of their ability, arguing that
life can never be without life. I will not spend time in discussing
the notion of the so-called "fifth body" which some writers have
devised as origin of the soul, in union with the familiar four
elements of our world. Either they mean the same thing by
"body" as we do, something extended in space of which any
part is less than the whole; or else they use the word "body"
for any substance or any changeable substance, recognizing
that not all substance is spatially extended in three dimen-
sions—in which case we need not quarrel with them over a
word.

10. If, in face of this diversity of opinion, one can perceive
that the nature of the mind is at the same time substantial and
non-corporeal (that is, that it does not occupy a smaller space
with a smaller part of itself and a larger space with a larger
part), one should at the same time observe that the error of
supposing it to be corporeal does not arise from ignorance of
the mind's nature, but from importing into it qualities supposed
essential to any conceivable existence. It is supposed that what
has to be conceived apart from all corporeal images must be
simply non-existent. But the mind has no need to look for itself
as though it were somewhere else. There is nothing more immediately present to cognition than what is present to the mind;
and there is nothing more immediately present to the mind than

---

6 These and other Greek theories of the soul's nature are discussed by
Aristotle in *De Anima*, I. The allusion which follows, to the theories of
believers in the soul's immortality, recalls the *Phaedo* of Plato, where the
idea of the soul as a "harmony" is refuted (*Phaed.*, 85E ff.). The "fifth
body" seems to refer to Aristotle's notion of the "ethereal matter" of
which he supposed the stars to be composed.

the mind itself. The very word "invention," used in the sense of "discovery," if we think of its derivation, suggests that to "invent" is to "come upon" what is sought. That is why things that come into the mind of their own accord are not usually said to be invented or discovered, though they may be called known; because we had not been making for them by a process of search, so as to "come upon" them, "invent" them. What is sought for with the eyes or any other of the senses, is sought by the mind itself, for it is the mind that directs the attention of the sense, and discovers ("invents") when the sense concerned "comes upon" what is being sought for. In the same way, what the mind must know by itself and not through the medium of any bodily sense, it discovers when it "comes upon" its object; whether in the higher substance, in God, or in other parts of the soul, as when it passes judgment upon the images of material things, "coming upon" their inward impressions as mediated to the soul by the body.

11 (viii). To ask then how the mind is to seek and find itself, in what direction it must seek, and at what point it will find, is to ask a paradoxical question. For nothing can be more certainly "in the mind" than the mind itself. But the mind is also "in" those things upon which it reflects with love; and since love has familiarized it with things sensible or corporeal, it has no power to be in itself apart from their images. The disfigurement of error fastens upon it from its inability to separate itself from the images of objects perceived by the senses, and see itself in isolation. They have stuck to it under the strange adhesive power of love; and its impurity, in the struggle to see itself by itself, arises from the supposition that it really is that which it cannot think itself without. Therefore what is required by the injunction to "know itself" is not that it should seek for a self that has been as it were removed from itself, but that it should remove its own additions to itself. For the mind itself is a more inward reality not only than the things of sense which are plainly external to it, but also than the images of them which exist in a certain part of the soul possessed by animals as well, though animals lack the intelligence which is peculiar to mind. To this inwardness of the mind it is a kind of outgoing from itself, when the passion of love is directed upon those images which are a sort of vestige left behind by many acts of attention. Such vestiges are imprinted upon the memory by the sensations derived from external bodies, so that even in the absence of the objects their images remain available for thought. The mind

then is required to know itself not by seeking for a self sup-
posedly absent, but by fixing upon itself the direction of the
will which was wont to stray elsewhere, and reflecting upon
itself. Then it will see that it has never been without either the
love or the knowledge of itself; but that through the love of
something else alongside itself it has confounded itself with that
and as it were coalesced with it, and so by embracing the
diverse as a unity it has come to believe that what are in fact
diverse are one and the same thing.

12 (ix). The mind's task is not to seek for the beholding of
an absent self, but to be sure that the self which is present is
clearly discerned: not to know itself as previously unknown, but
to distinguish itself from what it knows to be another matter.
Indeed it can take no steps to act on the words "know thyself,"
if it is ignorant of the meaning either of "know" or of "thyself."
If it knows both, it knows itself. For the saying "Know thyself"
has a different sense from a saying like "Know the Cherubim
and Seraphim": our knowledge of them is belief concerning
beings not present to us, based on the statement that they are a
kind of heavenly power. It is different again from saying "Know
the will of that man"—a thing which can only be perceived or
understood when conveyed to us by bodily signs, and leads
then rather to belief than to understanding. And it is different
from saying "See your face"—which can only be done in a
mirror. Our own face cannot be present to our observation
because it is not in a position that we can observe. But when
one says to the mind "Know thyself," in the moment of its
understanding the words "thyself," it knows itself: for the simple
reason that it is present to itself. If it does not understand what
it is told, of course it does not do it. What it is being enjoined
here to do is what it does in the act of understanding the
injunction.

13 (x). Thus, when the mind hears the command to know
itself, it must avoid the addition of any extraneous element to
what it knows itself as being. It knows at least that this command
is addressed to itself, that self which exists, and lives, and
understands. Existence belongs equally to the corpse, life to
the beast: understanding belongs to neither. The mind knows
therefore that its existence and life are the existence and life of
understanding. So it may suppose itself, for example, to be air:
it may suppose that air is intelligent; but it knows that itself
has intelligence, whereas it does not know but only supposes
that it is air. It must set aside what is supposition and look at

what is knowledge, retaining what was never doubted even by those who have supposed mind to be a body of one kind or another. Not every mind thinks itself to be air: some have thought themselves fire, some brain, others this or that other material substance, as noted above. But all alike know that they understand, exist, and live—understanding being relative to its object, while existence and life are absolute conceptions. It is beyond doubt that understanding implies life and life implies existence; from which it follows that the possessor of understanding has an existence and a life different from those of the lifeless corpse and the non-rational soul, of a peculiar and transcendent kind. Again, men know that they possess will, and they also know that will implies existence and life, and is relative to an object willed. They know that they have memory, and also that memory implies existence and life; memory itself being similarly relative to the thing remembered. Of these three functions, memory and understanding are the two in which our manifold experience and knowledge are embraced, while their enjoyment or their use depends on the application of will. We enjoy things known in which the will rests satisfied for their own sake; we use what we relate to something else as object of enjoyment. Nothing but wrong use or wrong enjoyment constitutes the faultiness and blameworthiness of human life. But that is not our present subject.[7] 14. We are concerned now with the nature of the mind; and we have to exclude from our consideration everything which enters our acquaintance from outside by the bodily senses, and concentrate our attention upon the points which all minds know with certainty about themselves. Whether the powers of life, recollection, understanding, will, thought, knowledge, judgment, are properties of air, or of fire, or of brain, or of blood, or of atoms, or of some "fifth body" distinct from the familiar four elements; or whether they could all be produced by the composition or harmonization of our fleshly substance—as to all this men have doubted; and one has attempted to affirm one theory, another another. But no-one can possibly doubt that he lives and remembers, understands, wills, thinks, knows, and judges. For even if he doubts, he lives: if he doubts what has made him doubt, he remembers; if he doubts, he understands that he is doubting; if he doubts, he wishes to be certain; if he doubts, he thinks; if he doubts, he knows that he is ignorant; if he doubts, he judges that he ought not to be hasty in assenting. A man may doubt everything else,

[7] Cf. above, p. 66 n.

but he should not doubt any of these facts; for if they were not so, he could doubt of nothing.[8]

15. The theories which treat the mind as material or as the compounding or harmonizing of matter, would represent all these activities as properties of a material subject: the real substance will be air or fire or whatever else of material nature is supposed to be the mind, while understanding is contained therein as a quality. The subject will be the mind, regarded as body: understanding, and the other activities which we have described as certainly belonging to us, will be properties of that subject. The view of those who deny that the mind itself is body, but make it the composition or harmony of a body, is much the same: the only difference is that the other theories maintain the mind to be the substance and subject of which understanding is a property, while this will have the mind itself to be a property of that bodily substance of which it is the compounding or harmonization. It must then consistently regard the understanding as a property of the same body which is its subject.

16. All these theories neglect the fact which we have demonstrated, that the mind knows itself even while it seeks itself. By no means can anything properly be said to be known in the absence of knowledge of its substance. Therefore when the mind knows itself, it knows its substance: when it is sure of itself, it is sure of its substance. That it is sure of itself is what our argument has proved. It is not at all sure whether it is air or fire or any material thing or condition of matter. Therefore it is none of these things; and the whole purport of its being bidden to "know itself" is to assure it that it is none of those things of which it is not sure, and to make it sure that it is and only is what alone it is sure of being. It has a particular way of thinking of fire, air, or any other material object; and it would be impossible for it to think of itself in the same way as it thinks of what is not itself. For it thinks of all those things, fire, air, this body or that, or some part, composition or harmony of body, by means of some representative image. It is not of course alleged to be all the things named, but only one or other of them. But whichever of them it were, it would think of it in a different way from the rest: I mean, not by any imagined picture, as we think of absent objects with which the bodily sense has brought us

---

[8] Augustine had used this argument, which anticipates Descartes, as early as the *De Libero Arbitrio* (II, 3) of 388 and the *De Vera Religione* (73) of 390. The famous *Si fallor, sum* comes from the *De Civitate* (XI, 26). See also *De Trin.*, XV, 21 (xii).

into contact (whether the picture be of the objects themselves or
of others of the same kind); but by a kind of inward presence,
real and not imaginary—for nothing can be more present to it
than itself—in the way that it thinks of its own living and remembering and understanding and willing itself. All this it
knows within itself, and does not imagine it as though previously
sensed by some external contact like the experience of material
objects. If it avoids tacking on to itself anything derived from its
thoughts of such material things, so as to suppose itself similar
in kind to them, then the account of itself which remains will be
the account of what alone it is.

17 (xi). And now, setting aside for the moment the other
activities which the mind is sure of its possessing, let us take for
particular consideration these three: memory, understanding,
will.[9] On these three points we are accustomed to examine the
capacities of children, to find what talents they display. The
more tenacious and ready is a boy's memory, the more acute his
understanding, the more eager his will to learn, so much the
more praiseworthy do we count his disposition. When, however,
it is a question of the learning of any individual, we enquire,
not how much strength and readiness of memory or sharpness
of understanding he possesses, but *what* he remembers and *what*
he understands. And seeing that a person is judged praiseworthy
not only according to his learning but also according to his
goodness, we take note not only of what he remembers and
understands but of what he wills: not simply of the eagerness of
his will, but first of what he wills and then of how much he wills
it. For a person who loves intensely only merits praise when
what he loves is what ought to be loved intensely. In the three
fields of disposition, learning, and practice or use, the test of the
first depends upon the individual's capacity in respect of memory, understanding and will; the test of the second, upon the
content of his memory and understanding, and the point to
which an eager will has brought him. But the third, use, belongs
entirely to the will as it deals with the content of memory and
understanding, whether as means relative to a particular end,
or as an end in which it may rest satisfied. To use, is to take a
thing up into the disposal of the will; whereas to enjoy is to use

[9] The choice of these three from among the various activities enumerated
in §14 above is not simply dictated by what Augustine knows he wants
to make of them. Of the others, "life" is not peculiar to mind, while
"thought," "knowledge," and "judgment" are forms of "understanding"
or "memory." For the meaning of the terms, see Introduction, *ad fin.*

with a satisfaction that is not anticipated but actual. Thus all
enjoyment is a kind of use, since it takes up something into the
disposal of the will for final delectation; but not all use is enjoyment, if what is taken up into the disposal of the will has been
sought after not for its own sake but as a means to something
else.[10]

18. Now this triad of memory, understanding, and will, are
not three lives, but one; nor three minds, but one. It follows
that they are not three substances, but one substance. Memory,
regarded as life, mind, or substance, is an absolute term: regarded as memory, it is relative. The same may be said of
understanding and of will; for both terms can be used relatively.
But life, mind, essence, are always things existing absolutely in
themselves. Therefore the three activities named are one, inasmuch as they constitute one life, one mind, one essence [11]; and
whatever else can be predicated of each singly in itself, is predicated of them all together in the singular and not in the plural.
But they are three inasmuch as they are related to one another;
and if they were not equal, not only each to each but each to all,
they could not cover or take in one another as they do. For in
fact they are covered, not only each by each but all by each. I
remember [12] that I possess memory and understanding and
will: I understand that I understand and will and remember: I
will my own willing and remembering and understanding. And
I remember at the same time the whole of my memory and
understanding and will. Whatever I do not remember as part
of my memory, is not in my memory; and nothing can be more
fully in my memory than the memory itself. Therefore I remember the whole of it. Again, whatever I understand, I know that
I understand, and I know that I will whatever I will; but whatever I know, I remember. Therefore I remember the whole of
my understanding and the whole of my will. Similarly, when I
understand these three, I understand all three in whole. For
there is nothing open to understanding that I do not understand
except that of which I am ignorant; and that of which I am
ignorant I neither remember nor will. It follows that anything

10 This is a refinement of the distinction between "use" and "enjoyment"
    into which Augustine is led *en passant*. It confuses rather than illuminates
    the distinction.
11 This phrase, repeated at the end of the section, had been used by Augus-
    tine of the "trinity" of being, knowing, and willing in *Conf.*, XIII, 12 (xi).
12 Note that Augustine is using "remember" not in the sense of actually
    recollecting, but in that of being able to recall: see Introduction, *ad fin.*,
    for the meaning of the terms "memory" and "understanding."

open to understanding that I do not understand, I neither remember nor will, whereas anything open to understanding that
I remember and will, I understand. Finally, when I use the
whole content of my understanding and memory, my will
covers the whole of my understanding and the whole of my
memory. Therefore, since all are covered by one another
singly and as wholes, the whole of each is equal to the whole
of each, and the whole of each to the whole of all together.
And these three constitute one thing, one life, one mind, one
essence.

19 (xii). We might now attempt to raise our thoughts, with
such power of concentration as is at our disposal, towards that
supreme and most exalted essence of which the human mind is
an image—inadequate indeed, but still truly an image. Yet it
may be better to illustrate more clearly the presence in the soul
of these same three functions, by means of our bodily sense perceptions of external objects, in which there is impressed upon
us in the process of time a knowledge of material things. We
found the nature of the mind, in its memory, understanding and
willing of itself, to be such that it must be apprehended as
always knowing and always willing itself; and therefore also
as always at the same time remembering itself, understanding
and loving itself,[13] although it does not always keep the thought
of itself clearly separated from things which are not identical
with it. This makes it difficult to distinguish in it the memory
of self and the understanding of self. When they are closely conjoined, neither preceding the other in time, it may look as
though they were not two, but one and the same thing under
different names. Even love may cease to be felt as such, if not
disclosed by the sense of want, as when its object is continually

13 In fact Augustine has so far nowhere said that the mind *always* possesses
the memory, understanding, and willing of itself—which would imply that
both understanding and will, like memory, exist in the mind unconsciously
before they are consciously realized. In Bk XIV, 9 (vi), he refers to what
he has said here, and proceeds to develop the distinction between "understanding" as a conscious act of "thought" (*cogitatio*) and the unconscious
"knowledge" on which it depends. It is only in the conscious act of understanding that he can find what he means by the "birth of the word."
Accordingly in Bk. XIV, though he maintains the idea of a permanent
and unconscious state of the triad (memory, understanding, will), it is
in its conscious realization that he has to look for his final demonstration
of the image of the Trinity (cf. Bk. XIV, 10 (vii), 13 (x)). In Bk. XV,
41 (xxi), however, he notes that in virtue of the inherence of understanding and will in memory, both can exist below the conscious
level.

present. All this may become clear to the slower thinker, in the course of an examination of those temporal processes which add to the content of the mind or otherwise affect it: when it remembers what it did not remember before, when it sees what it did not see before, and when it loves what it did not love before. This examination, however, demands to be taken in hand in the next Book.

BOOK XI

The Image in the Outward Man

ARGUMENT

[We are to look for a likeness of the inward man in the outward; and the particular sense we shall examine is that of sight.

1. We can distinguish (i) the external object of vision (ii) the perception of it in the sense-organ (iii) the mental attention which fixes the eye on the object.

(a) Sense and attention belong to the perceiving subject and are independent of the object. The form printed on the sense-organ is product of the object only, of which this form is a likeness or image, distinct from the object itself. Its existence in the sense-organ is proved, e.g., by our experience of the "after-image" of a luminous object on closing the eye, and the duplicated image of an unfocused vision. The three elements are thus diverse in substance; but the third (the voluntary act of attention) brings the two former into close union, and is capable, when its emotional tone is intense, even of producing changes in the body of the percipient. (b) When a remembered perception is recalled to mind, we can observe a corresponding "trinity of imagination," this time entirely within the mind, composed of memory, inward vision, and the will which directs attention upon the object in the memory. The resulting mental image may even be mistaken for the "real" thing, especially under the influence of strong desire or fear.

2. Both sense-perception and imagination can lead us astray. A life "according to the trinity of the outward man" is a bad life. This trinity, therefore, as belonging to the external and material world, cannot be a true image of God—though it may contain a "likeness" of him.—(a) In the trinity of sense, object and vision are heterogeneous, and cannot properly be styled "parent" and "offspring." The act of attention is a nearer

analogue of the Spirit, being neither "parent" nor "offspring": its "end" or realization in the vision can be related as a means to the will's pursuit of the ultimate Good.

(b) In the trinity of imagination, the thing remembered and the inward vision are no more than "quasi-parent" and "quasi-offspring"; for the inward vision, though taking form from the memory, existed before the impression on it of the particular form. The act of will is both homogeneous with the memory and in a sense "proceeds" from it: we cannot, e.g., want to recollect what we had for dinner yesterday unless we remember that we dined. Thought or inward vision can form images which may differ from the actual content of memory, though it is always dependent on memory, even when evoked by what is described by another person. Memory is to some extent controllable by the will, which can abstract the attention from what is presented to the senses.

3. In both "trinities" it is to be noted that the will's function is to link together, either (a) external object with sense-image, or (b) memory-image with thought-vision—each of these four being product or "offspring" of the preceding. Memory is limited by experience: imagination is not. We can think of black swans or four-footed birds. So we may see in memory, thought-vision, and voluntary attention, the "measure, number, and weight" of Wisdom 11:20, in which God has "ordered all things."]

BOOK XII

Knowledge and Wisdom

ARGUMENT

[Where is the link between outward and inward man?

1. We share sense-perception, and perhaps memory, with animals. Yet the rationality which distinguishes man from beast is in part concerned with direction of our bodily and temporal life, in part with our contact with eternal truth: it is partly active, partly contemplative. As in the union of male and female, there is here a binding together of "two in one flesh." The division in the human mind is one of function only. There may be a trinity in either function; but we shall have to seek the true image of God in the higher rather than the lower.

2. We must reject the idea that the Trinity is imaged in the triad of man, woman, and child. The "image of God" in Gen. 1:27 must be understood as an image of the Trinity and not of any one Person; but certainly Adam and Eve were not created with a son. Paul's saying in I Cor. 11:7 that man (as opposed to woman) is the image of God, is best interpreted in accordance with the distinction above suggested, of the double function, higher and lower, of the rational mind. In any case when he speaks of the "new man" in Col. 3:9, 10, he does not mean to exclude the Christian woman from renewal in God's image. Man and woman alike possess the same human nature in its completeness.

3. The Fall of man is the result of the "lower reason" throwing off the control of the "higher," and devoting itself to the pursuit of the material and temporal. Man seeks to be his own master, to have private possessions instead of his share in the universal good; and through preferring the knowledge which "puffs up" to the love of wisdom, sinks below the level of the rational. In the story of the forbidden fruit, is symbolized the

yielding of the higher reason (Adam) to the solicitations of the lower (Eve), which has already been perverted by the flesh (the serpent), so that sinful desire becomes sinful act. This is a better exegesis than to take the woman as symbolizing the bodily senses which we share with the beasts.

4. The lower reason has its proper place in the right use of things temporal, as means to eternal life. The distinction of knowledge and wisdom is suggested by I Cor. 13:8 and Job. 28:28. Knowledge ("abstaining from evil") is concerned with moral activity and the human history which instructs us therein. Wisdom is the contemplation of those eternal forms or principles of which Plato wrote; though his doctrine that the soul retains a memory of them from a former existence is unsatisfactory. It is better to believe that the mind is enlightened by a spiritual sun, as the eye by the physical.

5. Before we look for our image of the Trinity in that wisdom whereby the mind contemplates things eternal, we have to consider the likeness which may be traced in our knowledge of the temporal.]

Book XIII

The Trinity of Faith

ARGUMENT

[1. The distinction between higher and lower reason, wisdom and knowledge, laid down in Book XII, is illustrated by the Prologue of John's Gospel, where vv. 1–5 refer to things eternal, vv. 6–14 to things temporal, to known history and the faith based upon it. We have an immediate vision or knowledge of faith in ourselves, while we can only believe its presence in others.

2. Yet there are some beliefs and desires which are so generally entertained that we can almost regard them as universal. The desire for happiness (beatitude) is certainly universal, though the great variety of beliefs as to what constitutes happiness proves that the knowledge of it is by no means equally so. The true definition of happiness is not "living as you will," but the satisfaction of all wants when nothing is wanted wrongly. (For some objects of desire are bad, and cannot make us happy.) It is human perversity, when *both* these conditions of happiness are unattainable, to prefer the satisfaction of wants to the confining of wants to what ought to be wanted. In this life, happiness is never without alloy: if we truly desire happiness, we are desiring immortality; since if life ends, happiness ends, and the loss of happiness, even in expectation, cannot be good.

3. Faith alone can assure us of our capacity for immortality —in John's words, "power to become sons of God"; and this faith rests upon the Incarnation, Cross, and Resurrection of Christ. No other way could have been more fit to rescue us from despair than the assurance of God's love—the love for sinners who can have no merits that are not his gifts. This love, by which we are "justified in his blood," "reconciled by his death," is not the act of one Person of the Trinity, but the eternal love of Father, Son, and Holy Ghost.

95

4. By God's just and righteous permission, the sin of the first man put the whole race in the power of the devil—though the devil himself remains under the power of God. Both devil and fallen men pursue power rather than righteousness (justice); but righteousness is the condition of power and not *vice versa*, just as for happiness the good will must precede the power to live as we will. Therefore the devil's power could be overcome only by righteousness: the sinless Christ, submitting for righteousness' sake to an unjust death at the devil's hands, deprived him of his "right" to power over men; though the temporal sufferings and bodily death, which were the penalty of sin, remain for the trial of our faith. The death of Christ thus "justifies" us, because through faith we share in his righteousness, even as we had shared in Adam's sin.

5. The historic incarnation and atonement, on which our faith is based, thus fall within the sphere of knowledge rather than of wisdom. But in the Word made flesh are the "treasures of wisdom" as well as of "knowledge": in Christ we move through the latter to the former.

6. There is a "trinity of faith," when things believed are held in the memory, and recalled to thought by the act of will; and if their truth be accepted and loved, there is a life "according to the inward trinity." Yet it is not here that we can trace the full image of God.]

Book XIV

The Perfection of the Image in the Contemplation of God

ARGUMENT

[True wisdom in men is the worship of God (§§ 1, 2). Its object is the eternal and divine, while knowledge is of the temporal and human; and we have treated faith as belonging to the sphere of knowledge, so that the image of the Trinity to be discerned in faith must needs be a transient thing (§§ 3–5). The true image of God in the human mind must be permanent and unchanging, even though it be temporarily defaced (§ 6).

The existence of self-knowledge in the mind of the infant is problematical. In the adult, the mind comes "into its own view" only in the act of thinking, though always present to itself in the memory, which is the source from which its self-understanding is "begotten" (§§ 7, 8). In fact, apart from the conscious act of thought, there is always a sort of unconscious self-understanding and self-willing stored in the memory (§ 9). But since the act of thought is required for the production of the "word," we have a better image of the Trinity in the conscious act than in the unconscious memory (§ 10).

The mind is God's image *par excellence* in virtue of its capacity for knowing God. Its trinity is self-contained, and so distinguished both from the trinity of sense-perception, and from the trinity of faith (§ 11), which will pass away, as will the moral virtues appropriate to this life of action (§ 12). In the mind's self-knowledge there is nothing adventitious (§ 13); it is ever present to itself, and its "memory" is not related to past time (§ 14).

The perfection of the divine image in the mind is the divine gift of wisdom, by which the mind becomes aware of God (§ 15), and is not only "in" God, but "with" God (§ 16), through the revival in it of that "memory of God" which was never entirely obliterated (§ 17). The mind's self-love is true, that is, for its own good, only when grounded on the love of God (§§ 18, 19) —for which, as for the knowledge of God, it possesses a natural capacity, and which alone can satisfy its needs (§ 20).

The restoration of the image to its original perfection is the work of grace, enabling the mind to turn again to the light, of which even when it was averted therefrom it felt the touch—as shown, e.g., by its power of moral judgment (§§ 21, 22). This renewal "after the image of the Creator" is a gradual process, whereby the mind's love is re-directed upon God, and it reaches perfection only in the final vision of God (§§ 23, 24), when we shall be "like him, for we shall see him face to face." No true lover of wisdom can doubt the immortality of the soul (§ 25).]

THE TEXT

1. (i). We are now to consider the nature of wisdom; but not the Wisdom of God, which assuredly is God himself, for it is the name given to his only-begotten Son.[1] We are to speak of a human wisdom, which is yet a true wisdom as being in accordance with God, and consisting in his true and peculiar worship. This in Greek is denoted by the single word *theosebeia*, which our Latin translators, wishing to have one word to correspond to it, have rendered (as we have already noted) *pietas* or godly fear. The more usual Greek for *pietas*, however, is *eusebeia*. *Theosebeia* cannot be perfectly rendered in one word, and it is better to use two and call it *Dei cultus*, the worship of God. That this is man's wisdom (as laid down in the twelfth Book of the present work), is proved by the authority of Holy Scripture, in the Book of Job the servant of God. There we read that the wisdom of God has said unto man: "Behold, the fear of the Lord (*pietas*) is wisdom; and to abstain from evil is knowledge"[2]—or, as some have translated the Greek *episteme*, "discipline": which can stand for "knowledge," as being itself derived from *discere* or learning; for our purpose in learning anything is to know it. ("Discipline" has indeed another sense, as applied to the troubles suffered by a man for his sins with a view to correction. So the Epistle to the Hebrews says: "Who is the son to whom his father dealeth not discipline?" or again, more obviously; "All discipline for the time seemeth not to be joyous but grievous; but afterwards it shall yield the peaceable fruit of righteousness to them that have striven through it."[3])

[1] I Cor. 1:24.   [2] Job 28:28.   [3] Heb. 12:7, 11.

The supreme wisdom, then, is God himself; and the worship of God is the human wisdom, of which we are now speaking. For "the wisdom of this world is foolishness with God"[4]; it is of the wisdom which is the worship of God, that Holy Scripture says: "the multitude of the wise is the welfare of the world."[5]

2. But if it takes wise men to discourse of wisdom, we are in a difficulty. In order that our discourse of it may not be impertinent are we to presume so far as to profess wisdom? We should rather take warning from the example of Pythagoras, who dared not profess himself wise, and said in answer to his questioners that he was only a philosopher, that is, a lover of wisdom.[6] This was the origin of the name, which so approved itself to later thinkers that the greatest learning in matter of wisdom, whether claimed or acknowledged, would entitle a man to no more than the name of philosopher. Was the reluctance of such men to profess wisdom due to their supposing that the wise man must be altogether without sin? At any rate that is not the teaching of our Scriptures, which say: "Rebuke a wise man, and he will love thee."[7] To count a man in need of rebuke is surely to find him guilty of sin. But even so I would not dare to profess myself wise: it is enough for me that it belongs to the philosopher or lover of wisdom to discourse about wisdom. And that no-one can deny; for those who have professed themselves lovers of wisdom rather than wise have not ceased to discourse upon it.

3. Wisdom has been defined, in such discourse, as "the knowledge of things human and divine."[8] I too, in a preceding Book,[9] have expressed the opinion that acquaintance with both, things divine and human, can be called both wisdom and knowledge. But if we adopt the apostle's distinction—"to one is given the word of wisdom, to another the word of knowledge"[10]—it is proper for us to break up this definition, giving the name of wisdom in its strict sense to the knowledge of divine things, while of human things we speak, in the strict sense, of knowledge. This I have discussed in my thirteenth Book, where I assigned to this latter knowledge, not anything that a man can know of human affairs, a great part of which is matter of superfluous vanity or harmful curiosity, but only that by which the most wholesome faith that leads to true blessedness is begotten, nourished, defended, and strengthened.

[4] I Cor. 3:19.   [5] Wisdom 6:24.
[6] The story is told in Cicero, *Tusc. Quaest.*, V, 3.
[7] Prov. 9:8.   [8] Cicero, *De Off.*, II, 2.
[9] The reference is to Bk. XII, 22 (xiv).   [10] I Cor. 12:8

And in this knowledge many of the faithful are weak, though in the faith itself they are most strong. For it is one thing simply to know what is to be believed for the attainment of the eternal life which alone is blessed; it is another, to know how this faith gives succour to the godly and has its defence against the ungodly—which the apostle seems to describe by the particular term "knowledge." In speaking of it, I have already been concerned chiefly to commend the faith itself. I first briefly distinguished the eternal from the temporal, and proceeded to deal with the sphere of the temporal. I postponed to this Book the treatment of things eternal, but I showed that even of them there is a faith which is temporal indeed, and comes in process of time to dwell in the hearts of believers, yet is necessary for the attainment of the eternal. I argued the benefit, for this attainment, of that faith concerning the things which in time the Eternal wrought for us and suffered, in the man whose humanity he wore in time[11] and exalted to eternity; and I maintained that the virtues which give prudence, courage, temperance and justice to life in this temporal and mortal state, are true virtues only if they be related to this same faith, which, temporal as it is, conducts us to the things eternal.

4 (ii). It is written: "So long as we are in the body, we are sojourners away from the Lord; for we walk by faith, not by sight."[12] Accordingly, so long as the just lives by faith,[13] though his life be that of the inward man, he can only strive for the truth and make his way towards the eternal by means of the faith which is temporal: not yet can there be in the holding and contemplation and love of this temporal faith a trinity fit to be called the image of God. Else that which must be established in the eternal would seem to be established in things temporal. When the mind of man sees its own faith, believing what it does not see, it is not looking upon what is everlasting. What it sees will not be always so, will assuredly not be so, when at the end of the sojourning in which we are absent from the Lord and must walk by faith, shall come the turn of sight in which we shall see face to face.[14] We see not so now; but because we believe, we shall be found worthy to see, and shall rejoice that

---

[11] *Fecit et passus est in homine quem temporaliter gessit*—a phrase which is remarkable as combining the truths for which the Christologies of Alexandria and Antioch were about to contend. (See Sellers, *The Council of Chalcedon*, pp. 132–181.)   [12] II Cor. 5:6 f.   [13] Rom. 1:7.
[14] I Cor. 13:12. The contrast which Augustine draws between faith and sight governs the whole of the argument which follows. Cf. Introduction, p. 29 f.

faith has brought us home to sight. Instead of the faith by which
the unseen is believed, will come the sight by which things
formerly believed are seen. It may be then that we shall remember this mortal life that will be past, and recall our former
belief of what we did not see; but that faith will be set down
among things past and gone, not present and ever abiding. It
will be found, therefore, that the trinity which now appears in
the remembering, beholding and loving of the faith now present
and abiding, is then a thing not permanent but past and gone.
We must conclude that if that trinity is indeed the image of
God, this image itself must be counted as belonging not to that
which always is, but to that which passes away. (iii). But if the
soul's nature is immortal, so that after its original creation it
can never cease to be, God forbid that the soul's most precious
possession should not endure with its own immortality; and
what can be more precious in its created nature than its making
in the image of its Creator? Not therefore in the holding, contemplation, and love of faith, which may not be for ever, but in
what shall always be, we must find the image of God worthy of
that name.

  5. But let us test the truth of this conclusion by a closer and
more careful enquiry. It may be argued that this trinity does not
perish even when faith itself has passed away: on the ground
that just as now we hold the faith in memory, perceive it in
thought and love it in will, so then, when our former possession
of it shall be remembered and thought upon, and the memory
and reflection united by our will, the same trinity will remain
unchanged. For if it were to pass and leave no kind of trace in
us, then there would be nothing of it in our memory to which
we could recur in remembering it as past and linking by the
effort of attention the two elements—what was in the memory
without our thinking of it, and what is given form by thought.
This argument fails to notice the difference between two
trinities: one, when our present faith is held, seen, and loved
within us; and another which will exist when not faith itself but
a sort of imaged trace of it laid up in the memory is contem-
plated in recollection, and the will unites the content of memory
and the impression of it in the mind's view.

  To enable this to be understood, let us take an example from
the material world, which occupied us sufficiently in the
eleventh Book. In the ascent from lower to higher, or the entry
from outward to inward, we discovered a first trinity in the
material object of sight, the view of the beholder to which it

gives form in the moment of vision, and the exercise of will
which unites the two. We may postulate a trinity on similar
lines, when the faith now existing in us, like the material body
in space, is contained in our memory, and from it form is given
to the thought which recollects it, just as the bodily object gives
form to the view of the beholder. These two elements become a
trinity by the addition of the will, which links and joins together
the faith contained in the memory and the reproduction of it
imprinted in the recollecting contemplation: just as, in the
trinity of bodily vision, the form of the body seen and the conforming thereto of the beholder's view are united by the exercise of will. Now let us suppose that the material body which
was the object of vision has dissolved and perished, leaving
nothing of itself at any point in space to the sight of which the
eye could be re-directed. The fact that an image of the material
object, now past and gone, remains in the memory to give form
to the recollecting view, so that these two elements may be conjoined by the will, does not allow us to call the resulting trinity
the same as that which had existed when the real body was seen
in space. It is an entirely different one: not only does it belong
to the internal sphere whereas the other belonged to the external, but it is produced by the image of a body no longer there
instead of by the actuality of an existing body. So, in the case
under consideration, for the sake of which the parallel has been
drawn, the faith at present in our mind, like the body in space,
constitutes a kind of trinity in being held, regarded, and loved;
but the trinity will not be the same when this faith has ceased
to exist in the mind as the body has ceased to be in space. When
we come to recollect its existence in us as past and no longer
present, it will unquestionably be a different trinity. The one
we have now is produced by the presence of the thing itself and
its attachment to the believing mind: the one we shall have then
will be product of the picturing of what is no longer existent,
left behind in the memory as object of recollection.

6 (iv). We may say then neither that we shall have the
image of God in that trinity which does not exist at present, nor
that we have it now in the trinity which then will exist no
longer. We must find, in the rational or intellectual soul of man,
an image of its Creator planted immortally in its immortal
nature. We can speak of the soul's immortality only in a quali-
fied sense; for there is a death of the soul, when it is without that
bliss which must be accounted its true life. We call it immortal,
because even in utmost wretchedness it never ceases to live a

life of a sort. In the same way, though reason and understanding may at one time be dormant in it, and at others appear either small or great, the human soul is never anything but rational and intellectual; and for that reason, if its making in God's image represents its power to use reason and intellect for the understanding and the beholding of God, we may be sure that from the first beginning to be of so great and marvellous a creature, that image always remains, whether it be so faded that scarcely anything of it is left, whether it be obscured and defaced, or clear and fair.[15] We may appeal here to a text of God's Scripture which expresses his pity for the defacement of its dignity: "Although man walketh in an image, yet is he vainly disquieted: he heapeth up treasures, and knoweth not for whom he shall gather them."[16] Vanity would not be ascribed to the image of God, were it not seen to be defaced; and that no defacement can destroy its character as image is plain enough from the words: "though man walketh in an image." The sentence, then, will be equally true if its clauses are inverted, and we read: "Although man is vainly disquieted, yet he walketh in an image." Human nature is a great thing, but because it is not the highest it was liable to spoiling[17]; and although liable to spoiling because it is not the highest, yet because it has a capacity for the highest and is able to become partaker in it, it remains great.

We must look then, in this image of God, for a trinity of an unique kind—trusting in the help of him who made us in his image; for there is no other way of sound enquiry into the matter, or of discovery according to the wisdom which comes from him. But the reader will not need more words here upon the method to be followed, if what was said in earlier Books (especially the tenth) of the human soul or mind be remembered and re-considered, or reference be made to the pages containing that discussion.[18]

7. In the tenth Book it was said, among other things, that the mind of man knows itself.[19] For nothing can be better known to

---

[15] It is important to note that Augustine finds the *indelible* image of God in man, not in his rational nature as such, but in his "power to use" his rationality for attaining knowledge of God.

[16] Ps. 39:6. The "although" on which Augustine builds his fanciful exegesis may have been suggested by the LXX: it does not appear in the Vulgate.

[17] This follows from the doctrine that the only changeless "nature" is the divine.

[18] I.e. the discussion at the end of Bk. X of memory, understanding, and will.   [19] Bk. X, 10 (vii).

the mind than what is immediately present to it; and nothing can be more immediately present to the mind than itself. The point was also established to our satisfaction on other grounds. (v). What then are we to say of the mind of the child, as yet so small and so profoundly ignorant that its mental darkness is almost frightening to the more or less instructed adult? Perhaps even the child's mind may be thought to know itself, but to be so pre-occupied with experiences of the pleasures of sensation, all the greater for their novelty, that it cannot reflect upon itself, though unable to be ignorant of itself. The intensity of the child's interest in the external objects of sensation may be seen in the single example of its avidity for the light. If, from carelessness or ignorance of the possible effect, one puts a night-light by a child's cot, in a position where the child as it lies can turn its eyes towards the candle but is unable to move its head, it will gaze on the light so fixedly that cases are known where a squint has resulted, through the eyes retaining the position in which their delicate young structure has become set by habit. And we find the same intense concentration of interest, in the child's soul, upon the other bodily senses, so far as its age allows; so that strong repulsion or appetite will only be excited in it by what offends or attracts the flesh. Its thoughts are not turned inward upon itself, and introspection cannot be suggested to it; since it is still ignorant of the means of suggestion, which are principally the words of which (as of so much else) it knows nothing. But it was shown in the same Book that not to reflect upon oneself is a different thing from not knowing oneself.[20]

8. However, we may pass over the age of infancy, which we cannot question about its experiences, and which we ourselves have largely forgotten. It will be enough for us to take it as certain that when a man becomes able to think about the nature of his own mind and to discover the truth, he will not discover it elsewhere than in himself. And what he will discover is not something he did not know but something he did not think about. What can we know, if we are ignorant of what is in our own mind, since the mind is the necessary medium of all our knowledge? (vi). Yet such is the power of thought that it is only by thinking that the mind can set itself as it were in its own view. Nothing is in the mind's view but when it is thought about; and that implies that even the mind itself which is the only agent of thought can only be in its own view by thinking

[20] Bk. X, 7 (v).

about itself. The question how it can be conceived not to be in its own view when not thinking of itself, although it can never be separated from itself, is one that I cannot answer. It seems as if its "view" and "itself" were two different things—which is a reasonable enough way of speaking in the case of the bodily eye; for while the eye itself has its own fixed position in the body, its view is directed to external objects and can extend even to the stars. Nor is the eye in its own view at all, since it cannot see itself except as reflected in a mirror, as we remarked before[21]; whereas there is nothing to correspond with that reflection when the mind by the thought of itself places itself in its own view. We can hardly suppose that in thinking of itself the mind is seeing one part of itself with another part, as we see with one part of our body, the eye, other parts which can be in our view. The supposition and the statement of it are equally absurd. If the mind is removed, it is removed from itself: if it is set in its own view, it is set before itself. This implies a change in its position from the one occupied when it was not in its own view, as though it were removed from one place and set in another. But if it has shifted in order to be seen, where does it stay in order to see? Is there a sort of duplication of it, so that it can occupy two positions, one for seeing and another for being seen, in itself for seeing, before itself for being seen?

The truth will return none of these answers to our enquiries; for the fact is that this way of thinking is occupied with images drawn from material objects, and that the mind is no such thing is absolutely certain—at least for those few "minds" that can tell us the truth in this matter. It remains only for us to recognize that the "view" of the mind is something essential to its nature, to which it is recalled when it thinks of itself by no spatial movement but by a spiritual turning. And when it is not thinking of itself, though it is not in its own view and its seeing is not defined by its nature, yet it knows itself in its capacity as self-memory. In the same way, the knowledge possessed by the expert in a number of sciences is contained in his memory, and no part of it is in the view of his mind except when he thinks of it, the rest being shut away in that hidden storing place of knowledge which we call memory.

Hence we developed an account of the mental trinity, in which memory supplied the source from which the thinker's view receives its form, the conformation itself being a kind of image imprinted by the memory, and the agency by which the

[21] Bk. X, 5 (iii).

two are conjoined being love or will. Thus when the mind regards itself in the act of thought, it understands and takes
knowledge of itself: we may say that it begets this self-understanding and self-knowledge. For an object that is incorporeal
is seen when it is understood, and is known by the act of understanding. But this begetting by the mind of self-knowledge, when
it regards itself as understood in thought, does not imply that it
was previously unknown to itself. It was so known, in the way
that things held in the memory are known, though not thought
upon: as we say that a man knows letters, even when he is
thinking not of letters but of other things. And to these two, the
begetter and the begotten, we have to add the love which joins
them together, and is simply the will, pursuing or embracing
an object of enjoyment.[22] Accordingly, for the indication of our
mental trinity we found these three names appropriate: memory, understanding and will.

9. Towards the end of the same tenth Book we said that the
mind always remembers itself and always understands and
loves itself, although it does not always think of itself in isolation
from all that is of a different nature from itself.[23] We must ask,
then, in what sense understanding is to be assigned to the act of
thinking, while the knowledge of any object, which is in the
mind even when it is not being thought about, is properly
assigned to memory alone. If this is so, the three functions of
memory, understanding and love of itself will not have been
always present together in the mind. It will only have had the
memory of itself, and the understanding and love of itself will
have ensued when it began to think of itself. (vii). To meet
this difficulty, let us look more closely at the case previously
adduced to show the difference between not knowing a thing
and not thinking of it; so that it is possible for a man to know
something of which he is not thinking, when his thought is
occupied with something else. An expert in two or more arts
may, when he is thinking of one of them, know another or a number of others even if he is not thinking of them. But can we
properly say, "This musician knows music, but does not at this
moment understand it, because he is not thinking of it; but he
understands geometry at this moment, for geometry is what he
is thinking about?" Such a statement appears to be absurd; and
no less absurd would be the statement, "This musician knows

22 This definition well shows the relation in Augustine's language of "love,"
"will," and "enjoyment." Love does not cease to be love when its desire
is satisfied.   23 See note on Bk. X, 18 (xii).

music, but does not at this moment love it, since he is not thinking of it; but he loves geometry at this moment, since geometry
is what he is thinking about." What we may quite properly say
is: "This man whom you observe discussing geometry is also a
finished musician; for he remembers that art, understands it and
loves it; but while knowing and loving it, he is not at this
moment thinking of it because he is thinking of the geometry
which he is discussing." This suggests to us the existence "at the
back of our minds" of certain stores of knowledge of certain
things, which as it were come forward into the middle and take
more open position in the mind's view, when they become the
object of thought. Then the mind discovers that it remembered,
understood and loved what it was not thinking about while
thinking of something else. If there is a subject of which we have
not thought for a long time, and of which we cannot begin to
think unless it is suggested to us, then with regard to it we are
in the strange position (if the paradox may be allowed) of not
knowing that we know it. In fact it is proper for the giver of the
reminder to say to the receiver of it: "You know this, but you
do not know that you know it: I will remind you of it, and you
will find yourself knowing what you had thought you did not
know." The same is the effect of a book written on some
theme of which the reader is led by reason to discover the truth.
He does not take its truth on trust from the writer, as when he
is reading history: he himself finds it to be true, whether the
finding be his own or that of the very Truth which is the mind's
light. The man whose blindness of heart is such that no prompting can enable him to perceive such truths, is too deeply sunk
in the darkness of ignorance, and needs the miracle of divine
aid in order to reach true wisdom.

10. This was why I sought to illustrate the process of thought
by some kind of example which might show how from the content of memory the remembering attention takes form, and
something is brought to birth, in the person who thinks, of the
same kind as what was in him as the possessor of memory before
the thinking process. It is easier to distinguish things that are not
simultaneous, and where the parent is prior in time to the "offspring." If we look at the mind's inward memory whereby it
remembers itself, its inward understanding whereby it understands itself, and its inward will whereby it loves itself, we are
dealing with a state in which these three are ever present together and were ever present together from their beginning,
whether they were objects of thought or not. And thus it will

seem that the image of the Trinity belongs to the sphere of memory alone. Yet there can be no "word" without thought; for we think whatever we say, even if it be with the inward word that is of no particular language. So the image is to be discovered rather in the three functions of memory, understanding and will—"understanding" being here taken to denote the faculty by which we come to understand in the process of thought: that is to say, when our thinking takes form through the "bringing forth" of what was present to the memory but not thought of. And the word "will" means the love which unites the "offspring" and its "parent," and which is in a manner common to both.

It was, as I say, in order to make these distinctions easier for the reader to grasp that I used in the eleventh Book the field of external sense-perception to illustrate them; and thence advanced to the consideration of that faculty of the inward man which uses the power of reason upon things temporal, while I postponed for later treatment the other and sovereign faculty by which he contemplates things eternal. This occupied two Books, the twelfth dealing with the difference of one faculty from the other, as the lower from the higher to which it should be subordinate; and the thirteenth with the function of the lower, as including the salutary knowledge of human affairs which helps us in this temporal life so to act that we may attain to the life eternal. I treated of this as faithfully as I could, but in brief; for I had to cover in the limits of a single Book a subject of manifold and copious detail which has been the theme of many great works of many great writers. In this sphere also I pointed to a trinity, though still not such a one as to be called the image of God.

11 (viii). Now we have reached the point in our discussion at which we have undertaken to consider that highest element in the human mind whereby it knows or can know God, with a view to our finding therein the image of God. Although the human mind is not of that nature which belongs to God, yet the image of that nature which transcends every other in excellence is to be sought and found in the element which in our own nature is the most excellent. But first we have to consider the mind in itself, before it has participation in God, and discover his image there. We have said that it still remains the image of God, although an image faded and defaced by the loss of that participation. It is in virtue of the fact that it has a capacity for God and the ability to participate in God, that it is his image[24]:

24 Cf. 6 (iv), above, n. 15

only because it is his image can so high a destiny be conceived for it. Here then is the mind, remembering itself, understanding itself, loving itself. Perceiving this, we perceive a trinity—a trinity still less than God, but already an image of God. In this trinity, the memory has not imported from outside what it should retain, nor has the understanding discovered in the outer world the object for its beholding, like the body's eye. The will has not in this case made an outward union of these two, as of the material form and its derivative in the sight of the beholder. An image of the external object seen, taken up as it were and stored in the memory, has not been discovered by thought directed towards it, and thence form been given to the recollecting attention, while the two are united by the further activity of will. This was the system displayed in those trinities which we found to exist in material processes, or to pass somehow into our inward experience from the external body through the bodily sense. All this we discussed in the eleventh Book.

Nor is our present trinity the same as that which we found existing or presenting itself to us in our discussion of the knowledge (as distinct from wisdom) whose sphere is the activity of the inward man. The objects of this knowledge form an adventitious element in the mind: they may be introduced by historical information, like the things done and said, transacted and passing in time, or the things locally and geographically situated in the natural world; or they may arise from nonexistence within the man himself, either through the teaching of others or through his own reflections, like the faith which in the thirteenth Book we set forth at such length, or like the virtues which, if they are real, make the life of our present mortal condition good, in order that we may attain in the immortality which God has promised us the life which is blessed. These and the like matters are disposed in a temporal succession, which made it more easy for us to discover the trinity of memory, vision and love.[25] For some of them exist prior to the learners' knowledge of them: they are knowable before they are known, and beget the knowledge of themselves in the learners. Either they still exist in their own places, or they belong to time past: in the latter case, what exists is not themselves but certain signs of their past existence, the sight or hearing of which gives the knowledge that they once were and now are past. Such signs

[25] Here *visio* and *amor* are (exceptionally) substituted for *intelligentia* and *voluntas*.

may be locally situated, as memorials of the dead and the like. They may be preserved in credible works of literature, such as any reputable and authoritative history. Or they may be in the minds of men who already know the facts: what is already known to them is knowable for others, to whose knowledge it is prior, and who can come to know it through the instruction of those to whom it is known. All this, in the process of its being learnt, presents a kind of trinity: the reality which was knowable before it was known, the application to it of the knowledge of the learner which comes into existence with the learning, and thirdly the will which unites the two. And after the knowledge is acquired, another trinity appears in more inward form with its recollection in the mind itself, composed of the images impressed in the process of learning upon the memory, the form given to thought when the remembering attention is directed to them, and the will which unites the two. With regard to that which arises in the mind where it had not been before, such as faith and the like, this appears indeed to be adventitious in that it is implanted through teaching; but it is not, like the objects of belief, situated or transacted in the outer world, but originates entirely within the mind itself. Faith is not the object but the act of belief: the object is believed, the act is perceived. But since it originates in the mind, which was already mind before faith began to exist in it, it seems adventitious in character, and it will be counted among things past, when its place is taken by sight and itself ceases to be. The trinity composed by faith when it is present, as held, regarded and loved, is not, as we have already said, the same as that which will be traceable as a relic left in the memory by its passing.[26]

12 (ix). It may further be asked whether in the life to come the virtues which make life good in our state of mortality, must cease to be when they have brought the soul home to the eternal world; for they too have their beginning in the mind, which has a prior existence without them, in which it is none the less mind. Some have supposed that they will cease; and in the case of three of them, prudence, fortitude, and self-control, this view has much in its favour. But justice (or righteousness) at least is immortal, and will rather be made perfect in us in the life to come, than cease to be. Yet that great and eloquent writer, Cicero, in his dialogue *Hortensius*[27] argues as follows concerning

[26] Cf. 5 (iii), above.
[27] A lost work of Cicero which made a lasting impression upon Augustine in his youth (see *Conf.*, III, 7 (iv)).

all the four: "If, when we have passed out of this life, we should
be permitted, as stories tell, to live immortally in the islands of
the blest, what need should we have of eloquence, with no
courts to plead in, or even of the virtues themselves? We could
not require fortitude when no toil or danger confronted us, or
justice, when no other man's possessions could be coveted, or
self-control for the ruling of passions no longer existing, or even
prudence, when there would be no choice to make between good
and evil. Our blessedness would consist solely in the cognizance
and knowledge of nature, which alone makes admirable even
the life of gods. From which we may infer that all the rest is
grounded in necessity and only this in free will."—Thus the
great orator, when he comes to sing the praises of philosophy,
recalling his debt to the philosophers and expounding it with
mastery and charm, maintains that all four virtues are necessary
in this life only, full as we know it of cares and errors; but none
of them when we have passed out of it, if we are permitted to
live where life is blessed. He believes that the good soul is
blessed through nothing else but the cognizance and knowledge,
which is contemplation, of that Nature which is supremely good
and lovable—the Nature, that is, which has created and ordered
all natures else. If to be subject to that Nature's rule belongs to
justice, then justice certainly is immortal; nor will it cease to
exist in that blessed state, but will be of a perfection and a
greatness beyond the possibility of increase. Perhaps the other
three virtues also—prudence with no risk of error remaining,
fortitude without the trouble of ills to be endured, self-control
with no recalcitrant passions—may yet exist in that state of
happiness. It may be the act of prudence to think no good pre-
ferable or equal to God; of fortitude, to cleave to him immov-
ably; of self-control, to take pleasure in no harmful defection.
But the present work of justice, in supporting the oppressed, of
prudence, in taking heed of snares, of fortitude, in the endurance
of troubles, of self-control, in the restraint of corrupt pleasures—
of these there will be nothing in that life which will contain
nothing at all of evil. Accordingly, these activities of the virtues,
necessary to our mortal life as is the faith to which they must be
referred, will be accounted as things past; and the trinity now
composed when we hold, regard, and love them as present, is
not the same as that trinity which will exist when we find,
through those traces which their passing will leave in the memory, that they once were but are no longer. For there will be a
trinity, when of this so-called trace there is both a retention in

the memory and a true recognition, and a union of both by the will.

13 (x). In the knowledge of all those temporal matters, to which we have here referred, certain of the things knowable precede the knowing of them by an interval of time: such are the sensible properties which were already in the outward objects before they were perceived, and all the facts of historical knowledge. Certain others originate simultaneously with being known: if for example an object of sight which had no previous existence should arise before our eyes, it cannot precede our knowing of it; or if a sound is caused in the presence of a hearer, the sound and the hearing of it begin and cease simultaneously. But whether their origin is precedent or simultaneous, it is the "knowables" that beget the knowledge and not *vice versa*. And when the knowledge has been effected, and the things known take their place in the memory and are recalled to view in the act of recollection, it is obvious that the retention in the memory is temporally prior both to the recollecting vision and to the union of the two by will. It is not so however with the mind itself. It cannot be adventitious to itself, as though to a self already in being there should come from elsewhere an identical self previously non-existent, or as though, instead of coming from elsewhere, there should be born in the existing self an identical self which did not exist before, in the way that faith arises from non-existence in the existing mind. Nor does the mind, after coming to know itself, see itself by recollection as established in its own memory, as though it had not been there before becoming the object of its own knowledge. Assuredly, from the moment of its beginning to be, the mind has never ceased to know itself, to understand itself, and to love itself, as we have already demonstrated. Therefore, in its act of turning upon itself in thought, a trinity is presented in which it is possible to recognize a "word"—formed from the act of thinking, and united to its original by will. Here, then, is where we may recognize the image for which we are seeking.

14 (xi). It may be objected that the faculty by which the mind, which is ever present to itself, is said to "remember" itself, cannot properly be called memory. For memory is of things past, not of things present. Some writers upon the virtues, including Cicero, have analysed prudence into the three elements of memory, understanding and foresight,[28] assigning memory to what is past, understanding to what is present, and

28 Cicero, *De Inv. Rhet.*, II, 53.

foresight to what is future—the last being reliable only in those who have fore-knowledge of future events, an attribute which does not belong to men unless it be given from above, as to the prophets. So the scriptural Book of Wisdom says of men that "the thoughts of men are fearful, and our foreseeings uncertain." [29] Memory of things past, and understanding of things present, are reliable—that is, when the things present are incorporeal: for corporeal things are present, not to understanding but to the beholding of the bodily eyes. In answer to the objection that there is no memory of things present, we may point to an expression in secular literature, where there was more care for verbal correctness than for truth of fact:

> "Ulysses would not brook such outrage,
> Nor in that testing hour forget himself." [30]

When Vergil says that Ulysses did not forget himself, he is saying in other words that the hero remembered himself; and that, since he was certainly present to himself, could only be if memory were applicable to things present. Memory therefore in the case of things past denotes the faculty by which they may be reviewed and recollected; in the case of an object present, as is the mind to itself, the same name may be given without absurdity to the mind's possession of itself in such a way as to be understandable by its own act of thought, and to be capable of the union of possession and understanding through the act of self-love.

15 (xii). Now this trinity of the mind is God's image, not because the mind remembers, understands and loves itself; but because it has the power also to remember, understand and love its Maker. [31] And it is in so doing that it attains wisdom. If it does not so, the memory, understanding and love of itself is no more than an act of folly. Let the mind then remember its God, in whose image it was made, let it understand him and love him. In a word, let it worship the uncreated God who created it with the capacity for himself, and in whom it is able to be made partaker. For this cause it is written: "Behold, the worship of God is wisdom." [32] Wisdom will be the mind's, not by its own illumination, but by partaking in that supreme Light; and only when it enters eternity will it reign in bliss. But to say that a man may possess such wisdom is not to deny that it is the

[29] Wisdom 9:14.　　　　　　[30] Verg., *Aen.*, III, 628 f.
[31] The remaining chapters of the Book contain the climax of the whole argument.　　　　[32] Job 28:28.

property of God. God's is the only true wisdom: were it human, it would be vain. Yet when we call it the wisdom of God, we do not mean the wisdom wherewith God is wise: he is not wise by partaking in himself, as is the mind by partaking in God. It is rather as we speak of the righteousness of God, not only in the sense of that whereby God is righteous, but of that which he gives to man when he "justifies the ungodly": to which the apostle refers when he speaks of those who "being ignorant of God's righteousness, and willing to establish their own righteousness, were not subject to the righteousness of God." [33] In the same way we might speak of some who being ignorant of the wisdom of God, and willing to establish their own, were not subject to the wisdom of God.

16. There is an uncreated Being who has made all other beings great and small, unquestionably surpassing all that he has made, and so surpassing also the reasonable and spiritual being of which we have been speaking, namely the mind of man, made in the image of its Creator. And the Being surpassing all others is God. He is, indeed "not far from each one of us," as the apostle says; adding: "for in him we live and move, and have our being." [34] If this were spoken in a material sense, it could be understood of our material world: for in it too, so far as our body is concerned, we live and move and are. We must take the text, then, as spoken of the mind which is made in his image, and of a manner of being more excellent, not visible, but spiritual. What is there indeed that is not "in him," of whom Holy Scripture says: "for from him and through him and in him are all things"? [35] If in him are all things, in whom, save in him in whom they are, can the living live or the moving move? Yet all men are not with him after the manner of the saying "I am alway with thee." [36] Nor is he with all after the manner of our own saying, "the Lord be with you." It is man's great misery, not to be with him, without whom man cannot be. Certainly, man is never without him, in whom he is; yet if a man does not remember him, does not understand him, nor love him, he is not with him. But complete oblivion makes it impossible even to be reminded of what we have forgotten.

17 (xiii). We may take on this point an example from the visible world. A man whom you do not recognize says to you: "You know me"; and as a reminder, he tells you where, when, and how you became acquainted with him. If, after you have

33 Rom. 4:5; 10:3.   34 Acts 17:27 f.
35 Rom. 11:36.   36 Ps. 73:23.

been given all the clues which could revive your memory of him, you still do not recognize him, it means that you have forgotten him so completely that no trace of the former knowledge remains in your mind; and nothing remains but for you to believe his assurance that you once knew him—or not even that, if the speaker does not appear to you worthy of credit. If, however, you do remember, clearly you are going back to your memory, and finding there what had not been entirely forgotten and obliterated. Let us now return to the point which led us to draw this parallel from human intercourse. We find in the ninth Psalm the words: "Let the sinners be turned into hell, all the nations that forget God." [37] Or again, in the twenty-second: "All the ends of the earth shall be reminded, and shall turn unto the Lord." [38] These nations, then, had not so far forgotten God that they could not remember him when reminded. By forgetting God, as though forgetting their own life, they had been turned unto death, that is, into hell. But, on being reminded, they turn to the Lord, reviving again through the remembrance of their life, of which forgetfulness had deprived them. We may compare the text of the ninety-fourth Psalm: "Understand now, ye unwise among the people: return at last, ye fools, to wisdom. He that planted the ear, shall he not hear?" etc.[39] The words are addressed to those who through lacking understanding of God have spoken vain things concerning him.

18 (xiv). For the love of God, we can find many references in Scripture, where the presence of the other two elements in the mind is logically implied: in that no-one can love what he does not remember, or of which he is wholly without knowledge. Most familiar is the first great commandment: "Thou shalt love the Lord thy God." [40] The natural constitution of the human mind is such that it is never without the memory, the understanding, and the love of itself. But since with hate of a man goes the desire to do him hurt, it is with good reason that man's mind may be said to hate itself when it is hurtful to itself. Its ill-will to itself is unconscious, because it does not suppose that what it wants is injurious: yet in wanting what is injurious, it is willing evil to itself. So it is written: "He that loveth iniquity, hateth his own soul." [41] Therefore the man who knows how to love himself, loves God; while the man who does not love God, though he retains the love of self which belongs to his nature, may yet properly be said to hate himself when he does

[37] Ps. 9:17.   [38] Ps. 22:27.   [39] Ps. 94:8 f.
[40] Deut. 6:5.   [41] Ps. 11:5.

what is contrary to his own good and behaves to himself as an enemy. It is indeed a fearful delusion by which, though all men desire their own advantage, so many do only what works their ruin. A like distemper in dumb animals is described by Vergil in the words:

> . . . "God guard his servants from such error,
> And send it on his enemies!—to tear
> With naked fangs their mangled limbs". . . [42]

The poet can speak of a bodily disease as "error," inasmuch as every creature is naturally its own friend and guardian, and the effect of this disease was to make beasts mutilate the body whose well-being was their aim.

When the mind loves God, and consequently (as has been said) remembers him and understands him, there rightly follows the command concerning one's neighbour, to love him as oneself. For the mind's love of itself becomes right instead of perverted, when it loves God, by partaking in whom the image we speak of not only exists but is transformed from old to new, from disfigurement to shapeliness, from unhappiness to beatitude. The power of self-love is such that if a man must choose he will rather lose all that he loves in the world below him than himself be lost. Only with the God above him, to whom the Psalmist sings "My strength will I keep safe with thee," and again "Draw near unto him, and be lightened,"[43] can a man keep safe his strength and enjoy the divine light as his own. But the mind that forsakes the God above it becomes so feeble and darkened that, through loves it cannot quell and errors out of which it sees no way of return, it falls miserably away from itself into the things which are alien and inferior to itself. So the penitent, who already has knowledge of God's mercy, cries in the Psalm: "My strength hath forsaken me, and the light of my eyes is not with me." [44]

19. Yet even in such evil case of infirmity and error, the mind could not lose its natural memory, understanding and love of itself; and so is justified the saying quoted above [45]: "Though man walketh in an image, yet is he vainly disquieted: he heapeth up treasures, and knoweth not for whom he shall gather them." Why does he heap up treasures, but because his strength hath forsaken him—the strength in which, possessing God, he could have need of nothing? And why does he not know

42 Verg., *Georg.*, III, 513 f.   43 Ps. 59:9; 34:5.
44 Ps. 38:10.   45 Bk. XIV, 4 (ii).

for whom he shall gather them but because the light of his eyes is not with him?—so that he cannot see what the truth would tell him: "Thou fool, this night they require thy soul of thee; then whose shall those things be which thou hast prepared?" [46] Yet man, fallen as he is, still "walketh in an image," and his mind retains a memory, understanding, and love of himself; so that if it were made plain to him that he cannot have both, and a choice offered of one of the two with loss of the other—either the treasures which he has gathered, or his mind—there is no-one so mindless as to prefer treasures to mind. Treasures can very often overthrow the mind; but the mind that is not overthrown by treasures can live an easier and more unhampered life without any of them. Nor can there be any possession of treasures save by means of the mind. An infant born to the greatest riches, though master of all that is legally his, possesses nothing when his mind slumbers. How then can anything be possessed by one whose mind is lost? Indeed it is superfluous to urge that any man, confronted with the choice, must prefer the deprivation of treasures to the deprivation of mind. No-one could prefer treasures, or even compare them for value, to the eyes in his body, which give possession not as of gold to the favoured few but of the wide heaven to every man. By use of the bodily eyes everyone possesses all that he delights to see. Who then would not choose, if he could not keep both and must perforce be deprived of one, to lose his treasures rather than his eyes? Yet if he were asked on similar terms whether he would rather lose eyes or mind, every "mind" must see that he would keep his mind and lose his eyes. For the mind without the eyes of flesh is still human, but the eyes of flesh without mind are the eyes of a beast. Who would not rather be a blind man than a seeing beast?

20. My purpose in this argument has been to bring home in brief, to the least acute intelligence among those who may read or hear what I have written, the force of the mind's love of itself, even when it is weak and erring through the mistaken love and pursuit of what is beneath it. Now it could not love itself, if it were altogether ignorant of itself—that is, if it had no memory of itself—and did not understand itself. Such potency it has by virtue of this image of God that is in it, that it can be strong to cleave to him whose image it is. It has been set in that place in the order of reality (which is no spatial order) where there is none above it but God. And when its cleaving to him has become

[46] Luke 12:20.

absolute, it will be one spirit with him: witness the words of the apostle, "He that is joined to the Lord is one spirit." [47] The mind will be raised to the participation of his being, truth and bliss, though nothing thereby be added to the being, truth, and bliss which is his own. In that being, joined to it in perfect happiness, it will live a changeless life and enjoy the changeless vision of all that it will behold. Then, according to the promise of Holy Scripture, its "desire will be satisfied with good things," [48] with goods unchanging, the very Trinity itself, its God whose image it is; and, that never again despite be done to that image, it will abide "in the secret place of his countenance," [49] so filled with his abundant riches that sin can never more delight it.

But here and now, when the mind regards itself, the thing it sees is not unchangeable. 21 (xv). Of that it can have no doubt, since it is miserable and longs for blessedness: only because it can change, can it hope that blessedness is possible for it. For if it were unchangeable, it could pass neither from bliss to misery nor from misery to bliss. Nothing could have brought it to misery under a Lord omnipotent and good, but its own sin and its Lord's righteousness. Nothing will make it blessed, but its own desert and its Lord's rewarding; and even its desert is the grace of him whose reward its blessedness will be. [50] For it cannot give itself the righteousness which it has lost and lacks. In the creation of man it received that righteousness, and by its own sinning inevitably lost it. Therefore it must receive the righteousness for which it may deserve to receive beatitude. To a mind inclining to take pride in a good supposed of its own making, the truth is told by the apostle: "What hast thou that thou hast not received? and if thou hast received, why dost thou boast thyself as though thou hadst not received?" [51] But when it duly remembers its Lord, it receives his Spirit, and becomes fully conscious of the truth learnt from the indwelling Teacher, that it can rise only by his undeserved goodness, even as it could have fallen only by its own voluntary default. It has indeed no memory of its own blessedness; for that was once and is no longer, and the mind has totally forgotten it, so that no reminder can bring it back. It can only believe, on the faith of the Scriptures of its God, written by his prophet, the story of a happiness of paradise and

---

[47] I Cor. 6:17.   [48] Ps. 103:5.   [49] Ps. 31:20.
[50] "Man's good deservings are the gift of God" (*Enchirid.*, 28 (cvii)).
[51] I Cor. 4:7.

the account conveyed in narrative form of man's original good and evil. But it has the memory of the Lord its God. For he ever is—neither was and is not, nor is and was not, but never was not, even as never he will not be. And he is everywhere in his wholeness; so that in him the mind lives and moves and has its being, and therefore has the power to remember him. Not that it recollects having once known him in Adam, or anywhere else before this bodily life, or at its first making and planting in this body. Of none of these things has it any memory whatsoever: all of them are buried in oblivion. But it can be so reminded as to turn again unto the Lord, who is the light by which even in its turning away from him it was still somehow touched.[52] Hence comes the ability even in the godless to think of an eternal world, and rightly to assign blame and praise in the field of human morality. The norms by which they make such judgments must be those in which they see how every man ought to live, though their own lives be no example of it. Where do they see such norms? Not in their own nature; for while it is certainly the mind that sees them, their minds are admittedly changeable, and the changelessness of these norms is manifest to all who have the power to see it. Not in the fashion of their own mind; for the norms are norms of righteousness, and their minds are admittedly unrighteous. Where are the norms written, in which what is righteous is recognized by the unrighteous, in which he sees that what he has not is truly worth having? Where, but in the book of that light which is called truth,[53] out of which every righteous law is copied and passes into the heart of the man who works righteousness—passes not by transference but by impression, even as the seal of a ring passes into the wax without leaving the ring. But as for him who works not, and yet sees what right working is, he it is who turns aside from the light by which none the less he is being touched. The man who does not even see how he ought to live, sins with more excuse since he is not transgressor of a law he knows; yet even he may sometimes feel the touch of truth's omni-present shining, when he admits the justice of an admonition. 22 (xvi). Those who are moved by the reminder to turn again to the Lord, out of that state of deformity wherein worldly desires conformed them to this world, must receive from the Lord their re-formation, according to the apostle's saying: "Be not conformed to this world, but be reformed in newness of your mind"[54]; the

52 Augustine will not allow that the Fall has severed man's relation to God.
53 Cf. Bk. VIII, 9 (vi). 54 Rom. 12:2.

beginning of the image's re-forming must come from him who first formed it. The self which it was able to deform, it cannot of itself re-form. In another place the apostle says: "Be renewed in the spirit of your mind, and put on the new man, which is created after God in righteousness and holiness of truth." [55] The words "after God" correspond to what we read elsewhere: "in the image of God." [56] Through sin, righteousness and holiness of truth were lost; wherefore this image has become deformed and faded. The mind receives it again, when it is re-formed and renewed.

("The spirit of your mind" does not here imply two separate things, one the mind, and the other the mind's spirit. It means that while every mind is a spirit, not every spirit is a mind. God also is a spirit, who cannot be renewed since he cannot grow old. The word "spirit" is also used for something in a man which is not mind, and to which belong imaginings in the likeness of bodily objects: we find this in the text of the letter to the Corinthians, "If I pray with a tongue, my spirit prayeth, but my mind is unfruitful." [57] That describes what happens, when what is spoken is not understood. It could not be spoken, unless the images of material sounds were present in the thought of the spirit before their vocal enunciation. Again, the human soul may be called "spirit," as in the words of the Gospel: "He bowed his head and gave up his spirit," [58] signifying the body's death when the soul leaves it. "Spirit" may even be applied to a beast: this is explicit in the book of Solomon, Ecclesiastes, where we read: "Who knoweth the spirit of the sons of men whether it shall ascend upwards, or the spirit of the beast whether it shall go down into the earth?" [59] Also in the book of Genesis, concerning the death in the flood of all flesh, "that had in itself the spirit of life." [60] The word is used also of wind, a thing plainly material, as in the Psalms: "Fire and hail, snow and ice, the spirit of the storm." [61] "Spirit," then, having so many possible senses, Paul means by his phrase "the spirit of the mind," that spirit which we call "mind." Similarly, the same apostle writes: "in the putting off of the body of flesh." [62] Here there is no implication of two different things, one flesh and the other the body of flesh; but since many fleshless things may be called "body" (many bodies celestial and bodies terrestrial other than those of flesh), Paul uses "body of flesh" for that

[55] Eph. 4:23 f. [56] Gen. 1:27. [57] I Cor. 14:14.
[58] John 19:30. [59] Eccl. 3:21. [60] Gen. 7:22.
[61] Ps. 148:8. [62] Col. 2:11.

body which is flesh. And in the same way he uses "spirit of the mind" for the spirit which is mind.)

Elsewhere we find the image named more explicitly, as when the same exhortation is given in other words: "Putting off the old man with his doings, put on the new man who is renewed in the knowledge of God after the image of his Creator." [63] Where the former text has, "after God," the latter gives "after the image of his Creator"; and where the former has "in righteousness and holiness of truth," we have in the latter, "in the knowledge of God." Thus the renewal and reforming of the mind takes place "after God," or "after God's image": it is said to be "after God," to exclude its being supposed to be after some other creature; and "after God's image," to make it plain that the renewal is effected in the place where God's image is, that is, in the mind. In the same way we say of the faithful and righteous departed that he is dead "after the body," but not "after the spirit." Dead "after the body" means dead with or in the body, and not dead with or in the soul. To speak of a man as beautiful after the body, or strong after the body, not after the mind, is to say that his beauty and strength is not mental but bodily. The manner of speech is very common. [64] We are not, then, to understand "after the image of his Creator" as implying some other image after which man is renewed, rather than the actual image which is renewed.

23 (xvii). Of course, the renewal of which we speak is not effected in the single moment of return, like the renewal which takes place in baptism in a single moment through the remission of all sins—none whatsoever remaining unremitted. But it is one thing to be relieved of fevers, and another to regain health after the weakness which fevers have caused. It is one thing to withdraw a dart from the body, and another to heal by further treatment the wound it has inflicted. So here, cure's beginning is to remove the cause of sickness; and that is done through the forgiveness of all sins. Its furtherance is the healing of the sickness itself, which takes effect by gradual progress in the renewal of the image. Both are displayed in one text of the Psalm, where we read: "who shows mercy upon all thine iniquities"—which happens in baptism; and then: "who healeth all thy sicknesses" [65]—which is a matter of daily advances whereby the

[63] Col. 3:9 f.
[64] Less so in English than in Latin: the word "after" has been taken as the nearest equivalent of Augustine's *secundum*.
[65] Ps. 103:3.

image is made anew. Of this the apostle has spoken in plain terms: "If our outward man decays, yet is our inward man renewed from day to day" [66]—"renewed," as he has told us in the texts just quoted, "in the knowledge of God," that is, "in righteousness and holiness of truth." He who is thus renewed by daily advancing in the knowledge of God, in righteousness and holiness of truth, is changing the direction of his love from the temporal to the eternal, from the visible to the intelligible, from the carnal to the spiritual; diligently endeavouring to curb and abate all lust for the one, and to bind himself in charity to the other. In which all his success depends on the divine aid; for it is the word of God, that "without me ye can do nothing." [67]

When life's last day finds a man, in such advancing and increasing, firm in the faith of the Mediator, the holy angels will be waiting to bring him home to the God whom he has served and by whom he must be perfected; and at the world's end he will receive an incorruptible body, not for punishment but for glory. For in this image the likeness of God will be perfect only in the perfect vision of God: of which vision the apostle Paul says: "now we see through a glass darkly, but then face to face." [68] And again: "but we with unveiled face beholding the glory of the Lord, are transformed into the same image from glory into glory, as from the Spirit of the Lord" [69]—which describes the daily process in those who go forward as they ought. 24 (xviii). From the apostle John we have the saying: "Beloved, now are we sons of God, and it hath not yet appeared what we shall be: but we know that when he appears we shall be like him, for we shall see him as he is." [70] This shows that the full likeness of God is realized in his image only when it has attained the full vision of him. It may indeed be thought that the words of John refer to the immortality of the body; for in that too we shall be like to God, if only to the Son, since he alone in the Trinity has taken upon him a body in which he died and rose again, and which he carried with him into heaven. We may speak here also of an image of the Son of God, in which we shall have an immortal body like him, conformed in that particular to the image not of the Father or of the Holy Spirit but of the Son only. For of him alone do we read and receive in most wholesome faith, that "the Word was made flesh." [71] Thus the apostle says: "Whom he foreknew, them he also predestinated

66 II Cor. 4:16. 67 John 15:5.
68 I Cor. 13:12. 69 II Cor. 3:18.
70 John 3:2. 71 John 1:14.

to be conformed to the image of his Son, that he might be first-born among many brethren." [72] "First-born," indeed, "of the dead," in the words of the same apostle [73]—that death whereby his flesh was sown in dishonour and rose again in glory.[74] After this image of the Son, to which we are conformed through immortality in the body, we do according to another saying of Paul's: "As we have borne the image of the earthly, let us bear also the image of him who is from heaven." [75] That is, let us, who after Adam were mortal, believe with true faith and sure and steady hope that after Christ we shall be immortal. For so can we bear the same image now, not yet in vision but in faith, not yet in reality, but in hope. The apostle in fact was speaking of the resurrection of the body in the context of this saying.

25 (xix). But if we think of that image of which it is written: "Let us make man in our image and likeness," [76] not "in my image" or "in thy image"—we must believe that man was made in the image of the Trinity; and this is what we have devoted our best efforts to trace out and understand. Accordingly we may better interpret in the sense of this image the words quoted from John: "We shall be like him, for we shall see him as he is." The apostle is speaking here of him, of whom he has said: "we are sons of God." Moreover, the immortality of the flesh will be made perfect in the moment of resurrection, which (as Paul says) will be "in the twinkling of an eye, in the last trump: and the dead shall be raised uncorrupted, and we shall be changed." [77] For in the twinkling of an eye there shall rise again before the judgment, in strength, incorruption, and glory, that spiritual body which now is being sown, a natural body, in weakness, corruption, and dishonour. But the image that is being renewed in the spirit of the mind, in the knowledge of God, not outwardly but inwardly from day to day, will be made perfect by that vision, face to face, that shall be after the judgment—the vision which now is but a-growing, through a glass darkly.[78] And its perfecting is what we should understand by the words: "we shall be like him, for we shall see him as he is." This is the gift then to be given us, when we hear the call: "Come, ye blessed of my Father, possess the kingdom prepared for you." [79] Then shall be taken away the godless, so that he sees not the glory of the Lord, when those on the left hand go into

[72] Rom. 8:29.
[73] Col. 1:18.
[74] I Cor. 15:43
[75] I Cor. 15:49.
[76] Gen. 1:26.
[77] I Cor. 15:52.
[78] I Cor. 13:12.
[79] Matt. 25:34.

eternal punishment, and those on the right into eternal life.
And, as the Truth has told us, "this is life eternal, that they may
know thee the one true God, and Jesus Christ whom thou hast
sent." [80]

This wisdom of contemplation is, I believe, in its proper sense
distinguished in Holy Scripture from knowledge, and named
wisdom—a human wisdom, yet coming to man only from God:
partaking in whom, the reasonable and intellectual mind can
be made wise in truth. At the end of his dialogue *Hortensius*, we
find Cicero commending this same wisdom. "If," he says, "we
give day and night to such meditations, if we sharpen our
understanding which is the mind's eye, and take good heed that
it grow not dull—if, that is to say, we live the life of philosophy,
then we may have good hope: that if our power of feeling and
thought is mortal and transient, it will be pleasant for us to pass
away when the duties of our human life are done, nor will our
extinction be an offence to us but rather a repose from living;
and if, on the other hand, as the greatest and most famous of
ancient philosophers have believed, our souls are eternal and
divine, then we may fairly suppose that the more constant a
soul has been in following its own course, that is, in the pursuit
of reason and the ardour of enquiry, and the less it has mingled
and involved itself in the faults and errors of man, by so much
the easier will be its ascent and return to its heavenly country."
After which he adds this final sentence in which he resumes and
concludes his discussion: "Therefore, to end this long discourse,
if it is our will either to pass quietly into nothingness after these
pursuits have occupied our life, or to travel forthwith from our
present home to another that will be far better, to these studies
we ought to give all our energy and attention."

It is a wonder to me that so powerful a mind should offer to
men who live the life of philosophy, the life which gives blessedness in the contemplation of truth, a "pleasant passing away"
when the duties of their human life are done, if our power of
feeling and thought is mortal and transient; as though this
would be the death and destruction of something which we
loved so little, or even hated so fiercely, that its passing away
would be "pleasant" to us. He had learnt that, not from the
philosophers to whom he gives such high praise: his opinion
savoured rather of the New Academy, which had persuaded him
to scepticism even upon the most manifest of truths. The tradition which came to him from those philosophers who on his own

[80] John 17:3.

admission were the greatest and most famous, was that souls are eternal. For eternal souls, indeed, the exhortation is appropriate that they be found, when the end of this life comes upon them, "following their own course, that is, in the pursuit of reason and the ardour of enquiry," and that they should avoid the "mingling and involvement of themselves in the faults and errors of men," in order that their return to God may be the easier. But the course that is set in the love of truth and enquiry after it, is not enough for men unhappy as all must be whose mortality is supported by reason alone, without the faith of the Mediator. That is what I have done my best to show in earlier Books of this treatise, especially the fourth and thirteenth.

BOOK XV

Review and Re-valuation: Image and Original

ARGUMENT

[We have been seeking for an image of the Trinity in the highest of created things; and this search for God, even though it must be endless, is justified by Scripture (§§ 1–3).

Summary of the discussion in Books I–XIV (§§ 4, 5).

Our conception of the divine being is built up of a number of attributes which we derive from our rational judgments of value (§ 6). All these terms denote the one divine substance which belongs equally to the three Persons of the Trinity; but we may reduce them to the three attributes of eternity, wisdom, and blessedness (§§ 7, 8). Even these three might be regarded as all implied in one, viz. wisdom (§ 9). By reference to the image of God traced in his gift of wisdom to the mind, we may say that the divine wisdom is Trinity, in virtue of its own self-knowledge and self-love (§ 10).

Yet the analogy remains imperfect: (*a*) in that the human "trinity of wisdom" is *in* man, as a part of his nature, whereas the divine Trinity is itself constitutive of the divine nature (§ 11); (*b*) in that the human faculties of memory, understanding, and will are not interchangeable, whereas in God we cannot confine memory to the Father, understanding to the Son, and love or will to the Spirit (§ 12). Our temporal modes of existence and thought make it impossible for us to comprehend a wisdom which is both memory and fore-knowledge (§ 13). We see "in a glass, darkly" (§§ 14–16).

None the less, we can gain a certain understanding of the second Person's relation to the first, by considering the "inward speech" or unspoken word which takes place in our act of thinking (§§ 17–19)—the thought prior to all language, of which language is no more than a sign for the purpose of communication, like the flesh assumed by the divine Word. This human "word" is the source of all human activity, even as the divine Word is that through which all things were made (§ 20). But in many respects our human image of the divine Word is inadequate. (*a*) The knowledge which gives it form is scanty and uncertain. We have indeed some ultimate certainties, but they are few (§ 21). (*b*) God's knowledge is not acquired or conditioned from without: it precedes all his creative activity and is inseparable from his being (§ 22). (*c*) The correspondence of the divine Word to the divine knowledge is perfect (§ 23). (*d*) The human "word" is not always born of true knowledge (§ 24), and even a true "word" is not always present and actual, because it is not always the object of thought: at best it is "formable," not formed once and for all (§§ 25, 26).

The Holy Spirit, as proceeding from both Father and Son, may be regarded as the mutual charity of the first and second Persons (§ 27). But Scripture says that *God* is charity; and we have already seen the objection to identifying any Person of the Trinity with any one of the members of our mental triads (§ 28): only the terms "word," "gift," and "source" of generation or procession can rightly be assigned to the several Persons exclusively. Yet if the Word is more especially or appropriately named the wisdom of God, there may be a similar fitness in naming the Spirit charity (§§ 29, 30); and this is confirmed by the language of I John 4 (§ 31). Charity is indeed the supreme gift (§ 32), and Scripture is clear that the Holy Spirit is the gift of God (§§ 33–36). The Holy Spirit rightly may receive the name of charity, as proceeding from Father and Son and constituting the "communion" of both—for both are Spirit (§ 37). Charity, however, remains a term of the essence or substance of Godhead, and the heretical attempt to distinguish the divine will from the divine nature, in the interest of Arianism, must be rejected (§ 38).

Memory, understanding, and will, offer us an image of the Trinity, in so far as they are mutually inherent and inseparable activities (§§ 39–41). But the analogy is defective, in that the real actor is the human person or subject, possessed of these three powers or faculties, whereas the Trinity is not *in* one God, but is itself the one God, though constituting not one "Person" but three (§§ 42, 43). All discussion of the image in the human mind has value only as it is inspired by the faith that it *is* an image and no more, that it is sin which blurs the image and darkens our vision, and that only in the life to come shall we see face to face (§ 44).

For our present understanding it is hard to perceive the difference between generation of the Son and procession of the Spirit. We cannot speak of either in temporal terms (§ 45).—Christ gave the Spirit as God, received it as man (§ 46). But the procession of the Spirit is an eternal fact no less than the divine generation of the Son, to which there can be no parallel in our mental life: it is a fact in the being of the Father which with all else he imparts to the Son (§§ 47, 48). On this matter, the unbeliever must accept the teaching of Scripture before he can hope for any measure of understanding (§ 49).—We can but see, in our image of the Trinity, that thought or word is "begotten" of remembered knowledge, while will bears a different relation to both (§ 50).

Let us end our work not with argument but with prayer (§ 51).]

THE TEXT

1 (i). Our design of preparing the reader, by the study of the things that are made, for the knowledge of their maker, has brought us to the image of God which man presents, in virtue of that which sets him above all other animals: namely, reason or intelligence, with any other characteristic of the reasonable or intellectual soul that is properly to be assigned to what we call *mens* or *animus* (mind).[1] The word *animus* is used by some Latin writers as a technical term to distinguish the higher element in man, which is lacking in the beast, from the *anima* or soul which is present in beast as well as man. If we look for a being above this, and look for an existing reality, it must be God, the being not created but Creator. And whether this being is a Trinity is a question not only to be decided for faith by the authority of Holy Scripture; but one to which we ought, if we can, to give some rational answer, satisfactory to the understanding. My reason for saying "if we can," will emerge in the course of our actual discussion of the question.

2 (ii). The God whom we seek will, I doubt not, give us the help we need, that our labour be not fruitless. Then shall we understand what is written in the Psalm: "Let the heart of them rejoice that seek the Lord: seek the Lord and be strengthened; seek his face alway."[2] One might suppose that what is always sought is never found; and that the heart of them that seek must rather grieve than rejoice, if they cannot find what they seek.

[1] See Introduction, *ad fin.* Augustine here makes it clear that "reason" is not the *only* activity of *mens*. [2] Ps. 105:3 f.

It is not said, "Let the heart of them that find rejoice," but "of them that seek the Lord." Yet that the Lord God can be found through seeking, we are assured by the word of the prophet Isaiah: "Seek the Lord, and call upon him that ye may find him presently; and when he draweth near to you, let the ungodly leave his ways and the wicked man his thoughts." [3] If then, he can be found when he is sought, why are we bidden "seek his face alway"? Perhaps because even when he is found he must be sought. Enquiry concerning the incomprehensible is justified, and the enquirer has found something, if he has succeeded in finding how far what he sought passes comprehension. Comprehending the incomprehensibility of what he seeks, yet he will go on seeking, because he cannot slacken his pursuit so long as progress is made in the actual enquiry into things incomprehensible: so long as he is continually bettered by the search after so great a good—both sought that it may be found, and found that it may be sought: still sought that the finding may be sweeter, still found that the seeking may be more eager. So we may interpret the words put into Wisdom's mouth in the book Ecclesiasticus: "They that eat me shall still hunger, and they that drink me shall still thirst." [4] They eat and drink, because they find: because they hunger and thirst, they still seek. Faith seeks, understanding finds: wherefore the prophet says: "Unless ye believe, ye shall not understand." [5] And again understanding yet seeks him whom it finds: for "God hath looked upon the sons of men," we sing in the Psalm, "to see if there be one that is understanding, or a seeker after God." [6] Man is called to be understanding, to the end that he may seek after God.

3. Thus, the care with which we have dwelt on that which God has made will have been justified by its purpose, that thereby we might come to know the maker. "For the invisible things of him from the creation of the world, being understood through the things which are made, are clearly seen." [7] Hence the reproof in the Book of Wisdom, of those who "could not out of the good things that are seen know him that is; neither by considering the works did they acknowledge the artificer, but deemed either fire or wind or the swift air or the circling of the

---

[3] Isa. 55:6 f.   [4] Ecclesiasticus 24:21.
[5] Isa. 7:9. In this text, so important for Augustine's doctrine of "understanding" as the "reward" of faith, he retains the older Latin version from the LXX: the Vulgate represents the Hebrew with *non permanebitis*, "ye shall not endure."
[6] Ps. 14:2.   [7] Rom. 1:20.

stars or the violence of waters or the luminaries of heaven to be the gods which govern the world: with whose beauty if they were so delighted as to account them gods, let them know how much better the ruler of them is. For the first author of beauty hath created them. Or if they marvelled at their strength and working, let them understand from these things how much mightier is he that ordered them; for by the greatness of the beauty and the creation, the creator of them might recognizably have been discerned."[8] I quote these verses from the Book of Wisdom, that in my search for pointers to that supreme Trinity which we seek when we seek for God, I may not seem to any of the faithful to have wasted my labour in beginning with the creature, and so moving by stages through a number of special trinities up to the mind of man.[9]

4 (iii). The necessities of discourse and argument have obliged us to deal in the course of fourteen Books with many matters which we can hardly embrace in a single view, so as to apply them without hesitation to the point we desire to grasp. I shall therefore do my best, God helping, to summarize without discussion the results of our discussions in each Book, and so to make accessible at a glance, not the grounds of our conclusions but the conclusions themselves. In this way our later results will not be so far separated from the earlier that examination of the later will drive the earlier from our minds; or if it does, we shall be able readily to look back and recollect what was forgotten.

5. Book I showed the testimony of Holy Scripture to the unity and equality of the supreme Trinity.

Books II, III, and IV dealt with the same theme; but the detailed enquiry into the missions of the Son and of the Holy Spirit occupies the three Books. It was shown that the Person sent is not less than the Sender because of that relationship: the Trinity, which is equal throughout, working inseparably without any difference in the changelessness, invisibility and omnipresence of its being.

Book V met the argument that the substance of the Father and of the Son is not the same, on the ground that nothing can be predicated of God which does not denote substance, and that therefore begetting and being begotten, or the begotten and the unbegotten, being different predicates must denote different substances. It was shown that not all that is predicated

---

[8] Wisdom 13:1 ff.
[9] This hardly describes the procedure of the *De Trinitate* itself, in which *all* the "trinities" studied have been psychological.

of God denotes substance, as do the predicates "good" and
"great" and any others denoting what he is in himself; but that
there are also predicates of relation, denoting not what he is in
himself but what he is in relation to something which is not
himself; as he is called Father in relation to the Son, or Lord in
relation to the creature that is subject to him. If he is given a
relative predicate such as implies temporal process, as for example "Lord, thou hast become our refuge," [10] that does not
denote a happening to him involving change: he himself in his
nature or essence remains altogether changeless.

Book VI discussed the meaning of the apostolic titles of
Christ, "the power of God and the wisdom of God," postponing
for further consideration the question whether he of whom
Christ is begotten is not wisdom himself but only the Father of
his own wisdom, or whether wisdom has begotten wisdom. But
however that should be answered, this Book also served to make
clear the equality of the Trinity, and that God is not treble—
God three times over, but Trinity: Father and Son do not make
up a double as against the singleness of the Holy Spirit, and the
Three are not anything "more" than any one of them. The
Book ended with a discussion of the meaning of Bishop Hilary's
phrase: "Eternity in the Father, form in the image, use in the
gift." [11]

Book VII dealt with the question adjourned, to the effect that
God as begetter of the Son is not only Father of his own power
and wisdom, but also power and wisdom in himself; the same
holding of the Holy Spirit. Yet there are not three powers or
wisdoms but one power and one wisdom, as there is one God
and one essence. Then it was asked in what sense we speak of
one essence and three Persons, or in the Greek manner of one
essence and three substances. The terms were found to meet
the need of a form of speech that would provide a single answer
to the question "*What* are the three, whom we truly confess as
three?"—namely, Father, Son, and Holy Spirit.

Book VIII applied the method of reasoning to make it clear
to the understanding that in true substance not only is the
Father no "greater" than the Son, but neither are both together
a "greater" thing than the Holy Spirit alone; nor are any two
in the Trinity a "greater" thing than one, nor all three together

[10] Ps. 90:1.
[11] Hilary, *De Trin.*, II, 34. Augustine wrongly supposes that Hilary's term
usus, which referred to the work of the spirit in sanctification, was meant
to indicate the "embrace" or mutual enjoyment of Father and Son.

"greater" than each severally. Then I endeavoured to make intelligible, so far as that may be, the incorporeal and changeless nature of God: using the notions of the Truth which is understood and seen, the supreme Good from which all good proceeds, the righteousness for which a righteous soul is loved by one not yet righteous, and finally the charity which in Holy Scripture is called God, and in which an actual Trinity begins to show itself to the understanding, in the form of lover, the beloved, and love.

Book IX carried the argument to that image of God which is presented by man in his mental nature. There we find a kind of trinity, in the mind, the knowledge whereby it knows itself, and the love whereby it loves itself and its knowledge; and these three are shown to be equal to one another and of one essence.

Book X gave a more thorough and precise investigation to the same subject, which led to the discovery in the mind of a trinity more manifest, in the form of memory, understanding and will. But it was also found that the mind can never have been without the memory, understanding, and love of itself, although it does not always think of itself; and when it does, the same act of thought does not cause it to distinguish itself from what is corporeal. We therefore postponed our consideration of the Trinity of which this is an image, in order to discover a trinity in the actual process of bodily perception, and thereby to offer the reader a less obscure field in which to exercise his power of penetration.

Book XI accordingly took the visual sense as an example, findings in which could be recognized as valid for the other four senses. Thus was disclosed a trinity of the outward man, first in external vision, composed of the physical object seen, the form impressed from it upon the view of the beholder, and the act of voluntary attention which links the two. But the members of this triad are plainly neither equal to one another nor of one substance; and we proceeded to the discovery of another trinity in the mind itself, imported from the field of outward sense, in which the same three appeared as consubstantial: the imaging of the object as retained in the memory, the actualizing of the form derived from it when the thinker's view is directed thither, and the act of voluntary attention which unites them. Even this trinity was recognized as belonging to the outward man, inasmuch as it results from the perception of external objects.

Book XII laid down the distinction between wisdom and knowledge, and looked first in the inferior realm of knowledge in the strict sense of the word, for a special kind of trinity. This belongs indeed to the inward man, but cannot yet be regarded as the image of God, or so entitled.

Book XIII developed this enquiry by way of an exposition of Christian faith.

Book XIV proceeded to a discourse on man's true wisdom—the wisdom, distinct from knowledge, conferred by God's gift through a partaking in God himself; and this led to the emergence of a trinity in the image of God constituted by man in his mental nature, which is renewed in the knowledge of God after the image of him who created man in his image,[12] and in that renewal acquires the wisdom in which there is a contemplation of things eternal.

6 (iv). And now the time has come for us to direct our search for the Trinity, which is God, upon that eternal world, bodiless and changeless, in whose perfect contemplation we have the promise of a blessed life—the life that must needs be eternal. The being of God is not only asserted by the authority of divine Scripture. The universe of nature which environs us and to which we ourselves belong, proclaims its dependence on a supremely good establisher. He has given us a mind and a natural reason, whereby we discern the relative values of things: preferring the living to what is without life, the sentient to what is without feeling, the understanding to what is without intelligence; immortal to mortal, potent to impotent, righteous to unrighteous, beautiful to ugly, good to evil, incorruptible to corruptible, immutable to mutable, invisible to visible, incorporeal to corporeal, blessed to miserable. And inasmuch as we do not hesitate to set a higher value on the Creator than on things created, we are obliged to allow that he must have life at its highest, and awareness and understanding of all things; that he cannot suffer death, corruption, or change; that he is no body, but a Spirit most potent, righteous, beautiful, good, and blessed.

7 (v). But all these attributes, and any others that human modes of expression may worthily assign to God, belong both to the whole Trinity which is the one God and to the several Persons in that same Trinity. Neither of the one God, the Trinity itself, nor of Father or Son or Holy Spirit, may any man presume to speak as without life, sentience or understanding; or to suggest that any of them, in that being in respect of which they are accounted equal to one another, is either mortal or corruptible or changeable or corporeal; or to deny to any of

[12] Col. 3:10; Gen. 1:27.

them the fullest power, righteousness, beauty, goodness, and blessedness. If then these and all similar terms are to be predicated both of the Trinity itself and of the several Persons therein, where or how can they display the nature of Trinity?

Let us begin by reducing their indefinite number to something smaller. What we call "life" in God is his very essence and nature: the life by which God lives is what he is to himself. But that life is not the life of a tree, without understanding or sentience; nor the life of a beast, which possesses sentience in its five divisions, but no understanding. The life that is God has consciousness and understanding of all things; and its consciousness is mental not bodily, since God is spirit.[13] It is not through a body that God is conscious, like the embodied animal; for he is not composed of soul and body. His uncompounded nature is conscious as it understands, and understands as it is conscious: his understanding is the same as his consciousness. Nor is the life of God such as ever to cease or ever to begin, for it is immortal. Rightly is it said of him that he "alone hath immortality"[14]; for true immortality belongs only to him in whose nature there is no possibility of change. And the changelessness of God is the effect of his true eternity, without beginning, without end; from which follows his incorruptibility. So it is one and the same thing to call God eternal or immortal or incorruptible or changeless, and it is the same thing to call him living and understanding, which implies wisdom. He has not acquired a wisdom to make him wise, but is himself wisdom. And this is his life, and at the same time the strength or power, and the beauty, for which he is called potent and beautiful. Nothing could have more power and beauty than the wisdom which "reacheth mightily from one end to the other, and sweetly ordereth all things."[15] Again, goodness and righteousness cannot lie apart from one another in God's nature, as they do in his works: there are not two different qualities of God, one goodness, and another righteousness. His righteousness is his goodness, and his goodness is his blessedness. As for the term incorporeal, it is used of God simply in the sense that for our faith or understanding he is spirit and not body.

8. If then we call God eternal, immortal, incorruptible, changeless, living, wise, potent, beautiful, righteous, good, blessed, spirit—the last of these terms may be thought to denote substance only, and all the rest qualities of that substance. But

[13] John 4:24.   [14] I Tim. 6:16.   [15] Wisdom 8:1.

this distinction does not exist in the ineffable and uncompounded nature of God. Terms which appear to denote quality must here be taken as denoting substance or essence. We may never say that God is spirit in substance, and good in quality: he is both in substance. The same applies to all the terms we have applied to him: as we have argued at length in previous Books.[16]

The first four of these terms as above enumerated in order were eternal, immortal, incorruptible, changeless. Since these four denote one thing, as I have explained, let us select some one of them in order to concentrate our thought: say the one that comes first, "eternal." Let us do the same with the second four, living, wise, potent, beautiful. Here, we note that life of a sort belongs to the beast who is without wisdom; that wisdom and power may in a man be so contrasted with one another that Scripture can say: "Better is the wise than the strong"[17]; and that we normally use the word beautiful of bodily things. Our best choice among these four will therefore be "wise": although in God there is no inequality between the four, since the four words stand for one thing. In the case of the last group of four terms, it is true that righteousness in God is identical with goodness and blessedness, and "spirit" is identical with all three. But in men there can be an unblessed spirit, there can be one righteous and good who is not yet blessed; whereas none can be blessed who is not a spirit both righteous and good. Let us then choose the term which even in men must carry the three others with it, namely "blessed."

9 (vi). Can we then say that these three terms, "eternal," "wise," "blessed," constitute the Trinity which we call God? We have reduced our terms from twelve to three; but possibly we might make a further reduction of these three to some one of them. If wisdom and power, or life and wisdom, may be one and the same thing in the nature of God, why should not this hold of eternity and wisdom, or of blessedness and wisdom? Then, just as in our reduction of the larger to the smaller number it made no difference whether we used the twelve terms or the three, so it will make no difference whether we use the three, or the single one to which we have suggested that the two others might similarly be reduced. And then we shall hardly find a line of argument, a force or power of understanding, a vigour of reasoning or a penetration of thought, sufficient to

16 The reference is especially to Bks. V and VI.　17 Wisdom 6:12 (Vulgate).

show without regard to all the rest how the Trinity may be found in the application to God of this single term—wisdom. God does not learn wisdom from any other source as we do from him: he is his own wisdom, since, in him for whom to be is to be wise, his wisdom and his essence are not distinguishable things. It is true that in Holy Scripture Christ is called the power of God and the wisdom of God.[18] But we discussed in our seventh Book the interpretation of this text so as to avoid implying that the Son makes the Father wise; and our conclusion was that the Son is Wisdom from Wisdom, as he is Light from Light, God from God. And we were forced to extend the same argument to the Holy Spirit, admitting that he also is himself wisdom—all together constituting one wisdom, as they do one God and one essence. Of this wisdom, then, which is God, how shall we understand that it is Trinity? I do not say, How shall we believe? For of that there should be no question among the faithful. But if there is any way by which understanding may give us a vision of what we believe, what can that way be?

10. We may recall that it was in the eighth Book that the manifestation of the Trinity to our understanding began. There we essayed to lift up, so far as might be, the effort of our mind to the understanding of that most excellent and changeless being which is other than our mind. In contemplation we were aware of it as not far from us and yet above us—not spatially but by its own most reverend and wonderful excellence, so that we found it present in us in virtue of its own pervading light. But so far we had no glimpse of the Trinity, because we could not in that dazzling brightness direct our mind's eye steadily to look for it.[19] All that we could with some clearness distinguish was that it was no measurable mass in which the quantity of two or three must be believed greater than that of the two. Only when we came to consider charity, which in Holy Scripture is called God, the light began to break upon a Trinity, consisting in lover, the beloved, and love. But from that ineffable light our gaze flinched away: we had to confess that our mind in its weakness was not yet strong enough to be conformed to it. And therefore, in order to recruit our labouring efforts, we paused in the pursuit of our undertaking and turned back to the more familiar consideration of that same mind of ours, in which man has been made after the image of God; and from the ninth to the fourteenth Book we occupied ourselves with our own creaturely

[18] I Cor. 1:24.   [19] Bk. VIII, 3 (ii).

nature, in order that we might be able to apprehend and perceive the invisible things of God through the things that are made.[20]

And now the time has come, when after this exercise of our understanding in a lower sphere for so long as need required (and maybe for longer), we would lift ourselves up to perceive the supreme Trinity which is God. Yet our strength fails us. Many trinities we can see most surely. There are those which are produced by the action of bodily objects on the outward senses, and those which occur when the sense perception becomes matter of thought. There are trinities when things arising in the mind apart from the bodily senses are distinguished by clear reasoning and comprehended in knowledge, such as our faith, and those virtues which are ways of living. There are trinities when the mind itself, by which we know all that we truthfully claim to know, is known to itself or thinks of itself, or when it perceives an eternal and unchanging object other than itself. In all these processes we see trinities with assurance, since they occur or exist in us as we remember, regard, and will. But can we perceive therein by an act of understanding a Speaker and his Word, the Father and the Son, and proceeding thence the Charity common to both which is the Holy Spirit? It may be urged that while trinities belonging to the sphere of sense or mind are for us objects of sight rather than belief, the fact that God is Trinity must be believed rather than seen. If that be so, it must follow, either that the invisible things of him are nowhere apprehended and perceived by us through the things that are made; or, that in none of them which we perceive can we perceive the Trinity—that there is something in that sphere which we may perceive, but something also which we are obliged to believe though unperceived. Yet the eighth Book showed that we do perceive a changeless good, other than ourselves; and the same was indicated in the fourteenth Book when we spoke of the wisdom which comes to man from God. Why then can we not recognize there the Trinity? It is impossible to maintain that this wisdom which is called God neither understands nor loves itself; and it is patent that where there is no knowledge there cannot possibly be wisdom. That the wisdom which is God knows or loves other things but neither knows nor loves itself, cannot be asserted or believed without foolishness and impiety; and if so, here surely is Trinity: wisdom, its knowledge of itself, and its love of itself. That was how we discovered

[20] Rom. 1:20.

a trinity in man: the mind, the knowledge whereby it knows itself, and the love whereby it loves itself.

11 (vii). But these three are *in* man, without by themselves constituting man; for if we follow the definition of the ancients, man is a rational and mortal animal. The three things named are then man's highest part, but not by themselves man. Moreover, the one person which is the individual man possesses those three in his mind. Even if we adopt a different definition of man, to the effect that he is a rational substance composed of soul and body, it remains indubitable that man possesses a soul which is not body and a body which is not soul. And then our triad is not equivalent to man but belongs to man or is in man. If we set aside the body and think of the soul alone, we find that the mind is a part of it, as it might be its head or eye or face—though we may not think of the soul's parts as bodies. Thus it is not the soul but the highest thing in it which we call the mind. But we cannot say that the Trinity is in God in this manner—a part of God but not itself God. The individual man, who is called the image of God not in respect of all that belongs to his nature but in respect of his mind alone, is a personal unity, having the image of the Trinity in his mind. But the Trinity of whom he is image is as a whole nothing but God, is as a whole nothing but Trinity. Nothing belongs to God's nature that does not belong to this Trinity. The three Persons are of one essence, not like the individual man one person.

12. In another respect also there is a wide difference to be noted. In man, whether we speak of mind, its knowledge and its love, or of memory, understanding, and will, nothing in the mind is remembered but through memory, or understood but through understanding, or loved but through will. In the divine Trinity, reverence forbids us to say that the Father understands neither himself nor his Son nor the Holy Spirit, save through the Son, nor loves save through the Holy Spirit; or that through himself he does no more than remember either himself or the Son or the Holy Spirit. Or similarly, that the Son remembers himself and the Father only through the Father, and loves only through the Holy Spirit; while through himself he can only understand both Father and himself and Holy Spirit. Or in the same way that it is through the Father that the Holy Spirit remembers Father, Son, and himself, through the Son that he understands Father, Son, and himself, while through himself he can only love himself, the Father and the Son. This would amount to saying that the Father is memory of himself, Son,

and Holy Spirit, the Son is understanding of himself, Father, and Holy Spirit, the Holy Spirit is charity to himself, Father and Son. But to hold or express such opinions concerning the divine Trinity would be extreme presumption. If only the Son understands for himself and Father and Holy Spirit, we are back in the irrational notion that the Father is wise not of himself but by the Son: that wisdom has not begotten wisdom, but the Father is called wise in virtue of the wisdom he has begotten. For where understanding is lacking, there can be no wisdom: if the Father understands not for himself but the Son for the Father, clearly the Son makes the Father wise. And if for God to be is to be wise, and his essence is his wisdom, it will not be the Son who has his essence from the Father (as he truly does), but the Father who has his essence from the Son—which is entirely irrational and false. We may be satisfied with our discussion, refutation and rejection of this irrationality in the seventh Book. God the Father is wise by that same wisdom which is his own being; and the Son is the wisdom of the Father, as being derived from the wisdom which is identical with the Father of whom he is begotten. And accordingly the Father is understanding by the same understanding which is his own being; for wisdom implies understanding; and the Son is the understanding of the Father, as begotten of the understanding which is the Father's being. The same may properly be said of memory. He who remembers nothing, or does not remember himself, cannot be wise. Since therefore the Father is wisdom, and the Son is wisdom, the Son will remember himself no less than the Father remembers himself; and just as the Father remembers himself and the Son with a memory that is his own and not the Son's, the Son will remember himself and the Father with a memory that is not the Father's but his own. Finally, we cannot predicate wisdom where there is no love; from which it follows that the Father is his own love, no less than his own understanding and his own memory. We seem forced to the conclusion that our triad of memory, understanding and love or will, in that supreme and changeless essence that is God, are not to be identified with Father, Son and Holy Spirit, but with the Father by himself. And because the Son is wisdom begotten of wisdom, it is equally true that he understands for himself and not the Father or the Holy Spirit for him, and that neither does the Father remember nor the Holy Spirit love for him, but he does both for himself; for he is his own memory, his own understanding, his own love, though

that property comes to him from the Father of whom he is begotten. Again, since the Holy Spirit is wisdom proceeding from
wisdom, it is not true that the memory which belongs to him is
the Father, the understanding the Son, and the love himself;
for he would not be wisdom if another remembered for him,
and another understood for him, while for himself he did no
more than love. All three belong to him, and in such a manner
that he *is* all three; but this property comes to him from that
Source from which he proceeds.

13. No man can comprehend the wisdom by which God
knows all things, a wisdom wherein that which we call past does
not pass, and that which we call future is not awaited as though
not yet available, but both past and future are all together present with what is present: a wisdom wherein there is no thinking
on particular things severally, or movement of thought from
one thing to another, but the whole universe is presented
simultaneously in one single view. No man, I say, can comprehend such a wisdom, which is both foresight and knowledge;
inasmuch as even our own wisdom passes our comprehension.
We can perceive, in various ways, what is present to our senses
or our understanding: what is absent but was once present, we
know by memory if we have not forgotten it. We conjecture,
not the past from the future, but the future from the past,
though we cannot have certain knowledge of it. To some of our
thoughts we look forward with a degree of clearness and assurance as about to occur in the immediate future; but when we do
so with the maximum of security, we do it by an act of memory,
which is evidently concerned not with what is going to happen
but with what is past. This is open to experience in the case of
speeches or songs which we render from memory in a certain
order: did we not foresee in thought what comes next, we could
not speak it. But what enables us to foresee is not pre-vision but
memory. Until the whole speech or song is ended, there is
nothing in its recitation that was not foreseen and looked forward to. Yet in the process our singing and speaking is not
ascribed to pre-vision but to memory; and we remark, in those
who display exceptional powers of such extended recitation, a
strength not of foresight but of memory. We know, without
any doubt, that such processes are carried on in our mind, or
by our mind; but the more closely we try to observe the manner
of the process, the more surely does description fail us and effort
exhaust itself in the attempt to reach lucidity of understanding,
if not of language. Can we expect then that our feeble minds will

be able to comprehend the identity of God's providence with his memory and understanding—the providence of God who does not regard each thing severally in discursive thought, but embraces all that he knows in one eternal, changeless and ineffable vision? In the strait of such perplexity we may well cry out to the living God: "From myself thy knowledge has become wonderful: its strength is shown, and I shall not be able to reach it." [21] For from myself I understand how marvellous and incomprehensible is thy knowledge whereby thou hast made me; and yet in my meditation the fire is kindled, so that I seek thy face evermore.[22]

14 (viii). I know that wisdom is an incorporeal substance, a light in which are seen things not seen by the eye of flesh. And yet a man of such spiritual greatness as Paul says that "we see now through a mirror, in an enigma; but then face to face." [23] If we ask of what manner or of what nature is this mirror, we think immediately of the fact that in a mirror what is seen is no more than an image. What we have tried to do is to gain through this image which is ourselves some vision, as through a mirror, of him who made us. We find the same sense in other words of the apostle's: "We with unveiled face beholding in a mirror the glory of the Lord, are transformed into the same image from glory unto glory, as by the Spirit of the Lord." [24] (The word *speculantes* means "seeing in a mirror," not "observing from a watch-tower": as is clear in the original Greek, in which the *speculum* that reflects an image is described by a quite different-sounding word from the *specula* or height from the top of which we look out at distant objects, and it is plain enough that *speculantes*, in the phrase *gloriam Domini speculantes*, is derived from *speculum* and not *specula*.[25]) The words "transformed into the same image" refer to the image of God—the "same," that is, that very image which we behold in the mirror. For this same image is also the glory of God, as Paul says elsewhere: "the man ought not to veil his head, since he is the image and glory of God"[26] a text which we discussed in the twelfth Book. "We are transformed"—that is, we are changed from one form into another, from a form of obscurity into a form of clear light.

21 Ps. 139:6.   22 Ps. 39:3; 105: 4.
23 I Cor. 13:12.   24 II Cor. 3:18.
25 Augustine is probably right in agreeing here with A.V. and R.V. Mg. against R.V. text "reflecting." For a discussion of the text, cf. Kirk, *The Vision of God*, pp. 102 ff.
26 I Cor. 11:7.

Even in obscurity, the form is God's image; and if his image, then assuredly his glory, wherein we were created as men, excelling all other animals. For of human nature itself it is said that "a man ought not to veil his head, since he is the image and glory of God." And it is this nature, the most excellent of things created, which when justified by its Creator from its ungodliness is brought over from a form that is deformed into a form of perfect beauty. For even in its very ungodliness, the more severe our condemnation of its fault, the more unhesitating must be our appreciation of its natural dignity. Hence the addition of the words, "from glory into glory": from the glory of creation into the glory of justification. Another interpretation of these words is indeed possible: they may mean, from the glory of faith into the glory of sight: from that glory in which we are the sons of God into that glory in which we shall be like him, for we shall see him as he is. Finally, the words "as from the Spirit of the Lord" indicate that the blessing of a transformation so devoutly to be prayed for is granted to us by the grace of God.

15 (ix). These remarks have been suggested by the apostle's saying, that we see "now through a glass." The words which follow, "in an enigma," demand for their understanding some acquaintance with writers who have treated of the modes of expression called by the Greeks "tropes." We ourselves use this Greek word on occasion in place of the Latin "modes," just as we commonly speak of *schemata* rather than *figurae*. The names of the several modes or tropes are very difficult to render in Latin appropriately to each particular case without recourse to very unfamiliar terms. Hence certain of our translators, to avoid using the Greek word for the apostle's phrase, "which things are in an allegory,"[27] have employed the circumlocution: "which stand as signifying one thing by another." Of this particular "trope," the allegory, there are a number of kinds, among which is the so-called "enigma." The definition of the general term must of course cover all the kinds or species which it includes: thus, as every horse is an animal but not every animal a horse, so every enigma is an allegory, but not every allegory an enigma. The allegory is simply a trope in which one term is used to mean another, as for example in this passage from the Epistle to the Thessalonians: "Therefore let us not slumber, as others do; but let us watch and be sober. For they that sleep, sleep in the night, and they that are drunken, are

[27] Gal. 4:24.

drunken in the night. But let us, who are of the day, be sober." [28] This allegory is not an enigma; for the meaning lies to hand for all but the slowest wits. The enigma may be shortly described as an obscure allegory, such as "the leech had three daughters," [29] and the like. Where the apostle speaks of an allegory, he is applying the term not to a phrase but to a fact: for he shows that the two Testaments are signified by the two sons of Abraham, one of a bondmaid and the other of a free woman—a matter not of words but of history. But before his exposition of it, it remained obscure; and therefore such an example, included under the general name of allegory, might also have the special name of enigma.

16. However, it is not only people ignorant of literary discourse on the varieties of tropes who may question the meaning of the apostle's saying, that now we see in an enigma. The more instructed may still want to know what is the enigma wherein we now see. We must look therefore for a single meaning conveyed in both parts of the sentence: in the words "we see now through a mirror," and the addition, "in an enigma." It seems to me that as the word "mirror" was intended to signify an image, so the word "enigma" was meant to stand for a similitude, but one that is obscure and hard to discern. If then under the names of "mirror" and "enigma" we may understand the apostle to have expressed the notion of certain similitudes adapted for our understanding of God, in the manner in which such understanding is possible; it remains true that the similitude best adapted for that purpose will be that which deserves to be called his image. There need be no surprise that in the manner of seeing permitted us in this life, "through a mirror in an enigma," our struggle to see at all must be a hard one. If vision were easy, the word "enigma" would not be in place. The greater enigma lies in our not seeing that of which we cannot be without the vision. Can any man *not* see his own thought? And can any man see his own thought—I do not mean with his bodily eyes, but by an actual inward vision? Both not seeing and seeing are unimaginable. For thought is a kind of vision of the mind, whether in presence of the objects seen by the bodily eyes or felt by the other senses, or in their absence, when their likenesses are perceived by thought. And the same may be said when the object of thought is nothing of the kind, neither bodily things nor their likenesses, but such ideas as those of moral qualities, or of thought itself, the subjects of the sciences or

[28] I Thess. 5:6 ff.　　　　[29] Prov. 30:15.

liberal arts, or their higher causes and principles in the eternal world, or even notions of evil, vanity, and falsehood, held in the mind either without approval or with an approval inspired by error.

17 (x). We are now concerned with that which is object of our thought or matter of our knowing, though we may not be thinking of it; whether it belong to the contemplative faculty which I have argued should properly be called wisdom, or to the active which I would distinguish as knowledge. Both are at the same time faculties of the one mind—the one image of God. Yet when we are dealing with the lower faculty taken by itself, it is not to be called the image of God, although even then there is to be found in it a certain likeness of the divine Trinity. This we demonstrated in the thirteenth Book. We speak now of the whole range of human knowledge, in which we know all that is known to us: which must be true, or it could not be known. No-one can know what is false, except in the sense of knowing its falsity; and if that is known, the knowledge is true, inasmuch as it is the truth that the thing is false. We are dealing now with that of which we think as known, and which is known to us even if we are not thinking of it. Undoubtedly, if we would speak of it, we can only do so after thinking of it; for though no audible words be used, whoever thinks must be speaking in his heart. So we read in the Book of Wisdom: "they have said in themselves, thinking amiss" [30]—where "said in themselves" is explained by the addition of the word "thinking." There is a similar passage in the Gospel, where certain scribes, on hearing the Lord's word to the paralytic—"Son, be of good cheer, thy sins are forgiven thee"—"said within themselves, This man blasphemeth." "Said within themselves" can only mean "in thought." And the passage continues: "And when Jesus had seen their thoughts, he said, Why think ye evil in your hearts?"[31] So in Matthew's account: Luke tells the same story as follows: "The Scribes and Pharisees began to think, saying, Who is this that speaketh blasphemies? Who can forgive sins, but God only? But when Jesus knew their thoughts, he answered and said unto them, What do ye think in your hearts?" [32] Here the words "they thought, saying" is equivalent to the expression "they said, thinking" in the Book of Wisdom. In both places we are told that men speak within themselves and in their heart, that is, speak by thinking. They spoke within themselves, and were asked "What is it that ye think?" Again, of the rich man

30 Wisdom 2:1.   31 Matt. 9:2 ff.   32 Luke 5:21 ff.

whose field brought forth plentifully, our Lord himself says, "he thought within himself, saying." [33]

18. Thus, certain thoughts are locutions of the heart, which has its own "mouth," according to our Lord's saying: "Not that which entereth into the mouth defileth the man, but that which cometh forth from the mouth, this defileth the man." In this one sentence he speaks of two "mouths" in a man, one of the body, the other of the heart. What his hearers supposed to cause defilement, enters into the body's mouth: that by which our Lord says that a man is defiled, comes forth from the mouth of the heart. So runs his own explanation of his saying, given personally to his disciples: "Are ye still without understanding? Do ye not understand that whatsoever entereth into the mouth goeth into the belly and is cast out into the draught?" Here the "mouth" is plainly that of the body; but the next words point to a "mouth" of the heart: "But the things which come forth from the mouth proceed from the heart, and they defile the man. For from the heart proceed evil thoughts," etc. [34] The exposition could not be clearer. Yet when we say that thoughts are locutions of the heart, we are not denying that they are also visions, arising when they are true from visions of things known. In the external sphere of bodily activity, locution is one thing and vision another; but in the inward realm of our thoughts, both are one and the same. Hearing and sight are two different functions of the bodily sense, but in the mind there is no difference between seeing and hearing. That is why, although outward speech is not seen but heard, the holy Gospel can speak of the inward locutions which are thoughts as *seen* by our Lord and not heard: "They said within themselves, This man blasphemeth"; and then, "When Jesus saw their thoughts." He *saw* what they had said—saw in his own thought their thoughts, which they supposed visible to themselves alone.

19. It is possible therefore to understand the meaning of a word, not only before it is uttered aloud, but even before the images of its uttered sounds are rehearsed in thought; for there is a "word" which belongs to no tongue, to none (that is) of the "tongues of the peoples," of which our Latin language is one. Any man that can understand this unspoken word, can see through this mirror and in this enigma a certain likeness of that Word of which it is written: "In the beginning was the Word, and the Word was with God, and the Word was God." [35] When we speak the truth, that is, say what we know, there must

[33] Luke 12:17.   [34] Matt. 15:10 ff.   [35] John 1:1.

be born out of the knowledge held in our memory a word which corresponds in all respects to the knowledge of which it is born. The thought which has received form from the object of our knowledge is the word spoken in our heart—a word that is neither Greek nor Latin nor of any other tongue. Only when we need to convey it to the knowledge of those to whom we speak, do we employ some token by which to signify it. Usually a sound, but sometimes a gesture, is presented either to ear or eye, in order that by means of bodily tokens the word carried in our mind may be made known to the bodily senses. What indeed is beckoning but a kind of visible speech? We can quote Holy Scripture to the same purpose, where we read in John's Gospel: "Verily, verily I say unto you that one of you shall betray me. His disciples therefore looked upon one another, doubting of whom he might speak. There was one of his disciples, leaning upon Jesus' bosom, whom Jesus loved: Simon Peter therefore beckoned unto him, saying, Who is it of whom he speaks?" [36] The beckoning of Peter says what he did not dare say aloud. These and the like bodily tokens we apply to the ears or eyes of persons present and conversing with us; but we have also invented letters to enable us to converse with the absent— letters being tokens of uttered sounds, whereas the uttered sounds themselves are tokens in our speaking of the realities of which we think.

20 (xi). Accordingly, the word in its outward sounding is sign of the word that is inwardly luminous; and to this latter the name of "word" more properly belongs. What the mouth of flesh emits is the word's utterance, which itself is called "word" on account of that by which it is assumed for outward exposure. We may compare the manner in which our own word is made as it were a bodily utterance, through assuming that utterance as a means of displaying itself to men's senses, with that in which the Word of God was made flesh, through assuming that flesh as a means of displaying himself to men's senses. Even as our word is made utterance yet not changed into utterance, so the Word of God was made flesh, but most assuredly not changed into flesh. Our word is made utterance, the divine Word flesh, by an assumption of the outward form, and not by a consumption of itself and a passing into the other. He therefore who desires to arrive at some sort of likeness—unlike as it must be at many points—of the Word of God, should not regard the human word that sounds upon the ear, either in its vocal utterance or

[36] John 13:21 ff.

in the unspoken thinking of it. The words of every audible language may also be thought upon without speech: poems may be repeated mentally, while the bodily mouth remains silent—not only the series of syllables, but the notes of tunes, material as they are, and addressed to the material sense which we call hearing, may be presented through their material images to the thinking mind which rehearses them all in silence. We must go beyond all this, to arrive at that human word which may furnish some small measure of likeness for the beholding, as in an enigma, of the Word of God. We speak here not of that word which came to one or another of the prophets, of which it is said that "the word of God grew, and was multiplied" [37]; or again that "faith comes of hearing, and hearing through the word of Christ" [38]; or again: "when ye received from us the word of the hearing of God, ye received it not as the word of men, but as it is in truth, the word of God." [39] The Scriptures contain countless sayings of the kind concerning the word of God, which is spread abroad in many different tongues through the hearts and mouths of men. It is called God's word, as delivering a doctrine that is divine and not human. The Word of God of which now we seek to gain some scanty vision by way of this likeness, is that of which it is written, that "the Word was God"; that "all things were made by him"; that "the Word was made flesh"; that "a fountain of wisdom is the Word of God in the highest." [40] We must arrive at that human word which is the word of a reasonable creature, the word of an image of God not born of God but made by him, a word neither producing itself in sound nor object of thought in a likeness of sound, such as must needs belong to a particular language; but the word that precedes all the tokens by which it is signified, and is begotten of the knowledge which remains in the mind, in the moment when that knowledge is spoken inwardly and with truth to itself. The vision of thought is very like the vision of knowledge, When the word is spoken aloud or by means of any bodily token, it is not spoken as it truly is but in the manner in which it may be seen or heard through the medium of the body. Thus when the word's content is the same as the content of knowledge, it is then a true word—the truth that is expected of a man, wherein that which is in his knowledge is also in his word, and what is not in the one is not in the other. By this we recognize his "Yea, yea" and his "Nay, nay." [41] And so the

[37] Acts. 6:7.   [38] Rom 10:17.   [39] I Thess. 2:13.
[40] John 1:1, 3, 14; Ecclesiasticus 1:5.   [41] Matt. 5:37.

likeness of the created image approaches as nearly as it may to that likeness of the image begotten, by which God the Son is declared like his Father in all things according to substance.

There is a further likeness to the Word of God which we may observe in this "enigma." It is said of the divine Word that "all things were made through him" [42]; God is asserted to have created the universe through his only-begotten Word. So in the works of man there are none that are not first spoken in the heart, and hence it is written that "the beginning of every work is a word." [43] But here also there is beginning of a good work only when the word is a true word; and the word is true when it is begotten of the knowledge of good working. Here too the rule is "Yea, yea" and "Nay, nay": if "Yea" stands in the knowledge whereby men should live, it must be also in the word, through which man must work; if "Nay" is there, then "Nay" must be here also. Else such a word will be a lie and not the truth, and from it proceed sin and no right working.

Yet another likeness of God's Word may be seen in this likeness of our human word, in that a word of ours can be without a work following, while there can be no work without the preceding word. In like manner the Word of God was able to be, apart from the existence of any creature; but there could be no creature, save through that Word through whom all things were made. And accordingly it was not God the Father nor the Holy Spirit, nor the Trinity itself, but only the Son, the Word of God, that was made flesh—although the making was act of the whole Trinity. For the purpose was that we might live aright by our word following the pattern of his example; which means that in our word, whether in contemplation or in working, there be no manner of lie. But that is the perfection of the image, sometime to be. For the attaining of it we have the instruction of a good master in Christian faith and teaching of godliness: to the end that "with unveiled face"—removing the veil of the Law which is shadow of things to come—"beholding in a mirror the glory of the Lord," we may be transformed "into the same image from glory unto glory, even as from the Spirit of the Lord" [44]—according to the exposition of this text which was given above. 21. And when by that transformation the image in us will have been renewed unto perfection, we shall be like God, for we shall see him, not through a mirror but as he is [45]—in the apostle's words "face to face."

[42] John 1:3.
[44] II Cor. 3:18.

[43] Ecclesiasticus 37:16 (lxx).
[45] I John 3:2.

But for our present state, in this mirror, this enigma, this feeble trace of likeness, there remains a degree of unlikeness not easy for man to measure. Still, I will do what I can to suggest some few points in which the difference can be observed. (xii). In the first place, the knowledge itself from which our thought takes a form of truth, when we say what we know, must even for the most expert and learned of men be poor and scanty indeed. We need not dwell on what the mind receives from the bodily senses, in which the differences between appearance and reality are so many that a madman may think himself sane, in reliance on the plausibility of his sensations. Hence the prevalence of the Academic philosophy,[46] whose universal doubt was a madness even more pitiable. But apart from the mind's dependence on the senses, how few things remain which we know as surely as we know that we are alive? There at least we need not fear to be deceived by the plausibility of appearance, since it is certain that he who is deceived is alive; and this assurance does not come to us in the way of impressions from the outer world: in it there can be no optical illusion, as when the oar in water appears as broken, towers on the land seem to men on shipboard to be in motion, and in so many other cases of difference between appearance and reality. Here it is not the eye of flesh whereby we see: we know that we are alive by an interior knowledge, which cannot be touched by the suggestion of the Academic that we may be asleep without knowing it, and dream that we see. We all know that things seen by the dreamer are much like those seen by the waking man. But certainty in the knowledge of living leads a man to say, not "I know that I am awake," but "I know that I am alive": whether asleep or awake, he is living. In that knowledge he cannot be deceived by dreams; for it takes a living man both to sleep and to dream. Nor can the Academic dispute that knowledge by saying, "You may perhaps be mad without knowing it, for there is little difference between the impressions of madness and those of sanity." The madman must be alive; and the reply to the Academic is not "I know that I am not mad," but "I know that I am alive." Thus the claim to know that one is alive can never be convicted of illusion or falsity. Any number of deceptive impressions of all kinds may be urged against it; but he who makes

---

[46] The sceptical school to which Augustine himself was inclined for a time after his rejection of Manicheanism (*Conf.*, VI, 19 (x)), and which he set himself to refute after his conversion in the *Contra Academicos*. Cf. *De Trin.*, X, 14 (x).

the claim will remain entirely unmoved, since no man can be deceived who is not alive.

Nevertheless, if human knowledge includes no more than certainties of this kind, they are indeed few; though it may be possible to multiply them in each class so that instead of being few they are found to run to infinity. Thus, the assertion "I know that I am alive" is the assertion of a single item of knowledge; but if one adds, "I know that I know that I am alive," we already have two, and knowing that these two are known makes a third; and we can proceed in the same way, to add a fourth and a fifth, or as many as we will. Since however it is impossible either to comprehend an innumerable number by the addition of units or to express it without numeration, we can at least comprehend and express with complete certainty the fact that this knowledge is both true and innumerable, in the sense that its infinite number of items can truly be neither comprehended nor expressed. And we can note the same fact in regard to certainty of will. To the man who says, "I wish to be happy," you cannot have the face to retort, "Perhaps you are deceived"; and if he goes on to say, "I know that this is my wish, and I know that I know it," he can add to these two items his knowledge of them, to make a third, and a fourth, that he knows he knows those two, and so on to infinity. Again, take the assertion, "I do not wish to be mistaken": whether the asserter is mistaken or not, it will still be true that he does not want to be mistaken. And no-one could have the face to reply, "Perhaps you are deceived," seeing that in whatever other matter he may be deceived, he is not deceived about his unwillingness to be deceived. And if he says that he knows this, he can add any number of items known, clearly extensible to infinity. "I do not wish to be deceived, I know that I do not wish it, and I know that I know it" . . . however awkward the expression, the number of such knowables can be shown to be infinite. There are other conclusive arguments against the Academic contention that nothing can be known by man; but we must dwell on the point no longer, as it is not the purpose of our present work: we may refer to the three Books written soon after our conversion.[47] Those who are able and willing to read them and to read with understanding, will be disturbed by none of the various arguments alleged by the Academics against our apprehension of truth. Of things known there are two kinds, the one of those

---

[47] The *Contra Academicos*: in *Retract.*, I, 1, Augustine tells us that he wrote this work to clear his own mind of scepticism. Cf. above, 21 (xii) n.

things which the mind apprehends through the bodily senses, the other of what it apprehends through itself. These philosophers have been voluble in depreciation of the bodily senses; but they have failed altogether to cast doubt upon certain unshakable perceptions of truth which the mind reaches through itself, such as the judgment I have instanced, that I know that I am alive. Yet we are by no means to doubt the truth of what the bodily senses have taught us: for through them we have come to know heaven and earth and all that therein is known to us, in the measure in which he who has created us and them has willed that we should know them. Nor may we deny our knowledge of what we have learnt on the testimony of others: else we should be ignorant of the ocean, ignorant of the existence of lands and cities of which common report assures us, ignorant of the past history of men and their works, ignorant of all the events of which news comes to us every day from all parts, confirmed by the agreement and support of other information, ignorant finally of the places or the men from whom we have our own origin. All these things we have believed on the testimony of others. And if it be absurd to pretend such ignorance, we must admit that the bodily senses not only of ourselves but of strangers have made great additions to our knowledge.

22. All such knowledge in the mind of man, whether acquired through the mind itself, or through his bodily senses, or by the testimony of others, is preserved in the store-chamber of memory; and from it is begotten a true word, when we speak what we know. But this word exists before any sound, before any imagining of a sound. For in that state the word has the closest likeness to the thing known, of which it is offspring and image; from the vision which is knowledge arises a vision which is thought, a word of no language, a true word born of a true thing, having nothing of its own but all from that knowledge of which it is born. It matters not when it was learnt by the man who speaks what he knows: sometimes the speaking may immediately follow the learning. It will still be true if it arises from things known.

(xiii). But when we think of God the Father, of whom is begotten the Word that is God of God, can we suppose that the wisdom which is his own underived being has been learnt in part through a bodily sense and in part through himself? That would be to think of God as a rational animal, not as above the rational soul; but only thus can he be thought of by us men,

higher than all animals and all souls, though seen only through
a mirror, divined in an enigma, not yet face to face as he is. Of
God the Father we cannot say that what he knows, not through
the body (for he has none) but through himself, he has learnt
of any other source, or has stood in need of messengers or witnesses for the knowledge of it. His own perfection suffices him
for the knowledge of all that he knows. Messengers indeed he
has, in the angels, but not to bring him news of what he does not
know; for no such thing exists. The angels fulfil their being in
taking counsel of his truth for their own works; and when they
are said to be messengers to him of anything, it is not that he
may learn of them but that they may learn of him through his
Word, with no material sound. They are messengers of his will,
sent by him to whom he wills, having all their hearing of him
through that his Word: which means, finding in his truth what
they must do, the substance, the destination, and the times of
their messages. We too make our prayers to him, yet do not
instruct him of our needs: "for your father knoweth," as his
Word has said, "what is needful for you, before ye ask of him." [48]
Nor has he learnt the knowledge of this at any point in time.
All that was to be in time, what and when we were to ask of him,
to whose asking and to what requests he should hearken or not
hearken, were known to him beforehand without any beginning. Of all his creatures, both spiritual and material, his knowledge is not consequent on their existence; but their existence
consequent on his knowledge. He was never in ignorance of
what he was to create: he created therefore because he knew,
he did not know because he created. Nor was his knowledge of
them as created different from his knowledge of them as to be
created; for their being added nothing to his wisdom, which
stood fast as it ever was, while they came into being as it behoved them and when it behoved them. So it is written in the
Book of Ecclesiasticus: "all things were known unto him before
they were created, even so as after they were finished." [49] "Even
so," not otherwise: both "before they were created," and "after
they were finished," "even so" were they known to him. From
that knowledge, therefore, our own knowledge is widely different. What is knowledge in God is at the same time wisdom,
and what is wisdom is at the same time essence or substance.
For in the marvellous simplicity of the divine nature, to be wise
and to be are not different things: what constitutes wisdom,
itself constitutes being, as we have constantly maintained in

[48] Matt. 6 : 8.   [49] Ecclesiasticus 23:20.

previous Books.[50] Whereas our own knowledge in many matters is subject to loss and acquisition, since in us there is no identity of being and knowledge or wisdom: we may still have being, though we are ignorant or lacking in understanding of what we have learnt from external sources. For this reason, the unlikeness of our knowledge to the knowledge of God is paralleled by the unlikeness of the word in us, which is born of our knowledge, to the Word of God that is begotten of the Father's essence—which is as much as to say, of the Father's knowledge, or of the Father's wisdom; or, to express it more adequately, of the Father who is knowledge, the Father who is wisdom.

23 (xiv). Thus, the Word who is God the Father's only-begotten Son, in all things like and equal to the Father, God of God, Light of Light, Wisdom of Wisdom, Essence of Essence—that Word is entirely what the Father is, though he is not the Father since this is Son and that is Father. So he knows all that the Father knows, but his knowledge like his being is from the Father; for knowing and being here are one. Whereas the Father's knowledge, no more than his being, is derived from the Son. The Father's begetting of the Word, equal to himself in all things, is a kind of speaking of himself: he would not have spoken himself wholly and perfectly, if there were less or more in his Word than in himself. Here we see the supreme realization of "Yea, yea; Nay, nay." So that this Word is truly truth itself; for he contains all that is in that knowledge of which he is begotten, and nothing that is not in it. There can never in this Word be any falsity, since he disposes himself immutably as the Father disposes himself, from whom he is. "The Son can do nothing of himself, but what he sees the Father doing."[51] This "inability" is true ability, not weakness but the strength whereby truth is unable to be false. So the Father knows all things both in himself and in the Son, but in himself he knows all things as himself, in the Son as his Word, springing from all that is in himself. In like manner the Son knows all things: in himself, as what is born of that which the Father knows in himself, and in the Father, as that of which is born all that the Son knows in himself. Thus Father and Son know one another, the one by begetting, the other by being begotten. All that is in their knowledge, their wisdom, their essence, is seen by each of them in a single act, with no separation into parts or units, as though the sight should move from one point to another and back again, or transfer itself from this or that

[50] E.g., *De Trin.*, VI, 8 (vii). See Introduction, p. 21.   [51] John 5:19.

point to others in succession, unable to see one without losing others from view. All, I say, are seen together, and of them all there is nothing that is not always in sight.

24. We have seen that there is in ourselves a word that has no sound uttered or imagined, but belongs to a reality of inward vision and inward utterance, and therefore not to any spoken language. Hence there is in this "enigma" a kind of likeness to the Word of God which is also God; inasmuch as this word is born of our knowledge, as God's Word is born of the Father's. But in this word of ours, so recognized as having a certain likeness to God's, it must not irk us to observe and describe as fairly as we may the many elements of unlikeness.

(xv). First, can we say that the word in us is born only of our knowledge? Do we not say many things that we do not know—and not doubtfully but in the belief that they are true? If they happen to be true, the truth will lie in the things of which we speak and not in our own word; for there is no true word that is not begotten of a thing known. In this way our word may be false not through our lying but through our mistaking. When we are in doubt, the word is derived not from the thing of which we doubt but from the doubt itself. We may not know whether that of which we doubt is true; but we know that we doubt, and therefore when we say so the word is true, for we are saying what we know. Again, we may lie, in which case our word is wilfully and knowingly false, whereas the true word is that we are lying; for that is what we know. And when we confess a lie, we speak the truth, for we are saying what we know, which is that we have lied. But that Word which is God, and more powerful than us, has no power so to do. For "he can do nothing, but what he seeth the Father doing"; and he speaks not from himself, but has from the Father all that he speaks, since he himself is spoken by the Father alone. The high power of that Word is to have no power to lie: in him there is no "Yea and Nay," but "Yea, yea," and "Nay, nay." It may be objected that what is not true ought not to be called a word; and to that I willingly agree. But even when our word is true and so rightly called a word, can we say that as it may be called vision from vision, or knowledge from knowledge, it can also be called essence from essence—even as the Word of God is chiefly and most rightly so called? It cannot, because in us being and knowing are not identical. We know many things which have through our memory of them a kind of life, and when we forget them a kind of death: thus when they are no longer in our knowledge, yet we still exist, and when our knowledge has slipped from the mind and so perished for us, yet we are still alive.

25. There are indeed items of knowledge which cannot be lost, since their presence belongs to the nature of the mind itself —as for example the knowledge that we are alive, which must continue as long as the mind continues; and that means for ever. But this and any similar kind of knowledge, in which we may especially look for the image of God, though always known is not always object of thought. Since the word in us is spoken by thinking, it is not easy to see how the word of such knowledge can be called everlasting. The mind's life and the mind's knowledge that it lives are both everlasting; but its thinking of its life or of the knowledge of its life is not, since in passing from one thought to another it will cease to think of the former although it will not cease to know it. If then any everlasting knowledge can exist in the mind, but an everlasting thought of that knowledge cannot, and if the true inward word in us is spoken only when we think, it follows that God alone may be understood to possess a Word that is everlasting and co-eternal with himself. It may be suggested that a word as unbroken as the knowledge is to be found in the mere possibility of thought, in the fact that what is known is always potentially object of a true thought, even when it is not actually being thought of.[52] But what has not yet taken form in the mental vision is not in the proper sense a word: it cannot present a likeness to the knowledge of which it is born, if it has not the form of that knowledge, and is only called a word as having such form potentially. We might as well say that it should be called a word because it is one potentially. But what *is* this potential word that claims the name of word? What is this thing capable of form but still unformed, but a process in our mind, darting hither and thither with a kind of movement of passage, as we turn our thought from one object to another in the course of discovery or presentation? It becomes a true word, only when what I have called this darting movement of passage comes upon what we know and takes form from it, receiving its likeness at every point; so that the mode of thought correspond to the mode of knowledge, and its object be spoken in the heart without voice, uttered or imagined, such as must belong to a particular

---

52 We are reminded here of Augustine's assertion that memory, understanding, and will are always present in the mind, even if below the level of consciousness (cf. above, X, 19 (xii) n.). The following discussion brings out the difficulties of the conception with regard to "understanding."

language. We may allow, to avoid the appearance of verbal controversy, that the mental process capable of taking form from
our knowledge may be called a word even before the form is
taken, as being so to say formable. But who can fail to see the
unlikeness herein to that Word of God which is in the form of
God, not in the sense of having been first formable and later
formed, or able at any time to be without form, but as being a
form incomposite and equal without composition to him from
whom it is derived, and with whom it is in marvellous wise co-
eternal? We speak therefore of the Word of God, but not of
God's thinking, in order to exclude the notion of any passing
process in God, now receiving form and now regaining it in
order to become a word—capable therefore of losing its form
and passing through some unstable condition of formlessness.
That great master of language, Vergil, knew well the value of
words, with a sure insight into the nature of thought, when he
wrote in his poem:

> . . . "passes within himself
> The varied happenings of war" . . .[53]

which simply means "thinks." That is why the Son of God is
not called God's thought but God's Word. Our own thought
becomes our true word when it arrives at what we know and
takes form from it. The Word of God must be understood apart
from any thought of God, as a form in itself incomposite, de-
pending on no "formable" state that may as well lack form as
have it. The Scriptures do indeed speak of "thoughts" of God,
but only by the same mode of expression which also speaks of
God's "forgetting"—of which assuredly there can in strictness
be none in God.

26. Recognizing then so great an unlikeness to God and his
Word in this "enigma" as it now is, despite the measure of likeness we have found in it, we must admit that even when "we
shall be like him," when "we shall see him as he is" [54] (words
clearly implying awareness of our present unlikeness), we shall
yet have no natural equality with him. For the created nature
must always be less than the Creator. Then indeed our word
will not be false, for we shall neither lie nor be mistaken. Perhaps there will be no passage in our thoughts, of movement and
return from one thing to another, but we shall see all our knowledge in one simultaneous view. Yet even in that state, if we
reach it, the creature that was once formable will have achieved

[53] Verg., *Aen.*, X, 159 f.   [54] I John 3:2.

formation indeed, in such wise that nothing will be lacking to its destined form; but still it cannot be reckoned equal to that incomposite being in which there is nothing formed or re-formed that once was formable, but pure form, an eternal and immutable substance, neither formless nor formed.

27 (xvii). Concerning the Father and the Son we have now said as much as we have found possible to discern by means of the mirror and enigma of our human mind. It remains for us to consider, with such insight as God's gift may grant us, the Holy Spirit. Scripture teaches us that he is the Spirit neither of the Father alone nor of the Son alone, but of both; and so his being suggests to us that mutual charity whereby the Father and the Son love one another. But for the exercise of our under-standing, the inspired word has set before us truths not lying on the surface but to be explored in the depths and thence brought up to light; so that our search calls for the greater diligence. The Scripture has not said: "the Holy Spirit is charity." If it had, much of our enquiry would have been foreclosed. It has said: "God is charity" [55]; and so left us to ask whether God the Father be charity, or God the Son, or God the Holy Spirit, or God the Trinity itself. Now it is not open to us to say that God is called charity, not because charity is a substantive reality worthy to be named God, but because it is God's gift. In this latter manner, when God is addressed in Scripture in such terms as: "thou art my patience," [56] the meaning is not that our patience is the substance of God, but that it comes to us from him, as indeed we read elsewhere: "from him is my patience".[57] But this interpretation is at once refuted by the actual lan-guage of the Scriptures. "Thou art my patience" is like "Thou, Lord, art my hope," [58] and "My God is my compassion," [59] and many expressions of the kind. But we do not read: "the Lord is my charity," or "Thou art my charity," or "God is my charity," but "God is charity"—just as "God is a Spirit." Anyone who cannot see the difference must seek understanding from the Lord and not explanation from us; for we have no words to make the point more evident.

28. God, then, is charity. Our question is whether this be-speaks Father, or Son, or Holy Spirit, or the Trinity itself which is not three Gods, but one God. I have argued earlier in the present Book that the divine Trinity must not be so conceived, from the likeness of the three members displayed in our mental

[55] I John 4:16.   [56] Ps. 71:5.   [57] Ps. 62:5.
[58] Ps. 91:9   [59] Ps. 59:17.

trinity, as to make the Father memory of all three, the Son understanding of all three, and the Holy Spirit charity of all three. It is not as though the Father neither understood nor loved for himself, but the Son understood for him and the Holy Spirit loved for him, while he himself did nothing but "remember," both for himself and for them; nor as though the Son neither remembered nor loved for himself, but the Father remembered for him and the Holy Spirit loved for him, while he himself did nothing but understand both for himself and for them; nor as though the Holy Spirit neither remembered nor understood for himself, but the Father remembered for him and the Son understood for him, while he himself only loved both for himself and for them. Rather must we think that all and each possess all three characters in their proper nature; and that in them the three are not separate, as in ourselves memory is one thing, understanding another, and love or charity another: but that there is one single potency for them all, such as wisdom itself, so possessed in the nature of each several Person that he who possesses it is that which he possesses, i.e., the form of a changeless and incomposite substance. If this be understood and its truth manifest, so far as we may be suffered to see or to conjecture in these great matters, I see no reason why, just as Father, Son and Holy Spirit are each called wisdom, and all together are not three wisdoms but one, so Father, Son, and Holy Spirit may not each be called charity, and all together one charity. In the same way the Father is God, the Son is God, and the Holy Spirit God; and all together are one God.

29. Yet there is good reason why in this Trinity we call none Word of God but the Son, none Gift of God but the Holy Spirit, none of whom the Word is begotten and from whom the Holy Spirit originally proceeds, but God the Father. I add the word "originally," because we learn that the Holy Spirit proceeds also from the Son.[60] But this is part of what is given by the

[60] The doctrine of the "double procession" of the Holy Spirit, which led to the insertion of the *Filioque* clause into the Nicene Creed, was expressly maintained by Augustine. He argued that it was implied both by the Scriptural phrases "Spirit of the Son," "Spirit of Christ," and by the account in John 20:22 of Christ's insufflation of the Spirit upon his disciples after the Resurrection. See, e.g., *In Jo. Ev. Tr.*, XCIX, 6 ff. (quoted by Augustine below in Bk. XV, 48 (xxvii)), *Contra Maxim.*, II, xiv, 1.— At the same time Augustine always insisted (as here) that the procession of the Spirit from the Son is part of that which the Son receives from the Father in his eternal generation. There is thus no real difference between his position and the Eastern doctrine of the Spirit's procession from the Father through the Son.

Father to the Son, not as already existing without it, but given to him as all that the Father gives to his only-begotten Word, in the act of begetting. He is begotten in such wise that the common gift proceeds from him also, and the Holy Spirit is Spirit of both. And this distinction within the indivisible Trinity is not to be admitted in passing, but to be observed with all diligence. For hence it comes that the Word of God is by a special fitness called also the Wisdom of God, though both Father and Holy Spirit are wisdom. If then one of the three is by a special fitness to be named charity, the name falls most appropriately to the Holy Spirit. And this means that in the incomposite and supreme being of God, substance is not to be distinguished from charity; but substance is itself charity, and charity itself is substance, whether in the Father or in the Son or in the Holy Spirit, and yet by a special fitness the Holy Spirit is named charity.

30. We may compare the manner in which all the oracles of the Old Testament Scripture are sometimes denoted by the name of Law. A text quoted from the prophet Isaiah, where he says, "By other tongues and other lips I will speak to this people," is introduced by the apostle with the words "it is written in the law." [61] And our Lord himself says, "It is written in their law, that they have hated me without a cause," though we read the words in a Psalm. [62] But sometimes the title is assigned specially to the Law given through Moses, as in the texts, "the law and the prophets were until John," and "on these two commandments hang the whole law and the prophets." [63] Here certainly the Law is entitled in its special sense, as that coming from Mount Sinai. Again under the name of "Prophets" we find the Psalms denoted; though elsewhere the Saviour himself says: "it behoved all things to be fulfilled which are written in the law and the prophets and the psalms concerning me." [64] Here again the name "Prophets" excludes the Psalms. "Law," then, may be used in a general sense to include Prophets and Psalms, but also in a special sense of the Law given through Moses; and "Prophets" may be used as a common term including the Psalms, as well as in a special sense excluding them. And there are numerous other instances to show that many names can both be extended generally, and also applied in a special sense to certain things; but we need not dwell at length on so plain a matter. I am concerned only to

[61] Isa. 28:11; I Cor. 14:2. [62] John 15:25; Ps. 35:19.
[63] Matt. 11:13; 22:40. [64] Luke 24:44.

rebut the charge of impropriety in calling the Holy Spirit charity, if made on the ground that both God the Father and
God the Son are entitled to the same name. 31. We may say,
then, that just as we give the name of wisdom by a special fitness to the one Word of God, though in general both the Holy
Spirit and the Father himself are wisdom, so is the Holy Spirit
by a special fitness to be called charity, though both Father and
Son are charity in general. The Word of God, God's only-
begotten Son, is expressly named as the Wisdom of God in the
apostle's own phrase, "Christ the power of God and the wisdom
of God." [65] But we can also find authority for calling the Holy
Spirit charity, by a careful examination of the apostle John's
way of speaking. [66] After saying, "Beloved, let us love one another, for love is of God," he goes on to add, "and every one
that loveth is born of God: he that loveth not, hath not known
God, for God is love." This makes it plain that the love which
he calls God is the same love which he has said to be "of God."
Love, then, is God of (or from) God. But since both Son is born
and Spirit proceeds from God the Father, we must naturally
enquire to which of them applies the saying in this passage that
God is love. Only the Father is God without being "of God";
so that the love which is God as being "of God" must be either
the Son or the Holy Spirit. Now in what follows the writer
refers to the love of God—not that by which we love him, but
that by which "he loved us, and sent his Son as expiator for our
sins"; and bases thereon his exhortation to us to love one another, that so God may dwell in us, since God (as he has said)
is love. And there follows at once, designed to express the matter
more plainly, the saying: "hereby we know that we dwell in
him, and he in us, because he hath given us of his Spirit." Thus
the Holy Spirit, of whom he has given us, makes us dwell in
God, and God in us. But that is the effect of love. The Holy
Spirit himself therefore is the God who is love. A little further
on, after repeating his statement that "God is love," John adds
immediately, "and he that abideth in love abideth in God, and
God abideth in him": which corresponds to the earlier saying,
"hereby we know that we abide in him and he in us, because he
hath given us of his Spirit." It is the Spirit therefore who is signified in the text "God is love." God the Holy Spirit who proceeds from God, when he is given to man kindles him with the
love of God and of neighbour, and is himself love. For man has

---

[65] I Cor. 1:24.   [66] I John 4:7 ff.

no means of loving God, unless it comes of God: hence the following saying, that "we love him because he first loved us." It is the same in the apostle Paul: "the love of God is shed abroad in our hearts through the Holy Spirit which is given to us." [67]

32 (xviii). More excellent gift of God than this there is none. It alone divides between the sons of the eternal kingdom and the sons of eternal perdition. Other favours also are given through the Holy Spirit, but without charity they avail nothing. Unless the Holy Spirit be bestowed in such measure on any man as to make him a lover of God and of his neighbour, he cannot pass from the left hand to the right. The name of Gift belongs properly to the Spirit, only on account of love—the love which he that lacks, though he speak with the tongues of men and angels, is sounding brass and a tinkling cymbal: though he have prophecy and know all mysteries and all knowledge, and though he have all faith so as to remove mountains, he is nothing: and though he distribute all his substance, and give his body to be burned, it profits him nothing. [68] How great a blessing must this be, without which blessings so great can bring no man to eternal life! But suppose a man that does not speak with tongues, has not prophecy, knows not all mysteries or all knowledge, distributes not all his goods to the poor—whether because he has none to distribute or because some necessity forbids, nor gives his body to be burned—if he have no trial of such suffering to face. Love itself, or charity—both words mean the same thing— if such a man have it, will bring him to the kingdom: even to faith charity gives all its fruitfulness. For there may indeed be faith without charity, but not a faith that profits. So the apostle Paul says: "In Christ Jesus neither circumcision availeth anything, nor uncircumcision, but the faith which worketh through love" [69]: so distinguishing this faith from that whereby the devils also believe and tremble. [70] Thus the love which is of God and is God is specially the Holy Spirit, through whom is spread abroad in our hearts the charity of God by which the whole Trinity makes its habitation within us. And therefore is the Holy Spirit, God though he be, most rightly called also the Gift of God; and what can be the special sense of that gift but

[67] Rom. 5:5. This exegesis of I John, ch. 4 (for which cf. *In Ep. Jo. Tr.*, VII, 6; VIII, 12) is no doubt forced in so far as it attempts to prove an intentional *equation* of love with the Holy Spirit. But Augustine is not mistaken in finding both in John and Paul the doctrine that love is the unfailing evidence of the Spirit's presence and working.
[68] I Cor. 13:1 ff.   [69] Gal. 5:6.   [70] James 2:19.

charity, which brings us to God, and without which no other of God's gifts can bring us to him?

33 (xix). If proof be still awaited that the Holy Spirit is called in the inspired writings the Gift of God, we have the words of our Lord Jesus Christ in the Gospel according to John. "If any man thirst, let him come to me and drink. He that believeth in me, as the Scripture saith, out of his belly shall flow rivers of living water." To which the Evangelist adds his comment: "and this he said of the Spirit which they that believed on him were to receive." [71] Hence too the saying of the apostle Paul: "and we have all drunk of one Spirit." [72] It may be asked whether this water which is the Holy Spirit is actually called the Gift of God. The answer is that this water, found in that place to be the Holy Spirit, is found elsewhere in the same Gospel named as God's gift. When our Lord was talking at the well with the woman of Samaria, to whom he had said, "Give me to drink," and she answered that the Jews had no dealings with the Samaritans, Jesus answered and said unto her: "If thou hadst known the gift of God, and who he is that saith unto thee, Give me to drink, thou mightest have asked of him and he would have given thee living water. The woman saith to him, Lord, thou hast nothing to draw with, and the well is deep: whence then hast thou living water? . . . Jesus answered and said unto her: Every one that drinketh of this water shall thirst again; but he that shall drink of the water that I shall give him shall not thirst for evermore; but the water that I shall give him shall become in him a fountain of water springing unto eternal life." [73] Since this living water, according to the Evangelist's exposition, is the Holy Spirit, no doubt but the Spirit is that Gift of God of which our Lord here says: "if thou hadst known the gift of God, and who he is that saith unto thee, Give me to drink, thou mightest have asked of him and he would have given thee living water." The reference in the one passage, "Out of his belly shall flow rivers of living water," is the same as in the other: "shall become in him a fountain of water springing unto eternal life."

34. Paul the apostle also tells us that "to each one of us is given grace according to the measure of the giving of Christ"; and that the giving of Christ is the Holy Spirit is shown by his next words: "Wherefore he saith, he ascended on high and led captivity captive, and gave gifts to men." [74] Now we know well

71 John 7:37 ff.   72 I Cor. 12:13.
73 John 4:7 ff.   74 Eph. 4:7 f.

that our Lord Jesus, after his resurrection from the dead and ascension into heaven, gave the Holy Spirit, by whose inspiration the believers spoke with the tongues of all nations. The word "gifts," instead of "gift," need not disturb us, for it comes in a quotation from the Psalm; where, however, we actually read: "Thou hast ascended on high, thou hast led captivity captive, thou hast received gifts among men." [75] This is the reading of most manuscripts, especially the Greek; and so we have it as the translation of the Hebrew. The apostle follows the prophet in using the word "gifts," and not "gift"; but where the prophet says, "thou hast received gifts among men," the apostle chooses to say "gave gifts unto men." Thus we get the fullest meaning from both texts, the prophetic and the apostolic, as in both is the authority of the divine word. For both are true —both that he gave to men, and that he received among men: gave to men, as the head to his members; and received among men, himself in his members. On account of these his members he called from heaven, "Saul, Saul, why persecutest thou me?" and concerning them he says, "when ye did it unto one of my littlest ones, ye did it unto me." [76] Thus Christ himself both gave from heaven and received upon earth. On the other hand, both prophet and apostle have spoken in the plural of "gifts," because through the one Gift which is the Holy Spirit there is a distribution to the community of all Christ's members of many gifts, appropriated to each of them. Not every individual has all the gifts, but these have some and those others: though that one Gift, the Holy Spirit, by whom the rest are severally apportioned, is given to all. Paul in another passage, after mentioning the many gifts, says, "All these worketh one and the same Spirit, apportioning to every man as he will." [77] We find the same thought in the Epistle to the Hebrews: "God bearing them witness, with signs and wonders, and with divers miracles, and with distributings of the Holy Spirit." [78] In the text from which we started, after the quotation, "he ascended on high, led captivity captive, and gave gifts to men," Paul continues: "that he ascended, what is it but that he also descended into the lower parts of the earth? He that descended is the same that

[75] Ps. 68:18.
[76] Acts 9:4; Matt. 25:40. This principle of exegesis, based on the doctrine of the Church as Christ's mystical Body, which Augustine used as key to interpretation of the Psalms, he had learnt from the *Rules* of Tyconius the Donatist. For a possible explanation of Paul's variation from the Psalm text, see Armitage Robinson's commentary on Ephesians, *ad loc.*
[77] I Cor. 12:11.   [78] Heb. 2:4.

also ascended above all heavens, that he might fill all things. And he gave, some apostles, some prophets, some evangelists, some pastors and teachers." Here we see why "gifts" were spoken of. As Paul says elsewhere: "Are all apostles? are all prophets?" [79] And he concludes: "for the perfecting of the saints unto the work of ministering, unto the building up of the body of Christ." [80] That is the house, built up, as the Psalm has it, after the captivity; [81] for of those who are delivered from the devil, by whom they were held captive, is built up the house of Christ—the house which is called the Church. That captivity has been led captive by the conqueror of the devil, who has bound him, first with the chains of justice and then with the chains of power: [82] that he might not carry with him into eternal punishment those that were to be members of a holy head. So is the devil himself signified by the "captivity" led captive by him who has ascended on high and given gifts to men, or received them among men.

35. We have also the words of the apostle Peter, recorded in our canonical Acts of the Apostles. When by his speaking of Christ the Jews are stirred in their hearts, and ask, "What then shall we do, brethren? Show us," he answers: "Repent, and be baptized each one of you in the name of Jesus Christ for the remission of sins; and ye shall receive the gift of the Holy Spirit." [83] In the same book we read how Simon Magus would have given money to the apostles, in order that he might receive from them the power by which through the laying-on of his hands the Holy Spirit should be given. It is Peter again who answers: "Thy money perish with thee, because thou hast thought to possess the gift of God by money." [84] In another passage of the Acts, where Peter speaks to Cornelius and them that were with him, proclaiming and preaching Christ, the Scripture says: "While Peter yet spoke these words, the Holy Spirit fell upon all them that heard the word; and the believers of the circumcision, that had come with Peter, were amazed, because upon the Gentiles also was poured out the gift of the Holy Spirit. For they heard them speaking with tongues and glorifying God." [85] Afterwards Peter is called to give account to the brethren at Jerusalem, who were moved at the report of his action in baptizing men uncircumcised, because before they were baptized the Holy Spirit had come upon them, so as to cut away all ground

---

[79] I Cor. 12:29.   [80] Eph. 4:12.   [81] Ps. 127:1.
[82] See Bk. XIII, Argument.   [83] Acts 2:37 f.
[84] Acts 8:18 ff.   [85] Acts 10:44 ff.

for questioning; and his story ends: "When I had begun to speak unto them, the Holy Spirit fell upon them, as upon us in the beginning. And I remembered the word of the Lord, how that he said, John indeed baptized with water, but ye shall be baptized with the Holy Spirit. If therefore he hath given to them an equal gift as to us who have believed in the Lord Jesus Christ; who was I, that I should be able to prevent God from giving unto them the Holy Spirit?"[86]

There are many other Scripture texts which agree in their testimony that the Holy Spirit is the gift of God, inasmuch as he is given to them that love God through him. But it would be tedious to collect them all; and a man not contented by those we have quoted is likely to be content with nothing.

36. It may be necessary to point out, when the Scriptural appellation of the Holy Spirit as God's gift is recognized, that the phrase "gift of the Holy Spirit" is a form of expression of the same kind as "putting off the body of the flesh"[87]: just as "body of the flesh" means no more than "the flesh," so "the gift of the Holy Spirit" means no more than "the Holy Spirit." He is the gift of God inasmuch as he is given to those to whom he is given. In himself he is God, though he were given to no man; he was God, co-eternal with Father and Son, before being given to anyone. Nor is he a lesser than they because they are givers and he given. Though given as God's gift, he is as God the giver of himself. The Spirit who is said to "breathe where he listeth"[88] cannot be held to lack power over himself. Similarly the apostle's words already quoted: "all these worketh one and the same Spirit, dividing severally to every man as he will," indicate not a subjection of the given and a domination of the givers, but a concord of given and givers.

37. To sum up, Holy Scripture proclaims that God is charity. Charity is of God, and its effect in us is that we dwell in God and he in us. This we know, because he has given us of his Spirit. It follows that the Spirit himself is the God who is charity. If among God's gifts there is none greater than charity, and there is no greater gift of God than the Holy Spirit, we naturally conclude that he who is said to be both God and of God is himself charity. And if the charity whereby the Father loves the Son and the Son loves the Father displays, beyond the power of words, the communion of both, it is most fitting that the Spirit who is common to both should have the special name of charity. The sounder way of faith or of understanding is to hold that

[86] Acts 11:15 ff.   [87] Col. 2:11.   [88] John 3:8.

while charity in the divine Trinity is not the Holy Spirit alone, yet the reasons given justify applying to him this special name. So in the Trinity it is not he alone that is either Spirit or Holy, since the Father is Spirit and the Son is Spirit, the Father is Holy and the Son is Holy. Piety allows no doubt of that; yet we have reason for calling him in especial the Holy Spirit. Because he is common to both, he has in especial the name that belongs to both in common. If in the Trinity the Holy Spirit alone were charity, then the Son would be made out to be Son not of the Father alone but also of the Holy Spirit. Countless as are the texts which call him the only-begotten Son of the Father, the apostle's saying concerning God the Father remains true: "who hath delivered us from the power of darkness and translated us into the kingdom of the Son of his charity."[89] Not here, "of his Son"—though that would have had the truth of frequent usage —but "Son of his charity." If in the Trinity there is no charity of God save the Holy Spirit, then the Son is Son also of the Holy Spirit. That conclusion being absurd, the alternative must be accepted, that the Holy Spirit is not charity alone of the Trinity, but so called especially for the reasons sufficiently set forth. The phrase, "Son of his charity," means simply "his beloved Son"—in fine, the Son of his substance. For that charity of the Father that exists in his ineffably incomposite nature is nothing else than his very nature and substance—as we have so often said and must not weary of repeating. Thus the Son of his charity is no other than the offspring of his substance.

38 (xx). This shows the foolishness of the arguments of Eunomius, from whom the Eunomian heresy arose.[90] He could not understand, and would not believe that the only-begotten Word of God, through whom all things were made, was the Son of God by nature, that is, born of the Father's substance. Therefore he maintained that the Word was not Son of his nature, his

---

[89] Col. 1:13.
[90] Eunomius was the chief representative of the later "dialectical" Arianism, and both Basil and Gregory of Nyssa wrote to refute him. The particular doctrine that the generation of the Son was a creative act of the Father's will, had been held by Arians from the beginning, as well as by Eusebius of Caesarea. They could appeal to the language of earlier Fathers, including Origen who had said (De Princip., IV, 28) that the Son might be called Son of the Father's will, being the "Son of his love." See Athanasius, C. Arian., III, 59 ff. Eunomius distinguished the "essence" of God from his "activity" in creation and the time-process, the latter being identifiable with his will. The theory is stated in his Apologeticus, printed in Migne, P.G., XXX, with the works of Basil.

substance or essence, but Son of God's will. His intention was
to make the will by which the Father begot the Son an accident
in God: just as we will something at one time which we did not
will before. But that is why our own nature must be understood
as changeable—which we cannot possibly believe of God. It is
written that "there are many thoughts in the heart of a man;
but the counsel of the Lord abideth for ever" [91]; the whole purport of which is that we may understand or believe that the
counsel of God is unto eternity even as he is eternal, and therefore changeless as he is. And what is said of thoughts may with
equal truth be said of wills: "there are many wills in the heart
of a man; but the will of the Lord abideth for ever." Some have
sought to avoid speaking of the only-begotten Word as Son of
the counsel or will of God, by saying that the Word is himself
the Father's counsel or will. [92] But it is better, in my judgment,
to call him counsel from counsel or will from will, as he is substance from substance and wisdom from wisdom: in that way
we avoid the absurdity, already exposed, of saying that the Son
makes the Father wise or willing, the Father being without
counsel or will in his own substance. We may recall the pene-
trating answer once given to the heretic, [93] who ingeniously
enquired whether God begot his Son willingly or unwillingly:
if one should say, unwillingly, an impossible affliction would be
imposed upon God; if, willingly, the designed conclusion would
at once follow irresistibly, that the Son is son not of nature but
of will. To which the wary interlocutor rejoined with another
question: Is God the Father God willingly or unwillingly? If
the reply were unwillingly, again an affliction would be imposed upon God which it were insane to credit; if one should say
willingly, the answer would be that then God is God by will and
not by nature. The heretic thus had no resource but silence,
seeing himself caught by his own question in an inescapable
dilemma. If indeed any Person in the Trinity is to be termed
specially the will of God, the name is applicable rather, like
charity, to the Holy Spirit. For charity is strictly a form of
willing.

39. I believe that my treatment of the Holy Spirit in this
Book has given an exposition of Holy Scripture that may suffice
to the believer, who knows already that the Holy Spirit is God,

91 Prov. 19:21.
92 The reference may be to Athanasius himself, who answers Arius in this
way in the passage referred to above, note 90.
93 See Gregory of Nazianzus, *Theological Orations*, III, 6 (ed. Mason).

and is neither of another substance nor lesser than the Father and the Son: of which in earlier Books we have demonstrated the truth in accordance with the same Scriptures. Concerning the creature that God has made, we have done our best to encourage seekers after a reasoned knowledge to perceive the invisible things of him, being understood in the measure possible through the things that are made; and especially through the rational or intellectual creature that is made in the image of God. In it, as in a mirror, they may see, if they are able and as they are able, the Trinity of God, in our memory, understanding and will. Let a man have the lively perception of these three, existing naturally in his mind by the divine ordering. Let his memory recall, his understanding observe, and his love embrace, the greatness in that mind whereby even the Being that is everlasting and changeless can be remembered, viewed and desired; and there assuredly he will find an image of the supreme Trinity. Upon the remembering, beholding and loving of that supreme Trinity, that he may recall it, contemplate it, and delight in it, he ought to make all the life in him depend. But I have also given him such warning as appeared sufficient, that this image, made by the Trinity, is altered for the worse by its own fault: when therefore he compares it to the divine Trinity, he must not suppose it like in all respects; but rather discern even in its measure of likeness a great unlikeness also.

40 (xxi). Of God the Father and God the Son—God the Begetter, who has in a manner spoken in his own Word, co-eternal with himself, all that belongs to his own substance, and that same Word of his, God to whose own substance belongs all, in measure neither greater nor less, that is in him whose begetting of the Word is no lie but perfect truth: these two I have endeavoured to trace so far as possible, not as seen face to face, but by inference however remote from this likeness in an enigma, in the memory and understanding of our human mind. To memory we assigned all that we know even though we are not thinking of it, and to understanding the impartation of a certain definite form to thought. It is by thinking of a truth discovered that we are said especially to understand it: and afterwards we leave it once more in the memory. But it is in a more recondite depth of our memory that we find such truth when first we think of it; and so is begotten that inward word which is of no language, as a knowledge from knowledge, a vision from vision, and an understanding manifest in thought from understanding already present in the memory but hidden. Yet thought itself

must have some kind of memory of itself, else it could not return to things left in the memory when one thought is exchanged for another.

41. Of the Holy Spirit I have shown in this enigma of ours no apparent likeness but the will, or the love which is will in fuller strength; for the will which exists in us by nature acquires varying tones in relation to the objects present to it or meeting it, by which we are attracted or offended. But is it possible to say that our will, when rightly directed, is ignorant of what to seek or shun? If it is not, it must contain a knowledge of its own, such as cannot be without memory and understanding. We could never accept the suggestion that the charity which "does no wrong" [94] is ignorant of what it does. There is both understanding and love in that prime fount of memory, wherein we find ready and laid up the truth we can arrive at by the act of thought; for both of these we find there, present before we thought of them, when in the act of thought we discover our own understanding and love of any object. [95] There is both memory and love in the understanding which takes form in thought—the true word spoken inwardly without any specific language, when we say what we know; for our thought can only turn its observation upon anything by remembering, and will only be concerned to do so by loving. Love is that which takes the vision which has its seat in memory, and the vision of thought which thence receives form, and joins them together as parent and offspring; but in the same way unless it possessed the knowledge of purposive seeking, which involves memory and understanding, it would be ignorant of its own proper object.

42 (xxii). But when these three elements exist in a single person such as a man, an objector may make the point that this triad of memory, understanding and love, belong not to themselves but to *me*. What they do is done for me, not for them—or rather it is done by me through their means. It is I that remember by memory, understand by understanding, love by love. When I turn my thought's eye upon memory, and say within myself what I know, begetting out of my knowledge a true word, both are *mine*, both the knowledge and the word. *I* know, and *I* speak within myself what I know. And when in the process of thought I discover in my memory an existing understanding and love for something, an understanding and a love which were there already before I thought of them, it is *my* understanding

94 I Cor. 13:5.   95 See Bk. X, 19 (xii), 12.

and *my* love that I find in my memory, of which I am the subject and not they. Again, when thought performs the act of
remembering and by the act of will returns to what it had left
in the memory, wills to perceive it as understood and to speak
it as an inward word, the act of remembering is performed with
my memory, the act of will with *my* will, not its own. And when
my love remembers and understands what it ought to seek or
shun, it remembers by *my* memory not its own, and understands
whatever it loves with understanding, by *my* understanding and
not its own. In short: in all three it is I that remember, I that
understand, I that love, and I am neither memory nor understanding nor love but the possessor of them. They can be
enumerated by the one person who possesses the three of them
and is not identical with them. But in the uncompounded simplicity of the supreme being which is God, though there is one
God, there are yet three Persons, Father, Son and Holy Spirit.[96]

43 (xxiii). Thus there is a difference between the reality
of the Trinity and its image in another subject, the image in
virtue of which the mind embracing our three elements is itself
called an image; just as the word "image" is applied both to the
panel and to the painting on it, the panel being named an
image because of the picture it supports. The absolute trans-
cendence of the supreme Trinity defies comparison. A trinity
of men cannot be called one man; but such is the inseparable
unity of the divine Trinity, that in it both for our naming and in
reality there is one God; and the Trinity is not *in* one God but
is itself one God. Again, the image, the man in whom our triad
is contained, is a single person; the Trinity is three Persons,
Father in relation to Son, Son in relation to Father, Spirit in
relation to Father and Son. In our image of the Trinity, the
human memory, especially as distinguished from that of beasts
by containing ideas not conveyed to it through the bodily
senses, offers in its own measure a likeness, however inadequate,
of the Father. The human understanding which receives form
therefrom in the effort of thought, when the thing known is
spoken as an inward word belonging to no language, offers in
all its disparity a certain likeness of the Son. The human love,
which proceeds from knowledge and is a link between memory
and understanding, as being common to parent and offspring—
so that it cannot be identified with either—offers in that image
a likeness, even if an inadequate likeness, of the Holy Spirit.
But whereas in the image the three do not compose one man but

[96] See Introduction, p. 24.

belong to him, in the supreme Trinity whose image it is the three do not "belong" to one God but *are* one God, and the Persons are not one but three. And what is marvellously inexpressible, or inexpressibly marvellous, though the image of the Trinity is one person and the divine Trinity itself is three, yet the Trinity of three Persons is more inseparable than the imaged trinity of one. For the divine Trinity by the nature of its divinity —or Godhead if the term be preferred—is what it is, changelessly and always equal to itself. At no time was it not, or was different: at no time will it not be or be different. But the three elements contained in the inferior image, though not spatially separate (not being corporeal), yet in this present life are quantitatively variable. The fact that material mass is wanting does not prevent us seeing in one man more memory than understanding, in another the reverse; while in a third these two may be exceeded by love, whether they are equal to one another or not. Thus we may find a superiority of any one severally to the other two, of two together to any one severally, of any several one to any other, of the greater to the less. Even when they shall be made whole from all infirmity and equal to one another, the being that owes its constancy to grace will not attain equality to the being which is essentially changeless. There can be no equality between creature and Creator; and the making whole from all infirmity will itself be a change.

44. When the promised vision, "face to face," has come, we shall behold the Trinity—that Trinity which is not only incorporeal but perfectly inseparable and truly changeless—far more clearly and surely than we now behold its image in ourselves. This present vision, through a mirror and in an enigma, as vouchsafed to us in this life, belongs not to any who can perceive in their own mind all that we have here set out by our analysis; but to those who see the mind as an image, and so are able to achieve a certain relating of what they see to him whose image it is: to reach through their actual vision of the image a presumptive vision of the original which cannot yet be seen face to face. The apostle does not say, "We see now a mirror," but "We see now through a mirror." (xxiv). Those who see the mind as it may be seen, and in it that trinity of which I have attempted to give a variety of descriptions, yet without believing or understanding it to be the image of God: they are seeing a mirror, but so far from seeing through the mirror him who is now to be seen only in that way, they are unaware that the mirror seen *is* a mirror—which is to say, an image. If they knew

it, they might be conscious of the need to seek and in some measure even now to see, through this mirror, him whose mirror it is: their hearts being purified by faith unfeigned,[97] so that he who is seen now through a mirror may at last be seen face to face. But if they despise the faith that purifies hearts, no understanding of the most subtle analysis of our mind's nature can serve but to condemn them, on the testimony of their own understanding itself. The failure to reach any firm assurance despite all their struggles to understand, can be caused only by envelopment in a darkness which is punishment, and the burden of a corruptible body which presseth down the soul.[98] Such evil can have been incurred only by the guilt of sin; and the gravity of the evil should be their warning to follow the Lamb that taketh away the sin of the world.[99] (xxv). For men in his keeping, whose gifts of intellect are far less than theirs, when released from the body at this life's end are clear of all claim upon them by the powers of malice: those powers which the Lamb whom they slew without debt of sin vanquished by the right of his blood before overthrowing them by the might of his power.[1] Free from the power of the devil, they have welcome from the holy angels, delivered from every evil through the Mediator of God and men, the man Christ Jesus[2]: for the Holy Scriptures old and new are at one, both those that foretell the Christ and those that forth-tell him, in knowing "no other name under heaven whereby men must be saved."[3] Thus cleansed from every taint of corruption, the elect are established in peaceful dwelling-places until their bodies be given back to them, bodies corruptible no longer, for beauty not for burdening. For so the perfect goodness and perfect wisdom of the Creator has ordained, that the spirit of man in dutiful subjection to God should possess a body blessedly subject to itself, and that this blessedness should abide for ever.

45. There without any impediment shall we see the truth and enjoy it in perfect clarity and assurance. The mind will not pursue a knowledge by reasoning, but in contemplation will discern why Holy Spirit is not Son, though he proceed from the Father. In that light all such questioning will cease; though here its difficulty has been proved so great for me, and doubtless for all who read with care and understanding what I have written. In my second Book I promised to discuss the question in another place; but whenever I would have pointed out some

[97] I Tim. 1:5; Acts 15:9.   [98] Wisdom 9:15.   [99] John 1:29.
[1] Bk. XIII, Argument.   [2] I Tim. 2:5.   [3] Acts 4:12.

likeness to that truth in our creaturely being, I found no form
of words adequately corresponding to such understanding as I
had reached—though even in that understanding I am aware
of more endeavour than success. Again, when I found in the
single person of a man an image of the supreme Trinity, I sought
to make the likeness more easily apprehended in the sphere of
things changing, and to display it (particularly in the ninth
Book) [4] as existing in temporal succession. But, as we have
shown in this fifteenth Book, our human way of thinking cannot
fit the three entities in one person to the three divine Persons.
(xxvi). Moreover, in the supreme Trinity that is God there
is no temporal successiveness, whereby the question whether
first the Son is born of the Father and then the Holy Spirit proceeds from both, could be answered or even asked. Holy Scripture, indeed, calls him Spirit of both. It is he of whom the apostle
says: "Because ye are sons, God hath sent the Spirit of his Son
into your hearts" [5]; and it is he of whom the Son himself says:
"For it is not ye that speak, but the Spirit of your Father that
speaketh in you." [6] And there are many other texts of Scripture
which prove that he who in the Trinity has the special title of
Holy Spirit is Spirit both of Father and of Son. The Son again
says of him, "whom I will send to you from the Father"; and
elsewhere, "whom the Father will send in my name." [7] That
he proceeds from both may be learnt, first from the saying of
the Son, that he "proceedeth from the Father,"and secondly,
in that after his rising from the dead and appearing to his disciples, he breathed on them and said, "Receive ye the Holy
Spirit"[8]: so showing that the Spirit proceeds from himself. The
Spirit is that same "virtue," which (as we read in the Gospel)
"went from him and healed them all." [9]

46. If one ask why it was that after his resurrection he first
gave the Holy Spirit on earth and afterwards sent him from
heaven, my answer would be that by this gift is shed abroad
in our hearts the charity whereby we love God and our neighbour—according to those two commandments on which hang
all the law and the prophets.[10] To signify this, the Lord Jesus
gave the Spirit twice: once on earth for the love of neighbour,
and again from heaven for the love of God. But if the double
gift of the Holy Spirit should be otherwise explained, at least

[4] The reference to Bk. IX seems to be a slip: Augustine must be thinking
of Bk. XI. (Cf. Bk X, *ad fin.*)
[5] Gal. 4:6.   [6] Matt. 10:20.   [7] John 15:26; 14:26.
[8] John 15:26; 20:22.   [9] Luke 6:19.   [10] Rom. 5:5; Matt. 22:37 ff.

we may not doubt that it was the same Holy Spirit, given in the breathing of Jesus, of whom afterwards he says, "Go, baptize all nations in the name of the Father and of the Son and of the Holy Spirit." [11] It is the same Spirit, then, that was also given from heaven on the day of Pentecost, ten days after the Lord's ascension into heaven. He who gives the Holy Spirit must assuredly be God: nay, how great a God must he be who gives God! None of his disciples gave the Holy Spirit: they prayed that the Spirit should come upon those on whom they laid their hand, but they did not themselves give him. And the Church keeps now the same rule in her officers. Even Simon Magus, when he offers money to the apostles, does not say, "Give me also this power, that I may give the Holy Spirit," but "that on whomsoever I lay my hands, he may receive the Holy Spirit." The words of Scripture preceding were not: "Simon seeing that the apostles gave the Holy Spirit," but: "Simon seeing that by the laying on of the apostles' hands the Holy Spirit was given." [12] Accordingly the Lord Jesus himself not only gave as God the Holy Spirit, but also received him as man; and therefore he is said to be "full of grace," and "full of the Holy Spirit." [13] More expressly is it written of him in the Acts of the Apostles: "for God hath anointed him with the Holy Spirit" [14]—with no visible oil, but with the gift of grace, which is signified by the visible unction wherewith the Church anoints the baptized. Doubtless, Christ's own anointing with the Holy Spirit was not at that time when the Spirit descended upon him as a dove at his baptism. Then, it was his body that he deigned to represent, his Church in which particularly at baptism the Holy Spirit is received. The mystical and invisible anointing of him we must recognize at the moment when the Word of God was made flesh: that is, when human nature, with no preceding merits of good works, was so linked with God the Word in the virgin's womb as to become one person with him. [15] Therefore we confess him born of the Holy Spirit and the virgin Mary. It would be incongruous indeed to suppose that he received the Holy Spirit when he was already thirty years old, at which age he was baptized by John [16]: he must have come to baptism, as altogether without sin, so not without the Holy Spirit. If it is written of John his minister and fore-runner that "he shall be filled with

11 Matt. 28:19.   12 Acts 8:18 f.
13 John 1:14; Luke 4:1.   14 Acts 10:38.
15 Cf. *Enchirid.*, 36 (xi), and esp. *De Praed. Sanct.*, 30 f. (xv).
16 Luke 3:21 ff.

the Holy Spirit even from his mother's womb" [17]—since though engendered by the Father he yet received the Holy Spirit when he was formed in the womb—how are we to think or believe concerning the man Christ, the very conception of whose flesh was not fleshly but spiritual? When it is written of him that he received from the Father the promise of the Holy Spirit and poured it forth,[18] both natures are displayed, the human and the divine. He received as man, he poured forth as God. We can receive indeed the gift according to our capacity; but pour it forth upon others we cannot: for that, we must invoke upon them the God by whom it is performed.

47. We cannot then ask whether the Holy Spirit had already proceeded from the Father when the Son was begotten, or had not yet so proceeded but upon the begetting of the Son proceeded from both. For here nothing takes place in time. When we come to deal with the temporal we can suppose will first to proceed from the human mind, making a search for what may be called an offspring when it is found: with the "getting" or "begetting" of this, the act of will is completed, coming to rest in its object, so that the pursuit of the will that sought becomes the love of the will that enjoys[19]; and this love now proceeds from both, from the begetting mind and the begotten idea, as from parent and offspring. But it is impossible to look for parallels to this in a region where there are no temporal beginnings that can reach completion in process of time. Thus, given the power to understand the timeless generation of the Son from the Father, one must likewise understand the timeless procession of the Holy Spirit from both. Given power to understand, in the saying of the Son, "as the Father hath life in himself, so hath he given to the Son to have life in himself," [20] that the Father's gift of life is not to a Son previously existing without life, but that by this timeless generation the life given by the Father in his begetting is co-eternal with the life of the Father who gave it: one must likewise understand that as the Holy Spirit's procession from the Father belongs to the Father's own being, so has he given to the Son that the same Holy Spirit should proceed from him—in both cases timelessly. When it is said that the Holy Spirit proceeds from the Father, we understand that his procession from the Son comes likewise to the Son from the Father. If it is from the Father that the Son has all that he has, it must be from the Father that he has the

[17] Luke 1:15. [18] Acts 2:33.
[19] Cf. Bk. XIV, 8 (vi). [20] John 5:26.

proceeding from him of the Holy Spirit.[21] We must think here of no temporal before or after; for here there are no times at all. It would be wholly irrational to call the Spirit the Son of both; for while the Son receives his being, with no temporal origin and no mutability of nature, by generation from the Father, the Holy Spirit receives his being, with no temporal origin and no mutability of nature, by procession from both. We do not call the Holy Spirit begotten, but neither may we presume to call him unbegotten, lest the words suggest either two Fathers in the divine Trinity, or two Persons underived. The Father alone is underived, and therefore alone called unbegotten—not indeed in Scripture, but in the common usage of theologians, making discourse on such high matter as fitly as they can.[22] The Son is begotten from the Father; and the Holy Spirit proceeds, ultimately from the Father, and by the Father's gift at no temporal interval from both in common. He could be called son of Father and of Son, only if both had begotten him—a notion intolerable to all sound feeling. Thus he is not begotten of both, but proceeds from the one and the other as the Spirit of both.

48 (xxvii). To distinguish generation from procession in the divine Trinity, co-eternal, co-equal, incorporeal, beyond all expression changeless and inseparable, is indeed most difficult. For readers who find their thought here at the end of its tether, it may suffice for the moment to repeat what we have said in a sermon addressed to our Christian congregation, and afterwards put in writing. I had shown by texts of Holy Scripture that the Holy Spirit proceeds from both. "If then," I said, "the Holy Spirit proceeds both from the Father and from the Son, why has the Son said that he 'proceedeth from the Father?[23] It can only be after his manner of ascribing that which belongs to himself to him from whom he has his own being. For example: 'My doctrine is not mine, but his that sent me.'[24] Here, the doctrine he says is not his own but the Father's must yet be understood as *his* doctrine. No less must we understand in the text before quoted, where he says that the Spirit 'proceedeth from the Father' (not 'proceedeth not from me'), that the Spirit proceeds also from himself. The Son is

[21] Cf. above, 29 (xvii) and n.

[22] In particular, the Arian theologians, profiting from the confusion between the words *agennetos* (unbegotten) and *agenetos* (uncreated or eternal), had attempted to make "unbegottenness" the essence of Deity itself; whence they could argue that he who is "begotten" is not very God. See Athanasius, *De Decretis*, 28 ff.

[23] John 15:26.   [24] John 7:16.

God from God; and he from whom is derived the Godhead of the Son is the same from whom is derived the Holy Spirit's proceeding from the Son. So it is from the Father that the Holy Spirit has his procession from the Son, even as he proceeds from the Father. And this may enable us to understand, so far as understanding is possible for men like us, why the Holy Spirit is not called begotten, but is said to proceed. For if he also were called Son, he must be son of both the other Persons—which would be altogether irrational. A son can be son of two only if they be father and mother; and between God the Father and God the Son no relation of the kind is even to be thought of. Indeed no human son proceeds at one and the same time from father and mother: he does not proceed from the mother when he proceeds from father into mother, and he does not proceed from the father at the time of his proceeding from the mother into visible existence. Whereas the Holy Spirit does not proceed from the Father into the Son, and then from the Son to sanctify the creature: he proceeds at once from both, although his proceeding from the Son as from the Father is the Father's gift to the Son. We cannot say that while the Father is life and the Son is life, the Holy Spirit is not life. As, then, the Father who has life in himself has given to the Son to have life in himself, so has he given to the Son that life should proceed from him even as it proceeds from himself." [25] I insert this passage from a sermon into the present Book: it is addressed of course to the faithful and not to unbelievers.

49. Unbelievers indeed may lack the power to contemplate God's image in them, and to see the reality of the three elements in their own mind, which are three not as three persons but as all pertaining to the one person of a man. Then they had best believe what the holy Books contain concerning the supreme Trinity that is God, instead of demanding for themselves a perfectly clear and rational account such as weak and sluggish human minds cannot take in. By all means, once they have an unshakable belief in the truth of Holy Scripture's witness, let them go on by prayer and enquiry and right living to the pursuit of understanding—which means the seeing with the mind (so far as seeing is possible) of what is firmly held by faith. Who should forbid them? Who indeed would not encourage them to do so? But if they suppose that the reality must be denied because their minds are too blind to perceive it, then the blind from birth may with equal right deny the existence of the sun.

[25] In Jo. Ev. Tr., XCIX, 8 f. Cf. above, 29 (xvii) n.

The light shineth in darkness: if the darkness comprehend it not,[26] let those who are darkness first become enlightened by the gift of God into believing, and so begin in comparison with the unbelieving world to be light. Upon that foundation they may be built up to see what they believe, and in due course gain the power of sight. There are certain matters of belief, the sight of which is no longer possible. Christ can never again be seen upon the cross. But without belief in that which once happened and was seen, though there can be no expectation of its happening or being seen again, we can never reach that vision of the Christ which shall be without end. As for such discernment as is possible for the understanding of the supreme, ineffable, immaterial and changeless being of God: there is no field wherein the human mind can better train its insight, under the guidance of the rule of faith, than in that possession of human nature which is better than anything in the beasts, and better than any other part of the human soul, namely the mind itself. To it has been granted a certain vision of things invisible; it is the authority, raised upon the seat of honour in its inner chamber, for whose judgment the bodily senses deliver all their messages; above it there is none to whose ruling it is subject, save God.

50. In all this long discourse, I dare not claim to have said anything worthy of the unspeakable greatness of the supreme Trinity. I confess rather that "from myself his knowledge has become wonderful: its strength is shown and I cannot attain unto it." [27] And thou, soul of mine, where in all this dost thou find thyself, where liest thou, where standest thou, waiting for him who has shown mercy upon all thine iniquities to heal all thy sicknesses? [28] Doubtless thou seest thyself in that inn, whither the Samaritan brought him that was found half dead from the many wounds laid on him by the robbers. Yet thou hast seen many truths, not with the eyes that see the hues of bodily things, but with those for which the Psalmist made his prayer: "Let mine eyes look upon equity." [29] Thou hast seen many truths indeed, and not confused them with that Light that enabled thee to see them. Lift thine eyes to the Light itself and fix them upon it, if thou canst.[30] Then only shalt thou see the difference of the begetting of God's Word from the procession of God's Gift: wherefore the only-begotten Son has said that the Holy Spirit proceeds from the Father, and is not be-

26 John 1:5.   27 Ps. 139:6.   28 Ps. 103:3.
29 Ps. 17:2.   30 Cf. Bk. VIII, 3 (ii).

gotten of him so as to be his brother. Being a certain consubstantial communion between Father and Son, the Spirit is called the Spirit of both, never the son of both. But to perceive this plainly and clearly, thou art not able to keep thine eye fixed firmly: I know thou art not able. I speak truth to myself, I know what exceeds my power. Yet the light itself displays to thee those three elements in thyself, wherein thou mayest recognize the image of the supreme Trinity, whom thou hast not yet the strength to contemplate with unwavering eyes. The light itself shows thee that a true word is in thee, when it is begotten of thy knowledge, that is, when we say what we know; though it be with no people's tongue that we utter or think a sound with meaning, but our thought receives a form from the object of our knowledge. In the view of the thinker arises an image nearly alike to that knowledge which memory contained, while the will or love unites the two to one another, as parent and offspring. That will proceeds from knowledge, for no one wills a thing of whose being or nature he is altogether ignorant; yet it is not an image of knowledge. And thus there is a suggestion in this mental reality of the difference between begetting and proceeding, inasmuch as to view in thought is not the same as to pursue or to enjoy with the will. So much is to be perceived and discerned by him who is able. And thou too hast been able to perceive it, although thou couldst not and canst not set forth in adequate expression that truth which through the mists of material similitudes, that never cease to invade men's thinking, thou didst hardly see. Yet the light which is not thyself shows thee also that the immaterial likenesses of material things are wholly other than the reality which our understanding contemplates when they are rejected. This and the like certainties are manifested by that light to thine inward eye. Is there any reason why thou canst not behold the light itself with a gaze unwavering, but thine own infirmity? And what has made thee infirm but thine own iniquity? [31] Therefore there is none that can heal all thy sicknesses, but he that has mercy upon all thine iniquities. So were it better to bring this Book at last to an end, not with argument but with prayer.

51 (xxviii). O Lord our God, we believe in thee, Father, Son, and Holy Spirit. If thou wert not Trinity, the Truth would not have said: "Go ye, baptize all nations in the name of the Father and of the Son and of the Holy Spirit." [32] Nor wouldst thou, Lord God, have commanded us to be baptized in the

[31] Cf. Bk. VIII, 3 (ii).   [32] Matt. 28:19.

name of one who was not Lord and God. Yet, Trinity as thou art, wert thou not one Lord God, the divine word would not have said: "Hear, O Israel, the Lord thy God is one God." [33] Moreover, if thou wert thyself God the Father, and thyself Jesus Christ, the Son, thy Word, and the Holy Spirit, his Gift and thine,[33a] we should not read in the book of truth that "God sent his Son" [34]; nor wouldst thou, the only-begotten one, have said of the Holy Spirit: "whom the Father shall send in my name," and "whom I will send to you from the Father." [35]

Guiding the effort of my mind by this rule of faith, I have sought thee with all my power, with all the power thou hast created in me: I have desired greatly to see with my understanding that which I have believed; I have made much discourse, and much toil therein. O Lord my God, my one hope, hear me, that weariness may not lessen my will to seek thee, that I may seek thy face evermore with eager heart. Do thou give strength to seek thee, as thou hast made me to find thee, and given hope of finding thee ever more and more. My strength and my weakness are in thy hands: preserve the one, and remedy the other. In thy hands are my knowledge and my ignorance: where thou hast opened to me, receive my entering in; where thou hast shut, open to my knocking. Let me remember thee, understand thee, love thee: increase in me all these, until thou restore me to thy perfect pattern.

I know that it is written: "In much speaking thou shalt not escape sin." [36] Would that all my speaking were the preaching of thy word and the praise of thee! Then should I not only escape sin, how much soever I spoke, but gain desert of goodness. For it could not have been sin that a man blessed of thee enjoined upon his own son in the faith, to whom he wrote: "Preach the word, be instant in season, out of season." [37] In him who neither in season nor out of season kept back thy word, none can say there was not much speaking. And yet it was not much, when so much was needful. Deliver me, O God, from the plague of much speaking within mine own soul, a soul miserable in thy sight and fleeing unto thy mercy. For my thoughts are not always silent, though I keep silence from words. From this much speaking I would not ask for deliverance, if my thought were only such as should please thee. But my thoughts are

[33] Deut. 6:4.
[33a] i.e. if there were no distinction between the Persons.
[34] Gal. 4:4; John 3:17.   [35] John 14:26; 15:26.
[36] Prov. 10:19.   [37] II Tim. 4:2.

many, thoughts such as thou knowest, vain as thou knowest the thoughts of men to be. Grant me not to give way to them, but to reject them even when they delight me, and not to dwell upon them like a man falling asleep. Let them not have such power with me that aught of my working proceed from them; but let my mind at least and my conscience be kept safe from them by thy safe-guarding. A wise man, in that book of his we name Ecclesiasticus, spoke thus concerning thee: "We speak many things, and yet attain not: and the whole consummation of our discourses is himself." [38] When therefore we shall have attained to thee, all those many things which we speak, and attain not, shall cease: one shalt thou abide, all things in all [39]; one shall we name thee without end, praising thee with one single voice, we ourselves also made one in thee. O Lord, one God, God the Trinity, whatsoever I have said in these Books that comes of thy prompting, may thy people acknowledge it: for what I have said that comes only of myself, I ask of thee and of thy people pardon.

[38] Ecclesiasticus 43:27.   [39] I Cor. 15:28.

The Spirit and the Letter

INTRODUCTION

PELAGIANISM BEGAN AS A PROTEST AGAINST THE decay of Christian morals. In the last years of the fourth century, the proscription of paganism by the edicts of Theodosius brought into the Church large numbers of "converts" whose Christianity can hardly have gone deeper than acceptance of baptism and profession of the name. There was enough in the Church's official teaching upon the efficacy of the sacraments to encourage such nominal Christians in the belief that membership of the Church was all that was necessary for salvation. The growth and spread of monasticism, itself in great part a reaction against the worldliness of churchmen, had made familiar the notion of a double standard of morality: for those who would be "perfect," strict compliance with the severest exhortations of the Gospels; for the rest, a life of compromise in varying degrees. Moreover, in the Western Church human nature had for long been painted in darker colours than in the Eastern, with a greater stress upon the lasting consequences of the Fall. Men had learnt to acknowledge the universality of sin and the weakness of the human will as facts which compelled reliance upon those means of salvation which the Church provided.

We know nothing for certain about the early life of Pelagius. But he had certainly been in Rome for twenty years, perhaps for thirty, when the onset of Alaric and the Goths in 410 drove him with the crowd of refugees first to Africa and then to the East. He had come to Rome, likely enough, from his native Britain as a young man seeking to prepare himself for a civil career; but he had soon found his vocation, not in the priesthood nor in the monastery (though he was often called a "monk"), but in the exercise of a layman's mission to the upper circles of the more or less Christianized Roman society of the day. He saw himself called to "stop the rot"—to restore the slackened vigour of Christian life by recalling the Roman to his ancient ideal of manliness (*virtus*), and the Christian to the inflexible demands of Christ. We know that the first impression of Pelagius which Augustine derived from the reading of his book *On Human Nature* was that of "a man fired with a burning indignation against those who instead of laying the blame for their sins upon their human wills put it upon their natural constitution as men, and seek to make that nature their excuse." [1]

The religion of Pelagius was firmly based upon two axioms: that God is just, and that man is responsible—which means free. He thought of the divine justice as the character of a Lawgiver who is also Judge, who rewards and punishes men according to their deeds. In God's justice there can be no respect of persons: justice forbids the showing favour (*gratia*) to one man rather than another. A just God can give an unfair start to no-one. And he can command nothing which any man is unable to perform: the existence of a divine command necessarily implies ability in all to whom it is given to obey it. All men *can* keep the commandments of God "if they will." But that is to say that nothing counts for God's judgment of the individual but his own responsible actions. God will distribute his rewards and his punishments strictly according to merit, and merit is what each man *earns* by what he *does*. It is open to all Christians without exception to set themselves, by a life in accordance with the Gospel ideal of poverty, chastity, and well-doing, to earn the supreme rewards which only such a life can win. And if it is open to all, it is incumbent upon all.

A pastoral activity such as that of Pelagius, inspired by this rigid moralism, could no doubt be pursued for a time without compelling attention to its theological implications. But it could not long avoid a clash with the sacramental and devotional practice of the Church. It was too late in the day to open a campaign against infant baptism, and the Pelagians did not attempt it. But the Church knew one and only one baptism "for the remission of sins": the form of the sacrament was the same for infants as for adults. If there is no guilt but where there has been responsible action, how can the infant need forgiveness? and if he needs no forgiveness, has Christ not died for him? Again, the Pelagian homiletic insisted that sinlessness (*impeccantia*) was a condition achievable by any man in this life. Yet the universality

[1] *De Natura et Gratia*, 1 (i).

of sin was not only a fact asserted by unequivocal texts of
Scripture (Ps. 143:2; Rom. 3:23; I John 1:8): it was implied by
the petition for forgiveness in the Lord's Prayer, which every
Christian however saintly must repeat all his days.

It was therefore on these two points—the significance of infant baptism, and the possibility of avoiding sin—that Pelagianism was first challenged. Pelagius himself seems to have been
aware of the danger and anxious to avoid a conflict. It was the
common Christian tradition in East and West alike that Adam's
transgression involved the whole human race in a predicament
from which salvation is through Christ alone. But the Greek
Fathers in general thought of this predicament as *mortality*, and
they were not exercised by the question of fallen man's status
as a moral agent—the effect of the Fall upon man's capacity to
do right. They followed Origen in holding that self-determina-
tion is an essential characteristic of the created spirit: fallen man
retains that power of deliberate choice without which there can
be neither virtue nor vice. And this had been maintained in the
West, both by Tertullian as the basis of his doctrine of merit, and
later by Ambrose. But Tertullian had held the theory known as
Traducianism, according to which every child derives both soul
and body from his parents, and therefore inherits a nature in
which both soul and body suffer from corruption. Tertullian's
Traducianism, however, regarded the soul itself as material, and
was therefore unacceptable to later Latin Fathers in the form
he had given it. The alternative theory of the soul's origin was
Creationism, as generally held by the Greeks: viz, that every
soul is created at birth by the immediate act of God. But this
view made it difficult to attach any "original defect" (*vitium
originis*) to the soul, and so favoured the tendency, which in fact
displayed itself in Alexandrian theology, to find the source of
moral evil in the flesh. In the third century, Origen in Palestine
and Cyprian in Africa had suggested in similar though vague
terms that the baptism of infants implies some kind of defilement which is inseparable from the process of natural birth.
Here there was serious danger of playing into the hands of
Manichaeanism—a danger which the Pelagians were not slow
to detect and exploit.

The matter was bound up with the exegesis of Romans 5.
The argument of Paul in that chapter is best interpreted
as teaching not a physical inheritance of sin but a mystical
solidarity of mankind "in Adam" analogous to the unity of
Christians "in Christ." On these lines Ambrose, Bishop of Milan

when Pelagius settled in Rome, taught that "we have all sinned in the first man," that "Adam is in each one of us," that "in Adam I fell, and in him I have incurred guilt." At Rome, Pelagius had written his *Commentary on the Epistles of St. Paul*, in which he takes the language of Romans 5 to mean simply that "those who sin as Adam did, die in like manner," i.e., that both sin and the spiritual (not physical) death which is its consequence come from the following of Adam's example. Nevertheless, he had been careful (as Augustine noted when the *Commentary* first came into his hands) not to associate himself with the objections which he adduces, on Rom. 5:15, of "those who oppose the Traducianist doctrine"; though he added that the same school of thought, on the Creationist theory, will urge that "it is unjust that a soul born to-day and not derived from the substance (*massa*) of Adam, should bear the ancient sin of another," and that "reason forbids that God who remits a man's own sins should impute to him another's." [2] This last observation recalls a well-known phrase of Cyprian's, who in discussing infant baptism had said that the infant "receives remission not of his own but of another's sins." [3]

It was not Pelagius himself, but his less wary disciple Caelestius, whose activities provoked the first official condemnation of Pelagian doctrine. He had come to Africa like his master as a refugee from Rome in 410; and he was summoned before a synod of bishops at Carthage (at which Augustine was not present) to condemn a number of propositions attributed to him, of which the most important were (1) that Adam's sin had injured no-one but himself, (2) that infants come into the world in the same state of innocence as belonged to Adam before his fall, (3) that even before the coming of Christ there had been men whose lives were sinless (so that *a fortiori* under the Christian dispensation the avoidance of sin is no impossible ideal). Of Caelestius's defence we know only that he claimed (as he reasonably might) that the Traducianist theory of the transmission of sin was not Catholic dogma, and that he admitted the propriety of infant baptism. It is probable that he explained this admission by interpreting the sacrament as one of adoption into Christ's Sonship, and by making a distinction between "eternal life" and the "kingdom of heaven": saying that the unbaptized infant dying without actual sin is not excluded from

2 See the text in Souter's edition of Pelagius's *Expositions of Thirteen Epistles of St. Paul.*
3 Cyprian, *Ep.* LXIV, 5.

eternal life, whereas Christian baptism (in accordance with John 3:5) is necessary for entry into the "kingdom." [4]

Caelestius was condemned, and left Africa for the East. But the dissemination of his ideas had caused so much stir in Africa that Marcellinus, the imperial legate who presided in 411 at the great conference with the Donatists, wrote to consult Augustine, with whom he was intimate, on the questions at issue. Augustine, though at the moment much exercised by the troublesome aftermath of the conference, replied with the first of his anti-Pelagian works—*On the Deserts and Remission of Sins.* The first Book deals with the bearing of the Church's baptismal practice on the doctrine of "original sin," dismisses the attempted distinction between eternal life and the kingdom of God, and insists that the text of Rom. 5:12 can only mean that sin and death pass from Adam to his descendants "by propagation," not "by imitation." "As he in whom all are made alive not only offered himself as a pattern of righteousness to be imitated, but also gives to the faithful that altogether hidden grace of his Spirit, which he pours unseen even into infants: so he in whom all die not only is the example imitated by those who voluntarily transgress the commandment of God, but also has infected in himself with the hidden corruption of his carnal desire all those who come of his seed." [5] This passage makes it clear enough that Augustine sees the Pauline contrast between Adam and Christ as one between flesh and spirit: in his view, the mystery of original sin is bound up with physical heredity, while the mystery of grace is purely spiritual, though sacramentally conveyed.

The subject of the second Book is the Pelagian doctrine of "sinlessness." Augustine begins by admitting that we cannot deny the power of God to bring a man into a "state of grace" in which he should become altogether free from sin; but he thinks that the testimony of Scripture and of the confessions of holy men tends to show that no-one has in fact reached such a condition. He next asks, Why should this be so? "If it be possible, divine grace lending its aid to the human will, for men to be without sin, the question may be put, Why then are they not? A very simple and true answer would be, Because they have not the will. If I am asked, But why have they not?—we shall need longer to make that plain. I may however, without prejudice to more careful enquiry, say shortly this: Men *will* not do

---

[4] See Augustine, *De Peccato Originali*, 3 (iii) (iv).
[5] *De Pecc. Mer.*, I, 10 (ix).

what is right, either because the right is hidden from them, or because they find no delight in it. For the strength of our will to anything is proportionate to the assurance of our knowledge of its goodness, and to the warmth of our delight in it. Thus ignorance and infirmity are failings which hinder the will from being moved to perform a good action or to abstain from a bad one. But that what was hidden may become clear, what delighted not may become sweet—this belongs to the grace of God which aids the wills of men. If they lack that aid, the cause lies no less in themselves and not in God, whether they be predestined for damnation because of the wickedness of pride, or for judgment and instruction against their pride, if they be children of mercy." [6] This "short answer" gives us the essence of Augustinianism. Augustine could not know how much "longer" he would need to account for men's unwillingness to do the right. But what he has said here not only announces the theme which he was to develop in *The Spirit and the Letter*: it lays down the criterion by which he was always to test the claim of Pelagians that in their teaching the grace of God was upheld and not denied.

Marcellinus himself was the first to ask for a "longer" explanation. He thought it paradoxical to concede, as Augustine did, that the achievement of "sinlessness" was a theoretical possibility, and yet to deny not only that it ever has been achieved, but that there either has been or ever can be any instance of a completely sinless human life, except in the case of Christ himself. Augustine responded to his request for a solution of this difficulty by writing within the year (412) his treatise on *The Spirit and the Letter*, which is occupied entirely with an exposition of the doctrine of Grace, based on an exegesis of Paul's teaching in the Epistle to the Romans, with the saying of II Cor. 3:6—"the letter killeth, but the Spirit giveth life"—as text. Augustine agrees with the comment of Pelagius on this text, that the opposition of "letter" and "spirit" is not that of literal and allegorical (or "spiritual") interpretation of Scripture. But whereas Pelagius on Rom. 3:28 had taken the "works of the law," "apart from" which "a man is justified by faith," to mean the external ceremonies of circumcision, Sabbath, etc., Augustine shows convincingly that the whole argument of the Epistle is concerned with the law as a system of ethical precepts which can do nothing but convince of sin, and with grace as the divinely given power to fulfil these same

6 *De Pecc. Mer.*, II, 26 (xvii).

precepts: "what is enjoined under the law of works, is granted
under the law of faith" (§ 22). "The divine assistance for the
working of righteousness consists, not in God's gift of the Law,
full as it is of good and holy commands, but in that our will
itself, without which we cannot do the good, is aided and uplifted by the imparting of the Spirit of grace" (§ 20). "Grasp
this clear difference between the old covenant and the new:
that there the law is written upon tables, here upon hearts, so
that the fear imposed by the first from without becomes the delight inspired by the second from within, and he whom the
letter that killeth there made a transgressor, is here made a
lover by the Spirit that giveth life. Then you can no longer say
that God assists us in the working of righteousness, and works in
us both to will and to do according to his good pleasure, inasmuch as he makes us hear with the outward sense the commandments of righteousness. No, it is because he gives increase within
us, by the shedding abroad of charity in our hearts through the
Holy Spirit which is given us" (§ 42).

In all the long series of Augustine's anti-Pelagian writings,
there is none that can compare with *The Spirit and the Letter* for
calm and confident grasp of Christian principles. Here Augustine is not debating: there is none of the wearisome eristic of the
later treatises. He is going straight to the fountainhead of all
Christian faith in the grace of God, and triumphantly vindicat-
ing that faith with an understanding of Paul more profound
than any shown by earlier interpreters. Augustine's exegesis is
often mistaken in detail, and we know now that the Pauline
"justification" is not the equivalent, as he thought it was, of
"being made righteous." It remains true to-day that if we
would penetrate beneath the surface of language and logical
form to the vital springs of Paul's religion, we shall hardly find
a better guide than this little book.

For our understanding of Augustine himself, however, a
special interest attaches to the latter part of the work, in which,
having completed his exposition of Paul, he turns to examine
two objections to the doctrine of grace which has been set forth.

(1) If grace alone enables men to fulfil the law, what is to
be said of good works outside the Gospel and the Church? Paul
speaks in Rom. 2:14 of "Gentiles which have not the law,
doing by nature the things contained in the law." Now Augustine cannot surrender his conviction that saving grace is the
grace of our Lord Jesus Christ. He begins by suggesting that
Paul is here referring to Gentile *Christians*; but he is not quite

happy about this (clearly mistaken) interpretation, and expects it to be disputed. There is, he says, a possible alternative. The image of God belongs to the created nature of humanity, and it is ineffaceable however obscured by sin. Its survival may enable even the heathen to recognize and at least in part to perform the commandments of God. For what is written upon the heart in the new covenant is still the same law which "was not altogether effaced by growing old." But he will not admit that such "natural" righteousness can be inspired by the. true love of God which is the gift of grace. It cannot bring the salvation which is through grace alone: it can only avail, as no doubt it will in God's justice avail, for mitigation of punishment. Augustine could have reached no other conclusion without allowing the truth of one of the propositions charged against Caelestius, viz., "that the law admits to the Kingdom of Heaven as well as the gospel." With the general tradition of the Church, he believed that the saints of the Old Testament were not excluded from salvation, but this could only be because in the light of prophecy they had believed in the Christ who was to come.

(2) The second objection is one which is both more fundamental in itself and more important for the controversy. Does not the operation of grace, so conceived, violate human freedom? Augustine's answer is confused by his carelessness in the use of terms. He starts from the expression *liberum arbitrium*, usually translated "free will," but more properly "free choice" or "free decision"; and he maintains that it is something which has to be *conferred* by grace. In the order or process of salvation, faith comes first, then grace which heals the sick soul, then the *liberum arbitrium* which the healing makes possible, and then the love of righteousness which fulfils the law. Here *liberum arbitrium* is said not to exist before the work of grace: it is the Christian freedom which Augustine generally calls "liberty." But he proceeds to ask in what sense the faith with which the whole series begins can be said to be "in our power"; and he answers that the faith in God which is belief in his promises must like all belief be a voluntary act, and therefore is in our power because we "perform it if we will." Then arises the question, Whence comes the *will* to believe? From God's gift, or from the *liberum arbitrium* which is "implanted in us by nature"? And now this *liberum arbitrium* is described as a "neutral power," "conferred upon the rational soul in the way of nature" by God's creative act, and therefore itself (as Pelagius also insisted) the

gift of God. God will judge men according to their *use* of this gift. But the good use of *liberum arbitrium*, which shows itself in the will to believe, depends upon God's "calling" in the form of those presentations or "suasions" which come to us by his providence in our day-to-day experience. Sixteen years earlier, in his answer to the *Questions of Simplicianus* written before he knew anything of Pelagius, he had developed this idea of the calling of God. "We are enjoined to believe, in order that we may receive the gift of the Holy Spirit and the power to do good works through love. But who can believe, unless he be touched by some kind of calling, some testifying of the truth? Who has it in his own power to bring it about that his mind receive such impressions as may move his will to faith?" [7] In *The Spirit and the Letter*, the consent to this calling is said to "belong to our own will"—but only as the act of acceptance: the crucial text, "What hast thou which thou hast not received?" is still upheld, and God is said to "work in us the will to believe."

The later history of the Pelagian controversy does not concern us here. But it is worth while to examine the attempts of Pelagius, during the years that passed between 412 and his final condemnation in 418, to defend himself against the charge of making the grace of God of none effect. In 415 his treatise *On Human Nature* came into Augustine's hands, and Augustine quotes freely from it in his book *On Nature and Grace*, written in that year. Pelagius had begun by arguing for the *possibility* of being without sin—which (as we have seen) Augustine was prepared to allow. Pelagius went on to deny that sin could "weaken" or "alter" nature, and to assert that sin cannot be a personal action unless it is voluntary, which implies that it is avoidable. "I shall be told," he said, "that many are disturbed at my appearing to maintain a man's ability to be without sin, as though it did not come through the grace of God." And he exclaims indignantly that he has insisted upon the derivation of this very ability from God as the author of nature. That we are "able not to sin" is not, he says, a matter of will or choice (*arbitrium*) at all: it is a "natural necessity." We *cannot* be without the ability to avoid sin: that is how God has made us. [8]

In this same year (415) Pelagius had been acquitted of heresy by a synod of Palestinian Bishops. Confronted with statements of Caelestius to the effect that "the grace and help of God is not given for particular actions, but consists in the power of free choice, or in law and teaching," and that "God's grace is given

---

[7] *De Div. Quaest. ad Simpl.,* I, 21.   [8] *De Nat. et Grat.,* 52 ff.

according to our deserts, since if he gave it to sinners he must appear to be unjust," Pelagius had answered: "I have never held such views, and I anathematize anyone who may hold them."[9] Whether this disclaimer was entirely sincere it is diffi-cult to say. But in the long profession of orthodoxy which he submitted to the pope in 417, there were only a dozen words on the question of grace: "while confessing the reality of free choice, we maintain that we always have need of the help of God."[10]. What he meant by the "help of God," he had made clear enough in the work *On Freedom of Choice*, composed after his acquittal by the Palestinian Synod, from which we have extracts in Augustine's treatise *On the Grace of Christ*, written in 418 after the final condemnation of the heresy. Pelagius had analysed moral activity into (1) ability, (2) will, and (3) performance, ascribing the first to God's gift and the two latter to "our-selves." "It is God," he wrote, "who has given us the ability to will and to work, and by the help of his grace continually assists this ability itself"; and such assistance is given "through doctrine and revelation," whereby God "opens the eyes of the heart, shows what is to come, uncovers the wiles of the devil, and illuminates us with the gift of heavenly grace." God "works in us to will" by the promise of reward, by the revelation of wis-dom, and by all manner of good counsel. "That we are able to do what is good, comes of him who gave us this ability: that we do good, belongs to ourselves." It is Christ "who absolves be-lievers from all their sins through baptism, and then encourages them to perfect holiness by the imitation of himself, and over-comes the force of evil habit by his example of all virtues."[11]

The "divine aid" thus recognized by Pelagius appears to coincide closely enough with those presentations or "suasions," experienced by the individual in the course of his life, in which Augustine saw the calling of God, and which he commonly describes as the divine "preparation" of the will. If Augustine had maintained, consistently and unambiguously, that the will's "consent" to this calling must be a genuinely free act of personal decision, the cleavage between him and Pelagius would have been less complete: indeed his position would have superficially resembled what was later known as Semi-Pelagianism—the doctrine that men have power to make the initial act of faith

[9] *De Gest. Pelag.*, 30 (xiv).
[10] The *Libellus Fidei* is given in the Appendix to Tom. X of Augustine's works in the Benedictine edition.
[11] *De Grat. Christi*, 7, 8, 11, 26, 43.

"of themselves." He was aware that he himself had begun by holding a similar doctrine, and he dated his realization that faith is wholly the gift of God from that closer study of the Epistle to the Romans to which he had been drawn at the beginning of his episcopate. Yet in *The Spirit and the Letter*, as we have seen, he was still able to say that the consent of the will to the calling of God is "our own"; and he finds no occasion to correct this statement in the *Retractations*, in which the change in his views is frankly admitted. But in the work *On Grace and Free Choice*, written in 426 just before the *Retractations* were finished, he had declared roundly that "God brings about our willing *without us.*" [12] He seems never to have perceived that faith *is* the will's consent or response to the calling of God, and that this consent is not always once for all, but may need continually to be renewed. The effect of the Pelagian controversy was to sharpen the dilemma—either God's work *or* ours. That the dilemma is false, Augustine himself was able even in his old age to recognize on occasion. In his earliest attempt to deal with problems arising from the Epistle to the Romans, he had written: "That we believe, is our own act: that we work what is good, belongs to him who gives the Holy Spirit to them that believe." He comments in the *Retractations* (i, 23): "I should not have said that, if I had known then that faith itself is found among the gifts of God, which are given in the same Spirit. Both therefore [faith and works] are ours, through the choice (*arbitrium*) of our will, and yet both are given through the Spirit of faith and charity." That was to fall back upon the true paradox of grace as Paul expressed it: "Crucified with Christ, I live: yet not I, but Christ liveth in me." "He that is joined unto the Lord, is one Spirit."

There lies the ultimate difference between Pelagian and Augustinian religion. The theology of Pelagius was the theology of deism: his ethics were the ethics of naturalism. There was no room in his version of Christianity for "Christ in you, the hope of glory," nor for the real indwelling of the Holy Spirit in the believer. Augustine saw that in such a version the Gospel has disappeared; and we owe it to him that the Church has not parted company with Paul.

[12] *De Grat. et Lib. Arb.*, 33 (xvii).

The Spirit and the Letter

ARGUMENT

[The possibility of moral perfection for a man in this life may reasonably be allowed, even if Christ be the only instance of it. For God *could* do many things which he does not do; and human righteousness is itself a divine work (§§ 1–3).

What we cannot admit is that the human will is sufficient of itself to reach, or even to move towards, such perfection. For that, it must be divinely aided—and that not merely by its creation with freedom to choose, and by instruction in the moral ideal (§ 4). A man must also receive the Holy Spirit's gift of that delight in righteousness which is the love of God (§ 5).

Instruction in the Law of God is, by itself, the "letter that killeth" (II Cor. 3:6). The meaning of "the letter" in this text is not to be limited to Scripture as understood literally, as against its allegorical interpretation. The "letter" may also stand for the moral precepts of the Law, which must necessarily be taken literally; and so "the Spirit that giveth life" may mean, not "spiritual" or allegorical interpretation of Scripture, but the Spirit's gift of the desire for what is good (§§ 6, 7).

This can be shown by a study of Paul's argument in Rom., chs. 5–7. His subject is the contrast of Law and Grace (§§ 8–11), the grace which he knew from his own experience (§ 12). He meets the Jew's boast in the possession of the Law, by showing that the Law avails nothing if it be not kept. The Law brings only the knowledge of sin (§§ 13, 14); and the righteousness which keeps the Law is not product of men's will, but is the "righteousness of God," i.e., the righteousness which God imparts to men upon faith in Christ (§§ 15, 16). "Glorying," i.e., the conceit of righteousness, is "cut out" by the "law of faith," the thankful acknowledgment of the righteousness of God (§§ 17, 18), which Paul has proclaimed at the beginning of the Epistle, showing that if glory be not given to God only, the natural knowledge of God as Creator cannot save men from the corruption of sin (§§ 19, 20). Paul does not mean that the "law of works" belongs to Judaism and the "law of faith" to Christianity; for the moral law ("thou shalt not covet") is equally valid for both (§ 21). The difference between the two is that "what is enjoined with threatenings under the law of works, is granted to belief under the law of faith" (§ 22).

That the "letter that killeth" is in fact the moral law summarized in the Decalogue, is as plain from the whole context of II Cor., ch. 3 (§§ 23, 24), as from the argument of Rom., ch. 7 (§§ 25, 26). The passage of II Cor. suggests a contrast between Sinai and Pentecost, the "finger of God" which wrote the Law on tables of stone, and the "finger of God" as the Holy Spirit writing upon the heart (§§ 27, 28): the one working through fear, the other through love (§ 29), the one a "letter" which is external, the other an inward presence (§§ 30, 31).

In this same passage Paul refers to the new Covenant spoken of in Jeremiah 31 (§§ 32, 33). The new differs from the old, not by substituting a new law, but by giving the power to fulfil the Law (§ 34): the new Covenant heals the sickness of the "old" man (§ 35). Again, the promises attached to the old Covenant were earthly, material benefits (§ 36): the promise of the new Covenant is a spiritual good, the life which is the knowledge of God (§§ 37–39). The promise is given to the true Israel "after the spirit," that is, to God's elect (§ 40) to whom he grants the vision of himself (§§ 41, 42).

To the doctrine of Grace, so stated, it may be objected: (i) That Paul himself speaks of "Gentiles who do *by nature* the things contained in the Law" (Rom. 2:14). But this cannot contradict his teaching that all true righteousness is of grace (§ 43). Either (*a*) these Gentiles are Christian believers (§§ 44, 45), the Law being "written on their hearts" as heirs of the new Covenant (§ 46), and the "nature" by which they fulfil the Law being the image of God restored by grace (§ 47). Or (*b*) they are heathen in whom some trace of the divine image remains: as "strangers from the grace of Christ," their good works cannot bring them salvation, though they may receive a lighter punishment (§§ 48, 49). On either interpretation it remains true that no man can claim credit for his own fulfilment of the Law (§ 50): a man must be "justified" *before* he can do the works of which it is written that "if a man do, he shall live in them"(§ 51).

(ii) That the doctrine would deprive man of the freedom to choose. We may reply that this freedom is "established" by the grace which heals the soul (§ 52). But since the gift of grace only follows upon faith, we have to ask whether faith itself is "in our own power." Power may be defined as "will *plus* capacity to act" (§ 53). The act of belief involves the consent of the will: no one believes "unwillingly," nor is it true that all *willing* is of God, since in any case the evil will is not (§ 54). The belief in God, which is faith, is "in our power" because it is a willing act (§ 55); but it must be the belief of sons, not slaves, of love, not fear, and love is always the gift of the Spirit (§ 56).

Whence then comes the "will to believe"? from "nature" or from God's gift? In either case we ask, Why is it not universal? (§ 57). We may hold that the natural gift of freedom to choose is morally neutral, and that whether we use it rightly or wrongly the will of God is undefeated; for God renders to all according to their works (§§ 58, 59). But the will to believe is not only a function of the natural freedom of choice: it depends on the presentations which come to us in experience, whether objectively or subjectively caused; and of these God is the author. Our own consent to his calling is necessary, but this consent is itself an act of acceptance, by which we receive God's gift (§ 60).

Summary and conclusion (§§ 61–66)

Perfect righteousness in this life is not an impossibility, if we allow (as we must) that our righteousness is a work of God. For it presumes no more than the perfect knowledge of what is right, and an insuperable delight in it. Normally, both our knowledge of God's will, and our love of him, are in this life imperfect. The present life may indeed show a "lesser righteousness," in which there is no sin in the sense of consent to evil desire. But even so we must still pray: "Forgive us our trespasses." God *could* remove from a man all need for such a prayer; but as far as we know, he does not.]

THE TEXT

1 (i).

My beloved son Marcellinus,

I sent to you not long ago two essays, in the first of which I discussed the practice of infant baptism, and in the second the idea of moral perfection as an end never reached or likely to be reached by any man in this life, save only by the one Mediator who endured the trials of humanity in the likeness of sinful flesh, remaining altogether without sin. And now you tell me that you are struck by my speaking, in the second of these essays, of the possibility of a man's being without sin, if God's help be given and his own will not lacking, and yet asserting that there neither has been nor will be any man, except him alone in whom "all shall be made alive,"[1] to reach such perfection while he lives on earth. You think it a paradox to claim as possible a thing of which no instance can be given. Yet I suppose you would not doubt that there has been no case of a camel's passing through the eye of a needle, though Christ said that even this is possible for God.[2] Scripture tells you that twelve thousand legions of angels could have fought to save Christ from his passion; yet it did not happen.[3] Scripture tells you that the nations could have been cut off all at once from the land given to the children of Israel; yet God willed that it should only be by little and little.[4] We can think of any number of other things which we admit might have happened or may happen, though we can allege no instance of their occurrence. We should not then deny the possibility of a man's being without sin, simply because there is no man, save him who is not only man but very God, in whom we can show this perfection actually achieved.

2 (ii). You may object, that the cases I have mentioned of things possible yet not actual are works of God; whereas the avoidance of sin belongs to man's own working: man can do no better work than that which results in a righteousness full, perfect and complete in every part; and you think it not credible, if such a work can be achieved by man, that there neither has been nor is nor will be anyone in this life who has achieved it. But you should consider that though this pursuit is indeed man's business, it too is a divine gift; and so you should not doubt it to be a divine work. "For it is God," says the apostle, "who worketh in you both to will and to do, according to his good will."[5] 3. Accordingly we need not be disturbed by those who maintain that any man lives or has lived in this world entirely without sin: we must press them to establish their assertion if they can. There are texts of Scripture which seem to me to lay it down that no man in this life, free though he be to choose, is ever found without sin. For example: "Enter not into judgment with thy servant, for in thy sight shall no man living be justified."[6] If anyone can show that this and the like texts do not

---

[1] I Cor. 15:22.   [2] Matt. 19:24, 26.   [3] Matt. 26:53.
[4] Judg. 2:20 ff.   [5] Phil. 2:13.   [6] Ps. 143:2.

mean what they appear to say, and can prove that there has been a man or men whose life has been sinless, only a very grudging critic would refuse to accept his demonstration—I will not say without opposition, but rather with enthusiasm. On the other hand, supposing (as I incline to think) that no-one is or was or will be so perfect in purity, it would not so far as I can judge be an error either serious or mischievous to maintain the contrary, the mistake being naturally caused by a generous disposition; provided that the holder of such an opinion do not hold himself to be an example of perfection, unless his conscience has really and clearly declared it to him.

4. But there is an opinion that calls for sharp and vehement resistance—I mean the belief that the power of the human will can of itself, without the help of God, either achieve perfect righteousness or advance steadily towards it. When we press upon those who so think the presumption of supposing this to happen without divine aid, they check themselves from venturing a statement which they see would be irreligious and intolerable. But they say that the reason why it does not happen without divine aid is that God has both created man in possession of a will that chooses freely, and teaches him by the gift of his commandments the right way of life; so that God's help consists in the removal by instruction of man's ignorance, so that he can know what is to be avoided in his actions and what is to be sought; and thus, by means of the power of free choice belonging to him by nature, he may enter upon the road pointed out to him, and by a life of self-control, justice and piety may merit attainment to the life which is both blessed and eternal.

5 (iii). Our own assertion, on the contrary, is this: that the human will is divinely assisted to do the right in such manner that, besides man's creation with the endowment of freedom to choose, and besides the teaching by which he is instructed how he ought to live, he receives the Holy Spirit, whereby there arises in his soul the delight in and the love of God, the supreme and changeless Good. This gift is his here and now, while he walks by faith, not yet by sight: that having this as earnest of God's free bounty, he may be fired in heart to cleave to his Creator, kindled in mind to come within the shining of the true light; and thus receive from the source of his being the only real well-being. Free choice alone, if the way of truth is hidden, avails for nothing but sin; and when the right action and the true aim has begun to appear clearly, there is still no doing, no devotion, no good life, unless it be also delighted in and loved.

And that it may be loved, the love of God is shed abroad in our hearts, not by the free choice whose spring is in ourselves, but through the Holy Spirit which is given us.[7]

6 (iv). The truth is that the teaching which gives us the commandment of self-control and uprightness of life, remains, without the presence of the life-giving Spirit, a letter that killeth. That text—"The letter killeth, but the spirit giveth life"[8]—is naturally taken to mean that we are not to understand the figurative sayings of Scripture in their literal sense, which may be irrational, but to look for their deeper significance, and find nourishment for the inward man in a spiritual understanding of them[9]; inasmuch as "to be carnally minded is death, but to be spiritually minded is life and peace."[10] There is much for example in the Song of Songs which if carnally understood must encourage the passion of lustful desire and not the fruit of enlightened charity. But this is not the only meaning of the apostle's saying: "the letter killeth, but the Spirit giveth life." There is also, and perhaps more important, the sense which he clearly indicates elsewhere, in the words: "I was unaware of concupiscence, did not the law say, Thou shalt not covet." And a little further on: "Sin taking occasion by the commandment, deceived me, and through it slew me."[11] There is the letter killing! The words "Thou shalt not covet" are no figurative saying, not to be understood literally; they are a most plain and wholesome command, the fulfiller of which will be altogether without sin. The apostle has purposely chosen a general all-embracing precept, to convey the voice of the law forbidding all sin; for there is no sin whose commission does not begin with coveting. Accordingly, the law which gives this command is good and praiseworthy. But where the Holy Spirit's aid is not given, leading us to covet good[12] instead of evil, that is, shedding charity abroad in our hearts—there assuredly this law, good though it be, increases by its prohibition the evil desire. A continuing flow of water in the same

[7] Rom. 5:5; this text, to which Augustine is continually returning, remained for him the most conclusive scriptural refutation of Pelagianism. It must be noted that he always takes it to refer, not to God's love for us but to our love for God (cf. § 56, *ad fin.*); but since for him love in us is the product of God's love for us, he is not really misusing the text.

[8] II Cor. 3:6.

[9] This was the sense in which Augustine had heard the text employed by Ambrose at Milan, before his conversion (cf. *Conf.*, VI, 4).

[10] Rom. 8:6.   [11] Rom. 7:7, 11.

[12] Here Augustine uses the phrase *concupiscentia bona* as = *caritas*.

direction gains in impetus when an obstacle is interposed, and after overcoming its resistance breaks forth with added volume in a more headlong current. The coveted object grows somehow more attractive through being forbidden. That is how sin "deceives through the commandment, and through it kills," provoking the transgression which does not exist where there is no law.[13]

7 (v). It will be well to consider and (as God shall help us) expound this whole passage of Paul's Epistle. I wish to show, if I can, that the apostle's words: "the letter killeth, but the Spirit giveth life," do not refer primarily to figurative modes of speech—though that sense may also fit them—but rather to the law's express forbidding of what is evil. That being demonstrated, it will be the more evident that the good life is a divine gift: not only because God has given man the power of free choice, without which moral life were impossible; not only because he has given the commandment to teach us how to live; but because through the Holy Spirit he sheds abroad charity in the hearts of those whom he foreknew that he might predestinate, predestinated that he might call, called that he might justify, and justified that he might glorify.[14] If I can make this clear, I think you will see that the proposed objection falls to the ground: I mean the argument that nothing is to be called possible in the absence of an instance but works of God, like my case of the camel's passing through the needle's eye, and all else that with us is impossible but not with God; and that human righteousness cannot be included in this class, as belonging not to God's work but man's: so that there can be no reason for disbelieving in any example of its perfection, if that perfection is possible in this life. This argument, I say, must clearly fall to the ground, once we are assured that human righteousness itself, though not arising independently of man's will, is yet to be ascribed to the operation of God. We cannot deny the possibility of its perfection in this life, just because all things are possible for God—both what he does by his own will alone, and what he has ordained to be accomplished by himself with the co-operation of the wills of his creatures. Anything in either kind that he does not do will be without example in fact, but will have the reason of its possibility in God's power and the reason of its non-occurrence in God's wisdom. Such reason may be hidden from a man; but he must not forget his humanity, and attribute unwisdom to God because the wisdom of God exceeds his grasp.

[13] Rom. 4:15.   [14] Rom. 8:29 f.

8. Now consider the apostle's exposition in his Epistle to the Romans, in which he gives sufficient proof that his words to the Corinthians—"the letter killeth, but the Spirit giveth life"—are to be understood as we have said: in that the letter of the law, admonishing us to avoid sin, kills, if the life-giving Spirit be not present. For the law makes sin to be known rather than shunned, and, inasmuch as transgression of law is added to the evil of coveting, to be increased rather than diminished.

9 (vi). The apostle's aim is to commend the grace which came through Jesus Christ to all peoples, lest the Jews exalt themselves above the rest on account of their possession of the law. He says[15] that through one man sin and death entered into the human race, and through one man righteousness and eternal life—by the one pointing obviously to Adam and by the other to Christ. And he proceeds: "The law entered in that the offence might abound; but where the offence abounded, grace did much more abound, that as sin hath reigned unto death, even so might grace reign through righteousness unto eternal life by Jesus Christ our Lord." Next he puts to himself the question: "What shall we say then? Shall we continue in sin, that grace may abound? God forbid!" He has seen that perverse readers might put a perverse interpretation on what he has just said: "The law entered in that the offence might abound; but where the offence abounded, grace did much more abound." He might be taken to assert that because of the abounding of grace sin was profitable. He rejects this with his "God forbid!" and adds: "How shall we, that are dead to sin, live therein?" That is to say: "Since grace has effected for us our death to sin, to live therein would be nothing but ingratitude to grace." To praise the benefits of medicine does not imply a profit in the diseases and wounds which medicine heals. The higher our praise of medicine, the stronger is our censure and abhorrence of the hurts and diseases from which the admired art relieves us. So the praise and preaching of grace is the censure and condemnation of offences. Man needed to be shown the foulness of his malady. Against his wickedness not even a "holy and good" commandment[16] could avail: by it the wickedness was rather increased than diminished. For "the law entered in, that the offence might abound"; so that thus convicted and confounded he might see his need for God, not only as teacher but as helper to "direct his ways, lest any iniquity have dominion over him"[17]: that he should flee to the help of mercy for his healing, and so

15 Cf. Rom. 5:12—6:11.   16 Rom. 7:12.   17 Ps. 119:133.

where the offence abounded grace should yet more abound, not by the desert of the sinner, but through the aid of the succourer.

10. To this same healing medicine, mystically shown forth in Christ's passion and resurrection, the apostle points in his next words: "Know ye not, that so many of us as were baptized in Christ Jesus were baptized into his death? Therefore we are buried with him by baptism into death, that like as Christ rose from the dead through the glory of the Father, even so we also should walk in newness of life. For if we have been planted together in the likeness of his death, we shall be also in the likeness of his resurrection; knowing this, that our old man has been crucified with him, that the body of sin may be brought to nought, that henceforth we should not serve sin. For he that is dead, is justified from sin. Now if we be dead with Christ, we believe that we shall live together with him: knowing that Christ, rising from the dead, dieth no more, and death shall have no more dominion over him. For in that he died, he died unto sin once for all, but in that he liveth, he liveth unto God. So reckon ye also yourselves to be dead unto sin, but living unto God in Christ Jesus." It is plain enough that by the mystery of the Lord's death and resurrection is signified the setting of our old life and the rising of the new: there is shown forth the destruction of sin and the renewal of righteousness. Surely so great a benefit can come to man not by the letter of the law, but only by faith in Jesus Christ.

11 (vii). This holy consideration preserves the sons of men, who "hope in the protection of God's wings," that they may be "satisfied with the fatness of his house," and "drink of the river of his pleasures." For "with him is the fountain of life, and in his light we shall see light: he extends his mercy unto them that know him, and his righteousness unto them that are of an upright heart."[18] He extends his mercy, not because they know him but in order that they may know him: he extends his righteousness whereby he justifies the ungodly, not because they are upright in heart, but that they may become upright in heart. This consideration does not lead astray into pride—the fault that arises from trust in self and making the self the spring of its own life. To go that way is to draw back from the fountain of life, whose draught alone gives the righteousness which is good life, and from that changeless light by whose participation the reasonable soul is as it were set burning so as to be itself a light made and created. So was John "a burning and a shining

[18] Ps. 36:7 ff.

light,"[19] yet one that knew whence came his shining. "Of his fullness," says the Gospel, "we have received"—of the fullness, that is, of him in comparison with whom John was no light. For "that was the true light that lighteth every man that cometh into this world."[20] Accordingly, in the Psalm from which we have quoted the words: "Extend thy mercy to them that know thee, and thy righteousness unto them that are of upright heart:" it continues: "Let not the foot of pride come upon me, and let not the hands of sinners disturb me. There are they fallen, all that work wickedness: they are cast out, and were not able to stand." By the ungodliness which makes a man ascribe to himself what belongs to God, he is driven into his own darkness, the works of iniquity. Those works assuredly he does himself, and for their accomplishment he is sufficient to himself. But the works of righteousness he cannot do, except as he receives of that fountain and that light, where there is life in need of nothing, where there is no change nor shadow of alteration.[21]

12. Paul the apostle, who chose to be called Paul (as I think) instead of his former name of Saul, simply to indicate his "littleness" as "the least of the apostles," contends with such vigour and zeal on behalf of this grace of God against the proud and arrogant presumers upon their own works, just because the manifestation of grace had been in himself more especially plain and notable. His own work, in vehement persecution of the Church of God, had earned for him condign penalty; but instead of condemnation he received mercy, instead of punishment he met with grace. Rightly then is he loud and eager above all in the defence of grace: he cares nothing for the malice of men without understanding in this profound and inscrutable matter, who twisted his wholesome sayings into a perverted sense. Unhesitatingly he preaches the gift of God, by which alone salvation comes to the sons of promise, the sons of divine goodness, the sons of grace and mercy, the sons of the New Testament. His greeting is always in these terms: "Grace to you and peace from God the Father and the Lord Jesus Christ."[22] And in his letter to the Romans this very matter is almost his sole concern—waging his fight with such manifold argument as to weary the reader's endeavour to follow: yet such weariness is profitable and wholesome, training rather than enfeebling the physique of the inward man.

13 (viii). From this argument come the words which I

[19] John 5:35.   [20] John 1:16, 9.
[21] James 1:17.   [22] E.g., I Cor. 1:3.

have already quoted; and also the passage in which he convicts the Jew, saying that he is named Jew and yet by no means carries out what he professes. "If thou art called a Jew, and restest in the law and makest thy boast in God and knowest his will, and approvest distinctions, being instructed out of the law: if thou art confident that thou thyself art a guide of the blind, a light of them which are in darkness, an instructor of the foolish, a teacher of babes, having the form of knowledge and truth in the law— thou therefore which teachest another, teachest thou not thyself? Thou that preachest against stealing, dost thou steal? thou that speakest against adultery, dost thou commit adultery? thou that abhorrest idols, dost thou do sacrilege? thou that makest thy boast in the law, through breaking the law dishonourest thou God? For the name of God is blasphemed among the Gentiles through you, as it is written. Circumcision indeed profiteth, if thou keep the law; but if thou be a breaker of the law, thy circumcision is made uncircumcision. Therefore if the uncircumcised keep the righteous acts of the law, shall not his uncircumcision be counted for circumcision? and shall not uncircumcision which is by nature, if it fulfil the law, judge thee who by the letter and circumcision art a breaker of the law? For he is not a Jew which is one in appearance, neither is that circumcision which is apparent in the flesh; but he is a Jew which is a Jew in the unseen and by circumcision of the heart, in the spirit not in the letter, whose praise is not of men but of God."[23] Here is shown the meaning of the words: "Thou makest thy boast in God." If one that was a Jew indeed should make his boast in God in the manner called for by grace, which is given not according to the merits of works, but freely, his praise would be of God and not of men. But they made their boast in God, as though they alone had deserved to receive his law, according to that verse of the Psalm: "He hath not so done unto any nation and hath not shown forth his judgments unto them." [24] Yet this law of God they supposed themselves to fulfil by their own righteousness, though they were rather its transgressors. And so its working for them was wrath, as sin multiplied, committed by those who knew it for sin: even those who did as the law commanded, without the help of the Spirit of grace, did it through fear of punishment and not from love of righteousness. Thus in God's sight there was not in their will that obedience which to the sight of men appeared in their work; they were the rather held guilty for that which God knew they

[23] Rom. 2:17 ff.   [24] Ps. 147:20.

would have chosen to commit, if it could have been without penalty. By "circumcision of the heart," Paul means a will pure of all unlawful coveting; and this comes not of the teaching and threatening of the letter, but of the helping and healing of the Spirit. Therefore is the praise of such not of men, but of God who by this grace supplies that to which praise is due—God of whom the Psalm says: "in the Lord shall my soul be praised," [25] and to whom it says: "with thee is my praise." [26] This is not the mind of those who will have praise rendered to God because they are men, but to themselves because they are righteous. [27]

14. What is their answer? "We do give praise," they say, "to God as author of our justification, inasmuch as he gave the law, by the study of which we know how we ought to live." They are deaf to the Scripture: "because from the law shall no flesh be justified before God." [28] It may be so before men; but not before him who sees into the very heart and inward will, and there perceives, even though the fearer of the law act otherwise, how he would act if he were given licence. We cannot suppose that the apostle means here, by the law by which no man is justified, the law of ancient rites, in which many commandments were figuratively conveyed (as in that of circumcision itself, to be received by infants upon the eighth day); for he goes on immediately to define that law of which he was speaking, in the words: "for through the law is the knowledge of sin." It is then the same law of which he says later: "I have not known sin, but through the law; for I was unaware of concupiscence, did not the law say, Thou shalt not covet." [29] In other words: "through the law is the knowledge of sin."

15 (ix). Here, perhaps, it will be rejoined by that human presumption which is ignorant of God's righteousness and eager to establish its own, [30] that the apostle had good cause to say: "from the law shall no man be justified"; since the law does but point out what is to be done or not done, in order that the will may carry out its promptings, and so man be justified not by the law's command but by his own free choice. Nay but, O man, consider what follows!—"But now without law the righteousness of God hath been manifested, witnessed to by law and prophets." [31] Can even the deaf fail to hear? "The righteousness

---

[25] Ps. 34:2.   [26] Ps. 22:25.

[27] The "general" argument for grace against Pelagianism: righteousness is a greater gift than existence.

[28] Rom. 3:20.   [29] Rom. 7:7.

[30] Rom. 10:3.   [31] Rom. 3:21.

of God hath been manifested." This is that righteousness of which they are ignorant who would establish their own, and will not be subject to that other. "The righteousness *of God*"— not the righteousness of man or the righteousness of our own will—the righteousness of God, not that by which God is righteous, but that wherewith he clothes man, when he justifies the ungodly. To this, law and prophets bear witness: the law, inasmuch as by its commands and its threatenings, and its justifying of no man, it gives ample token that man is justified by the gift of God through the help of the Spirit; and the prophets, because Christ's coming has fulfilled that which they foretold. For how does the apostle continue?—"The righteousness of God through the faith of Jesus Christ": that is, the faith whereby we believe in Christ. The "faith of Christ" here meant is not that by which Christ believes, any more than the righteousness of God is that by which God is righteous. Both are our own; called "of God" and "of Christ," because bestowed upon us by his bounty. Thus "the righteousness of God without law" is yet manifested not without the law; otherwise it could not have been witnessed to through the law. It is indeed a righteousness of God without law, because God confers it upon the believer through the Spirit of grace, without the help of the law. The law, that is, contributes nothing to God's saving act: through it he does but show man his weakness, that by faith he may take refuge in the divine mercy and be healed. It is said of God's wisdom, that "she beareth law and mercy on her tongue"[32]: law, by which the proud are held guilty, mercy, by which the humble are justified. Accordingly, there is a "righteousness of God through the faith of Jesus Christ unto all that believe; for there is no difference: all have sinned and are in want of the glory of God"—not of their own glory; for "what have they which they have not received? and if they have received, why do they glory as though they had not received?"[33] They are in want of the glory of God; and (observe the conclusion!) "are justified freely by his grace." Justified, then, not by the law, not by their own will, but "freely by his grace": not that the justification is without our will, but the weakness of our will is discovered by the law, so that grace may restore the will and the restored will may fulfil the law, established neither under the law nor in need of law.

16 (x). "The law is not made for the righteous man"; yet it is good, "if a man use it lawfully."[34] In putting together these

[32] Prov. 3:16 (LXX).   [33] I Cor. 4:7.   [34] I Tim. 1:8 f.

two seemingly conflicting statements, the apostle prompts his
reader to the asking and answering of a question. In what sense
can it be said that the law is good, "if a man use it lawfully," if
the following words are true: "knowing this, that the law is not
made for the righteous"? For who but the righteous uses the
law lawfully? Yet it is not made for him, but for the unrighteous. The answer is that the unrighteous, in order that he may
be justified—that is, made righteous—must use lawfully the
law, as the "tutor" conducting him to grace,[35] through which
alone he can fulfil the law's commands. Through grace he is
justified "freely," that is, by no preceding merits of his own
works—"otherwise grace is no more grace"[36]: for it is given not
because we have done good works, but in order that we may
have power to do them, not because we have fulfilled the law,
but in order that we may be able to fulfil it. For of him who
said, "I came not to destroy the law, but to fulfil,"[37] it is written: "we beheld his glory, the glory as of the only-begotten
from the Father, full of grace and truth."[38] That is the glory,
of which it is said that "all have sinned and are in want of the
glory of God"; and that is the grace of which Paul speaks in the
same breath: "being justified freely by his grace." The unrighteous man, then, uses the law lawfully, in order that he
may be made righteous. When he has been made righteous, he
is to use it no longer, even as the use of a vehicle ceases at the
journey's end, or (in the apostle's own simile already mentioned) the use of a tutor when instruction is completed. If the
law is necessary for the righteous also, not to bring him while
as yet unrighteous to the grace which justifies, but to be used
lawfully by him after his becoming righteous, it is hard to see
how the law is not made for the righteous man. We may perhaps answer—indeed we may surely answer—that there is a
lawful use of the law by him who is already righteous, which
consists in his putting the fear of it upon the unrighteous. So,
when they too have found the plague of inveterate covetousness
worsened by the stimulus of prohibition and the multiplying of
transgression, they may take refuge by faith with the grace that
justifies, and escape the punishment threatened by the letter
through being brought by the Spirit's gift to delight in the
sweetness of righteousness. In this way there will be no con-
trariety nor conflict between the two positions, that the righteous also may use lawfully the good law, and yet the law be

35 Gal. 3:24.   36 Rom. 11:6.
37 Matt. 5:17.   38 John 1:14.

not made for the righteous. For he is justified not by it, but by the law of faith, through which he has believed that his own infirmity could in no way be enabled to fulfil the commands of the law of works, save by the succour of divine grace.

17. "Where then," asks the apostle accordingly, "is thy glorying? It is cut out. By what law? The law of works? Nay, but by the law of faith." 39 Here the "glorying" may be that commendable glorying "in the Lord," "cut out," not in the sense of being banished, but in that of being made to stand forth in relief. In this sense we sometimes call a worker in silver a "cutter-out"; and the same use is found in the Psalm-text: "that they who are approved by silver may be cut out" 40—which means that they who are approved by the word of the Lord may stand forth clearly, as it is said in another place: "the words of the Lord are pure words, silver tested in the fire." 41 Or it may be that Paul means the faulty "glorying" which comes of pride —the glorying of those who think their life is righteous and glory as though they had not received it; and this he says is "cut out," cast out and cast away, not by the law of works but by the law of faith, since it is by the law of faith that all must come to know that any good in their life is theirs by the grace of God, and that their perfecting in the love of righteousness can come about in no other way.

18 (xi). It is this consideration that makes a man God-fearing. For the fear of God—what the Greeks call *theosebeia*—is the true wisdom, the wisdom commended when man is told (in the Book of Job): "Behold, the fear of God is wisdom." 42 The Greek word *theosebeia* might according to its derivation be translated "the worship of God," of which the essence lies in thankfulness of soul: wherefore we are exhorted, in our liturgy of the one true Sacrifice, to "give thanks to the Lord our God." 43 But it will be thanklessness in the soul to attribute to itself that which comes to it from God—above all, to think of the works of righteousness as its own, as acquired by itself for itself. This is not the vulgar conceit of wealth or good looks or eloquence, or of any of those good things, of body, mind, or circumstance,

39 Rom. 3:27.
40 Ps. 68:30, where the Vulg. has *ut excludant eos qui probati sunt argento.* Augustine takes *excludant* here in the sense of *exclusor*, meaning a "silver-worker," and suggests that the word *exclusa* (which correctly translates the Greek) in Rom. 3:27 may have the same sense. The suggestion is clearly impossible.
41 Ps. 12:6.   42 Job 28:28.
43 The beginning of the Canon of the Mass.

which may equally be possessed by wicked men; it is a would-be superior pride in those goods which properly belong to the good. It is the fault which has caused even great men to fall away from the steadfastness of the divine being into the dishonour of idolatry.

So Paul begins this same Epistle, in which he is to speak so powerfully on behalf of grace, by acknowledging that he is debtor both to Greeks and barbarians, both to wise and unwise, and ready therefore so much as in him lies to preach the gospel to them that were at Rome.[44] "For I am not ashamed," he says "of the gospel; for it is the power of God unto salvation to everyone that believeth, to the Jew first and also to the Greek. For therein is the righteousness of God revealed from faith to faith, as it is written, "The righteous liveth by faith." This is the righteousness of God, which was hidden in the Old Testament and is revealed in the New: called the righteousness of God, because God by imparting it makes man righteous, even as it is "the Lord's salvation"[45] by which he causes men to be saved. And this is the faith, from which and to which it is revealed: that is, from the faith of those who proclaim it to the faith of those who are obedient to it. By the faith of Jesus Christ —the faith, that is, which Christ has conferred upon us—we believe that from God is given to us and will be given yet more fully the life of righteousness. Wherefore with that holy fear by which he alone is to be worshipped, we give him thanks.

19 (xii). With good reason, the apostle turns at this point to denounce those who, through the fault above mentioned, have mounted of themselves like blown-up bubbles into the empty air, and fallen down not to rest but to be shattered on the stones of idolatry. He had commended the true religion of faith, by which we should show thankfulness to God for our justification; and now he opposes to it the contrary state for our abhorrence. "For the wrath of God is revealed from heaven upon all ungodliness and unrighteousness of those men who hold the truth in iniquity; because that which is known concerning God is manifest in them, for God has manifested it to them. For the invisible things of him from the creation of the world are clearly seen, being understood through the things which are made, his eternal power also and divinity: that they may be without excuse, because though having a knowledge of God they glorified him not as God nor gave thanks, but became empty in their thoughts, and their foolish heart was darkened. Professing

[44] Rom. 1:14 ff.   [45] Ps. 3:8.

themselves to be wise, they were made fools, and changed the glory of the incorruptible God into the likeness of the image of corruptible man, of birds, of four-footed beasts, and creeping things." [46] Notice that Paul does not call them ignorant of the truth, but says that they held the truth in iniquity; and he does not fail to meet the natural question, Whence could they to whom God had not given the law have knowledge of the truth? For he says that through the visible things of the creation they reached an understanding of the invisible things of the Creator. There have, indeed, been great minds who sought earnestly for truth this way and were able to find it. [47] In what, then, lies their "ungodliness"? In that, having come to know God, "they glorified him not as God, nor gave thanks, but became empty in their thoughts." Emptiness is the peculiar disease of men who deceive themselves in the belief that they are something, when they are nothing. [48] They enter into the shadow of that swelling hill of pride, of whose foot the holy singer prays that it come not against him, saying "In thy light we shall see light." [49] Thus they have turned away from the very light of changeless truth, and "their foolish heart is darkened." For though they had known God their heart is not wise, but foolish, since "they glorified him not as God, nor gave thanks." For "to man he has said, Behold, the fear of God is wisdom." [50] Therefore, "professing themselves to be wise," which means simply, ascribing this same wisdom to themselves, "they have been made fools."

20. What need to tell the sequel? Through this godlessness those men, those very men who were able through the creation to reach a knowledge of the Creator, have fallen, because God resists the proud [51]—and to what depths they have sunk we may better learn from the following verses of the Epistle than here describe. It is not our purpose in this work to expound the Epistle to the Romans, but to use its testimony to prove as surely as we may that the divine aid for the working of righteousness consists not in God's gift of the law, full as it is of good and holy commands, but in that our will itself, without which we cannot do the good, is aided and uplifted by the imparting of the Spirit of grace. Without that aid, the teaching is a letter that killeth,

---

[46] Rom. 1:18 ff.
[47] Augustine is thinking of Plato and the Platonists, whom he always regarded as having reached a genuine apprehension of God. Cf. *Conf.*, VII, 9.
[48] Gal. 6:3.   [49] Ps. 36:11, 9.
[50] Job. 28:28.   [51] James 4:6.

since it rather holds men in the guilt of transgression than justifies the ungodly. To those who gained knowledge of the
Creator through the creature, that knowledge was of no avail
unto salvation, because "knowing God they glorified him not as
God, nor gave thanks, professing themselves to be wise." Even
so, those who through the law of God know how man ought
to live are not justified by their knowledge, since "willing to
establish their own righteousness they have not been subject to
the righteousness of God." [52]

21 (xiii). We shall do well then to consider the difference
between the law of works which does not "cut out" the glorying
spoken of, and the law of faith which does. But this requires an
effort of attention and discrimination. One might hastily conclude that the law of works belongs to Judaism and the law of
faith to Christianity, on the ground that the Jewish law pre-
scribes circumcision and suchlike works, which Christian practice has abandoned. The error in this distinction is what we have
all along been endeavouring to prove, and it may be have
proved already for clear-thinking readers—in particular for
yourself and for the like of you. Yet the matter is important
enough to warrant us for dwelling in its demonstration upon
still further evidences. The law of which Paul speaks, by which
no man is justified, is the same law which he says "entered
afterwards that the offence might abound." [53] But he defends it
against any ignorant argument or profane accusation. "What
shall we say then? Is the law sin? God forbid! Nay, I have not
known sin but by the law; for I was unaware of concupiscence,
did not the law say 'Thou shalt not covet.' Sin therefore, finding its opportunity through the commandment, wrought in me
all manner of concupiscence." [54] And again: "The law is holy,
and the commandment holy, just, and good; but sin, that it
might appear sin, wrought death in me by that which is good."
Therefore the law which says "Thou shalt not covet," is itself
"the letter that killeth"; and of it Paul says, in the words already
quoted: "through the law is the knowledge of sin. But now the
righteousness of God without law has been manifested, being
witnessed by the law and the prophets: even the righteousness of
God through the faith of Jesus Christ unto all who believe. For
there is no distinction: all have sinned and are in want of the
glory of God, being justified freely by his grace through the redemption that is in Christ Jesus; whom God has set forth to make
expiation, through faith, by his blood, for the showing of his

[52] Rom. 10:3.   [53] Rom. 5:20.   [54] Rom. 7:7 ff.

righteousness on account of the sins which have gone before under God's forbearance: to show his righteousness at this time, that he may be just and the justifier of him who is of the faith of Jesus."[55] Then follows the text with which we are now dealing. "Where then is thy glorying? It is cut out. By what law? Of works? Nay, but by the law of faith."

This law of works, then, is that same law which says "Thou shalt not covet," because by it is the knowledge of sin. I challenge anyone to tell me whether the law of faith does not say "Thou shalt not covet." If it does not, why may not we who stand under it sin with freedom and impunity? For that is what the apostle was supposed to imply, by those of whom he writes: "as some affirm that we say, Let us do evil that good may come: whose judgment is just."[56] But if the law of faith also says "Thou shalt not covet," as is constantly testified aloud by so many evangelic and apostolic precepts, why is not it too called a law of works? Because it no longer has the works of the old ordinances—circumcision and the like, it does not follow that the matter of its own ordinances, adapted to our own time, are not works. There was no question of the works of these ordinances,[56a] when reference was made to the law in respect that through it is the knowledge of sin, and accordingly no one by it is justified: so that glorying is cut out, not by it, but by the law of faith by which the just lives. Can it be that through the law of faith also comes the knowledge of sin, since it too says "Thou shalt not covet"?

22. Where then lies the difference? To put it in a sentence: what is enjoined with threatenings under the law of works, is granted to belief under the law of faith. The one says "Thou shalt not covet."[57] The other says, "Because I knew that no man can be temperate unless God grant it, and that to know of whose gift it came was a part of wisdom, I came near unto the Lord and besought him."[58] That is the wisdom which is called the fear of God, wherewith is worshipped the Father of light, from whom is every good and perfect gift.[59] He is worshipped by the sacrifice of praise and thanksgiving, that his worshipper may

---

[55] Rom. 3:20 ff. [56] Rom. 3:8.

[56a] "Ordinances" translates Augustine's word *sacramenta*. The "sacraments" of the old covenant have been replaced by others in the new: both are "works," but not by them but by the moral law common to both covenants comes the knowledge of sin.

[57] Ex. 20:17.

[58] Wisdom 8:21; note that Augustine can quote Apocrypha for the "law of faith." [59] James 1:17.

glory not in himself but in God.[60] So by the law of works God says, "Do what I command": by the law of faith we say to God, "Give what thou commandest." [61] The law commands, that we may be advised what faith must do: that the hearer of the command, if he cannot as yet perform it, may know what he should pray for; if at once he can and performs it obediently, he should know by whose gift he has that power. "For we have not received the spirit of this world," says the same most constant preacher of grace, "but the Spirit which is of God, that we may know those things which have been given to us by God." [62] What also is the spirit of this world but the spirit of pride, by which was darkened the foolish heart of those who knew God but glorified him not as God, by giving thanks?—the same spirit by which those men are deceived, who being ignorant of God's righteousness, and willing to establish their own, have not been subject to the righteousness of God. He that knows from whom he may hope to receive that which he has not yet is more a child of faith (I think) than he who ascribes to himself what he has; though better than either is he who both has and knows from whom he has it. Only let him not believe himself to be what as yet he is not, and so fall into the offence of the Pharisee who gave God thanks for what he had but asked for nothing to be given him—as though he stood in need of nothing for the increase and perfecting of his righteousness.[63]

The examination and discussion which we have carried out, to the best of that power which the Lord deigns to bestow, has led us to conclude that man is not justified by the precepts of the good life, but only through the faith of Jesus Christ: that is, not by the law of works but by the law of faith, not by the letter but by the spirit, not by the deserts of our actions but by grace freely given.

23 (xiv). The apostle's reproof and correction of those upon whom circumcision was being urged may seem to indicate that what he calls the law is circumcision and similar legal observances, which as shadows of what was to come are now rejected by Christians, who hold the reality of that which was promised in a figure through those shadows. But the law, by which he says that no man is justified, is meant by him to be taken in the sense not only of those ordinances which were given to them as

---

[60] II Cor. 10:17.
[61] The famous prayer of *Conf.*, X, 40, which gave offence to Pelagius (Aug., *De Praedest.*, II, 53).
[62] I Cor. 2:12.   [63] Luke 18:11 f.

figures of the promise, but also of the works in whose performance is the life of righteousness: whereto belongs the command
"Thou shalt not covet." To make our point the clearer, let us
look at the Decalogue itself. Undoubtedly Moses received on
the mount a law to be ministered to the people, written on
tables of stone by the finger of God.[64] It is comprised in ten
commandments, among which there is no charge of circumcision, nor of the animal sacrifices which by Christians are no
longer offered. In these ten commandments, apart from the
observance of the Sabbath, I would ask what the Christian is
not bound to observe: of the commands, not to make or worship
idols, or any other gods but the one true God, not to take God's
name in vain, to honour parents, to avoid fornication, murder,
theft, false witness, adultery, and the coveting of that which is
another's—which among these commands can be said not to
bind the Christian? It is impossible to suppose that what the
apostle calls "the letter that killeth" is not this law, written on
the two Tables, but that of circumcision and the other ancient
ordinances now done away; for in the law of the Tables comes
"Thou shalt not covet," the command by which (says Paul),
"though it is holy and righteous and good, sin deceived me and
thereby slew me"—which can only be "the letter killing."

24. It is still more patent that in the context of the Epistle
to the Corinthians, where the saying occurs that "the letter
killeth, but the spirit giveth life," the "letter" can only mean
the Decalogue, written upon the two Tables. The passage runs
thus[65]: "For ye are the epistle of Christ, ministered by us, written not with ink but with the Spirit of the living God, not in
tables of stone but in fleshy tables of the heart. And such trust
have we through Christ towards God; not that we are fit to
think anything as of ourselves, but our sufficiency is of God, who
also hath made us fit ministers of the new covenant, not of the
letter, but of the spirit. For the letter killeth, but the spirit
giveth life. But if the ministration of death, formed in letters of
stone, was made in glory, so that the children of Israel could not
stedfastly look upon the face of Moses, for the glory of his
countenance which is being done away, why shall not the
ministration of the Spirit be yet more in glory? For if
the ministration of condemnation is glory, much more shall
the ministration of righteousness abound in glory."

On this text much might be said; but it may be more in place
later. For the moment, note what is meant by the "letter that

[64] Ex. 31:18; Deut. 9:10.   [65] II Cor. 3:2 ff.

killeth," contrasted with the "Spirit that giveth life." Unquestionably it is "the ministration of death formed in letters of
stone": "the ministration of condemnation," because the law
"entered afterwards, that the offence might abound." [66] The
commandments themselves are profitable and wholesome to the
doer—so much so that only the doer of them can have life. But
can the Decalogue be called the letter that killeth because of
that one commandment which it includes concerning the Sabbath, on the ground that to continue the literal observance of
that day is to be carnally minded, and "to be carnally minded
is death"? [67] Can it be thought that the other nine commandments which it is still right to observe as they are written, belong
not to the law of works by which no man is justified, but to the
law of faith by which the just lives? It would be absurd to suppose
that the "ministration of death formed in letters of stone"
applies not to all ten commandments but to the single one
which deals with the Sabbath. What then are we to make of the
texts: "the law worketh wrath; for where no law is, there is no
transgression"; "until the law, sin was in the world; but sin
was not imputed when there was no law"; "by the law is the
knowledge of sin" (those words so often quoted); and above all,
the saying that admits no doubt as to its reference: "I was unaware of concupiscence, did not the law say, Thou shalt not
covet"? [68]

25. Consider the whole of this last passage, and see whether
it has any reference at all to circumcision, sabbath or any
ordinance that is a "shadow of things to come"; [69] or is not
entirely concerned to show that the letter forbidding sin does
not give life to man, but rather kills through increasing concupiscence and filling up iniquity with transgression—did not
grace bring deliverance through the law of faith which is in
Christ Jesus, when charity is shed abroad in our hearts through
the Holy Spirit which is given to us.

Paul has just said [70]: "that we should serve in newness of
spirit and not in the oldness of the letter." And he continues:
"What shall we say then? Is the law sin? God forbid. Nay, I
have not known sin but by the law: for I was unaware of concupiscence, did not the law say, Thou shalt not covet. But sin,
finding its opportunity through the commandment, worked in
me all manner of concupiscence. For without the law sin is dead.
At one time I lived without the law; but when the command-

[66] Rom. 5:20.   [67] Rom. 8:6.
[68] Rom. 4:15; 5:13; 3:20; 7:7.   [69] Heb. 10:1.   [70] Rom. 7:6 ff.

ment came, sin revived, and I died. And the commandment which was ordained unto life, I found to be unto death. For sin, finding its opportunity through the commandment, deceived me, and by it slew me. So the law indeed is holy, and the commandment is holy and just and good. Was then that which is good made death unto me? God forbid. But sin, that it may appear sin, has worked death for me through that which is good; that sin through the commandment may become exceeding sinful. For we know that the law is spiritual; but I am carnal, sold under sin. For that which I work, I know not; for what I would, that do I not, but what I hate, that I do. If then I do that which I would not, I consent unto the law that it is good. But as it is, it is no more I that work it, but sin that dwelleth in me. For I know that in me, that is in my flesh, good dwelleth not; for to will is present with me, but to perform the good is not. For the good that I would I do not, but the evil which I would not, that I do. Now if I do that which I would not, it is no more I that work it, but sin that dwelleth in me. I find then a law, that when I would do good, evil is present with me. For I delight in the law of God after the inward man: but I see another law in my members, warring against the law of my mind and making me captive in the law of sin which is in my members. O wretched man that I am! who shall deliver me from the body of this death?—The grace of God,[71] through Jesus Christ our Lord. Therefore I myself with the mind serve the law of God, but with the flesh the law of sin."

26. Thus it is manifest that the "oldness of the letter," if the "newness of the spirit" be lacking, rather makes men guilty by the knowledge of sin than delivers them from sin: with which agrees the saying in another place, "He that addeth to knowledge, addeth to sorrow."[72] Not that the law itself is an evil thing, but that it holds the good commandment in the letter that demonstrates, not in the spirit that brings aid. And if the commandment be done through fear of penalty and not through love of righteousness, it is done in the temper of servitude not freedom—and therefore it is not done at all.[73] For there is no good fruit which does not rise from the root of charity. The man in whom is the faith that works through love,[74] begins to delight in the law of God after the inward man; and that delight is a

[71] So the Latin versions, in place of "I thank God" or "Thanks be to God" in the Greek.   [72] Eccl. 1:18.
[73] Because the "new commandment" is the paradoxical command to love.
[74] Gal. 5:6.

gift not of the letter but of the spirit. It will work, even though there be still another law in the members warring against the law of the mind, until all that is old be changed and pass into that newness which day by day has increase in the inward man, as the grace of God delivers us from the body of this death through Jesus Christ our Lord.

27 (xv). This grace lay hidden in the Old Testament under a veil. It is revealed in the gospel of Christ, according to that perfectly ordered dispensation of history by which the wisdom of God disposes all things in their time. Perhaps we may discern its concealment in the fact that in the Decalogue given on Mount Sinai the only thing hidden under a figurative command is that which concerns the Sabbath. The Sabbath is a day of sanctification. It is not for nothing that among all the works which God made, the word "sanctification" is uttered first at that point when he rested from all his works.[75] This is not the place to discuss that matter: it is enough for our present question to observe that with good reason was the people commanded to abstain on that day from all "servile work," [76] which signifies sin; for to abstain from sin belongs to sanctification, that is, to the gift of God through the Holy Spirit. And this alone among the commandments of the law, written on the two tables of stone, is set under the shadow of a figure, whereby the Jews observe the Sabbath: to signify that in that time there was a hiding away of that grace which was to be revealed in the New Testament, through Christ's passion, as by the rending of the veil.[77] For "when thou shalt pass over unto Christ," says Paul, "the veil shall be taken away. 28 (xvi). Now the Lord is the Spirit; and where the Spirit of the Lord is, there is liberty." [78]

This is the Spirit of God by whose gift we are justified. Hereby it comes to pass in us that we find our delight in not sinning—which means liberty, whereas apart from the Spirit we find delight in sinning—which means servitude, from the works of which we are to abstain, that is, keep Sabbath in the spirit. That Holy Spirit, through whom charity which is the fulness of the law is shed abroad in our hearts, is also called in the Gospel the finger of God.[79] That those tables of the law were written by the finger of God, and that the finger of God is God's Spirit through whom we are sanctified, so that living by faith we may do good works through love—how striking here is

[75] Gen. 2:3.   [76] Lev. 23:7, etc.   [77] Matt. 27:51.
[78] II Cor. 3:16 f.   [79] Luke 11:20.

at once the agreement and the difference! Fifty days are counted from the celebration of Passover, which was commanded through Moses to be a figure, signifying by the killing of a lamb the Lord's passion that was to be, unto the day when Moses received the law on tables written by the finger of God[80]; and in like manner after the fulfilment of fifty days from the killing and the resurrection of him who was "led as a lamb to the slaughter,"[81] the faithful assembled together were filled by the finger of God which is the Holy Spirit.

29 (xvii). In this wonderful agreement there is the very great difference, that in the Old Testament the people is held back by a fearful dread from approaching the place where the law was given[82]; whereas in the New the Holy Spirit comes upon those who were assembled together waiting for his promised coming. There the finger of God worked upon tables of stone: here upon the hearts of men. So there the law was set outside men to be a terror to the unjust: here it was given within them to be their justification. "For this: thou shalt not commit adultery, thou shalt do no murder, thou shalt not covet, and if there be any other commandment"—written, as we know, upon those Tables—"it is briefly comprehended," said the apostle, "in this saying: Thou shalt love thy neighbour as thyself. Love worketh not a neighbour's ill: and charity is the fulness of the law."[83] This law is not written on tables of stone, but is shed abroad in our hearts through the Holy Spirit which is given to us. Therefore the law of God is charity. To it the mind of the flesh is not subject, neither indeed can be[84]; but when, to put fear into the mind of the flesh, the works of charity are written upon tables, we have the law of works, the letter killing the transgressor: when charity itself is shed abroad in the heart of believers, we have the law of faith, the Spirit giving life to the lover.

30. Now observe the tallying of this distinction with those words of the apostle which we quoted a while ago for another purpose, and postponed their closer consideration.[85] "Ye are manifestly declared to be the epistle of Christ ministered by us, written not with ink but with the Spirit of the living God, not in tables of stone, but in fleshy tables of the heart." He points, you see, to the fact that the one is written outside the man, to be a

---

[80] Deut. 16:9 ff; the harvest festival of Pentecost was held in later Judaism to commemorate the giving of the Law.
[81] Isa. 53:7.   [82] Ex. 19:10 ff.   [83] Rom. 13:9 f.
[84] Rom. 8:7.   [85] II Cor. 3:3 ff.

terror to him from without, while the other is written in the man himself, to justify him from within. By the "fleshy tables of the heart," he means not those of the "mind of the flesh," but that which is living and conscious in contrast with the unfeeling stone. When he says further on that "the children of Israel could not stedfastly behold the face of Moses," who therefore spoke to them through a veil, that signifies that the letter of the law justifies no man; but a veil is set over the reading of the Old Testament, until we pass over unto Christ and the veil is taken away: that is, pass over unto grace, and understand that from him we have the justification whereby we do what he commands. He commands, in order that we may take refuge with him when in ourselves we fail. And so when Paul has said that "we have such confidence through Christ unto God," he is most careful to add at once his explanation, lest this be attributed to our own strength: "not that we are fitted to think anything as of ourselves; but our sufficiency is of God, who also hath made us fit ministers of the New Testament—not of the letter, but of the Spirit: for the letter killeth, but the Spirit giveth life."

31 (xviii). Accordingly it is because the law, as he says elsewhere, "was set because of transgression,"[86] that is, the letter written outside the man, that he calls it the ministration of death and the ministration of condemnation; whereas the other, that of the New Testament, he calls the ministration of the spirit and the ministration of righteousness, because through the gift of the Spirit we work righteousness and are delivered from the condemnation of transgression. So the one is done away, while the other remains, since the tutor who puts in fear[87] shall be removed when fear has given place to charity: for "where the Spirit of the Lord is, there is liberty." That this ministration proceeds not from our deservings, but from mercy, is stated thus: "Therefore seeing that we have this ministration, as having obtained mercy, let us not be weakened, but cast away the hidden things of confusion, not walking in craftiness nor falsifying the word of God by deceit." By this craftiness and deceit he indicates that hypocrisy of the proud will that seeks to be accounted righteous. So in the Psalm which our apostle quotes in testimony of this same grace, we read: "Blessed is he to whom the Lord hath not imputed sin, nor is there deceit in his mouth."[88] That is the confession of humble saints, not boasting themselves to be what they are not. And so Paul continues: "For we preach not ourselves but Jesus Christ as Lord, and

[86] Gal. 3:19.   [87] Gal. 3:25.   [88] Ps. 32:2; Rom. 4:8.

ourselves as your servants for Jesus' sake: because God, who commanded the light to shine out of darkness, hath shined in our hearts the light of the knowledge of his glory upon the face of Jesus Christ." It is the knowledge of his glory whereby we know that he is the light by which our darkness is enlightened. Observe how he insists upon this very point. "But we have this treasure in earthen vessels, that the excellency of the power may be God's and not of us." Then, in more copious enlargement upon the same grace in the Lord Jesus Christ, he goes on to speak of that clothing with the righteousness of faith, clothed wherewithal we may not be found naked, and how for this cause we groan, burdened as we are with mortality and desiring to be clothed upon with our house which is from heaven, that what is mortal may be swallowed up of life. And he adds: "Now he that hath wrought us for the self-same thing is God, who hath given us the earnest of the Spirit;" and later concludes: "that we may be the righteousness of God in him"—the righteousness of God, not that by which he is righteous but that by which we are made so by him.

32 (xix). This and this only is the Christian faith, from which no Christian should stray. A man may shrink from saying in so many words that we make ourselves righteous without the grace of God working the same in us, because he sees such claims to be intolerable to the faithful and devout. But we must refuse the argument that we cannot be righteous without the operation of God's grace, merely because God gave the law, instituted the teaching, delivered good precepts. For all this, apart from the Spirit's aid, is indubitably the letter that killeth: only when the life-giving Spirit is present, does he cause to be written within, and loved, that which when it was written externally the law caused to be feared.

33. Look for a moment at the magnificent testimony rendered to this truth in the words of the prophet.[89] "Behold, the days come, saith the Lord, when I will consummate upon the house of Israel and the house of Judah a new covenant, not according to the covenant that I made for their fathers in the day when I took their hand to bring them forth from the land of Egypt; because they have not continued in my covenant, and I have let them go, saith the Lord. For this is the covenant that I will ordain for the house of Israel: after those days, saith the Lord, I will put my laws into their heart and will write them upon their mind; and I will be their God and they shall be my

[89] Jer. 31:31 ff.

people. And they shall teach no more every man his neighbour and every man his brother, saying, Know the Lord. For all shall know me, from the least of them unto the greatest of them; because I will forgive their iniquity, and their sins will I remember no more."

What shall we say of this? In the Old Testament it is difficult if not impossible to find outside this prophetic passage any mention of the new covenant in express terms. In many places it is signified or predicted, but not by its actual name. Consider then carefully the difference between the two covenants, the old and the new, to which God here bears witness.

34. After the words: "not according to the covenant that I made for their fathers in the day when I took their hand to bring them forth from the land of Egypt": it goes on: "because they have not continued in my covenant." It is accounted their fault that they have not abided by the covenant of God; lest it should appear that the law which then they received was to be blamed. It is the same law which Christ came not to destroy but to fulfil: though the ungodly are justified not through that law but through grace—that is by the action of the life-giving Spirit, apart from whom the letter kills. "For if there had been a law given which could have given life, righteousness would be altogether by the law. But the scripture hath shut up all under sin, that the promise by faith of Jesus Christ might be given to them that believe."[90] By this promise, that is, by the goodness of God, the law is fulfilled. Without it, men are made transgressors, whether in the actual doing of the evil work, where the flame of concupiscence has swept across the barrier of fear, or at least in the will, if fear of punishment overcomes the attraction of desire. The saying, that "the scripture hath shut up all under sin, that the promise by faith of Jesus Christ might be given to them that believe," shows the advantage of the "shutting up"; it is for the purpose presently named: "before faith came, we were kept in ward under the law, shut up unto the faith which afterwards hath been revealed." The law was given that grace might be sought; grace was given that the law might be fulfilled. For the non-fulfilment of the law was not through its own fault, but the fault of the "mind of the flesh"—a fault which the law must exhibit, and grace must heal. "What the law could not do, in that it was made weak through the flesh, God sent his Son in the likeness of the flesh of sin, and in regard to sin condemned sin in the flesh; that the righteousness of the

[90] Gal. 3:21 ff.

law might be fulfilled in us, who walk not according to the flesh but according to the spirit."[91] So we read in the prophetic testimony: "I will consummate upon the house of Israel and upon the house of Judah a new covenant"—"consummate" meaning "fulfil"—"not according to the covenant that I made for their fathers, in the day that I took their hand to bring them forth from the land of Egypt."

35. (xx). This was the "old" covenant, because the other is "new"; but why should they be distinguished as "old" and "new," if through the new covenant is fulfilled the same law which in the old said: "Thou shalt not covet"? The answer is, that "they have not continued in my covenant, and I have let them go, saith the Lord." It is because of the sickness of the old man, which the commands and the threatenings of the letter did nothing to heal, that the former covenant is called old, and the latter new with the newness of the Spirit, which heals the new man from his old failing. The words that follow set in the clearest light that truth which the self-confident refuse to look upon, "For this is the covenant that I will ordain for the house of Israel: after those days, saith the Lord, I will put my laws into their heart, and will write them upon their mind." Now we understand those words of the apostle, above quoted: "not on tables of stone, but on tables of the heart," because "not with ink, but by the Spirit of the living God." The reason, surely, for his mentioning the new covenant in this passage—where he says: "who also hath made us fit ministers of the new covenant, not of the letter but of the spirit"—must be that he had this prophecy in mind when he wrote the words, "not on tables of stone but on fleshy tables of the heart." For in the same prophecy where the new covenant is promised by that name, it is also said: "I will write them upon their hearts."

36 (xxi). It follows that the laws of God, written by God himself upon the heart, are nothing but the very presence of the Holy Spirit who is the finger of God; the presence by which charity, the fulness of the law and the end of the commandment, is shed abroad in our hearts. The promises of the old covenant are earthly promises. Certain of its ordinances were shadows of things to come, such as circumcision, the sabbath and other observances of days, rules as to particular foods, and the manifold ceremonial of sacrifices and holy rites, adapted to the old era of a fleshly law and the yoke of servitude. It is true that apart from these the old covenant contained precepts

[91] Rom. 8:3 ff.

of righteousness such as we are still enjoined to observe, especially those which are set forth in the two Tables with a literal and not allegorical significance: as "thou shalt not commit adultery, thou shalt do no murder, thou shalt not covet, and any other commandment which is summed up in this saying: thou shalt love thy neighbour as thyself."[92] Nevertheless, the promises there announced, as I have said, are earthly and temporal, good things of this corruptible flesh, even though they may be figures of the eternal and heavenly goods belonging to the new covenant. Whereas now there is promised a good of the heart itself, a good of the mind, a spiritual good, in the words "put my laws in their mind and write them in their hearts." They are to receive, in other words, not a law that menaces from without of which they must be in fear, but the very law of righteousness dwelling within them which they are to love.

37 (xxii). Finally, we are told of the reward: "I will be their God, and they shall be my people." This is that reward of which the psalmist speaks in his prayer: "For me to cleave unto God is good."[93]—"I will be their God, and they shall be my people." There can be no better good, no happier happiness than this: life for God, life from God, with whom is the well of life, in whose light we shall see light.[94] Of that life the Lord himself says: "This is life eternal, that they may know thee the one true God, and Jesus Christ whom thou hast sent"—that is, "thee and Jesus Christ whom thou hast sent, the one true God."[95] That is his own promise to his lovers: "He that loveth me, keepeth my commandments; and he that loveth me is loved of my Father, and I will love him and will show myself unto him"[96]—show himself in the form of God whereby he is equal to the Father, not in the form of a servant whereby he showed himself to the ungodly also. For then shall it be done as it was written: "let the ungodly be taken away, that he see not the glory of the Lord,"[97] when they on the left hand shall go into everlasting fire, but the righteous into life eternal. We have heard the definition of eternal life: "that they may know the one true God." With this agrees the saying of John: "Beloved, we are the sons of God, and it hath not yet appeared what we shall be. We know that when he appears, we shall be like him, for we shall see him as he is."[98] That likeness begins now to be

[92] Rom. 13:9.   [93] Ps. 73:28.   [94] Ps. 36:9.

[95] John 17:3; Augustine twists the text to make it conform to orthodox doctrine.

[96] John 14:21.   [97] Isa. 26:10.   [98] I John 3:2.

formed again, while man is renewed within from day unto day according to the image of him who created him.[99]

38 (xxiii). But between this and the perfection of that excellency which is then to be, what comparison is possible? The apostle, applying to those unspeakable things such distant analogy as he may from the familiar world, contrasts the age of infancy with the age of manhood. "When I was a child, I spake as a child, I understood as a child, I thought as a child: but when I became a man, I put away childish things"; and he goes on to point the bearing of his parable: "now we see in a mirror darkly, but then face to face; now I know in part, but then shall I know as also I have been known." [1]

39 (xxiv). In the same way, the word given to the prophet whose testimony we are examining leads to this indication that in God is our reward, in God our end, in God the perfection of our happiness, in God the sum of blessed and eternal life. After the saying: "I will be their God, and they shall be my people," there follows immediately: "and they shall not teach every man his neighbour and every man his brother, saying, Know the Lord; for they shall all know me, from the least unto the greatest of them." Assuredly, the time of the new covenant, promised through the prophet in the words of the passage quoted, is already here with us. Why then is it still said by everyone to his neighbour and his brother, Know the Lord? Is it not said, when the gospel is preached, when it is the very aim of the gospel's preaching that this be said everywhere? Does not the apostle call himself the teacher of the Gentiles, because it is happening as he says: "How shall they call on him in whom they have not believed? or how can they believe in him whom they have not heard? and how shall they hear without a preacher?"[2] Since then this preaching is now multiplied in all the world, how can it be the time of the new covenant, of which the prophet has written: "they shall not teach every man his neighbour and every man his brother, saying, Know the Lord; for they shall all know me, from the least unto the greatest of them"? We can only understand that here has been added the promise of that same new covenant's eternal reward, which is the most blessed contemplation of God himself.

40. "All, from the least unto the greatest of them," will then mean all who spiritually belong to the house of Israel and the house of Judah—that is, the sons of Isaac, the seed of Abraham. For that is the promise given in the words: "In Isaac shall thy

[99] Col. 3:10; II Cor. 4:16.   [1] I Cor. 13:11 ff.   [2] Rom. 10:14.

seed be called. For they which are sons of the flesh are not the sons of God, but the sons of promise are counted for the seed. And this is the word of promise: At this time will I come, and Sara shall have a son. And not only this, but Rebecca also, conceiving by our father Isaac two children at one time: of whom when they were not yet born, nor had done anything good or evil, that the purpose of God according to election might stand, not of works, but of him that calleth, it was said unto her that the elder shall serve the younger." [3] That is the house of Israel or the house of Judah (because of Christ's coming of the tribe of Judah), the house of the sons of promise—which means a house founded not on their own works but on the gracious act of God. For God promises that which he does himself: the promise is not his and the doing another's—which would be predicting, not promising. So it is "not of works, but of him that calleth," that it be not their own doing instead of God's, lest the reward be reckoned not of grace but of debt,[4] and so grace be no more grace—grace, whose powerful vindicator and maintainer is the "least of the apostles," who laboured more than they all, yet not he but the grace of God with him.[5] To return to the text: "they shall all know me." "All" are the house of Israel and the house of Judah; inasmuch as not all are Israel that are of Israel, but those who are addressed in the Psalm entitled "For taking up in the morning"—which we may interpret "For the new dawn," or the dawn of the new covenant: "Magnify him, the whole seed of Jacob: let all the seed of Israel fear him." [6] The whole seed without exception, truly all the seed of the promised and the called—but "the called according to his purpose." For "whom he did predestinate, them he also called; and whom he called, them he also justified; and whom he justified, them he also glorified." [7] "Therefore it is of faith, that according to grace the promise may be sure to all the seed, not to that only which is of the law"—which descends from the old covenant to the new—"but to that also which is of faith"—not a seed which has already received the law, but "of the faith of Abraham," that is, to those that copy the faith of Abraham, "who is the father of us all, as it is written, I have set thee as a father of many nations." [8]—In sum, these all, predestinate, called, justified, glorified, shall know God through the grace of the new covenant, from the least unto the greatest of them.

[3] Rom. 9:7 ff.   [4] Rom. 4:4.   [5] I Cor. 15:9 f.
[6] Ps. 22:23; for the title, cf. R.V. mg.—The LXX gives "for the morning aid.".   [7] Rom. 8:28, 30.   [8] Rom. 4:16 f.

41. Thus the law of works, written on tables of stone, and its reward in the land of promise which the house of Israel according to the flesh received after it was delivered out of Egypt, belongs to the old covenant; whereas the law of faith written in the heart, and its reward in the immediate vision of God which the spiritual house of Israel shall enjoy when it is delivered from this world, belongs to the new covenant. For then it shall be as the apostle says: "whether there be prophecies, they shall be brought to nought, whether there be tongues, they shall cease, whether there be knowledge, it shall be brought to nought."[9] He speaks of that knowledge of children, in which our life here passes, a knowledge "in part, through a mirror darkly." For because of it prophecy is needed, while past still gives place to future; because of it there is use for tongues, the variety of meanings whereby one thing is conveyed by another in allegory to the mind that cannot yet contemplate in purity the eternal light of transparent truth. But "when that which is perfect has come," and all that is in part has been done away, then the Word, which took flesh to appear to flesh, shall show himself to his lovers; then it will be life eternal for us to know the one true God; then we shall be like him, for then we shall know as we have been known; then "they shall not teach every man his neighbour and every man his brother, saying Know the Lord; for they shall all know him, from the least of them unto the greatest of them."

We may understand this in more than one sense. Perhaps it means that there also the saints differ from one another in glory, as star from star.[10] It is all one whether we say "from the least unto the greatest," or "from the greatest unto the least"; and this will hold, if we should understand by the "least" those who have attained only to faith, and by the "greatest" those who have reached also to such understanding as in this life is possible of the incorporeal and changeless Light.[11] Or may be the "least" means the later in time, and the "greatest" the earlier; for all at once are to receive the promised vision of God, because "they also foresaw better things for us, that without us they should not be made perfect"[12]—and so the "least" are found to be the "first," since their waiting has been less, as in the Gospel parable of the penny received first by those who came last into the

---

9 I Cor. 13:8 ff.   10 I Cor. 15:41.
11 For Augustine's distinction of "faith" and "understanding," see De Trin., Introduction, p. pp. 22 f., 35.
12 Heb. 11:40.

vineyard.[13] And there may well be some other way of which I cannot at the moment think, of taking "least" and "greatest" in the text.

42 (xxv). The point I have so laboriously endeavoured to make clear, and on which I would have you concentrate your mind, is this. In this promise of a new covenant, not according to the covenant before made with the people of Israel upon their deliverance from Egypt, the prophet has nothing to say of a change of sacrifices or outward ordinances of any kind; although that change was certainly to ensue in the manner we now see, to which the same prophetic scripture in many other places bears witness. He insists only upon this great difference between old and new: that God would put his laws into the mind of those who should belong to the new covenant, and write them on their hearts (whence the apostle drew his "not with ink but with the spirit of the living God, not on tables of stone, but on fleshy tables of the heart"); and that the everlasting reward of this "justification" or being made righteous is not the land from which were driven Amorites, Hittites and the rest of the nations recorded as dwelling in it, but God himself, unto whom to cleave is good, the love of whose goodness is the love of himself, from whom men are separated by nothing but their sins, which are remitted only by his grace. That is why the words "they shall all know me, from the least of them unto the greatest of them," are followed by the promise: "I will forgive their iniquity, and their sins I will remember no more." By the law of works the Lord says, "Thou shalt not covet." By the law of faith the Lord says, "Without me ye can do nothing"—meaning the good works which are the fruit of the vine-branches.[14]

Grasp this clear difference between the old covenant and the new: that there the law is written upon tables, here upon hearts, so that the fear imposed by the first from without becomes the delight inspired by the second from within, and he whom the letter that killeth there made a transgressor, is here made a lover by the Spirit that giveth life. Then you can no longer say that God assists us in the working of righteousness and works in us both to will and to do according to his good pleasure, inasmuch as he makes us hear with the outward sense the commandments of righteousness. No, it is because he gives increase within us, by the shedding abroad of charity in our hearts through the Holy Spirit which is given to us.

43 (xxvi). A difficulty, however, may be raised by the

13 Matt. 20:8 ff.   14 John 15:5

apostle's words: "When the Gentiles, which have not the law, do by nature the things contained in the law, these, having not the law, are a law unto themselves: which show the work of the law written in their hearts."[15] Does not this obscure the difference of the new covenant in which the Lord promised to write his laws in the hearts of his people—if the Gentiles have that by nature? We are presented with a serious problem, which is not to be shirked. The argument will run: If God distinguishes the new covenant from the old, in that he wrote his law upon tables in the old covenant, but upon hearts in the new, how are the faithful of the new covenant distinguished from the Gentiles, who have the word of the law written in their hearts, by which they do by nature the things contained in the law? It would seem that they have the advantage over the old Israel who received the law upon tables, and the priority over the new, to whom is conferred by the new covenant only that which nature has conferred upon the Gentiles.

44. It is possible that the Gentiles of whom the apostle speaks as having the law written in their hearts are those who belong to the new covenant. Let us see·how he comes to speak of them. First, he sets out the virtue of his gospel: "It is the power of God unto salvation to every man that believeth, to the Jew first and also to the Greek. For the righteousness of God is revealed in it from faith to faith, as it is written: The just liveth by faith."[16] Then he speaks of the ungodly whose pride made even the knowledge of God of no avail to them, because they glorified him not as God nor gave thanks. Then he passes to those who judge and yet do the things which they condemn. This no doubt refers to the Jews, who made their boast in the law of God; though he does not at first name them expressly. "Wrath and indignation," he says, "tribulation and anguish upon every soul of man that doeth evil, of the Jew first, and also of the Greek; but glory, honour, and peace to every man that worketh good, to the Jew first, and also to the Greek: for there is no acceptance of persons with God. For as many as have sinned without law shall perish without law; and as many as have sinned in the law shall be judged by the law. For not the hearers of the law are just before God, but the doers of the law shall be justified."[17] And this brings him to the matter of our question. He goes on: "For when the Gentiles which have not the law, do by nature the things contained in the law . . ." and so on as above quoted. Accordingly we may think that

15 Rom. 2:14 f.   16 Rom. 1:16 f.   17 Rom. 2:8 ff.

those here called Gentiles are none other than those before referred to under the name of "Greek," in the phrase "to the Jew first and also to the Greek." The gospel is "the power of God unto salvation to every man that believeth, the Jew first and also the Greek," but "wrath and indignation, tribulation and anguish upon every soul of man that doeth evil, of the Jew first and also of the Greek, but glory, honour and peace to every man that worketh good, to the Jew first, and also to the Greek." Now if it is this Greek who is signified under the Gentiles who do by nature the things contained in the law and have the work of the law written in their hearts, clearly these Gentiles who have the law written in their hearts belong to the gospel: they are believers to whom it is the power of God unto salvation. How could Paul promise glory, honour and peace to the good works of Gentiles placed outside the grace of the gospel? Because there is no acceptance of persons with God, and not the hearers but the doers of the law are justified, he argues that all, whether Jew or Greek (that is, all believers of the Gentiles), shall alike have salvation in the gospel. "For there is no difference," as he says later: "all have sinned and are in want of the glory of God, being justified freely by his grace." [18] How could he maintain that the Greek doer of the law is justified apart from the grace of the Saviour?

45. The words "the doers of the law shall be justified" cannot mean that they are justified by works and not by grace: that would be to contradict his own statement that a man is justified freely by faith apart from the works of the law[19]—where the word "freely" means simply that works do not come before justification. This he makes plain in another place: "if by grace, then not of works: else grace would be no longer grace."[20] That "the doers of the law shall be justified" must be taken in the sense that they can be doers of the law if, and only if, they be justified: so that justification does not follow but precede the doing. The word "justified" is equivalent to "made righteous" —made righteous by him who justifies the ungodly, so that he who was ungodly becomes righteous. The statement "men shall be made free" could only be understood to mean that freedom comes to persons who are already men. But the statement "men shall be created" could not possibly denote the creation of already existing men: it means the bringing of men into being as such by the act of creation. Similarly, if we were told that "the doers of the law shall be honoured," we should properly

18 Rom. 3:22 f.   19 Rom. 3:28.   20 Rom. 11:6.

understand that honour is to be given to those who are already doers of the law. But to say that "the doers of the law shall be justified" is equivalent to saying that "the just shall be justified"; for doers of the law are *ipso facto* just. We must take it therefore in the same way as we should understand "the doers of the law shall be created": not because they were, but in order that they may be. So it should be made clear even to the Jewish hearers of the law that they need the grace of the justifier in order that they may become doers.[21] Alternatively, we must suppose that "shall be justified" here means "shall be held just," "shall be accounted just"; as in the case of the lawyer in Luke of whom we read, "and he, willing to justify himself . . .,"[22] that is, with a view to being held or accounted just. So we say that God "sanctifies his saints" in a sense different from that of the prayer "let thy name be sanctified."[23] In the one case, "sanctify" means that God himself makes saints of men who were not saints: in the other, we pray that what is ever holy in itself may be held by men as holy, may be feared in holy wise.

46. In speaking, then, of Gentiles who do by nature the things contained in the law, and have the work of the law written in their hearts, Paul may have intended those who believe in Christ, because they come to the faith without having received the law beforehand as the Jews. Then we have no need to distinguish them from those to whom the Lord promised the new covenant by the prophet, saying that he would write his laws in their hearts; because they also, by the grafting done to the wild olive, belong to the one olive tree, the one people of God.[24] In this way the apostolic testimony will be in accord with the prophetic: to belong to the new covenant will be to have the law of God written not on tables but on hearts, that is, to embrace with inward affection the righteousness of the law, in which faith works through love. For God justifies the Gentiles by faith, as Scripture foresees in the prediction to Abraham that "in thy seed shall all the nations be blessed."[25] By this grace of the promise, the wild olive was to be grafted into the olive tree, and the faithful Gentiles become sons of Abraham in Abraham's seed, which is Christ[26]: following the faith of him, who before any law was given upon tables, and not yet having

---

21 This characteristically over-subtle piece of exegesis is the result of Augustine's misunderstanding of the Pauline "justification." In what follows here he glances at the possibility of a forensic interpretation of the word.   22 Luke 10:29.   23 Matt. 6:9.

24 Rom. 11:24.   25 Gen. 12:3.   26 Gal. 3:8, 16.

received circumcision, "believed God, and it was accounted to him for righteousness."[27] So the saying of the apostle about these Gentiles, that they have the work of the law written in their hearts, will be comparable with his words to the Corinthians: "not on tables of stone, but on fleshy tables of the heart." They become members of the house of Israel, when their uncircumcision is counted for circumcision, inasmuch as they do not display the righteousness of the law by the cutting of the flesh, but keep it in charity of heart: for "if the uncircumcision keeps the righteous requirements of the law, will not its uncircumcision be counted for circumcision?"[28] Therefore they are sharers in the new covenant in the house of the true Israel wherein is no guile; because God puts his laws in their minds and writes them in their hearts with his finger, the Holy Spirit, by whom there is shed abroad in those hearts the charity which is the fulness of the law.

47 (xxvii). This interpretation need not be disturbed by the saying of the text that they do the things contained in the law "by nature"—not by the Spirit of God, by faith, or by grace. For it is the work of the Spirit of grace to renew in us the image of God, in which "by nature" we were made. The fault in man is contrary to his nature, and is just that which grace heals—the grace besought in the prayer: "Have mercy on me, heal my soul, for I have sinned against thee."[29] Accordingly it is always "by nature" that men do the things contained in the law: those who fail so to do, fail by their own fault. By that fault the law of God was effaced from men's hearts; and so when it is written there through the healing of the fault, the things contained in the law are done "by nature"—not that nature is the denial of grace, but that grace is the mending of nature. For "by one man sin entered into the world, and through sin death, (and so it passed into all men), in whom all sinned."[30] Therefore, since "there is no difference," all are "in want of the glory of God, being justified freely by his grace."[31] By grace the righteousness which guilt had effaced is written in the inward man thus renewed; and this is God's mercy upon the human race through Jesus Christ our Lord. "For there is one God, and one mediator also between God and men, the man Christ Jesus."[32]

---

[27] Gen. 15:6.   [28] Rom. 2:26.   [29] Ps. 41:4.
[30] Rom. 5:12. The *in quo omnes peccaverunt* of Augustine's Latin version misrepresents the original Greek.
[31] Rom. 3:22 ff.   [32] I Tim. 2:5.

48. If this interpretation is rejected, and if those who "do by nature the things contained in the law" are not to be reckoned among those who are justified by the grace of Christ, then they must belong to the number of the heathen who worship not the true God in truth and righteousness, and yet do some things (known to us from books, observation, or report) which judged by the standard of right conduct call not only for the withholding of blame but even for merited and proper commendation. It is true that enquiry into the end or purpose of such actions would make it less easy to discover any that deserve the praise or the defence due to genuine righteousness.[33]

(xxviii). Yet we must remember that the image of God in the human soul has not been so completely obliterated by the stain of earthly affections, that no faint outlines of the original remain therein; and therefore it can rightly be said even in the ungodliness of its life to do or to hold some parts of the law. This may possibly be meant by the saying that the Gentiles, who have not the law (that is, the law of God) do by nature the things contained in the law, and that such men are a law unto themselves, and have the work of the law written in their hearts: namely, that the imprint of God's image in their creation has not been altogether effaced.[34] But even so there will be no shaking of the difference between old and new covenant, whereby the writing of the law of God in the hearts of the faithful through the new is opposed to its writing upon tables through the old. For what is now written by way of renewal is what was not altogether effaced by growing old. Just as by the new covenant there is a renewal in the mind of believers of that very image of God which ungodliness had not entirely done away— at the least there remained the essential rationality of the human soul—so even here what is written is undoubtedly that law of God which was never quite effaced by unrighteousness and now is renewed by grace. This writing, which is justification, could not be made effective in the Jews by the law written on tables: its effect was only transgression. Men indeed they were, and there was in them that natural impulse which gives the rational creature both a certain awareness of what is lawful and a certain

---

[33] Augustine could say (*De Civ.*, XIX, 25) that the virtues of the heathen are to be accounted "vices rather than virtues," because they are not "referred to God," i.e., God is not acknowledged as their source, and the love of him is not their motive. It is worth noting, however, that the phrase *splendida vitia* is *not* Augustinian. (See Mausbach, *Die Ethik des Heil. Augustinus*, vol. II, pp. 258 ff.)

[34] Cf. the important passage in *De Trin.*, XIV, 21 (xv).

power of doing it. But the religion that conveys to another life of blessedness and eternity possesses a law "unspotted, converting souls," [35] so that they receive of that Light renewal, and fulfilment of that which is written: "the light of thy countenance, O Lord, is marked upon us." [36] If men turn aside from it, they have deserved that it should fade away; renewal, save by the Christian grace which is the Mediator's intercession, they cannot have. "For there is one God, and one mediator also between God and men, the man Christ Jesus, who gave himself to be the redemption of all." And if those of whom we are speaking, those who do by nature the things contained in the law in the manner we have sufficiently set forth, are strangers from the grace of Christ, then the "thoughts" which "excuse" them can advantage them nothing in the day when God shall judge the hidden things of men—unless it be for a punishment less severe. Even as the righteous man is not held back from eternal life by those venial sins of which some in this life there must be, so for eternal salvation the ungodly has no advantage from some good works, which even in the life of the worst of men can scarcely be altogether absent. But as in God's kingdom the saints differ in glory like star from star, so in the condemnation of everlasting punishment it will be more tolerable for Sodom than for another city, and some will be twofold more than others the children of hell.[37] God's judgment will not fail to take account of it, if even in the ungodliness which must be condemned one has sinned more or less than another.[38]

49. The apostle is checking the self-glorification of the Jews. He has said that "not the hearers of the law are just before God, but the doers of the law shall be justified"; and he proceeds at once to speak of some who "not having the law, do by nature the things contained in the law." What is the point here made, if the reference is not to those who belong to the grace of the Mediator, but to those who without that worship of the true God which is true religion can yet show some good works in their ungodly life? It may be that this is his way of proving what he had already said, that there is no respect of persons with God,

[35] Ps. 19:7.   [36] Ps. 4:6.
[37] 1 Cor. 15: 41; Luke 10: 12; Matt. 23: 15.
[38] The Council of Carthage in A.D. 418 which condemned Pelagianism, rejected the belief in a "middle place" in the after life for unbaptized infants. Yet Augustine himself could say that they would receive *mitissima poena*, a "very gentle penalty": he clearly believes in "degrees" of punishment as of reward. See *Enchirid.*, 23, 29, and contrast the horrible arguments of *De Civ.*, XXI, 1–10.

and what he says later, that God is not God of the Jews only but also of the Gentiles; inasmuch as no works of the law, however small, could be found implanted by nature in those who have not received the law, unless it came from the relics of the divine image, which he in whom there is no respect of persons does not despise when they believe in him. Nevertheless, whether we accept this interpretation or the other, it holds good that the grace of God in the new covenant was promised also by the prophet, and that this grace is defined as consisting in the writing of God's laws in the hearts of men, so that they come to that knowledge of God in which "they shall not teach every man his neighbour or his brother, saying, Know God: for they shall all know him, from the least unto the greatest of them." And this is the gift of the Holy Spirit, by which charity is shed abroad in our hearts: that charity alone which is the love of God from a pure heart and a good conscience and a faith unfeigned.[39] By it the righteous lives in his pilgrimage here, and by it he is led on from mirror and dark saying, and all that was in part, to the region of sight, that he may know face to face, as also he has been known.[40] One thing he seeks from the Lord and requires the same, that he may dwell in the house of the Lord all the days of his life, to the end that he may contemplate in delight the fair beauty of the Lord.[41]

50 (xxix). No man therefore may boast of that which he seems to have, as though he has not received it[42]; or think that he has received it because the letter that comes from without has been set down for his reading or made to sound for his hearing. "For if righteousness is by the law, then Christ has died for nought."[43] If he has not died for nought, he has "ascended up on high, led captivity captive, and given gifts unto men."[44] Whoever has anything, has it from thence: whoever denies that he has it from thence, either has it not or else that which he has shall be taken away from him.[45] For there is "one God, who justifies the circumcision by faith and the uncircumcision through faith."[46] The change of preposition does not indicate any difference of meaning but serves simply to vary the phrase. Elsewhere, speaking of the Gentiles, that is, the uncircumcision, he says: "the Scripture, foreseeing that God justifies the Gentiles by faith";[47] and again, speaking of the circumcision to which he himself belonged; "we, Jews by nature and not sinners of the

39 I Tim. 1:5.   40 I Cor. 13:12.   41 Ps. 27:4.
42 I Cor. 4:7.   43 Gal. 2:21.   44 Eph. 4:8.
45 Luke 19:26.   46 Rom. 3:30.   47 Gal. 3:8.

Gentiles, knowing that a man is not justified by the works of the law but through faith of Jesus Christ, we also have believed in Christ Jesus." [48] Here we have both the uncircumcision said to be justified "by" faith, and the circumcision "through" faith— yet only if the circumcision hold to the righteousness of faith. For "the Gentiles which followed not after righteousness have laid hold on righteousness, even the righteousness which is of faith"—received it in answer to their prayer from God, not by counting upon themselves—"but Israel in following after the law of righteousness hath not attained to that law. Wherefore? because it was not by faith, but as though by works" [49]—as though they wrought it by themselves and not believing that God wrought it in them. "For it is God that worketh in us both to will and to work according to his good pleasure." [50] Therefore they "stumbled upon the rock of stumbling." [51] The meaning of Paul's actual words—"because it was not by faith, but as though by works"—is made quite clear in a following verse: "for they being ignorant of the righteousness of God and desiring to establish their own, have not been subject to the righteousness of God. For Christ is the end of the law unto righteousness to everyone that believeth." [52]

Can we still have any doubt what are those works of the law by which a man is not justified, if he regards them as his own, apart from the help and gift of God, which is by faith of Jesus Christ? Can we think for a moment of circumcision and such-like, because we read similar sayings about these ordinances in other places? Here at least it was not circumcision that they desired to establish as their own righteousness; for circumcision itself was established by the command of God. Nor can we suppose any reference here to those works, of which the Lord told them: "Ye do reject the commandment of God that ye may set up your traditions." [53] Paul's words are: "Israel in following after the law of righteousness attained not unto that law" [54]— not "following after their own traditions." The contrast lies entirely in the point that they ascribed to themselves the keeping of the law "Thou shalt not covet," and the rest of the holy and righteous commands of God. Man's power to accomplish them is wrought in man by God through faith of Jesus Christ, who is the end unto righteousness for everyone that believeth: in whom, that is to say, everyone that is incorporated through the Spirit,

---

48 Gal. 2:15 f.   49 Rom. 9:30 f.   50 Phil 2:13.
51 Rom. 9:32.   52 Rom. 10:3f.
53 Matt. 15:3.   54 Rom. 9:31.

and made a member of him, is enabled to work righteousness because he gives the increase from within. Of the works of such, the Lord himself has said that "without me ye can do nothing."[55]

51. The righteousness of the law, of which it is said that if a man do it he shall live in it,[56] is set forth to this end: that every man may recognize his own infirmity, and so, not in his own strength or through the letter of the law (which cannot be), but winning through faith the favour of the Justifier, may attain and do, and live in it. For the work which if a man do he shall live in it is done only by one who is justified: and justification is granted to the prayer of faith, of which it is written: "Say not in thy heart, who shall ascend into heaven? (that is, to bring Christ down), or who shall descend into the deep? (that is, to bring Christ back from the dead). But what saith the Scripture? The word is nigh thee, in thy mouth and in thy heart. That is (says the apostle) the word of faith which we preach. For if thou confess with thy mouth that Jesus is Lord, and hast believed in thy heart that God hath raised him from the dead, thou shalt be saved."[57] And righteous, inasmuch as saved. For by the same faith we believe that God raises up us also from the dead: for the time present in spirit, so that in newness of his grace we live soberly, righteously, and godly in this world,[58] and afterwards even in our flesh which shall rise again unto immortality. Such shall be the reward earned for flesh by spirit, which goes before it in a spiritual resurrection, that is, in justification. "For we have been buried with Christ by baptism unto death: that like as Christ rose from the dead through the glory of the Father, even so we also should walk in newness of life."[59] By faith of Jesus Christ is granted to us both the little beginning of salvation in possession, and its perfecting which we await in hope. "For every one that shall call upon the name of the Lord shall be saved."[60] "How countless is the sum of thy sweetness, O Lord," as the Psalm says, "which thou hast hidden from them that fear thee, but perfected unto them that hope in thee!"[61], From the law comes our fear of God, from faith our hope in him; but grace is hidden from those who are in fear of punishment. The soul that labours under that fear, not yet victorious over evil concupiscence and still held in the stern ward of that same fear, must take refuge by faith with the mercy of God, that he may grant what he commands, impart the sweet savour of

55 John 15:5.   56 Lev. 18:5.   57 Rom. 10:5 ff.
58 Titus 2:12.   59 Rom. 6:4.
60 Rom. 10:13.   61 Ps. 31:19.

grace, and by his Holy Spirit make the delight of his precepts greater than the attraction which obstructs the keeping of them. Thus that "countless sum of his sweetness," the law of faith which is the love of him written and shed abroad in our hearts, is perfected unto them that hope in him; so that the healed soul may work that which is good, not in fear of punishment, but through love of righteousness.

52. Do we then "make void" freedom of choice through grace? "God forbid! yea, we establish" freedom of choice.[62] As the law is not made void by faith, so freedom of choice is not made void but established by grace. Freedom of choice is necessary to the fulfilment of the law. But by the law comes the knowledge of sin; by faith comes the obtaining of grace against sin; by grace comes the healing of the soul from sin's sickness; by the healing of the soul comes freedom of choice[63]; by freedom of choice comes the love of righteousness; by the love of righteousness comes the working of the law. And thus, as the law is not made void but established by faith, since faith obtains the grace whereby the law may be fulfilled, so freedom of choice is not made void but established by grace, since grace heals the will whereby righteousness may freely be loved. All the links in that chain which I have drawn out are found speaking in the Holy Scriptures. The law says, "Thou shalt not covet."[64] Faith says, "Heal my soul, for I have sinned against thee."[65] Grace says, "Behold, thou art made whole: sin no more, lest a worse thing come unto thee."[66] Health restored says, "O Lord my God, I cried unto thee and thou hast healed me."[67] Freedom of choice says, "I will sacrifice freely unto thee."[68] Love of righteousness says, "The unrighteous have spoken unto me of delights, but not as thy law, O Lord."[69] Why then must wretched men be bold to vaunt themselves either of their freedom of choice before they are made free, or of their own strength, if the freedom has been given them? Why will they not hear in the very words "freedom of choice" the meaning of liberty? "Where the Spirit of the Lord is, there is liberty."[70] How, if they are slaves of sin, can they boast freedom of choice? "For of whom a man is overcome, to the same is he brought in bondage."[71] But if they have been made free, why boast of it as though it were their own work, and glory as though they had not received it?

[62] Rom. 3:31.   [63] See Introduction, p. 189.   [64] Ex. 20:17.
[65] Ps. 41:4.   [66] John 5:14.   [67] Ps. 30:2.
[68] Ps. 54:6.   [69] Ps. 119:85.   [70] II Cor. 3:17.
[71] II Pet. 2:19.

This is a freedom which will not have even him for master who says: "Without me ye can do nothing," and "If the Son shall make you free, then shall ye be free indeed." [72]

53 (xxxi). In this linked series which I have described, the beginning of salvation or of the way to it appears to be faith. The question will be asked, Is this faith itself placed in our own power? It will help us to see the answer, if we look somewhat more attentively into the nature of power. Willing is one thing, ability another; willing does not necessarily imply ability, nor ability willing: we sometimes will what we are not able to do, and sometimes are able to do what we do not will. The Latin words make it plain that will (*voluntas*) is derived from *velle*, power (*potestas*) from *posse*: he who wills has *voluntas*, he who is able has *potestas*. But will must be present for power to be operative: we do not call an unwilling act the operation of power. Yet on a closer analysis, it appears that even if you do a thing under compulsion, unwillingly, you do it by your will if you do it at all: you are said to do it against your will, that is, unwillingly, because you would prefer to act differently. You are compelled to act because of some evil, which it is your will to avoid or remove; and so you act under compulsion. If your will were strong enough to prefer the suffering of the evil to the doing of the act, you would of course resist the compulsion and refuse the act. Thus if you act, though it may not be with full or free will, it can never be without willing; and since the willing is carried into effect, we cannot say that the actor was powerless. If in yielding to compulsion you willed an act which you could not perform, we should say that the will was present, albeit forced, but the power lacking. But when you do not act because you will not, the power is there but the will is lacking, so long as your resistance to compulsion withholds the act. That is why, in the employment either of compulsion or of persuasion, it may be said: "Why not do what you have in your power, in order to escape this evil?" And one who is altogether unable to do that which he is being pressed to do on the supposition of his ability, may reply with the excuse: "I would do it if it were in my power." We have then a sufficient definition of power in the union of will with the capacity to act. We say that any man has in his power that which he does if he wills and does not if he wills not.

54. Now consider the question we raised for investigation: whether faith is in our power. We are speaking of the faith with

[72] John 15:5; 8:36.

which we respond in believing, not of that which we give when we make a promise. Here too we speak of "faith," but we use the word in different senses when we say "He had not faith in me," and when we say "He did not keep faith with me": the meaning in the first case is: "He did not believe what I said"; in the second, "He did not do what he said." By the faith wherewith we believe, we are faithful to God; by the faith wherewith his promises are performed, God himself is faithful to us: as the apostle says, "God is faithful, in not suffering you to be tempted beyond that which you are able." [73] It is the faith whereby we believe God or believe in God, of which we now ask whether it is in our power—the faith of which it is written: "Abraham believed God, and it was counted unto him for righteousness"; and again: "unto him that believeth in him that justifieth the ungodly, his faith is counted for righteousness." [74]

Ask yourself, then, whether anyone can believe if he will not, or not believe if he will. The supposition is absurd—for belief is simply consenting to the truth of what is said, and consent is necessarily an act of will. It follows that faith must be in our power. But, as the apostle says, "there is no power but of God." [75] There can be no reason, then, for excluding this power from the application of the words: "What hast thou which thou hast not received?" [76] Even our believing is a thing that God has granted to us. But nowhere do we read in the Holy Scriptures that "there is no will but of God"; and rightly so, for it is not true. Else, if there were no will but of him, God would be the author of sins—which God forbid! For the evil will by itself is sin, even if its effect be lacking, that is, if it have not power to act. When the evil will receives power to accomplish its intent, this comes of the judgment of God, in whom there is no unrighteousness: his punishment is carried out in this way as well as in others, and it is not the less just because it is hidden; though the wicked man only knows he is being punished, when manifest penalty makes him feel against his will the evil of the sin he wrought willingly. This is the meaning of what the apostle says of certain sinners: "God gave them over unto the lusts of their heart, to do the things which are unfitting." [77] And as the Lord said to Pilate: "Thou couldest have no power against me, unless it were given thee from above." [78] But the giving of power is not the imposition of necessity: the David who received the power

[73] I Cor. 10:13.
[74] Rom. 4:3, 5.
[75] Rom. 13:1; a misapplied text.
[76] I Cor. 4:7.
[77] Rom. 1:24.
[78] John 19:11.

to slay Saul, chose to spare and not to strike.[79] Thus we understand that the evil receive power for the condemnation of their evil will, but the good for the proving of their good will.

55 (xxxii). Faith, then, is in our power, because everyone believes when he wills, and when he believes, believes willingly. We must next enquire, or rather recall to mind, what is the faith that the apostle urges upon us with such force of argument. It is not any kind of believing that is good; or we should not be warned: "Brethren, believe not every spirit; but test the spirit which is of God."[80] Paul's words in his praise of charity, "believeth all things"[81], do not mean that we should depreciate the charity of any man who does not at once believe everything he hears. The same charity forbids us easily to believe any evil of a brother, and counts it rather as a part of itself not to believe, when it hears such evil spoken. The charity that "believeth all things" also "believes not every spirit." We are not told that it believes all men: it believes all things, but its belief is given to God. There can be no doubt that the faith commended by the apostle is that whereby God is believed.

56. But a further distinction is required. God may be believed as well by those who are under the law and try to work their own righteousness through fear of punishment; so that they cannot work the righteousness of God. For that is done by the charity that takes pleasure only in the lawful, and not by the fear that is compelled to act lawfully, while the will's desire would be to have licence (if that were possible) for the unlawful. They also believe God: if they were devoid of such belief, they would have no dread of the law's punishment. But this is not the faith commended by the apostle, who says: "Ye have not received the spirit of bondage again unto fear, but ye have received the spirit of the adoption of sons, whereby we cry, Abba, Father."[82] This fear then is the fear of slaves, and therefore, although it renders belief to the Master, there is in it no love of righteousness but only the fear of damnation. The cry of sons is, Abba, Father—two words that belong one to the circumcision and the other to the uncircumcision: "to the Jew first and also to the Greek"—"for there is one God that justifieth the circumcision by faith and the uncircumcision through faith."[83] Their cry is a petition, and its object is that for which they hunger and thirst: which can only be, as it is written of them: "Blessed are they which hunger and thirst after righteousness,

[79] I Sam. 24:10. [80] I John 4:1. [81] I Cor. 13:7.
[82] Rom. 8:15. [83] Rom. 1:16; 3:30.

for they shall be filled."[84] To this blessedness they that are under the law must cross over; the servants must become sons, yet not ceasing to be servants, but so as to render the free service of sons to their Master and Father. For this too is what they have received: "He," the only-begotten, "hath given power to become sons of God unto them that believe in his name."[85] He has counselled them to ask, to seek, to knock, that they may receive and find and that it may be opened unto them. To which he adds the rebuke of unbelief: "if ye being evil know how to give good gifts unto your sons, how much more shall your Father which is in heaven give good things to them that ask him?"[86]

The law which is the strength of sin, has fired the sting of death,[87] so that sin taking occasion by the commandment works all manner of concupiscence.[88] From whom then should we ask for continence but from him who knows how to give good gifts to his sons? The unwise, maybe, is ignorant that none can have continence unless God give it[89]: that he may know it, wisdom is what he needs. Let him listen then to the Spirit of his Father speaking through Christ's apostle, or to Christ himself saying in his Gospel: "Ask and ye shall receive"—speaking also in his apostle and saying: "If any one of you lack wisdom, let him ask of God, who giveth to all men liberally and upbraideth not, and it shall be given to him. But let him ask in faith, nothing doubting."[90]

This is the faith, by which the righteous lives. This is the faith that believes in him who justifies the ungodly. This is the faith through which glorying is "cut out,"[91] whether for the exclusion of that which is self-conceit or for the marking of that by which we glory in the Lord. This is the faith that gains the bountiful outpouring of the Spirit, of which it is said that "we through the Spirit await in faith the hope of righteousness."[92] (One may ask here whether righteousness is subject or object of the hope; for the righteous who lives by faith does indeed hope for eternal life, and the faith that hungers and thirsts after righteousness advances therein by the renewal of the inward man from day to day, and hopes to be satisfied therewith in that eternal life where the words of the Psalm shall come to pass: "who satisfieth thy desire with good things."[93]) This is the

84 Matt. 5:6.   85 John 1:12.   86 Matt. 7:7 ff.
87 I Cor. 15:56.   88 Rom. 7:8.   89 Wisdom 21:8.
90 James 1:5 f.   91 Rom. 1:17; 4:5; 3:27. 92 Gal. 5:5.
93 Ps. 103:5.

faith by which men are saved, according to the saying: "By grace ye are saved through faith; and that not of yourselves: it is the gift of God, not of works, lest any man be lifted up. For we are his making, created in Christ Jesus in good works, which God has prepared that we may walk therein." [94] This, finally, is the faith that works through love and not through fear, not dreading punishment but longing for righteousness. Whence comes that love, which is charity, through which faith works, but from the Source that granted it to faith's own petition? There could be no spark of it in us, however small, were it not shed abroad in our hearts through the Holy Spirit which is given to us. For this charity or love of God which is said to be shed abroad in our hearts is not his own love for us but that by which he makes us his lovers: like the righteousness of God by which we are made righteous through his gift, or the salvation of the Lord by which he causes us to be saved, or the faith of Jesus Christ by which he makes us faithful. That is the righteousness of God, which he does not only teach by the commandment of the law, but gives by the bestowal of the Spirit.

57 (xxxiii). There is, however, a further question to which we should give some consideration. Is the will by which we believe also the gift of God, or is it exerted by the freedom of choice which is implanted in us by nature? If we say it is not God's gift, there is a danger of our supposing that we have found an answer to the apostle's rebuke: "What hast thou that thou hast not received? But if thou hast received it, why dost thou glory as though thou hadst not received it?" [95] We may retort that we have the will to believe, which we have not received, and that gives us room to glory because we have not received it. If on the other hand we say that this act of will is nothing but the gift of God, again there will be danger lest the infidel and the godless be thought to have good ground for excusing their own unbelief on the plea that God has refused to grant them the will. When it is said that "it is God who worketh in us both to will and to work according to his good pleasure," [96] we are already in the sphere of grace, granted to faith, in order that man may have the good works, worked by faith through the love which is shed abroad in our hearts by the Holy Spirit which is given to us. But in order that this grace may be granted we believe, and our belief is an act of will. It is of this will that we ask whence it comes. If by nature, then why not to all, since the same God is the Creator of all? If by the gift of God, still why

[94] Eph. 2:8 ff.   [95] I Cor. 4:7.   [96] Phil. 2:13.

not to all, since he will have all men to be saved and come to the knowledge of the truth? [97]

58. Here the first point to be made, as a possible solution of the difficulty, is that the freedom of choice which the Creator has conferred in the way of nature upon the rational soul is a neutral power, which can either be exerted to faith or sink into unbelief. Accordingly it cannot be said that in the act of will whereby a man believes God, he possesses what he has not received, since it arises at God's call from the freedom of choice which he received in the way of nature at his creation. God wills all men to be saved and to come to the knowledge of the truth; but not so as to deprive them of that freedom of choice, for the good or evil use of which they are subject to the judgment of absolute Justice. By that judgment, the unbelieving act against God's will when they disbelieve his gospel; yet what they do is not to defeat his will but to cheat themselves of a supreme good and fall into the distress of punishment: in which they must learn the power of him whose mercy in his gifts they have despised. [98] Thus the will of God is ever undefeated: which would not be, had he no way of dealing with his despisers, or were there any escape for them from his sentence upon such. Suppose a master say: "I will that all these my servants work in the vineyard, and after their labour rest and feast; provided that any who will not so work shall grind for ever in the mill." It might appear that one who should despise the order is acting against his master's will; but he will only defeat it if in his master's despite he escapes also from the mill. And that under the power of God is altogether impossible. So it is written: "God spoke once"—which we understand in the sense of "unchangeably," though it might also be taken to mean a single utterance—and then we hear the matter of this unchangeable word: "these two things have I heard, that power belongeth unto God, and that mercy is thine, O Lord, who wilt render to every man according to his works." [99] The despiser of his mercy, which calls for belief, must bear under his power the sentence of condemnation. But whosoever believes, and trusts himself to God for the absolution of all his sins, for the healing of all his sicknesses, for kindling and illumination by the warmth and light of God, shall have by his grace those good works which lead to deliverance even in the

---

[97] I Tim. 2:4. Note that in this treatise Augustine does not find it necessary, as he did later, to explain away this text (cf. *Enchirid.*, 103).

[98] Here is the fatal distinction between God's power and his mercy, God's will and his love.   [99] Ps. 62:11 f.

body from the corruption of death, to crowning and satisfaction with the good things which are not temporal but eternal, above all that we ask or think.[1]

59. Such is the order set forth in the Psalm: "Bless the Lord, O my soul, and forget not all his rewardings, who forgiveth all thine iniquities, who healeth all thine infirmities, who redeemeth thy life from corruption, who crowneth thee with compassion and mercy, who satisfieth thy desire with good things."[2] And lest we despair of all these good things because of that deformity of old age which is our mortality, we hear the assurance: "thy youth shall be renewed like that of an eagle"—as much as to say: "all this that thou hast heard belongs to the new man and the new covenant." Dwell on it all with me, I pray you, and take your delight in the praise of mercy, which is the grace of God. "Bless the Lord, O my soul, and forget not all his rewardings"—not awardings but rewardings, because he rewards evil with good. "Who forgiveth all thine iniquities": that is done in the sacrament of baptism. "Who healeth all thine infirmities": that takes effect for the man of faith in this life, wherein the flesh lusteth against the spirit and the spirit against the flesh, so that we do not the things we would, wherein the other law in our members wars against the law of the mind, wherein to will is present but to perform the good is not; these infirmities of old age, if we persevere in going forward, are healed by the daily increase of new life in the faith that works through love. "Who redeemeth thy life from corruption": that comes to pass in the final resurrection of the dead. "Who crowneth thee with compassion and mercy": that will be in the judgment; then, when the King of righteousness sits upon his throne to render unto every man according to his works, who shall boast that he has a pure heart or is clean from sin?[3] Here, therefore, there was need to speak of the Lord's compassion and mercy, since in that judgment the exaction of debt and rendering of desert might seem to leave no place for mercy. He will crown with compassion and mercy; yet this too will be according to men's works. For it will be those set apart on his right hand who will hear him say: "I was hungry and thou gavest me to eat."[4] There is a "judgment without mercy," but it is "to him that showed not mercy," and "blessed are the merciful, for they shall obtain mercy."[5] Then those on the left hand shall go into everlasting burning, but the righteous into life eternal; and

---

[1] Eph. 3:20.   [2] Ps. 103:2 ff.   [3] Prov. 20:8 f.
[4] Matt. 25:35.   [5] James 2:13; Matt. 5:7.

according to the saying that "this is life eternal, that they may know thee the one true God and Jesus Christ whom thou hast sent," [6] so with that knowledge, that vision, that contemplation shall the desire of the soul be satisfied with good things. That and that alone suffices it, it has nothing more to seek, to long for, to require. It was the desire of that satisfaction that kindled the disciple's heart, who said to the Lord Christ: "Show us the Father, and it sufficeth us"; and received the answer: "He that hath seen me, hath seen the Father." [7] For eternal life itself is "that they may know the one true God, thyself, and Jesus Christ whom thou hast sent." And if to have seen the Son is to have seen the Father, no doubt to see the Father and the Son is to see the Holy Spirit of the Father and the Son.

Thus freedom of choice is undisturbed; and yet our soul may bless the Lord, not forgetting all his rewardings: it seeks not in ignorance of God's righteousness to establish its own, but believes on him who justifies the ungodly, and lives by faith till it be admitted into sight, by that faith which works through love. And this love is shed abroad in our hearts, not by the sufficiency of our own will nor by the letter of the law, but by the Holy Spirit which is given to us.

60 (xxxiv). If this line of argument be thought sufficient as answer to the question raised, well and good. It may, however, be replied that there is a danger of making God responsible for the sin committed by freedom of choice, if the reason for ascribing to God's gift the will to believe (in accordance with the saying: "What hast thou which thou hast not received?") be that it arises from that freedom of choice, which we received in our creation. But it should be observed that this is not the only reason. This act of will is attributable to the divine bounty, not only because it comes of the freedom of choice which was created with us in the way of nature. Besides that, God works for our willing and believing through the inducement of impressions which we experience: whether the impressions be external, as in the exhortations of the Gospel, in which case the law's commands have a certain effect, if by warning a man of his own weakness they make him seek refuge through believing with the grace that justifies; or internal, as in the ideas which enter the mind willynilly, though consent or refusal thereto is a matter of one's own will. In these ways does God work upon the reasonable soul to believe: indeed freedom of choice could produce no act of belief, were there no inducement or invitation to

[6] John 17:3.   [7] John 14:8 f.

belief. Assuredly then it is God who brings about in a man the very will to believe, and in all things does his mercy anticipate us; yet to consent to the calling of God or to refuse it, as I have said, belongs to our own will. Which, so far from conflicting with the text, "What hast thou which thou hast not received?", does even confirm it. For the soul cannot receive and possess the gifts there spoken of, but by consenting. What it is to possess, what it is to receive, pertains to God: the receiving and the possessing necessarily to him who receives and possesses.[8] There remains indeed the profound mystery, why this suasion in one man is effective, in another not. If I am pressed to attempt its fathoming, I can think at the moment of only two answers that I should like to give: "O the depth of the riches . . ." and, "Is there any unrighteousness with God?"[9] He whom the reply contents not may look for more instructed counsellors; but let him beware of finding such as are over-confident.

61 (xxxv). It is time to end this book. I cannot say whether its prolixity has achieved anything—I do not mean for you, whose faith I know, but for the minds of those on whose account you desired me to write. It is not against me, but (to refrain from any appeal to the authority of him who has spoken in his apostles) certainly against no less an apostle than Paul, speaking not in a single text but in a long argument of such power, intensity and vigilance, that they must defend, if they choose, their own opinion: instead of listening to him, as he entreats by the mercy of God, and bids them through the grace of God given unto him, "not to be wise overmuch beyond the wisdom that is fitting, but to be wise in soberness, according as God hath dealt to every man the measure of faith." [10]

62. But I may call your attention to the question which you put to me and to the upshot of my long and laboured argument. You were perplexed by the statement that a man may be without sin, if the divine aid be seconded by his own will, although there be no example, past, present, or future, of such perfect righteousness in this life. In the work previously addressed to you I had stated the matter in these terms: "If I am asked whether a man can in this life be without sin, I will allow that it is possible, through the grace of God and the man's free choice:

---

[8] For this passage, see Introduction, p. 190.

[9] Rom. 11:33; 9:14. Augustine habitually makes use of Paul's *O altitudo!*, in its context an outburst of praise for the great design of "mercy upon all," to quell heart-searchings over the problem of predestination.

[10] Rom. 12:3.

though I make no doubt that freedom of choice itself appertains to the grace of God, that is, to the things which he gives—and not only its existence, but its right direction, its turning to perform the Lord's commands; so that the grace of God not only shows what is right but also by its aid enables it to be done when it is shown." [11] You thought it irrational that there should be no example of a thing that is possible; and so arose the enquiry of this book, in which it lay on me to show that a thing may be possible even if example of it be lacking. Accordingly, we adduced instances at the beginning of our discussion, from the Gospel and the Law; such as the camel's passing through the needle's eye, the twelve legions of angels that might have fought for Christ had he so willed, the nations which God said he could have destroyed all at once from the face of his people—all being things that have not happened. One might add what we read in the Book of Wisdom, of the many strange torments which God could put forth against the wicked through the creature's obedience to his order [12]—which yet he did not; or one might quote the mountain which faith could shift into the sea, though we have no record or report of its ever being done. To say that any of these things is impossible to God, would be plain folly and contradiction of the truth of his Scripture. And many other cases of the same kind might occur to us in reading or reflecting, of which we could not deny the possibility with God, although example of them be lacking.

63. Since, however, it might be said that these are works of God, whereas righteous living is a matter of our own working, I undertook to show that this also is a divine work; and to the proof of this I have devoted the present book—perhaps with more words than were needed. Yet as against the enemies of God's grace I feel that I have said only too little. I am never so happy in speaking as when I have most ample support in the Scripture, and when the purpose is that whosoever glories may glory in the Lord, [13] and that in all things we may give thanks to the Lord our God, lifting up our hearts to heaven, whence from the Father of lights comes every best gift and every perfect gift. [14] If the fact that a thing is done by our hands or that we do it by God's granting makes it no work of God, then it is no work of God for the mountain to be carried into the sea, since the Lord has said that this can be done through the faith of men, and set it down to their own working in the words: "If ye have

[11] De Pecc. Mer., II, 7.   [12] Wisdom 16:24.
[13] II Cor. 10:17.   [14] James 1:17.

faith in you as a grain of mustard seed, ye shall say to this mountain, Be lifted up and cast into the sea, and it shall be done; and nothing shall be impossible to you." [15] Christ says "to you," not "to me" or "to my Father"; yet a man could by no means do such a thing, unless God granted and worked it. In this way we may see that perfect righteousness may be unexampled among men and yet be not impossible. It would come about, if there were brought to bear the will sufficient for such an achievement; and that might be, if all the requirements of righteousness were known to us, and if they inspired in the soul such delight as to overcome the obstacle set by any other pleasure or pain. That it does not happen is due not to its impossibility but to the judgment of God. For we are well aware that the extent of a man's knowledge is not in his own power, and that it does not follow that he will pursue what he knows to be worth pursuing, unless he delight in it no less than it deserves his love. But that depends upon the health of the soul.

64 (xxxvi). One might perhaps suppose that in regard to the knowledge of righteousness we have all we need; inasmuch as our Lord, summing and shortening his word upon the earth, [16] has said that upon two commandments hang all the law and the prophets, and put those commandments in the plainest words: "Thou shalt love the Lord thy God with all thy heart and with all thy soul and with all thy mind," and "Thou shalt love thy neighbour as thyself." [17] That in the fulfilling of these is the complete fulfilment of righteousness, is absolute truth. But to observe this must not be to forget how often we all go wrong in the belief that what we do is pleasing or not unpleasing to God; whereas his scripture or the clear assurance of reason may afterwards teach us to see that it is not pleasing to him, and we have to pray in penitence for his forgiveness. Human life is full of such records. And why is it that we know too little of what is pleasing to him, but because we know too little of himself? "For we see now through a glass darkly, but then face to face." [18] Who could dare to think that when we come to that state of which it is written, "that I may know even as also I am known," the love of God in those that behold him will be no greater than in the faithful here and now—or indeed that there can be any comparison between the one and the other? The greater the knowledge, the greater the love; and if that be so, then whatever now we lack in love must be thought lacking to the perfection of

15 Matt. 17:20 and Luke 17:6 (conflate).
16 Isa. 10:23.   17 Matt. 22:37 ff.   18 I Cor. 13:12.

righteousness. A thing can be known or believed, and yet not loved; but what is neither known nor believed cannot be loved. Through believing, the saints may have been enabled to reach that love than which by the Lord's own testimony there can in this life be no greater: namely, to lay down their life for the faith or for the brethren. But when we issue from this pilgrimage in which now we walk by faith, to the sight for which still unseen we hope and in patience wait,[19] most certainly will love itself be not only above that which we have here, but far above what we ask or think. Yet it can never be more than love with the whole heart, with the whole soul, with the whole mind; for there can be nothing remaining in us that could be added to the whole: otherwise it would not have been the whole. Accordingly this first commandment of righteousness, which bids us love God with our whole heart and with our whole soul and with our whole mind, on which follows the other concerning love of neighbour, will be fulfilled in the life to come when we shall see face to face. It is commanded to us even now, that we might be made aware of what faith must ask and whither hope must go ahead: what are those things that are before, unto which, forgetting the things that are behind, we must reach forth.[20] So, as it appears to me, in the righteousness that is to be made perfect much progress in this life has been made by that man who knows by his progress how far he is from the perfection of righteousness.

65. We may, however, speak of a lesser righteousness belonging to this life, and shown in the righteous man who lives by faith, though still absent from the Lord and therefore walking by faith and not by sight; and to this righteousness freedom from sin might not unreasonably be attributed. We cannot reckon it as guilt, if the love of God cannot yet reach the height appropriate to the full and perfect knowledge of heaven: it is one thing to fall short of charity in its wholeness, and another to follow after no evil desire. So it is the duty of a man, even though he loves God far less than he may love him when he is seen, to abstain from all pursuit of what is unlawful: just as, in the sphere of sense perception, the eye that cannot rest steadily upon a full blaze of light can refuse to take pleasure in darkness. Let us then imagine, in this corruptible body, a human soul wherein the most excellent perfection of charity has not yet absorbed and consumed every motive of earthly lust, but which is kept by this lesser righteousness from the least leaning towards

[19] II Cor. 5:7; Rom. 8:25.   [20] Phil. 3:13.

consent to such lust for the doing of any unlawful thing. Then
we can apply to our immortal life which is to come the rule:
"Thou shalt love the Lord thy God with thy whole heart and
with thy whole soul and with thy whole strength"; and to our
life here that other rule: "Let not sin reign in your mortal body,
to obey its desires." [21] There will be fulfilled the command:
"Thou shalt not covet"; here the command: "Go not after thy
concupiscences." [22] There we shall have nothing more to seek
but continuance in that state of perfection; here a man must
work to achieve his purpose, and hope for its perfecting as his
reward. There the righteous will live endlessly in the sight for
which here he longed; here the righteous will live by faith,
longing for that life which will most surely be his end.

On these premises, it will be sin for one who lives by faith to
yield any consent to any unlawful delectation, not only in the
committing of the more abominable misdeeds or crimes, but in
such more venial matters as lending ear to any word that ought
not to be listened to, or tongue to one that ought not to be
spoken; or having any thought in the heart that would desire
licence for a thing known by the commandment to be unlawful
and wrongly felt as delectable: for that itself is consenting to
sin, inasmuch as it would be done, but for fear of punishment.
But if the righteous who live by faith resist all such temptation,
does that mean that they have no need to say: "Forgive us our
debts, as we also forgive our debtors"? Do they confute the texts
of Scripture: "In thy sight shall no man living be justified"; "If
we say that we have no sin, we deceive ourselves, and the truth
is not in us"; "for there is no man that shall not sin," "for there
is no righteous man on earth that shall do good and not sin"? [23]
(Note that both these last texts speak not of the past but of the
future: not "has not," but "shall not sin".) These and other sayings of Holy Scripture in the same sense cannot be untrue. It
follows, as I see it, that in whatever kind or degree we may define righteousness in this life, there is in this life no man entirely
without sin: there is need for every man to give that it may be
given to him, to forgive that it may be forgiven him, and in
respect of any righteousness he possesses not to presume that
it has come of his own making, but to accept it as of the grace
of God who justifies; yet none the less to hunger and thirst for
the gift of righteousness from him who is the living bread and
with whom is the well of life—who so works justification in his

21 Rom.6:12.   22 Ecclesiasticus 18:30.
23 Ps. 143:2; I John 1:8; I Kings 8:46; Ecclesiastes 7:20.

saints that labour in the trial of this life, that there is always somewhat his bounty may add in answer to their prayer, or his goodness pardon upon their confession.

66. Let those who differ from us find a man, living under the burden of our corruption, whom God has no longer anything to pardon. If they can do so, they must either admit that he was enabled to that state, not by the gift of the law's teaching, but by the inpouring of the Spirit of grace, or else incur the guilt of no lesser sin than blasphemy itself. If they accept the sacred texts just quoted in their proper sense, their finding any such man is impossible. Nevertheless it may by no means be asserted that to God the possibility is not present of granting to the human will aid sufficient not only for the complete perfection, here and now, of the righteousness which is by faith, but even for that righteousness in which we shall hereafter live for ever in the contemplation of himself. Suppose God should will, here and now, to clothe in any man this corruptible with incorruption, and to bid him live immortal among mortal men—in such wise that all the old man in him were utterly done away, that there were no law in his members warring against the law of his mind, and that he knew the omnipresent God with that same knowledge which the saints shall have hereafter. Would anyone be mad enough to deny that God *could* do such a thing? Men will still question why he does not do it; but the questioners bethink themselves too little that they are men.

I know that there is neither impossibility nor unrighteousness with God; I know that he resisteth the proud and giveth grace unto the humble; and I know that the apostle to whom, lest he be exalted, was given a thorn in the flesh, an angel of Satan to buffet him, heard once again and yet a third time the answer to his prayer: "My grace is sufficient for thee: for strength is made perfect in weakness." [24] There lies therefore a secret in the hidden depth of God's judgments, that even of the righteous shall every mouth be closed in praise of self and opened only unto the praise of God. But that secret who can explore, who can search out, who can know? So "unsearchable are his judgments, and his ways past finding out. For who hath known the mind of the Lord? or who hath been his counsellor? or who hath first given unto him, and it shall be recompensed unto him again? For of him, and through him, and in him are all things. To him be glory for ever and ever. Amen." [25]

[24] Luke 1:37; Ps. 92:15; James 4:6; II Cor. 12:7 ff.
[25] Rom. 11:33 ff.

Ten Homilies
on the First Epistle General of St. John

INTRODUCTION

THE PELAGIAN CONTROVERSY WAS THE CHIEF
literary pre-occupation of Augustine from A.D. 411 (his
57th year) to his death in A.D. 430 at the age of 75. It
began as a controversy of a very different kind was ending. Ever
since his ordination to the priesthood in A.D. 391, his work had
been tormented by the Donatist schism; and he had taken the
leading part in the efforts to bring it to an end and to reunite the
Church in Africa, which culminated in the great Conference of
Carthage in A.D. 411—nominally a meeting of Catholic and
Donatist bishops to discuss their differences, but really a formal
execution of the Emperor's resolve to abolish a "new-fangled
superstition," the imperial "arbitrator" being that same Count
Marcellinus to whom Augustine was shortly to address *The Spirit
and the Letter*.

The schism in the African Church, from which Christianity
in Africa, despite the events of A.D. 411, was never to recover, had
lasted for a full century. It had arisen as an outcome of the Great
Persecution under Diocletian, in which many of the African
clergy had succumbed to the order for surrender of the books of
Scripture. Even before the famous Edict of Milan in A.D. 313
gave freedom of worship to Christians, rival bishops had been
set up in Carthage. The ostensible ground of objection to the
"Catholic" bishop Caecilian was that his consecration had been
invalid, because one of his consecrators had been a *traditor*, a
surrenderer of the Scriptures in the persecution. No such charge
was made against Caecilian himself, but he was accused of un-
christian conduct towards imprisoned confessors, and generally
of discouraging the cult of martyrs, which had long been a
cherished element of popular Christianity in Africa. In A.D. 313,

the Emperor Constantine instructed the Proconsul of Africa to restore to the Church the property of which it had been deprived, and made it clear that he regarded Caecilian as the legitimate bishop. The rival party immediately appealed to him for arbitration on their case by bishops from overseas. There was a series of investigations, by episcopal councils at Rome and at Arles in Gaul, by the Proconsul in Africa, and by the Emperor himself at Milan. Each time, judgment went against the Donatists; but they were defiant, and refused to surrender the churches which they held. An attempt was made to enforce the imperial decision by the secular arm, and the Donatists counted their first "martyrs" from this period. But Constantine had other matters on hand, the "persecution" was given up, and the African Church was left divided. Thirty years later, Donatus, who had given his name to the schismatic party and was still its leader, felt himself strong enough to ask the Emperor Constans for recognition as sole bishop of Carthage. By that time, his party had acquired supporters who were to prove a doubtful advantage to them. There had arisen a kind of chronic "peasant revolt," carried on by bands of religious fanatics known as Circumcellions, who combined the redress of agrarian grievances and the cancellation of debts with the pursuit of martyrdom, and terrorized the countryside under a Donatist war-cry. In A.D. 347, Constans sent a commission to Africa to pacify the Church, with offers of funds to both sides for the relief of distress. But Donatus rejected them, as well as the imperial intervention for which he had asked, with the protest which was to become notorious—"What has Emperor to do with Church?"—and appeasement was abandoned for repression. Troops were called in, and there was fighting and massacre. Donatus himself was exiled, and Donatism was confirmed in its representation of itself as the Church of martyrs, and of the "Catholics" as bloody persecutors. The accession of Julian the Apostate in A.D. 361, with his policy of general toleration for all religions and sects, allowed the leaders of the schism to return in full strength, and this time at least the Donatists were the aggressors. Africa was torn with communal rioting, violence and bloodshed. Despite the recovery of imperial favour by the Catholics after Julian's death, Donatism might well have advanced to final victory, if it had not lent its support once and again in the last quarter of the century to risings against Roman authority led by Moorish rebels. That, and the increasing scandal of Circumcellion outrages, convinced the Court that strong action was needed. In

A.D. 405, the existing laws against heresy were applied to the schismatics: their meetings and services were prohibited, and they became liable to heavy fines and economic disabilities, though there was no infliction of the death penalty. The desire of the Catholics, under Augustine's leadership, to represent their victory as one of reason rather than of force, was met by the formal hearing and dismissal of the Donatist case, at the Conference of Carthage in A.D. 411, after which Donatism was finally proscribed. But though it ceased to exist as an organized Church, and many of its congregations returned to the Catholic allegiance, there was no full reunion. Donatism survived the Vandal invasion which was swamping Roman Africa when Augustine died in A.D. 430, and it was still strong enough to trouble Pope Gregory at the end of the sixth century.

Augustine believed that the "origin and stubbornness of the schism" came from nothing else but the "hatred of brothers." That private and personal enmities had much to do with the original dispute, and that the violence and cruelties which accompanied its prolongation so exacerbated the issues as to make them irreconcilable, is sufficiently clear. But the trouble could not have lasted so long with such persistence and bitterness, had there not been deeper causes at work. The history of the schism shows at many points that social and economic factors were engaged as well as religious and ecclesiastical. The lines of cleavage between Donatist and Catholic ran in close parallel to those which in the Roman Africa of the fourth century divided native from immigrant, Punic or Berber from Latin speech, upland village from coastal town, peasant holder from wealthy land-owner—in short, a non-Roman and subject from a Romanized and dominant society. There was no clearcut geographical division, but the strength of one side lay in Numidia and of the other in the Old Province of proconsular Africa. It was by no accident that seventy Numidian bishops descended upon Carthage in A.D. 312 to consecrate a rival bishop in place of Caecilian, and that the great Donatus who soon succeeded their nominee as leader of the opposition was a Numidian from the High Plains. Numidia was always the stronghold of Donatism, while in the Old Province, even in Carthage itself, it was never more than a minority.

This does not mean, as has sometimes been suggested, that the schism was no more than an accidental symptom of African nationalism. Donatism arose at the moment when the Roman Empire turned from being the Church's persecutor to be its patron, and the Church from drawing life from the blood of its martyrs to be in large measure the pensioner of the State. The schism was a movement of revolt, but the revolt was at bottom religious and not political in motive. It is best understood as a protest against the subordination of the Church to the secular power which Christianity had resisted ever since its birth. That the Donatists were ready on occasion to appeal to the State or to take advantage of state legislation does not alter the essential character of their conflict with the established Church in Africa. For them, the perfect Christian must always be the martyr. Apostasy, the cowardly refusal to die for the faith, must always be unforgivable sin: the Christian priest who commits that sin can be priest no longer. More than that, he is a plague-spot that must infect all who hold communion with him. "Touch not the unclean thing."

The Donatists had a case, though they produced no one capable of stating it with the force needed to meet a controversialist of Augustine's calibre. Augustine argued, first, that they had failed from the beginning to establish the facts, connected with Caecilian's consecration, by which they justified their schism; and secondly, that even if the facts were established, the schism could be justified only by doctrines of the nature of the Church and the Sacraments which were untenable, and which in his view transformed it into a heresy. On the question of fact, it is now generally agreed that the documentary evidence, bearing upon the actions of African bishops in the Great Persecution and the events of A.D. 312, tells conclusively against the Donatist claims. The doctrinal issue is much more complicated. It centred upon the single point of church practice which divided Catholic and schismatic. In the time of Cyprian, the African Church had refused to recognize the validity of baptism conferred by any person outside Catholic communion, and so required the rebaptism of all converts baptized in heresy or schism. The Church of Rome had adopted the view that all baptism, performed as the Church performs it, is valid; and this had led to a sharp controversy between Africa and Rome in which neither side gave way—though (as Augustine was always reminding his Donatist adversaries) there was no breach of communion between the Churches. Rebaptism remained the African practice until the same Council of Arles in A.D. 314, which rejected the Donatist charges against Caecilian, pronounced against it. Thereafter, the Catholic Church in Africa fell into line with Rome. The Donatists maintained the practice of Cyprian and the doctrine which supported it: namely, that the Holy Spirit is given only in and through the Holy Church, and that outside the Church there is neither salvation nor sacrament of salvation. This meant that the validity of the sacrament could not be independent of the person of the minister who must represent the Church. Now Cyprian had declared it to be the duty of Catholic Christians to refuse the ministrations of unworthy priests; and there can be little doubt that he would have regarded apostasy in any form as a disqualification for the performance of priestly functions. The Donatists were fully justified in appealing to his authority as representing the common tradition of the Church in Africa: no *traditor* can perform a valid sacrament. The point was not really met when Augustine in turn appealed to Cyprian's use, against his own rigorist opponents, of the parable of the tares, to show that the Church in this world must tolerate the presence of sinners within her body. The Donatists pointed out, with some justice, that in the Gospel interpretation of the parable the "field" is not the Church but the world. They did indeed refuse to accept the Catholic argument that the holiness of the Church, "without spot or wrinkle," cannot be realized in this world. But there is no evidence that their ecclesiastical discipline was more rigorous than that of the Catholics, and it is a mistake to attribute to them a Puritan theory of the Church, like that of the Novatians with whom Cyprian had had to deal. Their real concern was with the status of the minister, not of the layman; and even in the case of the minister they recognized the fact that not all sin is open and notorious. What, in their view, must defile the Church and render the sacrament invalid is the attempted ministration of a priest *known* to be guilty of mortal sin. In their view, the "Catholics" of Africa had abandoned the sound tradition of her Church as a *quid pro quo* for the decision in their favour by the Council of Arles on the question of fact. It was thus Augustine and not the Donatist who was obliged to work out an ecclesiology to support an admitted innovation in practice. If we cannot regard his attempt as successful, that will be because he shared with his opponents the rigid dogma of Cyprian that there is no salvation outside the Church. It followed for him as for them that baptism and orders conferred outside the Church must so far be ineffectual. If such sacraments are not to be repeated when the recipient enters the Church, they must possess a *validity* which is unaffected by the status of the minister: the recipient in heresy or schism has *really* been baptized or ordained, because (so Augustine urged) the real minister in every sacrament is none other than Christ himself. "This is he which baptizeth with the Holy Spirit"(John 1:33). But if, as Augustine had to maintain, such sacraments possess no saving *efficacy* unless and until the recipient becomes a member of the Catholic Church, it has to be supposed that the Holy Spirit whom Christ gives through them remains as it were inactive so long as the recipient is outside that Church's communion.

This distinction between the validity and the efficacy of the sacrament has been almost exactly reversed in modern thought and usage: Catholics will now recognize that the sacraments of non-episcopal bodies have at least a measure of real efficacy in the fruits they bear, though they are "invalid" in the sense of irregular. Augustine tried to make sense of his own distinction by insisting that the Holy Spirit is the Spirit of *charity*, which is the "bond of perfectness" (Col. 3:14), and that the "unity of the Spirit" can be kept only in "the bond of peace" (Eph. 4:3). All schism, all separation from the Church, violates charity and therefore stifles the life of the Spirit. The great saying of Paul, that "neither circumcision availeth anything nor uncircumcision, but faith working through love" (Gal. 5:6), underlies all that has permanent value in Augustine's teaching on Church and Sacraments. In neither one nor the other can faith be efficacious, can it be Christian faith at all, unless it expresses itself in the "energizing" of charity. The principle is in theory inexpugnable. Its practical application by Augustine to the Donatist controversy involved him in the claim that the energizing of charity was in fact manifested in the Catholic Church and not in the schismatic. The Donatists rejoined that such a claim assorted ill with a record of persecution; and when Augustine began his struggle for reunion, he was insistent that the Church must avoid giving any occasion for such a rejoinder. He knew well the obstinacy of his opponents, yet he threw all his influence into the pursuit of a policy of reconciliation by peaceful discussion of differences. What made the policy so difficult to carry out was the fact that the Donatists with their Circumcellion "soldiers of Christ" were so often guilty of actions which were criminal by the law; and it was difficult to deny to the victims of such actions their proper legal redress. Even so, Augustine was able to persuade his Catholic colleagues to intercede frequently on behalf of the convicted Donatist for the remission or mitigation of the legal penalty. In the end, like the imperial authorities in their dealings with the Christians of the second century, Augustine himself gave up the attempt to distinguish between the "name" of Donatism and the "crimes attaching to the name," and accepted the proscription of Donatism as such. The Donatists themselves had constantly used force as a method of proselytizing: there seemed no answer but the legalized use of force against them, if the Church was to carry out her clear duty towards the many whom fear was retaining in schism against their will.

Hence the tragic capitulation of the great preacher of Christian charity to the principle of religious persecution. "Compel them to come in." It is upon this background that we must hear the impassioned encomia of charity in the *Homilies on St. John's Epistle*. Hippo lay within the border of Numidia, and Augustine's episcopate had always been the charge of a harassed minority. Vacillation on the side of the State, even after the decisions of A.D. 411, had delayed the effective enforcement of those decisions; and when, probably towards the end of the year 414, Augustine began to deliver his *Homilies on St. John's Gospel*, Donatism was still troublesome enough in his diocese to call for constant reference and systematic refutation in his exposition of the first few chapters: the fifth and sixth Homilies are entirely devoted to the application against the Donatists of the text John 1:32, 33, and we hear that the cathedral in spite of the very cold weather was crowded to hear them. At Eastertide A.D. 415 Augustine broke off his course on the Gospel to interpolate the *Homilies on the Epistle*, and both the choice of theme and the treatment of it show that the schism is still in the forefront of his concern. But soon after the resumption of the *Homilies on the Gospel*, references in them to Donatism cease almost completely. It is a reasonable inference that the long-drawn-out struggle ended in Hippo with the collapse of opposition just at this time.[1] Charity at last had won the day; but in celebrating its victory Augustine could not forget that the victory had not been achieved, as once he hoped it might be, by the spiritual arm alone. "Love, and do what thou wilt" is the most famous saying in the Homilies. Read in its context (Hom. VII, 8), it is the preacher's defence of compulsion in the service of love—the sad monument of an uneasy conscience, seeking to assure itself that the end justifies the means.

For the rest, the Homilies need no introduction. They are, of course, sermons and not a commentary, though they follow the

[1] See M. le Landais in *Études Augustiniennes*, pp. 72-80.

course of the Epistle verse by verse. Augustine's exegesis is often unsatisfactory, and his arguments on the text of Scripture are often forced: for example, he is at pains to reconcile the apparent contradiction between I John 1:8 and 3:9 by supposing that there is *one* sin and one only which he who "abides in Christ" can never commit, and that is the transgression of the new commandment of brotherly love. But if he is an indifferent exegete, he is an incomparable preacher. These Homilies show him at the summit of his extraordinary power to move the soul.

Ten Homilies
on the First Epistle of St. John

THE TEXT

PROLOGUE

As you know, my people, I have been giving you a course of
sermons on the Gospel according to John. During the present
holy festival, the Church gives us certain fixed Lessons to be
read year by year, which we must not alter; so that there will
have to be a short break in the course which we had begun, and
which we shall afterwards continue. I have considered what
part of Scripture would be a fitting subject on which to speak
to you, as the Lord may grant me ability, during this joyous
week, and which could be completed in these seven or eight
days; and I have chosen the Epistle of John. We shall then
still be listening to him whose Gospel we have for a while put
down. It is a book very sweet to every healthy Christian heart
that savours the bread of God; and it should be constantly in the
mind of God's Holy Church. But I choose it more particularly
because what it specially commends to us is charity. The man
who has in himself that of which he hears must rejoice at the
hearing. To him this reading will be like oil on the flame: if
there is matter in him for nourishment, it will be nourished, it
will grow and abide. For some, the Epistle should be like flame
to firewood: if it was not already burning, the touch of the word
may kindle it. In some, then, what is present is to be nourished:
in some, what may be lacking is to be kindled; so that we may
all rejoice together in one single charity. Where there is charity,
there is peace: where there is humility, there is charity. And
now let us hear John himself; and let me speak for your better
understanding whatever the Lord shall put into my mind as I
read the apostle's words.

FIRST HOMILY
I John 1:1–2:11

1. "That which was from the beginning, which we have heard, and which we have seen with our eyes, and our hands have handled, of the word of life."

There could be no handling with hands of the word, had not the Word been made flesh and dwelt among us. This Word, made flesh to be handled with hands, took its beginning as flesh from the virgin Mary; but it took not then its beginning as Word—for we read: "that which was from the beginning." Epistle is confirmed by Gospel, in which you have already heard: "In the beginning was the Word, and the Word was with God." [1] One might understand "the word of life" as a speaking about Christ, and not the actual body of Christ, handled with hands. But see what follows: "and the life itself was manifested." Christ, then, is the word of life. How "manifested"? He was from the beginning, but not manifested to man, though manifested to the sight of angels, feeding as it were upon their own Bread. But we read that "man did eat angels' food." [2] The Life itself has been manifested in flesh—set in manifestation, that what can be seen by the heart alone might be seen also by the eyes for the healing of hearts. Only by the heart is the Word seen: flesh is seen by the bodily eyes. We had the means of seeing the flesh, but not of seeing the Word: the Word was made flesh which we could see, that the heart, by which we should see the Word, might be healed.

2. "We have seen and are witnesses"—seen, that is, as manifested, and manifested by the light of this sun. The sun's Maker could only be seen by that sun's light, because he "set his tabernacle in the sun, going forth himself as a bridegroom out of his

[1] John 1:1.   [2] Ps. 78:25.

260

chamber, rejoicing as a giant to run his course." [3] He who was before the sun which he made, before the day-star and all stars, before all angels, the true Creator (for all things were made by him, and without him was nothing made),[4] that he might be seen by the eyes of flesh which see the sun, set his own tabernacle in the sun—showed his flesh in manifestation by this light: the Bridegroom's chamber was the virgin's womb, where Bridegroom and Bride, Word and flesh, were joined together. It is written: "And the two shall be in one flesh," or, as the Lord says in the Gospel, "therefore they are no longer two, but one flesh." [5] So finely does Isaiah make the two one, when he speaks in Christ's person, "He put a band upon my head as on a bridegroom, and adorned me as a bride with her ornaments." [6] The one speaker makes himself both Bridegroom and Bride; for they are "not two, but one flesh," since "the Word was made flesh and dwelt among us." When to that flesh is joined the Church, there is the whole Christ, Head and Body.[7]

3. "And we have seen, and are witnesses; and we make known to you the eternal life, which was with the Father and has been manifested among us: that which we have seen and heard, we make known to you."

They saw the Lord himself present in the flesh, and they heard the words of his mouth, and made them known to us. We also then have heard, but we have not seen. Are we less happy than they, who both saw and heard? No, for it goes on: "that ye also may have fellowship with us." They have seen, and we have not; yet we are their fellows, because we hold a common faith. There was one of them who saw, yet believed not, but would feel before he believed, saying: "unless I put my fingers into the print of the nails, and touch his scars, I will not believe." [8] So he who ever gives himself to be seen of angels gave himself for a time to be felt by the hands of men; and that disciple felt him and exclaimed, "My Lord and my God." Because he had touched a man, he confessed his God. And the Lord, for the comfort of us who cannot handle him with our hands now that he sits in heaven, but can touch him by faith, says to Thomas: "Because thou hast seen, thou hast believed: blessed are they who see not and believe."

It is we who are so described and designated. Let us then

[3] Ps. 19:5.　　　　　　　　[4] John 1:3.
[5] Gen. 2:24; Matt. 19:6.　　[6] Isa. 61:10.
[7] Augustine's constant doctrine, that the incarnate Christ and his Church are a single "whole."　　[8] John 20:25 ff.

receive the blessing which the Lord has promised: let us hold fast that which we see not, since they who saw have made it known to us.

"That ye also may have fellowship with us." You may think it no great matter to have fellowship with men. But see what follows: "and our fellowship be with God the Father and his Son Jesus Christ. These things we write to you that your joy may be full." That fulness of joy is in the fellowship, the charity, the unity itself.

4. "And this is the message which we have heard from him and make known to you . . . that God is light, and there is no darkness in him." The light and darkness here spoken of have nothing to do with our bodily eyes. As God surpasses the creature, as the Maker the thing made, as Wisdom itself surpasses that to which Wisdom has given being, so that light must far transcend all others. Perhaps we shall come near that light, if we know what it is and set ourselves before it that we may have enlightenment from it. In ourselves we are darkness: enlightened by it, we may become light: it will not confound us, because we confound ourselves. To confound myself is to know myself a sinner: not to be confounded by the light is to be enlightened by it. The man who sees himself darkened by sin and longs to be enlightened by the light, is drawing near to it. As the Psalm says: "Draw near to him and be enlightened; and your faces shall not be ashamed." [9] The light will not shame you, if it shows you your own ugliness, and that ugliness so offends you that you perceive the beauty of the light.

5. Have we expounded our text too hastily? We shall see as we proceed. Remember the words that came before: "that ye may have fellowship with us, and our fellowship be with God the Father, and his Son Jesus Christ." God is light, and there is no darkness in him, and we should have fellowship with him. The darkness must be driven from us, that the light may be in us; for darkness can have no fellowship with light—as Paul says.[10] But what follows? "If we say that we have fellowship with him, and walk in darkness, we lie." A man may well say to himself, "What can I do, how can I become light? I live in sins and iniquities." A gloomy despair creeps over him. There is no salvation but in fellowship with God. God is light, and there is no darkness in him. Iniquities are darkness: our iniquities overwhelm us, so that we cannot have fellowship with God. What hope is there?

[9] Ps. 34:5.　　　　[10] II Cor. 6:14.

Am I failing to keep my promise that in these days I should have a message of joy to speak to you? Listen: there may be a word of comfort, encouragement, and hope, that we faint not by the way. We are travellers, travelling to our home-land, and if we despair of reaching it, in our despair we faint. But he whose will it is that we should reach the home-land where he will keep us, nourishes us upon our journey. Listen: "If we walk in the light as he is in the light, we have fellowship with one another." And what of our sins? "The blood of Jesus Christ his Son shall cleanse us from all transgression." Great is the confidence that God has given us. Well may we celebrate our Paschal sacrifice, in which the Lord's blood is shed to cleanse us from all transgression. Let us rest confident: the devil held against us a bond of slavery, but Christ's blood has wiped it out.

Think for a moment of those brothers of ours whom we call "infants"[11]: but now, in the name of Christ whom they have confessed, all their sins have been washed away by his blood. They came, old, into the Baptistery and went out new—came in aged and went out infants. Their old life was somnolent age: their new life is the infancy of regeneration. But remember that past sins have been forgiven not only to them but to us. After the forgiving and wiping away of all sins, our life amidst the temptations of this world may not avoid all stain. Then let a man do what he can: let him confess what he is, that he may be healed by the one who never changes. For he alone ever was, and is: we were not, and we are.

6. "If we say that we have no sin, we deceive ourselves, and the truth is not in us."—If then you confess yourself a sinner, the truth is in you, for the truth itself is light. Your life is not yet perfect in brightness, for there are sins in it: yet your enlightenment has begun with your confession of sin. Read on: "but if we confess our transgressions, he is faithful and just to forgive us our transgressions and to cleanse us from all iniquity." Not only the transgressions that are past, but any that this life brings upon us; for so long as a man wears flesh, he cannot be without at least the lesser sins. But these that we call the lesser must not be made light of: if you make light of their gravity, you must tremble at their number. The many lesser make a large: many drops fill up a river, many grains make a lump. Where then is our hope? First of all, in confession; that none count himself righteous, man who was not, and is, lifting up his head before the eyes of God who sees what he is. First of all, then, confession,

11 The baptism of catechumens took place on Easter Eve.

and next, love; for of charity it is said that it covers the multitude of sins.[12] Let us see whether charity itself is not commended to us on account of the transgressions that steal upon us; for charity alone can quench transgression. Pride quenches charity: humility strengthens it: charity quenches transgression. Humility is part of our confession that we are sinners. But humility lies not in the spoken word, which might seek only to avoid the offence of arrogance in calling ourselves righteous. In wickedness and folly a man will say: I know that I am righteous, but I cannot say so openly, for folk will not suffer it: let my righteousness be known of God, and I will call myself a sinner—not because I am, but that I may not be set down as arrogant and offensive. No, say what you are, to man as well as to God. If you do not tell God what you are, he will condemn what he finds in you. If you would not have his condemnation, speak your own. If you would have his pardon, do you acknowledge your need of it: say to God, "Turn thy face from my sins"; say with the Psalmist, "For I acknowledge my iniquity."[13]

"If we confess our transgressions, he is faithful and just to forgive us our transgressions and to cleanse us from all iniquity. If we say that we have not sinned, we make him a liar, and his word is not in us." If you say, I have not sinned, you make him a liar in seeking to maintain your own truth; but how can God be a liar, and man true, in the face of Scripture: "Let every man be a liar and God only true"?[14] God in himself is true, you in yourself are a liar: in God you can be true.

7. These words, "faithful and just to cleanse us from all iniquity," might seem to offer impunity to sin. Men might say to themselves, "We can sin, we can do freely what we will, for Christ cleanses us, he is faithful and just, he cleanses us from all iniquity." This evil confidence must be taken from you, and a wholesome fear put in its place: be careful, not confident. He is faithful and just to forgive us our transgressions: but only if you are never self-satisfied, if you are always being made perfect through change. "My little children, these things I write to you that ye sin not." What then will happen, if, human as we are, some sin overtake us? Must we then despair? "If any man sin, we have an advocate with the Father, Jesus Christ the righteous; and he is the propitiator of our sins."[14a] Christ is the advocate. Strive yourself not to sin; but if human weakness suffers

---

[12] I Pet. 4:8.   [13] Ps. 51:9, 3.   [14] Rom. 3:4.
[14a] Augustine's version of this text varies between *propitiator* and *propitiatio*.

sin to overtake you, look to it instantly, let it instantly offend you, instantly condemn it; and having condemned it, you may come in confidence before the judge. For there is your advocate: do not fear to lose the cause in which you confess. If in the affairs of this life a man may commit himself to a clever speaker and so escape loss, shall you be lost if you commit yourself to the Word himself? Cry aloud, "We have an advocate with the Father."

8. See how John himself keeps humility. A righteous man, a great man, who from the Lord's breast drank deep mysteries, draughts of divinity from which he proclaimed: "In the beginning was the Word, and the Word was with God"—this John did not say, *You* have an advocate with the Father, but, If any man sin, *we* have an advocate. Neither, "you have," nor, "you have me": Christ, not himself, and "we" not "you." Rather would he set himself among sinners and have Christ for his advocate, than set himself as advocate in Christ's place and be found among the proud who face condemnation. My brothers, Jesus Christ the righteous is he whom we have as advocate with the Father: he is the propitiation of our sins. The man who held fast to this, caused no heresy, no schism. Schisms arise when men say, *we* are righteous; when they say, *we* sanctify the unclean, *we* justify the wicked, *we* ask, *we* obtain.[15] But what said John? "If any man sin, we have an advocate with the Father, Jesus Christ the righteous." You will say, But may not holy men ask on our behalf? May not bishops and rulers ask on behalf of the people? Look at the Scripture, and you will find rulers commending themselves to the people's prayers. The apostle says to his people, "Praying also for us." [16] The apostle prays for the people and the people for the apostle. We pray for you, my brothers; but do you also pray for us. Let all the members pray for one another, and let the Head intercede for all. No wonder then that what follows here should shut the mouths of those who divide God's Church. John has said that we have Jesus Christ the righteous, himself the propitiation of our sins; but he knew that there would be some who would set themselves apart, saying, "Lo, here is Christ, or lo, there!" [17] trying to show that he who purchased the whole and possesses the whole is only in the part.[18]

[15] Reference is to the Donatist principle that purity of conscience in the "giver" of the sacrament is needed for the cleansing of the conscience of the recipient: see *c. Litt. Petil.*, I, 2 (i) ff., and III, 9 (viii) ff.

[16] Col. 4:3.

[17] Matt. 24:23.

[18] Reference is to the Donatist assertion that the Catholic Church throughout the world has been polluted by communion with the polluted Church

Therefore he adds at once: "not only of our sins, but of the sins of the whole world." . . . Think, brethren, what that means. Surely we are pointed to the Church in all nations, the Church throughout the whole world. Be not led astray by those who pretend to justify but in fact mutilate. Abide in that mountain which has filled the world[19]; for Christ is "the propitiation of our sins, and not of ours only, but also of the whole world"—which he has won by his blood.

9. "And hereby we know him, if we keep his commandments." Which commandments? "Whosoever saith that he knows him, and keepeth not his commandments, is a liar, and the truth is not in him." You ask still, Which commandments? "Whosoever keepeth his word, truly in him is the love of God perfect." Maybe the commandment itself is named love. We asked, What commandments?, and we are told that "whosoever keepeth his word, truly in him is the love of God perfect." Turn to the Gospel and see if this is not the commandment: "A new commandment give I unto you, that ye love one another."[20] "Hereby we know that we are in him, if we are made perfect in him." It speaks of the perfect in love: what is love's perfection? To love our enemies, and to love them to the end that they may be our brothers. Love your enemies, desiring them for brothers: love your enemies, calling them into your fellowship. For so loved he who as he hung upon the Cross said, "Father, forgive them, for they know not what they do."[21] "Hereby we know that we are in him, if we are made perfect in him." It was of the perfection of love for enemies that the Lord said: "Be ye therefore perfect as your heavenly Father is perfect."[22] "He," therefore, "who says that he abides in him, ought himself to walk as he walked." And how is that, my brethren? What is "walking as Christ walked"? Walking upon the sea?[23] No, it is walking in the way of righteousness; and of that way I have already spoken. Nailed fast upon the Cross, he was walking in the way—the way of charity. "Father, forgive them, for they know not what they do." So then, when you have learnt to pray for your enemy, you will walk the way of the Lord.

in Africa. Augustine constantly appealed against them (as here) to the scriptural promises of a world-wide extension of the Church, and he seems never to have considered the possibility that these promises may have to wait much longer for their fulfilment.

[19] Dan. 2:35.   [20] John 13:34.
[21] Luke 23:34.
[22] Matt. 5:48.
[23] Matt. 14:25 ff.

10. "Beloved, I write not unto you a new commandment, but the old commandment which ye had from the beginning. The old commandment is the word which ye have heard." Old, that is, because you have heard it before. But he shows it to be also new, when he says: "Again a new commandment I write unto you." Not another commandment, but the same one that he called old, is also new. Why is this? "Which is true in himself and in you." You have heard why it is old: because you knew it already; but why is it new? "Because the darkness is passed, and the true light now shineth." That is what makes it new; for the darkness belongs to the old man, the light to the new. "Put off the old man," says Paul, "and put on the new" [24]; and again: "Ye were sometime darkness, but now light in the Lord." [25]

11. "He that saith he is in the light"—now the whole meaning is to be made clear—"He that saith he is in the light, and hateth his brother, is still in darkness." Ah, my brothers, shall I continue saying to you, Love your enemies? Are you sure that you are not still hating your brothers—which is worse than failing to love enemies? If you loved your brothers only, you would not yet be perfect, but if you hate your brothers, what and where are you? Look each one into his own heart: cherish no hate against a brother for some hard word: in a quarrel for earth, turn not to earth. Whoever hates his brother may not say that he walks in the light—still less, that he walks in Christ. "He who saith he is in the light and hateth his brother, is in darkness until now."—Such and such a man, who was a pagan, has turned Christian. Think what has happened: a pagan, he was in darkness; now, he has become a Christian. All rejoice for him with thanks to God. We repeat the apostle's greeting: "Ye were sometime darkness, but now are light in the Lord." He worshipped idols, but now God: he worshipped the work of his own hands, but now the God who made him. He is changed: thanks be to God, all Christians rejoice for him. Why? Because now he is a worshipper of Father, Son, and Holy Spirit, and a hater of demons and idols. But still John is anxious for him: in the general rejoicing there is still mistrust. My brothers, let us take to our hearts that motherly anxiety. Not without reason is the mother anxious for us, when others rejoice—I mean the mother Charity, who dwelt in the heart of John when he thus spoke. For there is that in us which makes him fear even when men rejoice over us: and what is his fear? "He who saith that he

[24] Col. 3:9 f.   [25] Eph. 5:8.

is in the light"—says that he is now a Christian—"and hateth
his brother, is in darkness still." There is nothing here to expound, but only that which must sadden if it comes to pass, and
gladden if it be avoided.

12. "He that loveth his brother, abideth in the light, and
there is no occasion of offence in him." Those who take or
cause offence are those who are offended in Christ and his
Church. If you keep hold of charity, you shall take offence
neither in Christ nor in the Church; and you will desert neither
Christ nor the Church. The deserter of the Church cannot be
in Christ, since he is not among Christ's members: he cannot be
in Christ, who is not in Christ's Body. It is they who desert
either Christ or the Church who take offence. But we can see
that in him who loves his brother there is no offence; for the
lover of his brother endures all things for unity's sake. In the
unity of charity brotherly love consists. You are offended by
such and such a man, whether he be really evil, or evil only in
your belief or only in your pretence; and you abandon all the
many good. What sort of brotherly love has been shown in our
Donatists? Because of their charge against Africans they have
abandoned the world.[26] Were there no saints in the world at
large? Was it right for you to condemn them unheard? No, if
you loved your brothers, there would be no occasion of offence
in you. What does the Psalm say?—"Great peace have they
which love thy law, and there is no offence for them." [27] So they
who take offence, lose their peace; and they who do not take or
cause offence are the lovers of God's law, so that their dwelling
is charity. If it be said that the Psalm speaks of the lovers of
God's law and not of brothers, then hear the Lord's words: "A
new commandment give I unto you, that ye love one another."
Law and commandment are one. And not taking offence is but
forbearing one another, according to Paul's saying: "forbearing one another in love, striving to keep the unity of the
Spirit in the bond of peace." [28] And that this is the law of Christ
is shown by the same apostle's enjoining of that law: "Bear
ye one another's burdens, and so shall ye fulfil the law of
Christ." [29]

13. "For he that hateth his brother is in darkness, and walketh in darkness, and knoweth not whither he goeth; because the
darkness hath blinded his eyes."—There is no blindness like
that of those who hate their brothers. The proof is, that they

26 Cf. above, c. 8, n. 18.   27 Ps. 119:165.
28 Eph. 4:2 f.   29 Gal. 6:2.

stumble on the mountain.[30] We know that the stone cut from the mountain without hands is Christ who came of the kingdom of Jewry without human father: the stone that shattered all the kingdoms of the earth, all the tyrannies of idols and devils; the stone that grew and became a great mountain, and filled the whole world. We do not have to point out that mountain with the finger, as we sometimes point out the new moon to the short-sighted. This is a mountain that fills the whole face of the earth, the city of which it is written, "a city that is set on a hill cannot be hid."[31] And our Donatists stumble on the mountain, and when we tell them "Go up!" they say, "There is no mountain there," and will sooner strike their face against it than seek a dwelling on it. Yesterday we read the text of Isaiah: "In the last days the mountain of the Lord's house shall be manifested, made ready on the summit of the mountains; and all nations shall come together unto it."[32] Who can go astray on that mountain? Who can break his head by stumbling upon it? Who cannot recognize the city set on a hill? No wonder that it is not recognized by those who hate their brothers; for they walk in darkness and know not whither they go; for the darkness hath blinded their eyes. That is the proof of their blindness: they hate their brothers. Because they find cause of stumbling in Africa, they cut themselves off from the world: to brethren whom they slander they refuse toleration for the sake of the peace of Christ; while to others, whom they condemn, they grant it for the sake of the party of Donatus.[33]

[30] Cf. c. 8 above: the allusion is to Dan 2:34 f.
[31] Matt. 5:14.
[32] Isa. 2:2.
[33] Augustine frequently taxed the Donatists with inconsistency in recognizing the sacraments of the Maximianists, a sect which had split off from the main body of their Church.

SECOND HOMILY

I John 2: 12–17

1. All that we read in Holy Scripture for our instruction and salvation demands an attentive ear. You have just heard how the eyes of those two disciples upon whom the Lord came in the way were held so that they did not know him.[1] He found them in despair of the redemption that was in Christ, supposing him now to have suffered and died as a man, not imagining him to live for ever as the Son of God. And then he opened unto them the Scripture, and showed them that it behoved the Christ to suffer, and all things to be fulfilled that were written concerning him in the law of Moses and the prophets and the psalms—so embracing the whole of the Old Testament. Everything in those Scriptures speaks of Christ, but only to him that has ears. He opened their mind to understand the Scriptures; and so let us pray that he will open our own.

2. What was it then which the Lord showed as written concerning himself in law, prophets, and psalms? The evangelist has set it down in few words, that we might know what in all that extent of Scripture we should believe and understand. There is many a page, many a book; but the content of all is in these few words of the Lord to his disciples: "that it behoved the Christ to suffer, and to rise again on the third day."[2] So much we learn of the Bridegroom; and what of the Bride? Wherefore must Christ suffer and rise again? Because "all the ends of the world shall remember and turn unto the Lord, and all the kindreds of the nations shall worship before him."[3] So here our minds are led on from Bridegroom to Bride; "and that in his

[1] In one of the special lessons for Eastertide to which Augustine refers in the *Prologue*: Luke 24: 13 ff.

[2] Luke 24:46.   [3] Ps. 22:27.

270

name repentance and forgiveness of sins should be preached through all nations, beginning from Jerusalem." [4] Brethren, you hear: mark it well. Let none doubt that the Church is of all nations: let none doubt that it began from Jerusalem and filled all nations.

3. When we tell the Donatists that if they are Catholic Christians they must be in communion with that church from which the gospel has been spread throughout the world, they answer: "We have no communion with the city where our King was slain, our Lord was slain." But he loved that city and had compassion on it: therefore he said that the preaching of himself should begin from Jerusalem. You shrink in horror from the communion of that city which he made the starting-point for the preaching of his name. No wonder! The severed branch may hate the root. But he told his disciples: "tarry ye in the city, because I send my promise upon you." [5] He willed that his disciples should tarry there, and that there he should send them the Holy Spirit. The Church began in that place where the Holy Spirit came from heaven, and filled a hundred and twenty persons as they sat together. The number of the apostles was multiplied tenfold: there sat in that place a hundred and twenty persons, and the Holy Spirit came and filled all the place: there was a sound as of a rushing mighty wind, and cloven tongues as of fire. You have heard to-day the Lesson from the Acts: "They began to speak with tongues as the Spirit gave them utterance." [6] And all that were there, Jews coming from divers nations, heard each one his own tongue, and marvelled how these unlearned and ignorant men should suddenly have learnt, not one or two strange tongues, but the tongues of all peoples. That speaking in the beginning in all languages was a sign that men of every language should believe. But our Donatists, whose love for Christ is such that they refuse communion with the city that killed him, give to Christ the strange honour of confinement to two languages—the Latin, and the Punic or African! Christ is to possess two tongues only; for these two alone, no more, are spoken by the followers of Donatus. [7] Brethren, let us keep our minds awake! Let us see rather the gift of God's Spirit: let us believe what was foretold concerning him, and let us see the fulfilment of the psalmist's prophecy: "There is neither speech nor language, whose voices shall not be heard." [8] That this means, not the assembling of tongues in

[4] Luke 24:47.   [5] Luke 24:49.   [6] Acts 2:4.
[7] Cf. *Hom.*, I, 8, 12.   [8] Ps. 19:3 ff.

one place, but the coming of the gift of Christ to all tongues, is clear from what follows: "Their sound is gone out into all the earth, and their words unto the end of the world." And this, because "he hath set his tabernacle in the sun"—that is, where all may see it. His tabernacle is his flesh: his tabernacle is his Church—set in the sun, in the day, not in the night. Why then do they not acknowledge it? Turn again to where we ended yesterday's reading, and you will see the reason. "He that hateth his brother walketh in darkness, and knoweth not whither he goeth; because the darkness hath blinded his eyes." Let us then read on, and not be in darkness. We shall not be in darkness if we love the brethren; and the proof of love for the brotherhood lies in not rending our unity, in maintaining charity.

4. "I write unto you, little children, because your sins are forgiven you through his name." "Little children," because new-born by the forgiveness of sins. But whose is the name through which sins are forgiven? Certainly not the name of Augustine; and therefore not the name of Donatus either. But no need to mention Augustine or Donatus: it is not even the name of Paul or the name of Peter. When the Corinthians were dividing their Church, and setting up parties instead of unity, mother Charity, travailing with her children in person of the apostle, opens her bosom and speaks as if tearing her breast: she weeps for the sons whom she sees borne out to burial, she recalls to the one Name those who would enrol themselves under many, she sends them back from the love of herself to the single love of Christ: "Was Paul crucified for you? or were ye baptized in the name of Paul?"⁹ In other words: "If you would be with me, you must not be mine: be with me, and all of us are Christ's, who died for us, was crucified for us." And so in our text: "your sins are forgiven you through his name"—not through the name of any man.

5. "I write unto you, fathers." Why do "children" come first? "Because your sins are forgiven you through his name," and you are born again into a new life—which makes you children. And why "fathers"? "Because ye have known him who is from the beginning"; and there is a beginning in all fatherhood. Christ is new in the flesh, ancient in divinity; "before Abraham, I am."¹⁰ And not before Abraham only: heaven and earth were made, before there was any man. Before them the Lord was, or rather is: most truly does he say, not "before

⁹ I Cor. 1:13.   ¹⁰ John 8:58.

HOMILIES ON I JOHN

Abraham I was," but "before Abraham, I am." That of which we say that it was, is not; and that of which we say that it will be, is not yet. He knows only *being*: begotten of the eternal Father, begotten from eternity, in eternity; with no beginning, no end, no local extension; because he is that which is, because he is he who is. That is the name he told to Moses: "thou shalt say unto them, He who is hath sent me unto you." [11] Therefore, to say "before Abraham," "before Noah," "before Adam," is not enough. Hear the Scripture: "before the morning star I have begotten thee." [12] And the last word must be "before heaven and earth"; for "all things were made through him, and without him nothing was made." [13] Thus you may know who are fathers; for they become fathers by knowing that which is from the beginning.

6. "I write unto unto you, young men." There are children, fathers, and young men: children, because they are born, fathers because they know the beginning, and why "young men"? "Because ye have overcome the evil one." To children belongs birth, to fathers age, to young men strength. If the evil one is overcome by young men, he still fights with us—fights but vanquishes not. Is that because we are strong, or because he who was found weak in the hands of persecutors is strong in us? He who resisted not his persecutors has made us strong; for he was crucified in weakness, but lives in the power of God. [14]

7. "I write unto you, children"—children, "because ye have known the Father." "I write unto you, fathers"; and here he repeats, "because ye have known him who is from the beginning." Remember that you are fathers: if you forget him who is from the beginning, you have lost your fatherhood. "I write unto you, young men": once more, bear in mind your youth: fight, that you may overcome: overcome, that you may be crowned; be humble, lest you fall in the battle. "I write unto you, young men, because ye are strong, and the word of God abideth in you, and ye have overcome the evil one."

8. Brethren, all that is said here—that we have known that which is from the beginning, that we are strong, that we have known the Father—all this seems to commend knowledge; does it not also commend charity? If we have known, let us love; for knowledge without charity cannot save. "Knowledge puffeth

11 Ex. 3:14.   12 Ps. 110:3 (LXX and Vulg.).
13 John 1:3.   14 II Cor. 13:4.
A.L.W.—18

up, but charity edifieth." [15] If you would confess, but not love, you make yourselves like the demons: they confessed the Son of God, they said, "What have we to do with thee?" [16] and they were driven back. Do you confess, and embrace. They feared for their iniquities: do you love the forgiver of your iniquities. But we cannot love God, if we love the world: if we love the world, it will separate us from the love of God which is charity. The apostle makes us ready, then, to have charity dwelling in us. Two loves there are, of the world and of God: if the love of the world dwells in us, the love of God can find no entrance. The love of the world must depart, the love of God come in to dwell: make room for the better love. Once you loved the world, now cease to love it: empty your heart of earthly love and you shall drink of the love divine: charity will begin its dwelling in you, and from charity nothing evil can proceed. Hear then the words of the apostle who now would cleanse you. He sees men's hearts as a field, and in what condition? If he finds weeds, he roots them up; if he finds clean land, he plants—that tree which he would fain plant, which is charity. The weeds that he would root up are love of the world. Hear the rooter-up of weeds: "Love not the world, nor the things that are in the world. If a man love the world, the love of the Father is not in him."

9. You hear this. Brethren, let none say in his heart that this is not true. It is God's word spoken by the Holy Spirit through his apostle, and nothing can be truer: "if a man love the world, the love of the Father is not in him." Would you have the love of the Father, and be fellow-heir with the Son? Love not the world. Shut out the evil love of the world, that you may be filled with the love of God. You are a vessel that was already full: you must pour away what you have, that you may take in what you have not. We know that these our brethren have been born again of water and the Spirit, [17] even as we were so many years ago. It is good for us not to love the world, lest there remain in us only sacraments for our condemnation, and not stays for our salvation. The stay of salvation is to have charity at the root, to have the virtue of godliness and not the form only. The form is good and holy; but it avails nothing apart from the root. The severed branch is cast into the fire. You should keep the form, but in union with the root; and there is no way to be firmly rooted, but by holding fast to charity, according to the words of the apostle Paul: "rooted and grounded in charity." [18]

[15] I Cor. 8:1.
[16] Matt. 8:29.
[17] Cf. *Hom.*, I, 5.
[18] Eph. 3:17.

10. "Because all that is in the world is the desire of the flesh, and the desire of the eyes, and the pretensions of this life"— three things, "which are not of the Father but of the world. And the world passeth away, and the desires thereof; but he that doeth the will of God abideth for ever, as he abideth for ever."

Why may I not love what God has made? Make your choice: either to love things temporal and pass away with time's passing, or not to love the world, and to live for ever with God. The river of time sweeps us on; but there, like a tree growing by the river, is our Lord Jesus Christ. He took flesh, died, rose again, ascended into heaven. He willed to plant himself as it were beside the river of things temporal. If you are drifting down to the rapids, lay hold of the tree: if you are caught up in the world's love, lay hold of Christ. He for your sake entered into time, that you might win eternity; for by his entering into time he did not cease himself to be eternal.

11. Let us not love the world, nor the things that are in the world. For the things that are in the world are "the desire of the flesh and the desire of the eyes and the pretensions of this life." The naming of these three forestalls objection. A man might say: "The things that are in the world are what God has made—heaven and earth, sea, sun, moon, stars, and all the furnishings of the heavens. Why should I not love what God has made?" Let God's Spirit indeed be in you to show you that all these things are good; but beware of loving things created and forsaking their Creator. You find them fair; but how much fairer is he that formed them! Think, my friends: you may learn by a parable, lest Satan get advantage of you, saying as he is wont: "Be happy in God's creation: he made it only for your happiness!" So men's wits are stolen, and they perish in forgetfulness of their Maker: they use the creature with lust instead of temperance, and the Creator is despised. Of such the apostle says: "They worshipped and served the creature rather than the Creator, who is blessed for ever." [19] God forbids you not to love them, but he will not have you seek your bliss in them: the end of your esteem for them should be the love of their Maker. Suppose, my brethren, a man should make for his betrothed a ring, and she should prefer the ring given her to the betrothed who made it for her, would not her heart be convicted of infidelity in respect of the very gift of her betrothed, though what she loved were what he gave. Certainly let her love his gift; but if she should say "The ring is enough, I do not want to see his

[19] Rom. 1:25.

face again," what should we say of her? Should we not all abhor such frivolity, and charge her with the mind of an adulteress? "Gold is more to you than a husband, a ring more than your betrothed: if it is in you to transfer your love from your betrothed to the ring and not to want the sight of him, he will have given you a pledge not for security but for divorce." Yet surely the pledge is given by the betrothed, just that in his pledge he himself may be loved. Even so, God has given you all these things: therefore, love him who made them. There is more that he would give you, even himself, their Maker. Though God has made these things, if you love them and are careless of their Creator—if you love the world, must not your love be set down for adulterous?

12. "World" is the name not only for this fabric that God has made, of heaven, earth and sea, of things visible and invisible. We use the word "world" also for the dwellers in it, just as we do the word "house" both for the structure and its occupants. Sometimes we approve the house while we condemn the occupants. Now just as men may dwell in heaven by lifting up their hearts, though in the flesh they walk on earth, so all lovers of the world are dwelling in the world by their love, and thus may themselves be called the world. And in them there is nothing but these three—the desire of the flesh, the desire of the eyes, and the pretensions of this life. They desire the pleasures of food, drink and sex. But in such things there is a due limit. When you are told not to love them, it does not mean that you are forbidden to eat or drink or beget children; but for the Creator's sake there is a limit set, so that the love of all this does not make prisoner of you—lest your love of what you should possess for use become the love of final enjoyment.[20] The test comes only when the choice between this and that is set before you: "Money or the right?" "I am without the wherewithal to live, the wherewithal to eat and drink." But what if you can only gain that wrongfully? Were it not better to set your love on what you cannot lose, than to commit a wrong? You have eyes for the gain of money, not for the loss of faith. Here then, he tells us, is the desire of the flesh, the desire, that is, of what belongs to the flesh, food and sex and so forth.

13. "And the desire of the eyes." By this he means all that itch for marvels which I call curiosity. It has a very wide scope.

[20] For the distinction of "use" and "enjoyment," cf. De Trin., X, 13, 17; and for detailed discussion, De Div. Quaest. LXXXIII, 30, and De Doctr. Christ., I, 4.

The public spectacle, the theatre, the devil's mysteries, the arts of magic and sorcery, all pander to curiosity. But sometimes it may try the servants of God, making them wish to be wonder-workers, to try whether God will hear them by a miracle. That is curiosity, the desire of the eyes: it is not of the Father. If God has given you such power, use it: he has offered it for your use; but the lack of it will prevent no one from belonging to the Kingdom of God. When the apostles rejoiced because the devils were subject to them, what said the Lord to them? "Rejoice not in this: but rejoice, because your names are written in heaven."[21] He would have his apostles rejoice for the same cause as you too have for rejoicing. It will go hard with you, if your name is not written in heaven; but will it go hard if you have not raised the dead? if you have not walked upon the sea? if you have not cast out devils? If you have received the power to do such things, use it in humility and not in pride. For the Lord has said even of certain false prophets, that they should do signs and wonders. Therefore shun the "pretensions of this life." The pretensions of this life are pride. Men desire to vaunt themselves upon their honourable positions: they think themselves great because of their wealth or powerful standing.

14. Apart from these three things, you will find nothing that tempts human covetousness—nothing but desire of the flesh or desire of the eyes or pretensions of this life. By these three was the Lord tempted of the devil.[22] He was tempted by desire of the flesh, when it was said to him: "If thou art the Son of God, command these stones that they become bread"—when he was hungry from fasting. Remember how he repulsed the tempter, and taught his soldiers to fight: saying, "Man liveth not by bread alone, but by every word of God." He was tempted again by desire of the eyes, for a miracle, when the devil said: "Cast thyself down, for it is written, He hath charged his angels to bear thee up, that thou strike not thy foot against a stone." So did he resist the tempter; for if he had worked a miracle, he must have appeared either to have yielded or to have done it for "curiosity's" sake. He did indeed work miracles when he would, as God, but for the sake of healing the sick. If at that time he had done so, it would have seemed as though his only purpose was to work a miracle. But, to avoid such misapprehension, observe how he answered; and if ever such temptation comes to you, do you answer as he did: "Get thee behind me, Satan; for it is written, Thou shalt not tempt the Lord thy God"—meaning

[21] Luke 10:20. [22] Matt. 4:1 ff.

"if I do this, I shall be tempting God." Our Lord spoke as he would have you speak. If the Enemy should whisper to you: "A poor sort of man, a poor sort of Christian must you be! Have you worked a single miracle, have the dead arisen at your prayer, have you healed the fever-stricken? Were there really anything in you, you would do some mighty work!"—answer him and say, "It is written, Thou shalt not tempt the Lord thy God; I will not tempt God, as though I should belong to him if I wrought a miracle, but not otherwise. How then should he have said, Rejoice that your names are written in heaven?" And lastly, our Lord was tempted with the pretensions of this life: when the devil raised him up on the height, and said to him, "All these things will I give thee, if thou wilt fall down and worship me." He would have tempted the King of ages with the exaltation of an earthly kingdom; but the Lord that made heaven and earth trod the tempter under foot. No wonder, indeed, that the Lord should vanquish the devil; but his answer to the devil was to teach you your own: "It is written, Thou shalt worship the Lord thy God, and him only shalt thou serve."

Hold to the Lord's answers, and you will be free from all lusting after the world: in that freedom, you will be enslaved neither by desire of the flesh nor by desire of the eyes nor by the pretensions of this life; and you will make room for the coming of charity, which is the love of God. If your heart is occupied by love of the world, the love of God will not be in it. Hold to the love of God, that you may stand fast for ever as God stands: for the being of every man is according to his love. Dost thou love the earth? To earth thou shalt turn. Dost thou love God? I would not dare to say, A god thou shalt be; yet we have the word of Scripture, "I have said, Ye are gods, and ye are all the sons of the Most High." [23] If then you would be gods and sons of the most high, "love not the world, nor the things that are in the world. If any man loveth the world, the love of the Father (which is charity) is not in him. For all that is in the world is the desire of the flesh and the desire of the eyes and the pretensions of this life: which are not of the Father but of the world (that is, of men who love the world). And the world passeth away, and the desires thereof; but whosoever doeth the will of God, abideth for ever, even as God abideth for ever."

---

[23] Ps. 82: 6.—Augustine is chary in use of the characteristically Greek idea of the "divinization" of the Christian by grace.

THIRD HOMILY

I John 2:18–27

1. "Children, it is the last hour."—In this text, he addresses us as children, that we may hasten to grow—because it is the last hour. Bodily age is not a matter of will; no one grows in the flesh when he wills, as no one is born when he wills. But where birth lies in the will, so does growth. No man is born of water and the Spirit save willingly: therefore if he wills, he grows; if he wills, he diminishes. To grow is to go forward: to diminish is to go back. The man that knows he has been born must learn that he is a child, an infant: he must set his lips eagerly to his mother's breast, and he will grow quickly. Now the mother is the Church, and her breasts are the two Testaments of Holy Scripture. From them let him suck the milk of all the mysteries enacted in time for our eternal salvation, that he may come nourished and strengthened to eat that food of which the Gospel tells: "In the beginning was the Word, and the Word was with God, and the Word was God." Our milk is Christ in his humility: our food is the same Christ in his equality with the Father.[1]

3. But, lest we be slow to go forward, let us pay heed: "Children, it is the last hour." Go forward, run, and grow: it is the last hour. The last hour is long, but it is the last. It means, the last time; for in the last times shall come our Lord Jesus Christ. But some would say, "It cannot be the last time, the last hour: surely Antichrist must come first, and then the Day of Judgment." Such thoughts were known to John, and to rouse men from the security of imagining that this is not the last hour

---

[1] Cf. *De Trin.*, Bk. XIII, in which "knowledge" of the historic Incarnation is set forth as the necessary preparation for the "wisdom" which is contemplation of the Eternal Word.

279

because Antichrist is yet to come, he tells them: "as ye have heard that Antichrist cometh, even now have there been many Antichrists." In what hour but the last could there be many Antichrists?

4. He goes on to explain of whom he is speaking. "Wherefore we know that it is the last hour": we know, because there are many Antichrists. "They went out from us"—now we recognize them—"they went out from us," so that we must lament our loss; yet there is comfort—"but they were not of us." All heretics, all schismatics, have gone out from us, that is, from the Church; but they would not go out, if they were of us. Therefore, before their going out, they were not of us; and if that be so, there may be many within who have not gone out and yet are Antichrists. We make bold to say this, only to the end that none who is within becomes an Antichrist. John is about to describe and designate the Antichrist: we shall soon see who they are; and every one must question his own conscience whether he be such. Antichrist means one contrary to Christ: and what that means, you are to learn from the apostle's account of it, and understand that none can go out but Antichrists, whereas those that are not contrary to Christ can by no means do so. For he that is not contrary to Christ, is set firm in his Body and reckoned a member; and members are never contrary to one another. The wholeness of the Body is constituted by all the members together, and for the concord of the members we have Paul's word, that "if one member suffer, all the members suffer with it, and if one member is glorified, all the members rejoice with it." [2] If that be true, the concord of the members must exclude the Antichrist.

5. "They went out from us, but"—grieve not, for "they were not of us." And the proof is, that "if they had been of us, they would have remained with us." So, my friends, you are to see that many who are not of us may receive with us the sacraments, may receive with us baptism and all that the faithful know themselves to receive—blessing, and Eucharist, and all the sacred mysteries—may receive with us the very communion of the altar, and yet they are not of us. That they are not of us, is proved in the hour of trial: when trial comes to them, like a gust of wind, they are scattered abroad; for they were not grain but chaff. They will all be scattered, as we must never forget, on that day of judgment when threshing begins in the Lord's floor. Beloved, you may be very sure of this: that any who have gone

2 I Cor. 12:26.

out and afterwards return are not Antichrists, not contrary to
Christ. It is impossible for those who are not Antichrists to
remain without; but it is of his own will that every man is
either in Christ or against him. "They went out from us, but
they were not of us; for if they had been of us, they would have
remained with us; but that it should be made manifest that not
all were of us." "That it should be made manifest," because,
while yet within, they are not of us; but this is not manifest
till it is shown by their going out. "And ye have an anointing
from the Holy One, that ye may be manifest to yourselves."
This spiritual anointing is the Holy Spirit himself of whom the
visible anointing is the sacrament; John tells us that all who have
this anointing of Christ's can recognize evil and good: they
have no need to be taught, for their anointing teaches them
of itself.

6. "I write unto you, not that ye have not known the truth,
but because ye know it, and because no lie is of the truth." Here
we are given warning how to recognize the Antichrist. Christ
is the truth: he said, I am the truth.[3] But "no lie is of the truth,"
therefore none that lie are yet of Christ. It is not said that *some*
lie is of the truth, and *some* lie not of the truth. Take heed of the
words as they stand, and shun all flattery of yourselves, all deceiving of yourselves. "*No* lie is of the truth."—But let us see the
manner of Antichrist's lying: for there is more than one kind of
lie. "Who is the liar, but he that denieth that Jesus is the
Christ?"

7. Ask the heretics, and you will find none that denies that
Jesus is the Christ. My friends, there is a mystery here: give heed
to what the Lord God shall put into our mind, and what I
would make you understand. Here are men who have gone out
from us and become Donatists: we ask them whether Jesus is the
Christ, and they straightway confess that he is. If then he is Antichrist who denies that Jesus is the Christ, neither can they give
the name to us nor we to them; for both we and they confess the
same. But if neither may call the other Antichrist, then neither
have they gone out from us nor we from them. But if there has
been no going out from us, we are in unity; and then whence
come the two altars in this city? whence come divided houses
and homes, the sharing of the marriage-bed and the division of
Christ. Our text gives us warning and requires us to confess the
truth. Either they have gone out from us, or we from them. But
the latter is unthinkable: we have the testament of the Lord's

3 John 14:6.

inheritance, we read the Psalm and find it said: "I will give the nations for thine inheritance, and the ends of the earth for thy possession."[4] We hold Christ's inheritance: they do not, for they will not have communion with the world, with the universal company of them that are redeemed by the Lord's blood. We stand secure in the unity of the inheritance, and whoever refuses communion therewith has gone out from it.

8. If then they have gone out from us, they are Antichrists: and if Antichrists, then liars; and if liars, then guilty of denial that Jesus is the Christ. We come back to our problem. Ask each one singly and they will confess that Jesus is the Christ. Let us then enquire who it is that denies; and let us consider not words, but deeds. Let the tongue keep silence awhile, and put your question to the life. If we can find assurance from Scripture that actions may deny as well as tongues, we can indeed point to many Antichrists who profess Christ with their mouth and depart from him in their ways. And we have that assurance from the apostle Paul: speaking of such men, he says, "they profess to know God, but in works they deny him."[5] There you have the Antichrist—every one that denies Christ by his works. There is no liar like the Antichrist who professes with his mouth that Jesus is the Christ, and denies it by his actions. He is a liar, because he says one thing and does another.

9. But it follows from this, my brethren, that if deeds are what we must question, we shall find not only many Antichrists who have gone out from us, but many still concealed who have not gone out at all. If there are within the Church perjurers, defrauders, workers in magic, dabblers in divination, adulterers, drunkards, usurers, slave-dealers, and such—whom we cannot enumerate—all these things are contrary to the teaching of Christ and the word of God; for the Word of God is Christ, and all that is contrary to God's Word is in Antichrist, that is, contrary to Christ. The openness of their resistance to Christ can easily be shown. For some evil action that they do, they incur rebuke; and not daring to slander Christ they slander his ministers from whom the rebuke comes. If you show them that you are speaking Christ's words and not your own, they do their best to convict you of using words that are your own and not Christ's; but if it be too plain that your words are Christ's words, they will even set upon Christ and begin to find fault with him. "How," they say, "and why has he made us

4 Ps. 2:8; for the argument, cf. *Hom.*, I, 8, 13.
5 Tit. 1:16.

such as we are?" Is not that the daily excuse of men convicted of their own ill-doing? Perverted by crookedness of will, they accuse the craftsman; and the heavenly craftsman, our Maker and our Re-maker, cries aloud to them: "But what was it that I made in you? A man, not avarice; a man, not robbery; a man, not adultery!" Do you put right what you have made, that the making of God in you may be preserved! If you will not, if you love and cling to your sins, you are contrary to Christ: whether within or without, you are Antichrist; whether within or without you are chaff and not grain—not without, only because you have not yet faced the wind.

10. Brethren, the point is clear. Let no man say, I worship not Christ but God his Father. "Every one that denieth the Son, hath neither the Son nor the Father; and he that confesseth the Son hath both the Son and the Father." He speaks to you that are good grain; but let them that were chaff give heed and be changed into grain. Let each one consult his own conscience, and if he is a lover of the world, let him change: let him become Christ's lover, not Christ's enemy. Tell a man that he is Antichrist, and he gets angry and thinks an outrage done him: maybe he threatens a libel action, if his adversary calls him by that name. Christ says to him: "Be patient. If the charge is false, you may rejoice with me, for I too am falsely charged by Antichrists. But if it is true, summon your conscience; and if you fear the name, fear yet more the deserving of it."

11. "Let that therefore abide in you, which yourselves have heard from the beginning. If that which ye have heard from the beginning shall abide in you, ye also shall abide in the Father and the Son. This is the promise that he hath promised us." Perhaps you would ask of the reward, and say: "Suppose I guard in myself obediently what I have heard from the beginning: for the sake of that abiding I endure perils, toils and trials. What is my profit, my reward? In this life I see that I must labour under trials: what then will God give me hereafter? Here I see there can be no rest: mortality weighs upon the soul, and the corruptible body presses me downwards [6]; but I bear it all, that what I have heard from the beginning may abide in me, and that I may say to my God, "Because of the words of thy lips I have kept to hard ways." [7] But for what reward?" Hear, and faint not: or if you were fainting under your labours, let the promised reward make you strong. No worker in the vineyard will dismiss from his mind what he is to receive: if he

[6] Wisdom 9:15.　　　　[7] Ps. 17:4.

should forget his reward, his hands will fail him. The recollection of the promised reward gives perseverance in the work—even when the promiser is a man that can deceive. In the field of God, how much greater should be your strength, when the promise has come from the truth that can neither die nor give place to another, nor deceive him who has had its promise! What then is the promise?—let us look to that. Is it gold—so much loved by men in this world—or silver? Is it possessions, for which men pour out the gold they love so much—pleasant estates, large houses, numerous servants, herds of cattle? That is not the kind of reward which he encourages us to expect, that we may hold fast in our labour. The reward is named—what? Eternal life. You hear, and you cry out with joy.[8] Set your love then on that which you have heard, and look for enfranchisement from your labours into the repose of eternal life. Eternal life—that is what God promises; and what he threatens is eternal fire. To those set on his right hand he says, "Come, ye blessed of my father, receive the kingdom prepared for you from the beginning of the world"; and to those on his left, "Depart into eternal fire, prepared for the devil and his angels."[9] If you cannot yet desire the one, at least fear the other.

12. Remember, then, my brethren, that eternal life is Christ's promise. "This is the promise which he hath promised to us, even eternal life. These things have I written to you concerning them that lead you astray." Let none lead you astray unto death: set your heart upon the promise of eternal life. Whatever the world may promise, it promises to one who may die to-morrow; and then how will you face him that abideth for ever? You say, I am driven to do wrong by the threatenings of powerful persons. What do such threats amount to? Prison, fetters, brandings, the rack, the beasts? Yes, but not eternal fire. Tremble at the threatenings of the Almighty, and desire the promises of the Almighty: then the whole world's terrors will be of as little account as its promises.

"These things have I written to you concerning them that lead you astray; that ye may know that ye have an anointing, and that the anointing which we have received from him may abide in you." The anointing has its outward sign or sacrament: the power of it is invisible. The unseen anointing is the Holy Spirit: the unseen anointing is the charity which is the living root of everyone in whom it is found, the root that cannot

---

[8] The congregation has applauded. Cf. *Hom.* VII. 10.

[9] Matt. 25:34, 41.

wither, let the sun be never so hot; for every plant that is well-rooted is nourished and not withered by the sun's heat.

13. "And ye have no need that any man should teach you; because his anointing teacheth you concerning all things." What then are we about, my brethren, in offering you teaching? If his anointing teaches you all things, our labour is to no purpose: we may spare our breath and leave you to his anointing, that itself may teach you. Yet this question that I have just asked myself may be asked even of the apostle. Let John deign to hear it put to him by a lesser man, who asks: "Had they to whom thou didst speak an anointing? Surely; for thou didst say, his anointing teacheth you concerning all things. Why then write such an Epistle? What teaching, what instruction, what edification wast thou giving by it?" You see here, my brethren, a great mystery. The sound of our words strikes the ear, but the Master is within.[10] You must not think that anyone learns from a man. The noise of our voice can be no more than a prompting; if there be no teacher within, that noise of ours is useless. Brethren, do you need that I should explain further? Have you not all heard this sermon? Yet how many will leave this place untaught! For my part, I have spoken to all; but those who hear not the inward speech of that same anointing, those whom the Holy Spirit teaches not inwardly, go home untaught. Outward teachings are but a kind of helps and promptings: the teacher of hearts has his chair in heaven. Therefore he says himself in the gospel: "Call no man your master upon earth; for one is your master, even Christ."[11] Let him then speak to you within, when no man is there: indeed there may be no man in your heart, though a man be at your side. But it is not well that there be none in your heart: let Christ be in your heart, let his anointing be there, lest your heart be left alone to thirst, with no water-spring to refresh it. He that teaches is the inward Master, Christ and his inspiration. Where that inspiration and that anointing are lacking, the noise of words from without is vain. Brethren, these words that we speak to you from without are like the husbandman to the tree: his is an outward working, he gives water and careful tillage. But whatever his outward application, it is not he that forms the fruit, that clothes the bare branches with the shade of leaves, that acts inwardly in any such manner. Who it is, you may learn from the apostolic husbandman, and see what we are, and listen

[10] Augustine always teaches that we can recognize truth only through the presence within us of the *Magister interior* who is Christ.

[11] Matt. 23:8 f.

to the inward Master. "I planted, Apollos watered, but God gave the increase; for neither he that planteth is anything, nor he that watereth, but God who giveth the increase." [12] This then is our word to you: whether we plant or water through our speaking, we are nothing. All is of him who gives his increase, even God: that is, his anointing that teacheth you concerning all things.

[12] I Cor. 3:6 f.

FOURTH HOMILY

I John 2:27–3:8

1. Our reading of yesterday, my brethren, ended as you will remember with the words: "Ye have no need that any man should teach you: the anointing itself teacheth you concerning all things."

2. It goes on: "And it is true"—this same anointing: that is, the Spirit of the Lord, the teacher of men, cannot lie. "It is no liar. Even as it hath taught you, so abide in it. And now, little children, abide in him; that when he shall be manifested, we may have confidence in his sight, that we may not be put to shame by him at his coming." You see, my brethren: we believe in Jesus whom we have not seen, and we await his coming. All who await him in faith will rejoice when he comes: those that are without faith will be ashamed when what they see not now has come. And their confounding will not be for a moment, and then pass, as is the way with men who are confounded when detected in some fault, and meet the tauntings of other men. This confounding will set the confounded upon the left hand where they will hear their sentence: "Depart ye into eternal fire, which is prepared for the devil and his angels."[1] Let us then abide in his words, that we be not put to shame when he comes.

3. "If ye know that he is righteous, know also that every one that doeth righteousness is born of him." Perfect righteousness is not yet in any but the angels: in us it has only its beginning, by faith, after the Spirit. You heard in the reading of the Psalm: "Begin unto the Lord with confession."[2] "Begin"—and the beginning of our righteousness is the confession of sins. If you

[1] Matt. 25:41.
[2] Ps. 147:7. The Latin versions of the Psalms regularly use *confiteri* and *confessio* for "thanksgiving." Augustine's own *Confessions* were meant to be thankgivings as much as "confessions" of his sins.

have begun to make no defence of your sin, you have already taken the first step in righteousness. It will be made perfect in you, when the doing of nothing else shall delight you, when death shall be swallowed up in victory. Then, when no evil desire shall stir within you, when there shall be no striving with flesh and blood, when shall come the crown of victory, the triumph over the adversary—then shall righteousness be perfect. Here as yet we are engaged in fight: as fighters we stand in the arena, strokes are given and received: the issue of the battle is awaited. But victory goes to him who thinks not to deal his strokes in his own arm's strength but by the encouragement of God. In the fight against us, the devil stands alone: if we stand with God, we overcome the devil. For to fight alone against the devil is to court defeat: he is a practised enemy that has won many a trophy. And so hear what follows in our Epistle: it tells us to overcome the devil, but not of ourselves. "If ye know that he is righteous, know also that every one that doeth righteousness is born of him." Born of God, born of Christ; these words, "is born of him," are for our encouragement. Because we are born of him, our perfecting is already sure.

4. "Behold, what manner of love the Father hath given unto us, that we should be called, and be, the sons of God." To be called and not to be, to have the name and not the reality, avails no one. There are many called physicians who cannot cure: there are many called watchers that sleep all night. So are there many called Christians that are not found such in fact; because what they are called they are not in life, in manners, in faith, in hope, in charity. But what is it, brethren, that these words tell you?—"Behold what manner of love the Father hath given unto us, that we should be called, and be, the sons of God. For this cause the world knoweth us not, because it hath not known him: so the world knoweth not us." There is a whole world of Christians, and a whole world of ungodly; for ungodly and godly are both spread through all the world, and we can see that the first know not the second, because they revile men of good life. Consider, whether there be not such among yourselves. Any one of you that lives a godly life, thinks little of worldly matters, will not frequent the public shows, will not make festivals an excuse for drinking, or—what is worse—seek the protection of holy days for uncleanness [3]: is not one that

---

[3] Augustine had hard work to purge the observance of Christian holy days from the customs associated with pagan religious festivals. See his *Ep.* XXIX, to Alypius, and cf. *Serm.* 311, 352.

abstains from such things reviled by them that do them? and would he be so reviled if he were recognized? He is not recognized, because the world does not recognize him. By the world, as I have often said and need not weary you by repeating, is meant the dwellers in the world, as we use the word "house" for its inhabitants. So when you find "world" used in a bad sense, you are to understand only the world's lovers: those who dwell in the world by their love of it, and earn their name from that in which they dwell. "For this cause the world knoweth us not, because it knew not him." The Lord Jesus Christ himself walked on earth, God was in flesh, his strength hidden in weakness. And why was he not known? Because he convicted men of all their sins. They could not recognize God because they delighted in the pleasures of sin: the desires kindled by their fever made them do violence to the physician.

5. What then of ourselves? Here already we are "born of him"; but because our life is in hope, there is more to be said. "Beloved, now are we the sons of God." Now? and what then do we wait for, if we are already sons of God? "And it is not yet manifest what we shall be." What shall we be, more than sons of God? Listen! "We know that when he shall have appeared, we shall be like him; for we shall see him as he is." Set your minds upon this: it is a great matter. Ponder that word "is": do you know its meaning? That which is said to "be," and not only said to be, but truly "is," is changeless: it abides for ever, it knows no change, no element of decay, it neither advances, for it is perfect, nor goes back, for it is eternal. And what is it? "In the beginning was the Word, and the Word was with God, and the Word was God." [4] What is that Word? He "who being in the form of God, thought it not robbery to be equal with God." [5] The Christ who is thus in the form of God, the Word of God, one with the Father, equal to the Father, evil men cannot see. The Word as made flesh, the wicked also will be able to see; for he will come to judge even as he came to be judged. They will see the form of the servant, not the form of God; because they are godless, and the Lord himself says, "Blessed are the pure in heart, for they shall see God." [6] Brethren, what we are to see is a vision, that neither eye hath seen nor ear hath heard nor hath come up into the heart of man[7]—a vision surpassing all earthly beauties, of gold or silver, of woods or fields,

4 John 1:1.   5 Phil. 2:6.
6 Matt. 5:8.   7 I Cor. 2:9.

the beauty of sea and sky, of sun, moon, and stars, the beauty of angels: excelling all these things, for all have their beauty from him.

6. And when we see this, what shall we be? what is the promise given us? "We shall be like him; for we shall see him as he is." The spoken word has done all it could: the rest must be pondered in the heart. In comparison of him who "is," what could John say, and what can be said by us whose desert is so far below his? We must go back to the anointing of which he has spoken, that anointing which teaches inwardly what passes utterance; and since as yet you cannot see, your work must lie in longing. The whole life of the good Christian is a holy longing. What you long for, as yet you do not see; but longing makes in you the room that shall be filled, when that which you are to see shall come. When you would fill a purse, knowing how large a present it is to hold, you stretch wide its cloth or leather: knowing how much you are to put in it, and seeing that the purse is small, you extend it to make more room. So by withholding the vision God extends the longing, through longing he makes the soul extend, by extending it he makes room in it. So, brethren, let us long, because we are to be filled. See how Paul stretches out his purse so that it may have room for that which is to come. "Not that I have already received," he says, "or already am made perfect. Brethren, I count not myself to have apprehended."[8] We ask, What then is your business in this life, if you have not yet apprehended? He answers: "One thing: forgetting the things that are behind, and stretching out to the things that are before, according to my purpose I follow after the prize of the upward calling." He speaks of himself as stretching out, and following according to his purpose: he felt himself too small to take in that which eye hath not seen nor ear heard, nor hath come up into the heart of man. That is our life, to be trained by longing; and our training through the holy longing advances in the measure that our longings are severed from the love of this world. I said once before: Empty out that vessel that is to be filled; you are to be filled with good, pour away the evil. God would fill you, shall we say, with honey: where can you put it, if you are full of vinegar? What your vessel held must be poured away, and the vessel cleansed: cleansed, were it with toil and chafing, so that it be fit to hold—did we say honey? Gold? Wine? Speak as we may of that which cannot be spoken, call it what

8 Phil. 3:13 f.

we will, its proper name is—God. Even in this word, "God," what have we said? Is that single syllable the whole of that for which we wait? Nothing that we have power to name is high enough. Let us stretch ourselves out towards him, that when he comes he may fill us full. For "we shall be like him; because we shall see him as he is."

7. "And every one that hath this hope in him" . . . He sets us, you see, in hope. Notice the agreement of Paul with his fellow-apostle: "By hope are we saved; but hope that is seen is not hope, for what a man sees, why should he hope for? If we hope for that which we see not, we wait for it in patience." [9] Patience itself trains up the longing. Wait, for he waits: walk on steadfastly, that you may reach the end: he will not leave that place towards which you are moving. Listen again: "And every one that hath this hope in him, purifieth himself, even as he is pure." Notice that these words, "purifieth himself," preserve our freedom of choice.[10] None but God can purify us, but God purifies you not against your will. You purify yourself in uniting your will to God. You purify yourself, not by yourself but by him who comes to dwell within you. Yet because there is here an act of your own will, to you too there is something assigned; and it is assigned to you that you may say with the psalmist, "Be thou my helper, forsake me not." [11] Thus to ask for help means that you do something; for if you do nothing, how can he help you?

8. "Every one that committeth sin, committeth wickedness." You cannot distinguish sin and wickedness; you cannot say, I am a sinful man, but I am not wicked. For "sin is wickedness." How then shall we deal with our sins and wickednesses? Let us hear what John says: "And ye know that he hath been manifested to take away sin; and in him is no sin." He in whom there is no sin has come to take away sin. Were there sin in him, it must needs have been taken away from him—not by him. "Every one that abideth in him, sinneth not": that is, in so far as a man abides in him, he does not sin. "Everyone that sinneth, hath not seen him nor known him." That seems very difficult; yet it is not strange. We have not seen him, but we are one day to see him: we have not known him, but one day we shall: we

---

[9] Rom. 8:24 f.
[10] One of the few echoes in the *Homilies* of the Pelagian controversy: in his preaching Augustine always insists on the part of the will in right action and the reality of free choice.
[11] Ps. 27:9.

believe in him whom we have not known. May we say that we have known him by faith, but not as yet by sight? Surely, in faith we have both seen and known; for if faith does not yet see, why are the faithful called the "enlightened"? [12] There is one enlightenment of faith, another of sight. In our present pilgrimage we walk by faith, not by sight [13]; so that our righteousness also is by faith and not by sight. When the time of sight has come, our righteousness will be perfect; meantime we may not let go of the righteousness which is of faith, for "the just lives by faith," as the apostle says. [14] "Everyone that abideth in him, sinneth not"; for "every one that sinneth hath not seen him, nor known him." The man that sins, does not believe: if he believe, he does not sin, so far as he belongs to the faith of Christ.

9. "Little children, let no man deceive you. He that doeth righteousness is righteous, even as he, Christ, is righteous." We must not suppose, because it is said that we are righteous, "even as he," that we are on an equality with God. You must take the sense of this word "as." A little back, we read: "purifieth himself even as he is pure"; but none would dare to say that our purity is equal to the purity of God, or our righteousness to his. "Even as" does not always imply equality. Consider, for example, the difference between a man's face and its image in a mirror. There is a face in the image and a face in the body, but the image exists as a likeness, the body as a reality. Yet we say that there are eyes and ears here, *even as* there. There is disparity in the object; but what "even as" implies is likeness. So there is an image of God even in ourselves, but not that image which is in the Son as the Father's equal. Yet if we according to our capacity were not "even as" he, there would be no ground for calling us "like" him. Thus he purifies us even as he is pure; but his purity is of eternity, ours of faith. We are righteous even as he is righteous; but he is righteous in changeless everlastingness, we by believing in him whom we see not, in order that at last we may see. Even when our righteousness has been perfected, when we have been made equal to the angels, it will still not be the equal of his righteousness. How far then must it fall short of him now, if not even then will it be equal!

10. "He that doeth sin is of the devil; for the devil sinneth from the beginning." "Is of the devil" means, as you know, that he imitates the devil. The devil has made no one, begotten or

[12] "Enlightenment" was a term very early in use for Christian baptism.
[13] II Cor. 5:7.
[14] Rom. 1:17.

created none. But anyone who imitates the devil, as though born of him, becomes the devil's son by imitation though not by a true birth. You are a son of Abraham, but Abraham did not beget you; the Jews that were sons of Abraham became sons of the devil[15] because they imitated not the faith of Abraham, though they were born of his flesh. So, if those that had their birth of him were disinherited because they failed to imitate him, you, though not so born, are made his son, and his son you shall be, by imitation. In the same way, if you imitate the devil in his pride and impiety against God, you will be his son—by imitation, not by creation or begetting.

11. "Unto this end the Son of God was manifested." Ah, my brethren, all sinners are born of the devil, inasmuch as they are sinners. Adam was made by God: but when he consented to the devil, he was born of the devil; and all that he has begotten are as he was. With concupiscence itself we were born, and our birth comes of that condemnation, before we add to it debts of our own. If we are born with no sin, there is no reason for hastening with our infant children to baptism for their absolution.[16] There are two births for your understanding, my brothers, of Adam and of Christ: two men, but of them one man is man, the other man is God. Through the man that is man we are sinners: through the Man that is God we are justified. One birth has cast us down to death; the other has raised us up to life. One draws sin along with it, the other delivers from sin. For to this end came Christ as man, that he might do away with the sins of man. "To this end the Son of God was manifested, that he might destroy the works of the devil."

12. For the rest, my beloved, I must not overburden you to-day. There is a question, hard for us to answer, that arises from our speaking of ourselves as sinners. If a man says that he is without sin, he is a liar. You will remember the earlier words of this very epistle of John: "If we say that we have no sin, we deceive ourselves and the truth is not in us." Yet in this later chapter you are told that "whosoever is born of God sinneth not . . . he that doeth sin, hath not seen him nor known him . . . everyone that doeth sin, is of the devil." Sin is not of God.

Once again we are put in fear. How can we be born of God, and confess ourselves sinners? To say that we are not born of God would be to take all meaning from the sacraments applied to

15 John 8:44.
16 Stock defence of the doctrine of original sin.

infants. Yet John has said that "whosoever is born of God, sinneth not"; and the same John again has told us that "if we say that we have no sin, we deceive ourselves and the truth is not in us." It is a serious and difficult question, and I would have your minds set upon finding its answer. To-morrow, in the Lord's name, we will discourse of it as he shall enable us.

FIFTH HOMILY

I John 3:9–18

1. I ask to-day for your closest attention, since we have no light matter for our considering. Indeed the interest with which you listened to yesterday's sermon assures me that it will be even keener to-day. For the question to be raised is a very difficult one. We are asking what is meant by this text in our epistle: "He that is born of God sinneth not"—in view of that earlier saying in the same epistle: "If we say that we have no sin, we deceive ourselves and the truth is not in us."

2. Now give your minds to these words. I want you to face the difficulty, so that your earnest attention may be a prayer on my behalf as well as yours, and God may grant us enlargement and open the way out: that none may find occasion of falling away in his word, the word that is neither preached nor written but for healing and salvation.

"Every one that is born of God committeth no sin, because his seed remaineth in him; and he cannot sin, because he is born of God." This is put very strongly. But maybe the words "sinneth not" refer, not to any sin, but to some particular sin. Then by the saying, "He that is born of God sinneth not," we may understand some special kind of sin, which a man that is born of God cannot commit—a sin of such a kind that its commission binds all other sins upon us, whereas if it be not committed the others may be absolved. What is that sin? Transgression of the commandment. And what commandment? "A new commandment give I unto you, that ye love one another."[1] Consider. This commandment of Christ has the name of love; and through that love are sins absolved. If it be not kept, not only is the sin grave but it is the root of all sins.

[1] John 13:34.

3. Consider this, my brethren. The suggestion we have made is one that may give the key to our problem when rightly understood. There is a sin that cannot be committed by him who is born of God. If that sin be not committed, others are absolved: if it be committed, others are bound fast. And this sin is the transgression of Christ's command, the new covenant: "A new commandment give I unto you, that ye love one another." The man that acts contrary to charity, contrary to brotherly love, may not dare to boast that he is born of God. But for him who is established in brotherly love, there are certain sins that he cannot commit, above all the hating of a brother. And as for all other sins, of which it is said that "if we say that we have no sin we deceive ourselves, and the truth is not in us"—for them he may take confidence from another text of Scripture: "Charity covereth the multitude of sins." [2]

4. Charity, then, is the theme of our exhortation, as it is the theme of this epistle. The Lord after his resurrection put no other question to Peter but "Lovest thou me?" [3] Once was not enough: a second time he asked the same, a third time the same. And though at the third questioning Peter was distressed, as though the Lord did not believe him, as one ignorant of what was passing in his heart; yet the question was asked once, twice, and thrice. Fear had three times denied, love three times confessed. Peter loves his Lord; and what shall he offer him? His own trouble had found utterance in those words of the Psalm: "What shall I return unto the Lord for all that he hath returned to me?" [4] For the psalmist's mind was set upon the great things that God had done for him: he sought for what he might do in return, and could not find it. For there is nothing that one would return which one has not received from him for the return of it. And so we see that what he found to return was what he had received from God. "I will receive the cup of salvation, and call upon the name of the Lord." None had given him that saving cup but he to whom he would make the return. But to receive the saving cup, and to call upon the name of the Lord, is to be filled full with charity—so full that not only will you not hate your brother, but you will be ready to die for him. That is the perfection of charity—to be ready to die for your brother; and this our Lord displayed in himself, by dying for all, and praying for those by whom he was crucified, with the words: "Father, forgive them; for they know not what they do." [5] But if he were

2 I Peter 4:8.   3 John 21:15 ff.
4 Ps. 116:12 f.   5 Luke 23:34.

the only one so to act, he had been no teacher, as having no disciples. Disciples there were who followed him and did the same. As Stephen was stoned, he fell upon his knee and prayed: "Lord, lay not this sin to their charge."[6] He showed his love for his murderers, in that he died for them. So we find Paul saying, "I would myself be spent in behalf of your souls"[7]; for among those souls were some for whom Stephen prayed when he was dying at their hands.

That is the perfection of charity. Charity is perfect in him whom it makes ready to die for his brethren; but it is never perfect as soon as it is born. It is born that it may be perfected. Born, it is nourished: nourished, it is strengthened: strengthened, it is made perfect. And when it has reached perfection, how does it speak? "To me to live is Christ, and to die is gain. My desire was to be set free and to be with Christ; for that is by far the best. But to abide in the flesh is needful for your sake."[8] He was willing to live for their sakes, for whom he was ready to die.

5. To teach us that this is the perfect charity, which he that is born of God cannot violate or sin against, the Lord says to Peter: "Peter, lovest thou me?" And Peter answers, "I love thee." What return could Peter make to him that loved him? This: "Feed my sheep." That is, "Do for thy brethren what I have done for thee. I have redeemed all by my blood. Do not shrink from dying for the confession of the truth, that others may follow your example."

6. But this, my brothers, as I have said, is perfect charity, possessed by him that is born of God. Think, my dear people, and understand what I am saying. The person that is baptized has received the sacrament of birth. He possesses the sacrament —a sacrament great, divine, holy, unspeakable. Consider its purport: to make a new man through the remission of all his sins. Yet he must look well into his heart and see whether that which has been done in his body is made perfect there. Let him see whether he has charity, and then say, "I am born of God." If he has not charity, the Master's mark is on him, but he is a deserter straying from the ranks. Let him have charity, or else let him not say that he is born of God. He may say, "But I have the mystery of the sacrament." The apostle will answer him: "If I know all mysteries, and have all faith, so as to remove mountains, and have not charity, I am nothing."[9]

6 Acts 7:60.   7 II Cor. 12:15.
8 Phil. 1:21 ff.   9 I Cor. 13:2.

7. You will remember that when we were beginning the reading of this Epistle I asked you to bear in mind that charity is what above all else it enjoins upon us. The writer may appear to pass from one subject to another, but to this always he returns: he means all that he says to be brought into relation with charity. So let us see whether he does so here. Listen: "Every man that is born of God, doth not commit sin." If we take this to mean *any* sin, it will conflict with that other saying, "If we say that we have no sin, we deceive ourselves and the truth is not in us." And so we ask, What sin? and look for some pointing from the writer himself; lest I may have been over-hasty in suggesting that this sin is the violation of charity, because of his saying above: "He that hateth his brother is in darkness, and walketh in darkness, and knoweth not whither he goeth, because the darkness hath blinded his eyes." But perhaps in the words which follow here we shall find express mention of charity. You will see that indeed the turning of the sentence leads us to that very conclusion. "Every one that is born of God, sinneth not, because his seed abideth in him." (The seed of God is God's word: as the apostle puts it: "I have begotten you through the gospel."[10]) "And he cannot sin, because he is born of God." We look now to be told *wherein* he cannot sin. "In this are manifested the children of God and the children of the devil. Everyone that is not righteous, is not of God; and he that loveth not his brother."

He that loveth not his brother: the reference of these last words is clear. Love is the only final distinction between the sons of God and the sons of the devil. All may sign themselves with the sign of Christ's cross: all may answer Amen, and sing Alleluia: all may be baptized, all may come to church and line the walls of our places of meeting. But there is nothing to distinguish the sons of God from the sons of the devil, save charity. They that have charity, are born of God: they that have not charity are not. There is the great token, the great dividing mark. Have what else you will; if this one thing you have not, all is to no purpose. If you lack all the rest, have this, and you have fulfilled the law. "For he that loveth another," says the apostle, "hath fulfilled the law"; and "charity is the fulness of the law."[11] This, I would say, is the pearl which the merchantman in the Gospel went seeking: who found one pearl, and sold all that he had, and bought it.[12] Charity is that precious pearl, without

10 I Cor. 4:15.   11 Rom. 13:8, 10.
12 Matt. 13:46.

which all that you have profits you nothing, and which suffices you if you have nothing else. Now your vision is by faith, then it will be by sight; and if we love while we do not see, with what ardour shall we embrace when we have seen! But how are our hearts to be trained? Through love of the brethren. You may say, "I have never seen God"; you cannot say, "I have never seen a man." Love your brother; in loving the brother whom you see, you will see God at the same time. For you will see charity itself, and there within is God dwelling.

8. "He that is not righteous, is not of God; and he that loveth not his brother. For this is the message"—note how proof is given!—"this is the message that we have heard from the beginning, that we should love one another." The writer points clearly to his authority: whoever transgresses that commandment, is involved in that abominable sin into which they must fall who are not born of God. "Not as Cain, who was of the evil one, and slew his brother; and wherefore slew he him? Because his works were evil, and his brother's righteous." Thus where envy is, there cannot be brotherly love. Consider this, my people. Envy and love exclude one another. In the envious is the devil's sin; for it was by envy that the devil cast man down: he fell, and envied him that stood upright. He sought to cast down, not that he himself might stand, but that he might not be alone in his fall. Keep in your minds what the apostle's comment teaches, that in charity there can be no envying. You have the express saying, in the praise of charity: "Charity envieth not."[13] There was no charity in Cain, and had there not been charity in Abel, God would not have accepted his sacrifice. When both brought their offering, the one from the fruits of the earth, and the other from the young of sheep, it is not to be thought that God cared not for the fruits of the earth and loved the lambs. God looked not at that which was in their hands, but saw what was in their heart; and seeing the one offer in charity, had respect unto his sacrifice: seeing the other offer in envy, from his sacrifice turned away his eyes. The "good works" of Abel mean nothing but charity: the "evil works" of Cain mean nothing but hatred of a brother. More than hating his brother, he envied his good works; and because he would not follow his example, he resolved to slay him. Herein he showed himself a son of the devil, as Abel showed himself a righteous man of God. Herein, therefore, my brethren, is the proving of men. We are to observe not what men say, but their deeds and

13 I Cor. 13:4.

their heart. A man that will not do his brethren good, shows what he has in him: by temptation men are tested.

9. "Marvel not, my brethren, if the world hateth us." I should not need to keep telling you what "the world" means. It is not heaven or earth, or the works of God's making, but the lovers of the world. I know that some of you must find such repetition tedious; but it is not for nothing, if some cannot tell, when they are asked, whether the preacher said it! So let me try by hammering it in to leave something sticking in my hearers' minds![14] The world, in its good sense, is heaven and earth and God's works in them, as when it is said: "the world was made by him."[15] Again, the world may mean the fulness of the earth, as in John's own words: "he is the propitiator not only of our sins but of the sins of the whole world."[16] Here "world" means all the faithful, scattered in all parts of the earth. But in its bad sense, the world is the world's lovers; and those who love the world, cannot love their brother.

10. "... if the world hateth us: we know"—and what is it that we know?—"that we have passed from death unto life"—and how do we know that?—"because we love the brethren." Let there be no questioning of another. Let each man turn to his own heart, and if there he finds charity towards his brothers, let him be sure that he has passed from death unto life. His place already is on the right hand; he need not be concerned that his glory is at present hidden; when the Lord comes, then he will appear in glory. He has the vigour of life, though it is still winter: his root is vigorous, though the branches be dry: there is life in the pith, the leaves and fruit are ready there within, waiting for the summer. Therefore "we know that we have passed from death unto life, because we love the brethren. He that loveth not, remaineth in death." And lest you suppose it a light thing, my brothers, to hate or not to love, hear the warning that follows: "Every one that hateth his brother is a murderer." If there were any that made light of hatred for brothers, can he in his heart make light of murder? He may not lift his hand to kill, yet already he is counted by the Lord a murderer. The brother may live, but he is already judged as the shedder of blood. "Every one that hateth his brother is a murderer, and ye know that no murderer hath eternal life abiding in him."

11. "Hereby we know love." He speaks now of love's perfection, that perfection on which we have dwelt. "Hereby we know

[14] A pleasant example of the preacher's knowledge of his congregation.
[15] John 1:10.　　　　　[16] I John 2:2.

love, in that he laid down his life for us; and we ought to lay down our lives for the brethren." Here is the bearing of the Lord's words: "Peter, lovest thou me? Feed my sheep." Peter's feeding of his sheep was to mean the laying down of his life for them: as we may learn from the saying that followed. "When thou wast young, thou girdedst thyself, and went whither thou wouldest; but when thou shalt be old, another shall gird thee, and carry thee whither thou wilt not. And this he said," adds the evangelist, "signifying by what death he should glorify God"—teaching the man he had charged to feed his sheep to lay down his life for the sheep.

12. Brethren, how does charity begin? Wait a moment. You have heard how it is made perfect: the end of it and the form of it has been enjoined by the Lord in the gospel: "greater charity hath no man than this, that he lay down his life for his friends."[17] Thus is the perfection of charity shown in the gospel, and thus commended here. But you will be asking among yourselves, When shall we be able to possess such charity? Do not too soon despair of yourself. Perhaps it is already born, but not yet grown to perfection: cherish it, so that it be not stifled. You may say, But how am I to know? We have been told how it is perfected, but we would hear how it begins. This is what John goes on to say: "He that hath this world's goods, and seeth his brother an-hungered, and shutteth up his bowels of compassion from him, how shall the love of God be able to dwell in him?" There is where charity begins. If you are not yet capable of dying for your brother, show now your capacity to give him of your goods. Let charity even now be stirring your inmost heart to do it, not for display but out of the very marrow of compassion, thinking only of the man and his need. If you cannot give of your superfluity to your brother, are you going to be able to lay down your life for him? In your purse lies money, of which thieves may rob you; and if they do not, still you must part from it when you die, though it part not from you while you live. What are you going to do with it? Your brother is hungry, in want: maybe he is in trouble, hard pressed by some creditor. He has not what he needs, you have. He is your brother, he and you were purchased together, one price was paid for both of you, both were redeemed by the blood of Christ. Is there pity in you for him, if you have this world's goods? Do you ask, What concern is it of mine? Am I to give my money to save him from inconvenience? If that is the answer your heart gives you, the love of the Father

17 John 15:13.

dwells not in you; and if the love of the Father dwells not in you, you are not born of God. How can you boast of being a Christian? You have the name and not the deeds. If the work goes with the name, call you pagan who will, you prove yourself Christian by your deeds. For if your deeds prove not your Christianity, then though all may call you Christian, the name without the reality can avail you nothing. "He that hath this world's goods, and seeth his brother have need, and shutteth up his bowels of compassion from him, how can the love of God dwell in him?"   And then it goes on: "Little children, let us not love in word only and in tongue, but in work and in truth."

SIXTH HOMILY

I John 3:19–4:3

1. You remember, my brothers, that we ended our sermon of yesterday with that sentence, which, as it was the last you heard, should certainly have stayed and still remain in your mind: "Little children, let us not love in word only and in tongue, but in work and in truth."

2. We ask, What is this work and this truth? Can there be a work more apparent than giving to the poor? Yet many do it for display and not for love. Can there be a greater work than dying for the brethren? Yet even of this many seek only the reputation, ambitious of acquiring the name, and not in truly heartfelt love. The true lover of his brother is he who before God assures his own heart, wherein God alone sees, who puts to his heart the question whether what he does is indeed for love of the brethren; and has witness borne him by that eye that penetrates the heart, which no man can observe. So the apostle Paul, ready as he was to die for his brethren, saying, "I will myself be spent for your souls,"[1] yet because that motion of his heart was visible to God only and not to the man to whom he spoke, he tells them: "To me indeed it is a very small thing to be judged of you, or by any day of man."[2] And in another place the same Paul shows that such things may be done for empty display, not in the solid strength of charity. In his commending of charity itself he says: "If I give all my goods to the poor, or give my body to burn, and have not charity, it profiteth me nothing."[3] Can anyone so act without charity? It is indeed possible. Look among those who for lack of charity have brought division upon our unity: you will see many who give much to the poor; you will see others so ready to face death that when

[1] II Cor. 12:15.   [2] I Cor. 4:3. See R.V. mg.   [3] I Cor. 13:3.

303

the persecutor stays his hand they hurl themselves to destruction.[4] Such men, certainly, do this without charity. Back, then,
to the voice of conscience, of which the apostle says: "For this
is our glory, the testimony of our conscience."[5] Back to the
voice of conscience, of which the apostle says again: "Let each
man prove his own work, and then shall he have glorying in
himself and not in another."[6] Let each one of us prove his own
work, whether it issues from the pulse of charity, whether the
branches of good works spring forth from the root of love. "Let
each man prove his own work," says Paul, "and then shall he
have glorying in himself and not in another"—when witness is
borne him not by another's tongue but by his own conscience.

3. This, then, is what our Epistle here teaches us. "Hereby we
know that we are of the truth,"—when we love in work and in
truth, not in words and tongue only—"and assure our heart
before him." "Before him"—that is, where God sees him. So
says the Lord himself in the Gospel: "Take heed that ye do not
your righteousness before men, to be seen of them: else ye shall
have no reward with your Father who is in heaven." What else
is the meaning of the saying: "Let not thy left hand know what
thy right hand doeth,"[7] but that the right hand is a pure conscience, and the left the desire of the world? From desire of the
world, many perform many a wonder: but it is the work of the
left hand, not the right. The right hand must do the work, and
without the left hand knowing it, lest worldly desire intrude
itself when we do a thing in the love of what is good. And how
can we be sure of this? You stand before God: ask your own
heart, look at what you have done and what was your purpose
in it—your own salvation, or the empty praise of man. Look
within; for a man cannot judge one whom he cannot see.

If we assure our heart, let us do so in God's presence. "For if
our heart feel evil," that is, charges us inwardly of not acting
with the right intention, "God is greater than our heart and
knoweth all things." You may hide your heart from man: hide
it from God if you can. How shall you hide it from him to whom
a sinner of old time spoke in trembling confession: "Whither shall
I go from thy spirit? and whither shall I flee from thy presence?"[8] He sought a place of escape from God's judgment, and
found none: for where is God not? "If I climb up into heaven,

---

[4] So the Circumcellions were reported to do in their fanatical zeal for
  martyrdom.
[5] II Cor. 1:12.   [6] Gal. 6:4.
[7] Matt. 6:1, 3.   [8] Ps. 139:7 f.

thou art there; if I go down into hell, thou art with me."
Whither are you to go, whither can you flee? If you will hear
counsel, flee to God himself if you would flee from him: flee to
him by confessing, not by hiding; for hide you cannot, but confess you can. Say unto him, "Thou art my refuge" [9]; and let the
love which alone opens the way to life be nourished in you. Let
witness be borne you by your conscience, for it is of God; and if
it is of God, desire not to display it before men; for neither can
their praises exalt you to heaven nor their censures pull you
down from thence. Let his eyes be on you, who gives the crown,
let him be the witness by whose judgment you receive it. "God
is greater than our heart, and knoweth all things."

4. "Beloved, if our heart feel no evil, we have confidence
unto God." "Feel no evil"—that is, tells us truly that we love,
and that the love in us is true love, sincere, not feigned, seeking
our brother's good, looking for no profit from our brother but
his own well-being. "We have confidence unto God; and whatsoever we ask, we shall receive from him, because we keep his
commandments." Our confidence then is not in the sight of
men, but where God himself sees, in the heart; and we shall
receive from him whatsoever we ask, only because we keep his
commandments. What are his commandments? Need we always be repeating it?—"A new commandment give I unto you,
that ye love one another." [10] The duty of which our text speaks
is charity, charity is what it enjoins. Whoever has charity for
the brethren and has it before God, in the place where God sees,
and whoever's heart, when honestly examined, gives to his
questioning no answer but that it holds the true root of charity,
whence good fruits proceed—he has confidence with God, and
whatever he asks he shall receive from him, because he keeps
his commandments.

5. But there is a difficulty here. Of you or me, or of any man
of our time, who may ask something of the Lord our God and
not receive it, it is easy to say, "He has not charity." One man
may think as he will of another. But a more serious question
arises, when we consider those men whom all acknowledge to
have written as saints and now to be with God.

6. You and I are nothing but the Church of God, known to
all: if God will, we belong to his Church, and if we abide in her
by love, we must so persevere if we would show the love we have.
But how are we to think evil of the apostle Paul? Did he not love
his brethren? Did he not have the witness of his conscience in the

9 Ps. 32:7.   10 John 13:34.

sight of God? Was there not in Paul that root of charity whence all good fruits proceeded? It would be madness to deny it. Yet we find him asking and not receiving. "Lest I be exalted by the greatness of the revelations, there was given unto me a pricking of my flesh, a messenger of Satan to buffet me. Concerning which I besought the Lord three times that he would take it away from me; and he said unto me, My grace is sufficient for thee; for strength is made perfect in weakness."[11] You see, his prayer that the messenger of Satan might be taken away from him was not heard. But why? Because it was not for his good. Thus he was heard unto his own good, though not heard according to his desire. This is a great mystery, which I would have you, my people, understand and always remember in your temptations. The prayers of the saints are heard unto their good in all things, always heard unto their eternal good. And that is what they desire: to that end they are always heard.

8. So we should understand that though God gives not what we wish, he gives what is for our good. When you are ill, you may ask for something that is bad for you, which the physician knows to be so. Suppose you ask for cold water: if it is good for you, the doctor will give it at once; if it is not, he will refuse it, but that does not mean that he does not hearken. In denying you your wish, he has hearkened to you for your health. So let charity, brethren, be in you: let charity be in you, and you need have no care. Even when your request is not granted, you are heard, though you know it not. Many are left to themselves, to their hurt, of whom the apostle says: "God gave them over to the desires of their heart."[12] A man that has asked for great wealth may have received it to his own hurt. While he was without it, he had little to fear; as soon as he has possession of it he has become a prey to the stronger. His wish to own what brings the robber's hand upon him, when in his poverty none attacked him, has indeed been granted to his hurt. Learn so to make your requests to God, as trusting the physician to do what he knows best. Confess your sickness, and let him apply the remedy: only hold fast yourself to charity. Let him use knife or cautery as he wills: if under the cutting, the burning, and the pain your cry is not heard, he knows how far the gangrene goes. You want him to withdraw his hand, while he searches the wound: he knows how deep he must press to reach the end. He does not hear you as you would, but as your cure demands. Be

11 II Cor. 12:7 ff.   12 Rom. 1:24.

sure, then, my brethren, that the apostle's words are true: "For we know not what to pray for as we ought; but the Spirit himself maketh intercession for us with groanings that cannot be uttered, because it is he that intercedeth for the saints."[13] The Spirit that intercedes is nothing but the same charity which the Spirit has wrought in you: as the same apostle says, "The charity of God is shed abroad in our hearts through the Holy Spirit that is given to us."[14] Charity itself groans in prayer, and he who gave it cannot shut his ears to its voice. Cast away care, let charity make request, and the ears of God are ready to listen. The answer comes, not what you want, but what is to your advantage. Therefore, "Whatsoever we shall ask, we shall receive from him." Here, as I have said, there is no difficulty, if we understand that the receiving is for our good: otherwise the difficulty is so great as to lead you into calumny of the apostle Paul. "Whatsoever we shall ask, we shall receive from him; because we keep his commandments, and do what is pleasing to him in his sight."—"In his sight"—that is, in the inward place where he sees us.

9. And what are these commandments? "This is his commandment, that we should believe the name of his Son Jesus Christ, and love one another." You see what the commandment is, and you see that its transgressor commits the sin from which every man that is born of God must be free. "As he gave us commandment"—namely, to love one another. "And he that keepeth his commandment"—remember that it enjoins upon us nothing but love of one another—"he that keepeth his commandment shall abide in him, and he in him. And hereby we know that he abideth in us, from the Spirit which he hath given us." Is it not plain that the Holy Spirit's work in man is to cause love and charity to be in him? Is it not plain that, in the words of the apostle Paul, "the charity of God is shed abroad in our hearts through the Holy Spirit that is given to us"? John was speaking of charity, and saying that we ought to question our own heart in the sight of God. "But if our heart feel no evil"— that means, if the heart confess that any good work is wholly performed from love of brother. And if that were not enough, he adds when speaking of the commandment: "This is his commandment, that we should believe the name of his Son Jesus Christ, and love one another. And he that doeth his commandment abideth in him, and he in him. Hereby we know that he abideth in us, from the Spirit which he hath given us." If you

[13] Rom. 8:26 f.   [14] Rom. 5:5.

find charity in yourself, you have the Spirit of God to give you understanding; and that is a thing most necessary.

10. At the Church's beginning the Holy Spirit fell upon the believers, and they spoke with tongues unlearnt, as the Spirit gave them utterance. It was a sign, fitted to the time: all the world's tongues were a fitting signification of the Holy Spirit, because the gospel of God was to have its course through every tongue in all parts of the earth. The sign was given, and then passed away. We no longer expect that those upon whom the hand is laid, that they may receive the Holy Spirit, will speak with tongues. When we laid our hand upon these "infants,"[15] the Church's new-born members, none of you (I think) looked to see if they would speak with tongues, or, seeing that they did not, had the perversity to argue that they had not received the Holy Spirit, for if they had received, they would have spoken with tongues as happened at the first. If then the Holy Spirit's presence is no longer testified by such marvels, on what is anyone to ground assurance that he has received the Holy Spirit? Let him enquire of his own heart: if he loves his brother, the Spirit of God abides in him. Let him see himself, examine himself before the eye of God: let him see if there is in him the love of peace and unity, love of the Church that is spread throughout all the world. Let him look for love, not only of the brother present at his door. We have many brothers whom we do not see, yet are we linked to them in the unity of the Spirit. That not all are here with us is natural; but all of us are in one Body, and have one Head in heaven. My brothers, our eyes cannot see themselves, they are as it were unknown to themselves; but we cannot say that they know not themselves in the charity of a single bodily organism. That they know themselves in charity's union is plain from the fact that when both are open, the right eye cannot mark anything unmarked by the left. You cannot turn one upon its object without the other: they go together, and turn together: they have one direction, though their positions are separate. If then all who love God with you share with you a single direction, do not think of your bodily separation from them in space: together you have set your heart's eye upon the light of truth. And so, if you would know that you have received the Spirit, ask your own heart: it may be that the sacrament is yours without the virtue of the sacrament.[15a] Ask your heart; and

15 Cf. *Hom.* I, 5.
15a In schism the sacrament *must* be without its "virtue": within the Church it *may* be. Cf. Introduction, p. 256.

if the love of brother is there, your mind may be at rest. There can be no love without the Spirit of God. Paul cries aloud: "The charity of God is shed abroad in our hearts through the Holy Spirit which is given to us."

11. "Beloved, believe not every Spirit." This is because he had said: "Hereby we know that he abideth in us, from the Spirit which he hath given to us." Now you are to observe how the Spirit himself is recognized: "Beloved, believe not every spirit, but test the spirits, if they be of God." And who is to be the tester of the spirits? The task set before us is a hard one, my brethren, and it were good for us to be taught by the apostle how we are to discern the truth. He will teach us, no fear; but first observe with attention, and see how the chicaneries of idle heretics have their source here exposed. Observe: "Beloved, believe not every spirit; but test the spirits if they be of God." The Holy Spirit is described in the Gospel under the symbol of water, when the Lord cried, saying: "If any man thirst, let him come to me and drink: he that believeth on me, from his belly shall flow rivers of living water." And the evangelist expounds the meaning of the saying, in the next verse: "this he spake of the Spirit which they that should believe on him were to receive."[16] There were not many baptized by our Lord: it says, "the Spirit was not yet given, because Jesus was not yet glorified." Some were already baptized, but they had not yet received the Holy Spirit, whom the Lord sent from heaven on the day of Pentecost. For the giving of the Spirit, the Lord's glorifying was waited for. Yet before he was glorified and sent the Spirit, he was calling men to prepare themselves to receive that water of which he said: "Let him that thirsts come unto me and drink"; and, "He that believeth on me, from his belly shall flow rivers of living water." What are "rivers of living water"? What is this "water"? No need to ask me: the Gospel tells you. "This he spake of the Spirit, which they that should believe on him were to receive." There is a difference, then, between the water of the sacrament and the water that signifies the Spirit of God. The water of the sacrament is visible: the water of the Spirit is invisible. The former washes the body, and signifies what happens in the soul: by the Spirit the soul itself is cleansed and nourished. This is the Spirit of God that cannot be possessed by heretics, or any that sever themselves from the Church. Moreover, all they who are so severed, not by their own express act but by reason of their wickedness, and thus become

[16] John 7:37 ff.

chaff, tossed about within the threshing-floor, and not grain, all these possess not the Spirit—that Spirit signified by our Lord with the name of water.

12. It still remains for us to discover how the presence of God's Spirit is to be tested. We are given an indication, though not perhaps a simple one; but let us see. We shall be brought back to charity, the charity which instructs us, because it is our anointing. But what is said here? "Test the spirits, if they be of God; for many false prophets have gone out into the world." There we are pointed to all that is heresy or schism. And the means of testing is now to be given. "Hereby is known the Spirit of God." Open your heart's ear! We have been asking in our perplexity, who can know or discern? Now we are to receive a sign. "Hereby is known the Spirit of God. Every spirit that confesseth that Jesus Christ is come in the flesh, is of God. And every spirit that confesseth not that Jesus Christ is come in the flesh, is not of God; and this is Antichrist, of whom ye have heard that he is to come: and now is he in the world." We are listening eagerly for the discernment of spirits, and what we have heard seems to give us no help in discerning them. What are we told? "Every spirit that confesseth that Jesus Christ is come in the flesh, is of God." But then the spirit that is in heretics will be of God; for many of them confess that Jesus Christ is come in the flesh.

13. Ah, my brethren, but we must pay heed to men's actions and not to the noise of their words! Let us ask why Christ came in the flesh; then we may find who are they that deny his coming so. If you pay heed to words, you will hear many a heresy confessing that Christ has come in the flesh; but truth convicts them. Why did Christ come in the flesh? Was he not God? Is it not written of him: "In the beginning was the Word, and the Word was with God, and the Word was God"?[17] Was he not then, as he is now, the food of angels? Did he not come to this world without leaving heaven, and again ascend without leaving us alone? Why then did he come in the flesh? Because it needed that we should be shown the hope of resurrection. He was God, and he came in the flesh. Death was not possible for God: for the flesh it was; and he came in the flesh in order that he might die for us. And how came he to die for us? "Greater charity hath no man than this, that a man lay down his life for his friends."[18] Charity therefore it was that brought him to death; and it follows that whoever has not charity, denies Christ's coming in the flesh.

[17] John 1:1.   [18] John 15:13.

Now put the question to every heretic.[19] "Did Christ come
in the flesh?" "He did: so I believe and confess." "Nay, but you
deny it." "How so? You hear me assert it." "Nay, I convict you
of your denial: you assert it with the voice and deny it with the
heart; you assert it in words, but deny it in deed." "In what
way do I deny it in deed?" "Because Christ came in the flesh
in order that he should die for us, and he died for us because he
taught the height of charity: 'Greater charity hath no man
than this, that he lay down his life for his friends.' You have
not charity, because you break up unity to do yourself honour."
—Hence, then, you may know the Spirit that is of God. Tap
with your finger on the vessel of earthenware, and see whether
the sound it gives be cracked or false. See if it sounds true and
whole: see if charity is there. You are removing yourself from
the world's unity, you are dividing the Church by schisms, you
are rending the Body of Christ. He came in the flesh to gather
men together: you cry aloud to scatter them abroad. Therefore
the Spirit of God is he that maintains Christ's coming in the
flesh, not in word but in deed, not by loud noises but by love.
He is not the Spirit of God who denies Jesus Christ's coming in
the flesh, whose denial also is not by his tongue but by his life,
not in words but in deeds. So it is clear how we are to know the
brethren. Many are within the Church that are within in seeming only; but none are without that are not without in reality.[20]

[19] But of course Augustine is thinking of Donatists.
[20] Augustine would however have added that some of those who are
"without" are nevertheless predestinate members of the Church.

SEVENTH HOMILY

I John 4:4-12

2. "Now ye are children of God, and ye have overcome him."
Overcome, that is, the Antichrist; for he had said above:
"Every one that dissolveth Jesus Christ, and denies that he is
come in the flesh, is not of God." We have explained, as you
remember, that all who violate charity deny Jesus Christ's coming in the flesh, because there was no cause but charity for the
coming of Jesus. It is that same charity here enjoined upon us,
which he himself enjoins in the Gospel: "Greater love can no
man have than this, that a man lay down his life for his friends." [1]
By no means could the Son of God lay down his life for us, but
by clothing himself with the flesh in which he might die. Therefore whoever violates charity, let his tongue say what it will, by
his life denies Christ's coming in the flesh; and that man is
Antichrist, wherever he is and into whatever place he has
made his way. And to them who are citizens of the home-land
after which we sigh, John says: "ye have overcome him." How?
"Because greater is he that is in you than he that is in this
world." He would not have them ascribe the victory to their
own strength, and so be overcome by the presumption of pride;
for the devil overcomes every man that he makes proud. So,
with intent that they may keep humble, John says, first, "ye have
overcome him." That word "overcome" might make any man
raise his head, hold himself upright, and look for praise. But be
not uplifted, see whose is the victory in you: you have overcome,
"because greater is he that is in you than he that is in this
world." Be humble, carry your Master, go quietly under your
rider. It is good for you that he have the reins, and use them. If
you have not him on your back, you may throw up your head

[1] John 15:13.

and heels, but, riderless, it will go ill with you: that freedom will despatch you to the wild beasts as their prey.

3. "They are of the world: therefore speak they of the world, and the world heareth them." They who speak of the world, you must observe, are they who speak against charity. You have heard the Lord's saying: "If ye forgive men their sins, your heavenly Father also will forgive you your sins; but if ye forgive not, neither will your Father forgive you your sins." [2] There is the sentence of truth: deny it, if it be not the Truth who speaks. If you are a Christian and believe the Christ, he said: "I am the truth" [3]: that sentence is true and fast. Now hear the men that speak of the world: "Are you not to have your revenge? Is he to tell the tale of what he has done to you? No, let him feel that he is dealing with a man!" We hear that sort of thing every day, from those who "speak of the world"; and the world hears them. Such things are said only by those who love the world; and only by those who love the world are they listened to.

You have been told that he who loves the world and is regardless of charity, denies the coming of Jesus in the flesh. What if the Lord himself had so acted in the flesh: if when struck by men's hands, he had been moved to avenge himself; if, hanging on the cross, he had not said: "Father, forgive them, for they know not what they do"? If he, who had the power, would use no threatenings, why should you, that are subject to another's power, go puffing and blowing? [4] He died because he willed to die, and threatened not: are you to threaten, who know not when your death shall be?

4. "We are of God." Let us see why that is so: whether there is any reason but charity. "We are of God: he that knoweth God, heareth us; he that is not of God, heareth us not. Hereby know we the spirit of truth and of error." Because he that hears us, has the spirit of truth, and he that hears us not, has the spirit of error. Now let us see how he counsels us, and let us hear his counsel as given in the spirit of truth: counsel given not to Antichrists, not to lovers of the world, not to the world. If we are born of God, "Beloved," he goes on—and remember what he has said: "We are of God; he that knoweth God, heareth us: he that is not of God, heareth us not. Hereby is known the spirit of truth and of error." Our attention is roused: he that knows God, hearkens, he that knows not, hearkens not; and

[2] Matt. 6: 14 f.   [3] John 14:6.
[4] Augustine has the homely expression *Quid sufflas?*

here lies the discerning of the spirit of truth and of error. Let us see what is to be the counsel, wherein we should hear him. "Beloved, let us love one another." Why? Because this is a man's counsel? "Because love is of God." It is a strong commendation of love, to say that it is of God; but there is more to come, and let us listen with all our ears. "Love," he has said, "is of God; and everyone that loveth is born of God, and knoweth God. He that loveth not, knoweth not God." Why? "For God is love." My brothers, what more could be said? If nothing else were said in praise of love, in all the pages of this Epistle, nothing else whatever in any other page of Scripture, and this were the one and only thing we heard from the voice of God's Spirit—"For God is love"—we should ask for nothing more.

5. See now, that to act contrary to love is to act contrary to God. Let no man say: "When I do not love my brother, I sin against a man";—note this well—"sin against a man is a small thing, it is only against God I may not sin." How can you not be sinning against God, when you sin against love? "God is love." The words are not mine. If it were I that said, "God is love," any of you might take offence, and say, "What was that? What did he mean, 'God is love'? God has given love, God has granted love."—"Love is of God: God is love." There, my brethren, is God's Scripture before you: this is a canonical Epistle, read in every nation, maintained by universal authority, on which the world itself has been built up. Here you are told by the Spirit of God, "God is love." Now, if you dare, act against God, and refuse to love your brother.

6. But how do these two texts stand to one another? First, "Love is of God," and now, "God is love." God is Father, and Son, and Holy Spirit. The Son is God of God; the Holy Spirit is God of God; and these three are one God, not three Gods. If the Son is God, and the Holy Spirit is God, and he in whom the Holy Spirit dwells is a lover; then God is love—but God because of God. In the Epistle you have both: "Love is of God," and "God is love." Of the Father alone, Scripture never says that he is "of God." So when we read the words "of God," we must understand them either of the Son or of the Holy Spirit. And from the saying of the apostle: "The charity of God is spread abroad in our hearts through the Holy Spirit that is given to us,"[5] we may understand that in love is the Holy Spirit.[6] It is the Holy Spirit himself, whom evil men cannot receive, who is that fountain of which Scripture says, "Let thy fountain of

[5] Rom. 5:5.   [6] The same exegesis is developed in *De Trin.*, XV, 31.

water be thine own, and let no stranger share with thee." [7] For all who love not God are strangers, Antichrists. Though they enter our churches, they cannot be counted among the sons of God: that fountain of life belongs not to them. The evil man as well as the good can possess baptism: the evil man as well as the good can possess the gift of prophecy. King Saul possessed it: he persecuted the saintly David, and was filled by the spirit of prophecy and began to prophesy. The evil man as well as the good can receive the sacrament of the Body and Blood of the Lord; for of such it is written: "he that eateth and drinketh unworthily, eateth and drinketh judgment to himself." [8] The evil man as well as the good can have the name of Christ, can be called a Christian: of such it is written: "They defiled the name of their God." [9] All these sacraments may be possessed by the evil man; but to have charity and be an evil man is not possible. This therefore is the peculiar gift of the Spirit: he is the one and only fountain. To drink of it, God's Spirit calls you: God's Spirit calls you to drink of himself.

7. "Hereby is manifested the love of God in us." See now, we have our calling to love God. Could we love him, did he not first love us? If we were slow to love, let us not be slow to the return of love. He first loved us—not as we love ourselves. He loved wicked men, but did away their wickedness; he loved wicked men, but not for wickedness did he bring them together into one; he loved sick men, but visited them for their cure. Then—"God is love. Hereby is manifested the love of God in us, in that he sent his only-begotten Son into this world, that we might live through him." Even as the Lord himself says: "Greater love can no man have than that he lay down his life for his friends"; and in this is proved Christ's love towards us, that he died for us. Wherein is proved the Father's love towards us? In that he sent his only Son to die for us; as Paul the apostle also says: "He that spared not his own Son, but delivered him up for us all, how hath he not also with him given us all things?" [10] Christ was delivered up by the Father, and delivered up by Judas: is there no seeming likeness between these two acts? Judas is a betrayer; then is God too a betrayer? God forbid, you say. But what makes the difference between the Father delivering up the Son, the Son delivering up himself, and Judas the disciple delivering up his Master? In that Father and Son did it in charity, Judas in treachery. You see, we have to look, not at

[7] Prov. 5:16 f.   [8] I Cor. 11:29.
[9] Ezek. 36:20.   [10] Rom. 8:32.

what a man does, but with what mind and will he does it. We find God the Father in the very same act in which we find Judas; we bless the Father, and we execrate Judas. Why so? Because we bless charity, and execrate wickedness. How vast a good has come to mankind from the delivering-up of Christ! But that was not what was in the mind of Judas. In the mind of God was the salvation whereby we are redeemed: in the mind of Judas the money for which he sold his Lord. The Son himself thought upon the price he paid for us: Judas upon the price he took for selling him. The difference in intention makes a difference in the acts. Though the thing is one, yet when we measure it by the difference of intention, the one lovable, the other damnable, we find that one is to be glorified and the other execrated. Such great virtue has charity: you see that it alone divides, it alone distinguishes the actions of men.

8. We have been marking this in similar actions. When we look at differing actions, we find that charity may cause a man to be fierce, and wickedness to speak smoothly. A boy may be struck by his father, and have fair words from a slave-dealer. Were you to offer a choice between blows and smooth words, who would not choose the fair words and shun the blows? But if you look to the persons from whom they come, it is charity that strikes and wickedness that ingratiates. You see the point we are making, that the actions of men are discerned only according to their root in charity. Many things can be done that look well, yet do not issue from the root of charity. Thorns too have their flowers. Some actions seem harsh or savage, but are performed for our discipline at the dictate of charity. Thus a short and simple precept is given you once for all: Love, and do what you will.[11] Whether you keep silence, keep silence in love; whether you exclaim, exclaim in love; whether you correct, correct in love; whether you forbear, forbear in love. Let love's root be within you, and from that root nothing but good can spring.

9. "Herein is love. Herein is manifested the love of God towards us, that God sent his only-begotten Son into this world, that we might live through him. Herein is love, not that we loved him, but that he loved us." We did not first love him. He loved us, to the end that we might love him. "And he sent his Son to be the propitiator for our sins"—propitiator, that is, offerer of sacrifice.[11a] He offered sacrifice for our sins. Where did

11 See Introduction, p. 257, and cf. below, §11.
11a Here Augustine has *litator* instead of the consistent Vulgate *propitiatio*.

he find the offering, the pure victim that he would offer? Because he could find no other, he offered himself. "Beloved, if God so loved us, we ought also to love one another." "Peter," the Lord says, "lovest thou me?" And Peter said: "I love thee." "Feed my sheep."

10. "No man hath seen God at any time." God is an invisible reality: he is to be sought, not with the eye, but with the heart. If we would see the light of the sun, we must keep clear the bodily eye which is our means of beholding it. So if we would see God, let us cleanse the eye with which God can be seen. And the place of that eye we may learn from the Gospel: "Blessed are the pure in heart, for they shall see God."[12] Only let not the "desire of the eyes" fashion our thought of God. One may easily imagine for oneself some vast form, or some measureless immensity extended through space, as it might be this light which our eyes can see, increased to the limit and flooding the landscape; or one may picture some old man of venerable aspect. But our thoughts are not to go that way. There is true matter for your thought, if you would see God. "God is love." What outward appearance, what form, what stature, hands or feet, has love? None can say; and yet love has feet, which take us to the Church, love has hands which give to the poor, love has eyes which give intelligence of him who is in need—as the Psalm says: "Blessed is he who bethinks himself of the needy and poor."[13] Love has ears, of which the Lord says: "He that hath ears for hearing, let him hear."[14] All these are not members set each in their own place: he that has charity sees the whole at once with the understanding's grasp. Dwell there, and you shall be dwelt in: abide, and there shall be abiding in you. My brothers, one does not love what one cannot see. Why then, when you hear the praise of charity, are you stirred to acclamation and applause? What have I displayed to your eyes? No vivid colours, no gold or silver, no gems of the treasure-house. My own face has not changed in speaking: this body of mine looks as it did when I entered the church, and so do all of you. You hear the praise of charity, and your voices ring out. Certainly there is nothing for you to see. But let that same delight in charity which makes you acclaim it, lead you to hold it fast in your heart. Listen to me, my brothers: here is a great treasure, which I would urge you with all the power that God gives me to win for yourselves. Suppose you were shown some cup, finely wrought and gilded, which charmed your eye and

[12] Matt. 5:8.   [13] Ps. 41:1.   [14] Luke 8:8.

compelled your admiration, delighting you by the artist's skill, the weight of the silver and the gleam of the metal. Any of you might exclaim: "If only that cup were mine!" The words would be wasted, for you could not make them come true. Or if one were bent on possessing it, he might meditate the stealing of it out of the owner's house. Now you have heard the praise of charity: if it delights you, take it for your own—no need to commit any robbery, no need to think of the purchase price. It is yours for nothing. Take hold of it, clasp it to yourself: no possession can be sweeter. If it be such to the hearing of it, what must it be in the owning!

11. If there be any of you, my brothers, that would get charity and keep it, you must above all avoid thinking of it as a poor, inactive thing, wanting no more than a sort of gentle mildness for its keeping, or even a careless indifference. Charity is not kept in that way. You are not to suppose that you love your servant when you do not beat him, or love your son when you relax your discipline over him, or love your neighbour when you never find fault with him. That is not charity, but weakness. Let charity be zealous to set right, to correct faults, to delight in good behaviour, but to correct and improve what is bad. Love the man, not his errors; for God made the man, his errors are his own doing. Love what God has made, not what man has done. In loving the first, you remove the second: in loving the one, you amend the other. And if sometimes you must be harsh or angry, let it be for love of righting the wrong. That is why charity is shown by the dove which came down upon the Lord. The appearance of the dove was that under which came the Holy Spirit, by whom charity was to be poured into us; and the reason is that the dove has no gall, and though it fight for its nest with beak and wings, its anger is without bitterness. So does a father act: when he chastens his son, his purpose is discipline. As I said before, the kidnapper who would sell the boy, gives him fair words with a foul intent; the father who would correct him, puts no gall into his chastising. Be so yourselves with all men. Here, my brothers, is a good pattern, a good rule: all of you have sons or hope to have them, or if any of you have resolved to have no sons of your body, he will desire spiritual children. Is there one that does not correct his son, or any son who does not receive discipline from his father? Yet there must be an appearance there of anger. Love can be angry, charity can be angry, with a kind of anger in which there is no gall, like the dove's and not the raven's.

And this suggests to me, my brethren, a word on that schism which violators of charity have brought about. For their hatred of charity has been matched by their hate for the Dove. But the Dove convicts them, the Dove that comes forth from heaven, as the heavens are opened, and stays over the Lord's head. And wherefore so? For the hearing of these words: "This is he that baptizeth."[15] Back, brigands! Back, usurpers of Christ's estate! Upon those estates, over which you seek to rule, you have dared to post the title-deeds of a greater owner. He recognizes his titles and claims his own estate: he will not erase the titles, but he will enter and possess his own. So, when one comes into the Catholic Church, there is no cancelling of his baptism, no erasing of the Emperor's title. The title is acknowledged: the owner enters under his own titles where the brigand had entered under a title that was not his.

[15] John 1:33; see Introduction, p. 256.

EIGHTH HOMILY

I John 4:12–16

4. It may have occurred to some of you, since we have been
expounding this Epistle of John, to ask why the charity
which he so strongly commends is only brotherly love. He
speaks of "him that loveth his brother," and of the "commandment given to us that we love one another." Brotherly charity
is continually spoken of; but of the charity of God, the charity
(that is) whereby we love God, there is not such constant mention—though it is not altogether passed over in silence. On the
other hand, there is scarcely a word in the whole Epistle about
the love of enemies. In all his urgent preaching and commendation of charity, he does not tell us to love our enemies, only to
love our brethren. Yet just now, in our reading of the Gospel, we
heard the text: "If ye love them that love you, what reward have
you? Do not the publicans the same?"[1] How is it then that John
the apostle enjoins brotherly love upon us as the great means
towards our perfecting, while our Lord says that it is not enough
for us to love our brothers, but that love itself must stretch so
far as to reach our enemies? The reaching to enemies does not
mean the passing over of brothers. Our love, like a fire, must
first take hold of what is nearest, and so spread to what is further
off. A brother is nearer to you than a casual stranger: and again
you are closer to the man whom you do not know but who is not
opposed to you, than to the enemy who is. Your love should
extend to your neighbours; but that is not to be called extension. Love for those who are linked to you is much the same
as love for yourself. Extend it to such as you do not know,
who yet have done no harm to you; and now go further than
them, and reach to the love of enemies. That, certainly, is our

[1] Matt. 5:46.

320

Lord's command. Why then has John said nothing of loving an enemy?

5. All love, even the love we call carnal—for which the more usual Latin word is not *dilectio* but *amor*, *dilectio* being commonly used and understood in a higher sense—all love, my dear brothers, implies necessarily an element of goodwill towards those who are loved. Whether we use the word *diligere* or *amare* —as the Lord did when he said to Peter, Lovest (*amas*) thou me?—we should not, indeed we cannot love men in the sense in which a glutton will say, I love partridges: the object of his love being the killing and eating them. He says he loves, but the effect for the partridges is to put an end to their existence: he loves their destruction. The love of food can only purport its consumption and our own refreshment. Men are not to be loved as things to be consumed, but in the manner of friendship and goodwill, leading us to do things for the benefit of those we love. And if there is nothing we can do, goodwill alone is enough for the lover. We should not want there to be unfortunates, so that we may exercise works of mercy. You give bread to the hungry; but it would be better that no one should hunger, and that you should not have to give. You clothe the naked; would that all were so clothed that there were no need for it! You bury the dead: but we long for that life in which there is no dying. You reconcile men at law with one another: but we long for the ever-lasting peace of Jerusalem where all quarrels are at an end. All these are the services called out by man's needs. Remove distress, and there will be no place for works of mercy. Works of mercy will cease, but there will be no quenching of the fire of charity. You may have the truest love for a happy man, on whom you have nothing to bestow: such love will have a greater sincerity and a far more unspoilt purity. Once you have bestowed gifts on the unfortunate, you may easily yield to the temptation to exalt yourself over him, to assume superiority over the object of your benefaction. He fell into need, and you supplied him: you feel yourself as the giver to be a bigger man than the receiver of the gift. You should want him to be your equal, that both may be subject to the one on whom no favour can be bestowed.

8. The true Christian will never set himself up over other men. God gave you a place above the beasts, in which you are of more value than they. That is your natural privilege, always to be better than a beast. If you would be better than another man, you will grudge to see him as your equal. You ought to

wish all men equal to yourself; and if you have gone beyond another man in wisdom, you should want him too to show himself wise. While he is still backward, he may learn of you: while he is ignorant, he has need of you; and you appear as teacher, he as learner. As teacher, you are the superior; as learner, he is the inferior. Unless you want him to be your equal, you will be for having him always as the learner, and that will make you a grudging teacher. But what sort of teaching will a grudging teacher give? I can only beg you not to teach him your grudgingness. Listen to the apostle's words, which come from the true heart of charity: "I would that all men were such as I myself."[2] See how he wanted all to be his equals; and just because charity made him so desire, he was raised above all. Man has transgressed his proper limit: created higher than the beasts, he has let covetousness carry him away, so that he might be higher than other men. And that is pride.

9. Consider now the works that pride may do: notice how they may resemble or even equal those of charity. Charity feeds the hungry, so does pride: charity, to the praise of God, pride, to the praise of itself. Charity clothes the naked, so does pride; charity fasts, so does pride; charity buries the dead, so does pride. All the good works that are willed and done by charity, may be set in motion by its contrary pride, like horses harnessed to a car. But when charity is the inward driver, pride must give place—pride which is not so much misgoverning as misgoverned. It goes ill with the man who has pride for his charioteer, for he is sure to be overturned. How can we know or see that it be not pride which governs the good deed? Where is the proof? We see the works: hunger is fed by compassion, but also by pride; strangers are entertained by compassion, but also by pride; poverty is protected by compassion, but also by pride. In the works themselves we can see no difference. I would go further—though it is not I, but Paul who says it: charity goes to death, a man (that is) who has charity confesses the name of Christ and becomes a martyr; and pride also may do both. The one has charity, the other has not; but let this other mark the apostle's words: "If I give all my goods to the poor, and if I give my body to burn, and have not charity, it profiteth me nothing."[3] So Holy Scripture recalls us from all this outward showing, recalls us from the surface appearance displayed before men, to the inward truth. Come back to your own conscience, and question it: pay heed, not to the visible flowering

[2] I Cor. 7:7.   [3] I Cor. 13:3.

but to the root beneath the ground. Is covetousness at the root? Then you may have a show of good deeds, but of works truly good there can be none. Is charity at the root? Be easy, for no evil can be the issue. The proud may speak fair words, love may show anger: the one may clothe, the other may smite: the one clothes for the pleasing of men, the other smites for the correction of discipline. The stroke of charity is more to be welcomed than the alms of pride. Come back, then, my brothers, into the place within, and in whatsoever you do, look for the witness of God. See, as he sees, the intention of your acts. If your heart does not accuse you of acting for the sake of display, it is well, you may be easy. And when you do well, have no fear of another's seeing. Fear only to act so that you may have praise for yourself; let the other see, so that God may have the praise. If you hide what you do from man's eyes, you are hiding it against man's imitation, and robbing God of his praise. There are two parties for whose benefit you give alms, two are hungry, the one for bread, the other for righteousness; for it is written, "Blessed are they that hunger and thirst after righteousness, for they shall be filled." [4] Between these two hungering ones, you are set for the working of good: if charity is the worker, it has compassion for both, it seeks to give help to both. For while the one looks for food, the other looks for an example to follow. As you feed the first, offer yourself to the second, and you have given alms to both. You have enabled the one to give thanks for the ending of his hunger, the other to imitate the example shown him.

10. Let your works of mercy, then, proceed from a merciful heart; for then even in your love of enemies you will be showing love of brothers. Do not think that John has given no charge concerning love of one's enemy; for he has said much of brotherly charity, and it is always the brother that you love. How so? you ask. I ask in turn, Why do you love your enemy? Because you wish him to have good health in this life? but suppose that is not in his interest? Because you wish him to be rich? but if riches themselves should rob him of his sight? To marry a wife? but if that should bring him a life of bitterness? To have children? but suppose they turn out badly? Thus there is uncertainty in all the things you seem to desire for your enemy, because you love him: uncertainty everywhere. Let your desire for him be that together with you he may have eternal life: let your desire for him be that he may be your brother. And if that

4 Matt. 5:6.

is what you desire in loving your enemy—that he may be your brother—when you love him, you love a brother. You love in him, not what he is, but what you would have him be. Once before, if I remember right, my dear people, I put to you this parable: Imagine the trunk of a tree lying before you: a good carpenter may see such a piece of timber, unhewn, as it was cut in the forest. He loves it at sight, but because he means to make something out of it. The reason for his love is not that it may always remain as it is: as craftsman, he has looked at what it shall be, not as lover at what it is; and his love is set upon what he will make of it, not upon its present state. Even so has God loved us sinners. God, we say, has loved sinners; for we have his word, "They that are whole need not a physician, but they that are sick." [5] But surely his love for us sinners is not to the end that we remain in our sin. Like trees from the wood, we have been looked on by the Carpenter, and his thought turns to the building he will make of us, not to the timber that we were. So may you look upon your enemy, standing against you with his angry passion, his biting words, his provoking insults, his unrelenting hate. But in all this you need think only that he is a *man*. You see all the hostility to yourself as of the man's making; and you see in himself God's making. That he was made to be a man, is the act of God: his hatred of you, his malice against you, is his own. And what do your say in your heart? "Lord, have mercy on him: forgive him his sins: put fear in him, and change him." You love in him, not what he is but what you would have him be; and thus when you love your enemy, you love a brother. Therefore the perfection of love is the love of an enemy, and this perfect love consists in brotherly love. It is not to be held that the apostle John enjoins upon us a lesser degree of charity, and the Lord Jesus a greater. John, indeed, instructs us to love our brothers, Christ to love even our enemies. But you must consider why Christ has bidden you love your enemies. It cannot be with the intent that they should always remain such: that would be an instruction to hate, not to love. Consider the manner of his own love for them, which was a will that they should not continue his persecutors: "Father," he says, "forgive them, for they know not what they do." [6] The will for their pardoning was a will for their transformation: in willing that they should be transformed, he deigned to make brothers out of enemies; and so in very truth he did. He was killed, and buried. He rose again

[5] Matt. 9:12.   [6] Luke 23:34.

and ascended into heaven, he sent the Holy Spirit upon his disciples. They began with confidence to preach his name, they worked miracles in the name of the crucified and slain; and those who had done the Lord to death saw what was done: that blood which they had shed in fury, they drank in faith.

11. I have spoken of all this, my brethren, somewhat lengthily; but if charity was to be urged upon you, my people, with the force demanded, there was no other way. If there is in you nothing of charity, all I have said comes to nothing. But if it exists at all in you, my words should be as oil upon the flames; and perhaps they may have kindled it even where it was not. In one, what was already there will have grown: in another, what was not may have begun to be. I have spoken in order to stir up your backwardness in the love of enemies. If a man is passionate against you, meet his passion with prayer: if he hates you, meet his hatred with pity. It is the fever in his soul that hates you: when he is cured, he will show his gratitude. Think of the physician's love for the sick: he does not love them *as* sick men. If he did, he would want them always to be sick. He loves the sick, not so that they may remain sick men but so that they may become healthy instead of sick. And how much he may have to suffer from them in their delirium—abuse, not seldom blows! The physician attacks the fever and excuses the man: is this loving his enemy? Truer to say that he is hating his real enemy, disease: that is what he hates, while he loves the man that strikes at him. His hatred, then, is for the fever; for the blows are struck at him by the disease, the sickness, the fever. The physician takes away the thing that shows hostility to him, in order that the man may live to give him thanks. So with you. If your enemy hates you, and hates you unjustly, you know that it is because the lusts of this world have the mastery in him. If you meet his hate with hate, you are returning evil for evil; and what comes of that? I had to lament for one sick man, who hated you: now, if you are hating also, I must mourn for two. But, you say, he has attacked your property, he is robbing you of some earthly possession or other: you hate him, because he is making this life strait for you. You need not suffer such straitening: for you can take your journey into the heaven above, lifting up your heart to the wide realm of freedom where in the hope of life eternal there is no straitness to be borne. Think what it really is of which he would rob you, and remember that he could not even do that, were he not permitted by

the Father who "chasteneth every son that he receiveth." [7]
Your enemy himself is as it were God's operating instrument to
work your own healing: if God knows it to be for your good that
he should despoil you, he allows it; if God knows it to be for
your good to be beaten, he allows your enemy to strike you.
God is using him to make you whole; pray that he too may be
given healing.

12. "No man hath ever seen God." See, my beloved! "If we
love one another, God shall abide in us, and his love shall be
perfected in us." Make a beginning of love, and you shall be
made perfect. For if you have begun to love, God has begun to
dwell in you: love him who has begun to dwell in you, so that
by a more perfect indwelling he may make you perfect.
"Hereby we know that we abide in him, and he in us, because
he has given us of his Spirit." It is well: thanks be to God! We
know that he dwells in us; and how do we know that we know
it? Because John himself tells us, that "he has given us of his
Spirit." How do we know that? How do you know that he has
given you of his Spirit? Ask your heart: if it is full of charity,
you have the Spirit of God. How do we know that this is
evidence for you of God's Spirit dwelling in you? Ask Paul the
apostle: "Because the charity of God is shed abroad in our
hearts through the Holy Spirit that is given us." [8]

13. "And we have seen, and are witnesses, that the Father
sent his Son to be the Saviour of the world." Sick men, be at
your ease: if such a physician has come to you, there can be no
despairing. Grave were your diseases, incurable your wounds,
desperate your sickness. But if you think of the gravity of your
trouble, think also of the omnipotence of the Physician. You
are desperate, but he is omnipotent; and his witnesses are they
who first were healed, and who now proclaim the Physician—
although their own healing were in hope rather than in fulfilment, as the apostle says: "In hope we are saved." [9] So we have
begun to be healed in faith, and our salvation will be perfected, when this corruptible shall have put on incorruption,
and this mortal shall have put on immortality. That is hope,
not fulfilment; but he that rejoices in hope shall lay hold
of the fulfilment, to which he that has not hope can never
attain.

14. "Whosoever confesses that Jesus is the Son of God, God
abideth in him, and he in God." We need not now insist at
length, that this confessing must be not in word but in deed,

7 Heb. 12:6.   8 Rom. 5:5.   9 Rom. 8:24.

not of the tongue but of the life; for there are many that confess
in words what their deeds deny. "And we have known,
and have believed, what love God hath in us." Again, how
have you known this? "God is love." He has said it before, and
now says it again. You could not have a fuller commendation
of love than the naming of it with God's name. You might
possibly have thought little of God's gift, but can you think little
of God? "God is love, and he that abideth in love, abideth in
God and God abideth in him." There is a mutual indwelling
of the holder and the held: your dwelling in God means that
you are held by him, God's dwelling in you means that he holds
you, lest you fall. Think of yourself as being made a house of
God, but not like the house of bricks and mortar that carries
you in the body. If that house should go from under you, you
fall; but God does not fall, if you go from under him. He is whole
and entire, when you desert him, whole and entire when you
return to him. Your healing brings no gift to him: it is you that
are cleansed, you that are amended and re-created. He is medicine to the unhealthy, rule to the crooked, light to the darkened,
dwelling to the homeless. The imparting is all to you, and you
may not suppose that when you come to God there is aught
imparted to him—even the possession of a slave. God will not
lack servants, though you refuse, though all refuse his service.
God has no need of servants, but servants have need of God.
Hence the words of the Psalm: "I have said unto the Lord,
thou art my God"—yes, God is the true Lord—"because thou
needest not my goods."[10] You need the good your servant provides. He needs the good you provide for him in feeding him,
and you need the good he provides for you by his service. For
yourself you cannot do all the drawing of water, the cooking,
the running before your carriage, the grooming of your beast.
You are in want of the good your servant furnishes, you are in
want of his attendance; and inasmuch as you want an inferior,
you are no true lord. The true lord is he who seeks nothing
from us; and it goes ill with us, if we seek not him. He seeks
nothing from us, yet he sought us when we were not seeking him.
One sheep had gone astray: he found it and brought it home
upon his shoulders rejoicing.[11] Was the sheep a necessity for
the shepherd, or not rather the shepherd a necessity for the
sheep?

I am loth, you see, to reach the end of this Epistle, just because
there is no theme on which I would fainer speak than charity;

[10] Ps. 16:2.   [11] Luke 15:4 f.

and no other Scripture extols charity with greater warmth. For you there can be no sweeter matter of discourse, no food more healthful for your souls—but only if by good living you confirm in yourselves the gift of God. Be not unthankful for this wondrous grace of God—God, who, possessing one only-begotten Son, willed not that Son to be alone, but adopted us to be his brothers and share with him eternal life.

NINTH HOMILY

I John 4:17–21

1. You will remember, my dear people, that we have still to treat and expound to you, as the Lord shall enable us, the last part of John's Epistle. I have not forgotten my debt, and you should not forget to demand it of me. For that same charity which is the chief, if not the sole theme, of this Epistle, will make me most faithful in acknowledging my debt, and you most welcome in demanding it. Most welcome in demanding: for demands are unpleasant, where there is not charity, but where there is, they are welcome; and for him on whom they are made, though they involve labour, yet the labour is lightened or even nullified by charity itself. Can we not see, even in dumb, unreasoning creatures, where there is no spiritual charity but only one that belongs to the fleshly nature, with what eager insistence the mother's milk is demanded by her little ones? Yet however rough be the suckling's onset upon the udder, the mother likes it better than if there were no sucking, no demanding of the debt that charity admits. Indeed we often see the bigger calf butting with its head at the cow's udders, and the mother's body forced upward by the pressure; yet she will never kick her calf away, but if the young one be not there to suck, she will low for him to come to it. Of spiritual charity, the apostle says: "I have become little among you, like a nurse cherishing her children."[1] If such charity be in us, we cannot but love you when you press your demand upon us. Backwardness in you we do not love: it makes us afraid of the failing of your strength.

The occurrence of certain set Lessons for the festal days, which we were obliged to read and discourse upon, has compelled us to leave for a time the text of our Epistle; but now we are to

[1] I Thess. 2:7.

return to the course which was broken, and I ask your devout attention to what remains.

2. "Herein is love made perfect in us, that we may have confidence in the day of judgment; because, as he is, so are we in this world." This tells us how every man may test the progress of charity in him—or rather his own progress in charity: for if charity is God, in God there can be neither progress nor regress; and charity is only said to make progress in you, inasmuch as you make progress in charity. Ask therefore how far you have progressed in charity, and listen to the answer of your heart, that you may know the measure of your progress. John has promised to show us how we may know it, saying: "Herein is love made perfect in us." Herein—"that we may have confidence in the day of judgment." In every man that has confidence in the day of judgment, charity is made perfect. To have confidence in the day of judgment is not to fear its coming. There are men who do not believe in a day of judgment, and they cannot have confidence in a day which they do not believe will come. We can leave them aside: may God awaken them into life, but of the dead we will say nothing. They do not believe in a coming day of judgment, and neither fear nor desire that in which they do not believe. But for any man that has begun to believe in a day of judgment, the beginning of belief is the beginning of fear. So long as he fears, he cannot have confidence in the day of judgment, and not yet is charity made perfect in him. Yet there is no cause for despair: where you see a beginning, why despair of the end? And fear itself is a beginning—as Scripture says: "The fear of the Lord is the beginning of wisdom." [2] A man has begun to fear the day of judgment: let fear make him amend himself; let him keep watch against the sins that are his enemies; let him begin to renew the life within him, and as the apostle says, to "mortify his members that are upon the earth." [3] The "members upon the earth" mean the spiritual things of wickedness, the "greediness and uncleanness" and the rest, which the text proceeds to recount. In the measure in which he that has begun to fear the day of judgment mortifies his members upon the earth, the heavenly members arise and gain strength. These heavenly members are all kinds of good works; and as they arise, the man begins to desire that which he was fearing. He feared lest Christ should come and find in him godlessness for condemnation: now he desires Christ's coming, because he is to find godliness ready to

[2] Ps. 11:10.   [3] Col. 3:5 f.

be crowned. When the soul has begun to long for Christ's coming, the chaste soul that longs for the husband's embrace, she forswears the adulterer, becoming inwardly virgin in the power of faith, hope, and charity; and now she has confidence in the day of judgment: there is no inner conflict in her prayer, "Thy kingdom come." He who fears the coming of God's kingdom, must fear lest this prayer be heard; and it is a strange sort of prayer that fears to be heard. But he who prays in the confidence of charity, truly desires that the kingdom may come. And so, my brothers, do all that you can to train yourselves to long for the day of judgment. For the perfection of charity is attested only when a longing for that day has begun to arise. To long for it is to have confidence in it; and to have confidence in it is to have no alarm of conscience, in the charity that is perfect and pure.

3. "Herein is his love made perfect in us, that we may have confidence in the day of judgment." Wherefore shall we have confidence? "Because, as he is, so are we in this world." The meaning of this is to be understood in reference to charity itself. The Lord says in the gospel: "If ye love them that love you, what reward have you? Do not the publicans the same?" [4] Then he tells us what he would have us do. "But I say unto you, Love your enemies, and pray for them that persecute you." And for the command to love our enemies, he gives us our pattern in God himself, saying: "that ye may be sons of your Father which is in heaven." God loves his enemies, for God is he "who maketh his sun to rise on the good and the evil, and raineth upon the just and the unjust." Thus the perfection to which God calls us is that of loving our enemies as he has loved his own; and so our confidence in the day of judgment is because, as he is, even so are we in this world. As he loves his enemies, making his sun to rise on the good and the evil, and raining upon the just and the unjust; so we, though we cannot give sun and rain to our enemies, may give them our tears when we pray for them.

4. And now observe what the Epistle says about this very confidence. How are we to recognize the perfection of charity? "There is no fear in charity." What then of the man who has begun to fear the day of judgment? If charity were perfect in him, he would not fear; for perfect charity would make perfect righteousness, and he would have no cause for fear: rather he would have cause for longing that wickedness pass away and God's kingdom come. Therefore, "there is no fear in charity."

[4] Matt. 5:44 ff.

But this is true, not of charity's beginnings: "perfect charity," he continues, "casteth out fear." Fear, then, may be a starting-point; for "the fear of the Lord is the beginning of wisdom." Fear, as it were, prepares the place for charity; but when charity has taken up its dwelling, the fear that prepared the place for it is expelled. As one grows, the other diminishes: as charity moves to the centre, fear is driven outside. The greater the charity, the lesser the fear: the lesser the charity, the greater the fear. But if there has been no fear, there is no way for charity to enter. When we sew a seam, the thread must be let in by the needle: the needle goes in first, but it must come out if the thread is to follow. So fear takes first hold upon the mind, but does not stay there, because the purpose of its entry was to let charity in. And once the quiet of fearlessness is established in the soul, what joy is ours, whether in this world or in the world to come! Even in this world, who shall harm us if we are filled with charity? Hear the apostle's triumphant cry: "Who shall separate us from the charity of Christ? Shall tribulation, or distress, or persecution, or hunger, or nakedness, or peril, or sword?" [5] And again, in the words of Peter: "And who is he that can harm you, if ye be followers of that which is good?" [6]

"There is no fear in love: but perfect love casteth out fear; because fear hath torment." The heart is tormented by consciousness of sins: justification has not yet come, there is that within which pricks and stings. So in the verses of the Psalm which speak of the perfecting of righteousness: "Thou hast turned for me my mourning into joy: thou hast stripped off my sackcloth, and girded me with gladness, so that my glory may sing unto thee, and my pricking is ended." [7] Pricking is ended, when the goad of conscience is stilled. Fear is a goad; but you are not to fear, for charity enters, with healing for the wound of fear. The fear of God wounds like the surgeon's knife: it cuts out the festering part, and seems to enlarge the wound. When there was festering in the body, the wound was smaller, but it was dangerous. The pain was not so sharp as now at the touch of the surgeon's knife. The treating of it may hurt more than if it had no treatment; but the added pain in the application of the cure serves to end pain for good by the recovery of health. Therefore let fear take hold of your heart, that it may give an entry to charity: let the surgeon's knife make way for the healing scar. Such is our Surgeon's skill, that not even a scar may show: you have only to submit yourself to his hand. For if you are

[5] Rom. 8:35.　　　[6] I Peter 3:13.　　　[7] Ps. 30:11 f.

without fear, you will not be able to be justified. That is the
word of Scripture: "He that is without fear shall not be able
to be justified." [8] So there must needs first enter fear, by means
of which charity can come in. Fear is the remedy, charity is
health. "He that feareth is not made perfect in love." And that
is because "fear hath torment," like the surgeon's incision.

5. There is indeed another text which may seem to contradict this, if it be not rightly understood. We read in a certain
passage of the Psalms: "the fear of the Lord is pure, enduring
for ever and ever." [9] That points us to an everlasting fear, that
yet is pure. But if so, is there a contradiction to it in the words
of our Epistle: "there is no fear in charity, but perfect charity
casteth out fear"? Let us enquire of both these oracles of God.
The Spirit that speaks is one, though there be two books, two
mouths, two tongues. One and the same breath may blow two
flutes, and cannot one and the same Spirit fill two hearts and
set two tongues in motion? But if two flutes, filled by one spirit,
one breathing, may sound in harmony, is it possible that two
tongues, moved by the Spirit of God, should be discordant?
There must then here be some harmony, some concord, that
demands a sympathetic ear. The Spirit of God has filled by his
inspiration two hearts and two mouths, has moved two tongues:
of one tongue we hear, "there is no fear in charity, but perfect
charity casteth out fear"; of the other we hear, "the fear of the
Lord is pure, enduring for ever and ever." Well! Is there a dis-
cord between the sounds? No: you must listen with care and
observe the melody. Not for nothing does the word "pure"
come in the one saying, and not in the other: there must be one
kind of fear that is called pure, and another kind that is not.
Let us distinguish these two fears, and then we may grasp the
harmony of the flutes. How shall we do this? Listen, my people.
There are men who fear God because they fear to be cast into
hell, to burn with the devil in everlasting fire. This is the fear
that makes an opening for charity; but it enters only to go out
again. If as yet it is the thought of punishment that makes you
fear God, not yet do you love him whom so you fear: you are not
longing for good things, you are but apprehensive of evil. But
that very apprehension leads you to amend yourself, and so to
begin to long for the good things; and when you begin to do

[8] Ecclesiasticus 1:22. The text has: "Unrighteous anger shall not be able
to be justified." Augustine may be quoting from memory as often: the
context in Ecclesiasticus is "the fear of the Lord."
[9] Ps. 19:9.

that, the pure fear will arise in you—the fear of losing what is good. It is one thing, you see, to fear God, lest he send you to hell with the devil: it is another, to fear God, lest he depart from you. The first fear is not yet pure, for it comes not of the love of God but of the fear of punishment. But when you fear God lest his presence leave you, you are embracing him, and longing to enjoy him.

6. The difference between these two fears—the one which charity casts out, and the other pure and enduring for ever— may best be shown by thinking of two married women, differing in character. Suppose one of these two to be drawn towards adultery, to take pleasure in the wicked desire, but to fear the judgment of her husband. She fears her husband, but this fear comes of her still loving wickedness; to her the husband's presence is not welcome but burdensome; and if she does live in sin, she fears her husband's coming. (Of such are they who fear the coming of the day of judgment.) Suppose the other to love her husband, to own her duty to him in pure embraces, never admitting a stain of infidelity upon her thoughts. This one will long for her husband's presence; yet there will be fear in her no less than in the other. How are the two fears to be distinguished? You may put the same question to both of them: "Do you fear for your husband?" Both will answer: "I do"—the same words, but with a different meaning: for if you go on to ask "Why?", the one will say: "I am afraid of his coming," and the other: "I am afraid of his going away." One says: "I fear to be found guilty," the other: "I fear to be left alone." Now apply this to the mind of the Christian, and you will find the fear that charity casts out, and the other pure fear that endures for ever and ever.

7. Let us then address ourselves first to those who fear God with the fear of the woman who finds pleasure in wickedness, fearing her husband's judgment on her guilt. "Soul," we will say, "thou that fearest God for his judgment, as the woman who finds pleasure in wickedness fears her husband: if such a woman be misliking to thee, mislike thyself. Would you have your own wife fear you for that reason? Would you not rather she were chaste for love of you and not for fear? Then show yourself to God as you would that your wife should be to you. Pray God to look upon you, and turn his face from your sins. There is only one way of deserving that God's face be turned from your sins, and that is never to turn your own face from them. You have the very words in the Psalm: "For I confess my

wickedness, and my sin is ever before me."[10] Do you make confession, and God will pardon.

8. Such is our address to that soul in which is still the fear that does not endure for ever and ever, but is shut out and banished by charity. Let us speak now to that other soul which possesses already the pure fear, enduring for ever and ever. Can we suppose that this soul is to be found and addressed? Is there such, do you think, among our people? In this church? In this whole earth? Such there must be, though unseen. It is winter, but within there is freshness and vigour at the root. Maybe our words will reach that soul's ears; but wherever it be, I would fain come upon it, and rather than have it listen to me, lend it my own ears. It should teach me rather than learn of me. A holy soul, all aflame with longing for God's kingdom, it shall hear not me but God himself speaking to it, and comforting its patient sojourn on this earth with words like these: "Already thou wouldest I should come, and I know that thou wouldest it: I know what thou art, that thou mayest await my coming with confidence. I know that the waiting is irksome to thee: yet wait the rather, and be patient; I come, and I come quickly." Yet to the lover it seems slow. You may hear that soul's yearning song, like a lily among the thorns—hear her sighs: "I will make music with understanding in the unspotted way: when wilt thou come unto me?"[11] But in the unspotted way there is no need for fearing; because perfect charity casteth out fear. Yet even when she has reached the embrace of her beloved, she will fear, though without anxiety. She will take heed and watch against her iniquity, lest she fall again into sin: fearing, not to be cast into hell fire, but to be left by him alone. So there will be in her the "pure fear that endureth for ever and ever."

Such is the music, the harmonious music, of our two flutes. Both tell of a kind of fear; but one tells of the soul's fear of judgment, the other of the soul's fear of desertion. One is the fear which charity excludes; the other is the fear that endures for ever and ever.

9. "We are to love, because he first loved us." How indeed should we love, had he not first loved us? Through loving we have become friends; but it was as enemies that he loved us, in order that we might be made friends. He first loved us, and bestowed on us the power to love him. As yet we loved him not: through loving we are made fair. An ugly and misshapen man may love a beautiful woman, or an ugly and misshapen woman

[10] Ps. 51:3. [11] Ps. 101:1 f.

of dull complexion may love a handsome man; but love can make beautiful neither the man nor the woman. The man loves a fair woman and when he looks on himself in the glass, he is ashamed to raise his face to the beauty of her whom he loves. He can do nothing to make himself beautiful: if he waits for beauty to come to him, waiting will make him old and his face plainer. There is nothing he can do, no advice you can give him but to restrain his passion and venture no more to set his love upon an unequal match: if he loves and would marry a wife, he must desire modesty in her and not physical charm. But our soul, my brethren, is ugly through its iniquity: through loving God it is made fair. What manner of love is this, that transforms the lover into beauty! God is ever beautiful, never ugly, never changing. He that is ever beautiful, he first loved us—and loved none that were not ugly and misshapen. Yet the end of his love was not to leave us ugly, but to transform us, creating beauty in place of deformity. And how shall we win this beauty, but through loving him who is ever beautiful? Beauty grows in you with the growth of love; for charity itself is the soul's beauty. "We are to love, because he first loved us."

10. "If any man say, I love God" . . . Ask anyone you will to tell you if he loves God: he will make loud profession, "I do love God, God knows it!" But there is another matter on which he may be questioned. "If any man says, I love God, and hateth his brother, he is a liar." Why is he a liar? Because "he that loves not his brother whom he sees, how can he love God whom he sees not?" Does it then follow that he who loves his brother loves God also? Of necessity he must love God: of necessity he must love love itself. He cannot love his brother and not love love: he cannot help loving love. And if he loves love, he needs must love God: in loving love, he is loving God.[11a] You cannot have forgotten the words that came a little earlier: "God is love." If God is love, whoever loves love, loves God. Therefore love your brother, and have no other care. You cannot say, I love my brother, but not God. Just as to say, "I love God," when you do not love your brother, is to lie; so when you say, "I love my brother," you are deceived, if you imagine that you do not love God. You love your brother, and must needs love love itself; but love is God; therefore whoever loves his brother must needs be loving God.

If you do not love the brother whom you see, how can you love God whom you do not see? Why does a man not see God?

[11a] Cf. the same argument in *De Trin.*, VIII. 10 (vii) ff.

Because he has not love. He has not love because he does not love his brother; and it follows that the reason for his not seeing God is that he has not love. If he had love, he must see God; for God is love. By love the heart's eye must continually be cleansed and strengthened for the sight of that changeless Being, in whose presence the lover may ever delight, and enjoy it in the society of angels unto all eternity. But now he must run his course, so that one day he may rejoice in his true fatherland. He may not love his pilgrimage or the way along it. Nothing may be sweet to him save the God who calls us, until the day that we cleave fast to him, saying with the psalmist: "Thou hast destroyed all them that commit fornication against thee." [12] The fornicators against him are they that turn aside and love the world. Your part is told you in the verse that follows: "for me it is good to cleave fast unto God." That is my whole good, to cleave unto God, looking for nought else. If you ask, "Why cleave to God?", and a man should say "For that which he will give me," ask him again what God will give him. God made the heaven, God made the earth: what is there for him to give you? If already you cleave fast to him, what better thing can you find? If you could, he would give it.

11. "He that loves not his brother whom he sees, how can he love God whom he sees not? And this commandment we have from him, that he who loves God, love his brother also." Proudly you spoke the word, "I love God"—and you hate your brother! Murderer that you are, how can you love God? Did you not hear earlier in the Epistle, that "he that hateth his brother is a murderer"? "Indeed, indeed," you say, "I love God, though I hate my brother." Indeed, indeed, if you hate your brother you do not love God. Let me prove it by another text: again we read that "He gave us a commandment that we should love one another." [13] Can you love him whose commandment you hate? Can anyone say, "I love the emperor, but I hate his laws"? It is by the observation of his laws, published through his empire, that the emperor is aware of your love for him. Our emperor's law is this: "A new commandment give I unto you, that ye love one another." [14] You say you love Christ: then keep his commandment and love your brother. If you do not love your brother, how can you love him whose commandment you despise?

My brothers, I can never tire of speaking in Christ's name of charity. The more you covet possession of it, the more (I hope)

12 Ps. 73 : 27 f.   13 I John 3 : 23.   14 John 13 : 34.

will charity itself grow within you, casting out fear, so that there remain the pure fear that endures for ever and ever. Let us bear this world, bear all its afflictions, bear the offences of our temptations. Let us never go back on our journeying; let us hold to the Church's unity, hold to Christ, hold to charity. Let us not be sundered from the members of his Bride, nor sundered from the faith, that we may make our boast in his presence; and so we shall abide safe in him—in this present time by faith, and in the time to come by sight, whereof in the gift of the Holy Spirit we have so sure a pledge.

TENTH HOMILY

I John 5:1-3

1. Those of you who were present yesterday will remember, no doubt, the place our exposition has reached in the course of this Epistle. "He that loveth not his brother whom he sees, how can he love God whom he does not see? And this commandment we have from him, that he who loves God, love his brother also." That was the verse at which we ended: now let us see what comes next.

"Every one that believeth that Jesus is the Christ, is born of God." Who is the man that does not believe that Jesus is the Christ? He that does not live as Christ commanded. There are many that say, "I believe"; but faith without works cannot save. The work of faith is love, according to the apostle Paul's saying: "Faith which worketh through love." [1] That is the faith that Jesus is the Christ, as it is believed by Christians who are such not in name only but in deed and in life. It is not as the devils believe: they believe, as Scripture says, and tremble. [2] One might suppose that devils' faith could go no further than the confession: "We know who thou art, the Son of God." [3] What the devils said was what Peter said. When the Lord asked who he was and what men called him, the disciples answered: "Some call thee John the Baptist, others Elias, others Jeremias or one of the prophets." [4] And when he asked again: "And whom say ye that I am?"—Peter answered and said: "Thou art the Christ, the Son of the living God." Then came the Lord's saying to him: "Blessed art thou, Simon Bar-Jona; for flesh and blood hath not revealed it unto thee, but my Father which is in heaven." See what commendation is given to this faith of Peter's: "Thou art

[1] Gal. 5:26. [2] James 2:19.
[3] Matt. 8:19. [4] Matt. 16:13 ff.

339

Peter, and upon this rock will I build my church." "Upon this rock" means "Upon this faith," [5] upon the saying: "Thou art the Christ, the Son of the living God." "Upon this rock," says the Lord, "I will build my church." A high commendation indeed! Thus Peter says: "Thou art the Christ, the Son of the living God"; and the devils say: "We know who thou art, the Son of God, the Holy One of God." What Peter says, the devils say also: the words are the same, but not the thought. Peter's words, we may be sure, were spoken with love; for love goes with the Christian's faith, but not with the devils'. For Peter's words were meant to embrace the Christ, the devils' were meant to make him depart from them. For before saying, "We know who thou art, thou art the Son of God," they had said: "What have we to do with thee? Why art thou come before the time to destroy us?" It is one thing to confess Christ in order that you may hold to him: another thing to confess Christ in order that you may thrust him from you. You see then that the words of our text, "He that believeth," denote a faith of a special kind, not the faith that may be held by many. Therefore, my brothers, let no heretic say to you, "We also believe." I have given you the example of the devils, that you may examine the deeds of men's lives before rejoicing at the words of their belief.

2. Let us see then what is meant by belief in Christ, by belief that Jesus is the Christ. Our text goes on: "Every one that believeth that Jesus is the Christ, is born of God." But what does this belief mean? "And every one that loveth him that begat him, loveth him that is begotten of him." With faith the apostle straightway conjoins love; for without love faith is vain. The Christian's faith has love together with it: the devils' faith is loveless. Those who do not believe at all are in worse state than the devils, falling behind them in apprehension. The man who will not believe in Christ has not come so far as to do what the devils do. He may reach the point of believing, yet still hate him in whom he believes: the confession of his faith being through fear of punishment, not love for the offered prize; and now he is like the devils who dreaded the punishment in store for them. To such faith love must be added, so that it becomes the faith that Paul describes, the "faith that worketh through love"; and then you will have the Christian, the citizen of

[5] In *Retr.*, I, 21, Augustine refers to two other interpretations of the text which he has given: one, that the "rock" is Peter, another that the "rock" is Christ. Between these two, he invites the reader to choose which he thinks the "more probable."

Jerusalem and fellow-citizen of angels, the pilgrim toiling eagerly on his way. Join him, for he is your good comrade, travel with him—if only you be what he is.

3. "Every one that loveth him that begat him, loveth him that is begotten of him. Hereby we know that we love the sons of God." What does this mean, my brothers? The apostle has just spoken of the Son of God, not of sons: the one Christ was set forth for our contemplation in the words, "Every one that believeth that Jesus is the Christ is born of God; and every one that loveth him that begat"—that is, the Father—"loveth him that is begotten of him"—that is, his Son our Lord Jesus Christ. And he goes on: "hereby we know that we love the sons of God." We should have expected: "Hereby we know that we love the Son of God." But John, having just spoken of the Son of God, now speaks of God's sons. It is because the sons of God are the Body of God's only Son; because he is Head, and we are members, the Son of God is still one. Therefore to love the sons of God is to love the Son of God; to love the Son of God is to love the Father; none can love the Father unless he love the Son; and he that loves the Son, loves also the sons of God. These sons of God are the members of God's Son; and he that loves them, by loving becomes himself a member: through love he becomes a part of the structure of Christ's Body. And thus the end will be the one Christ, loving himself; for the love of the members for one another is the love of the Body for itself.[6] "If one member suffer, all the members suffer with it; and if one member have glorying, all the members rejoice with it."[7] On which the apostle concludes: "Now ye are the body of Christ, and members of him." So John, speaking a little earlier of brotherly love, has said: "He that loveth not his brother whom he sees, how can he love God whom he sees not?" If you love your brother, can it be said that you do so and yet do not love Christ? Impossible—when it is Christ's members that you love. Loving the members of Christ, you are loving Christ; loving Christ, you are loving the Son of God; loving the Son of God, you are loving the Father. There can be no separation of love: you may choose for yourself what you will love, and all the rest will follow. You may say, "I love God only, God the Father." That is not true. If you love him, you cannot love him only: if you love the Father, you are

6 This celebrated passage is the crown of Augustine's doctrine of the unity of Christ and his Church.

7 I Cor. 12:26 f.

loving the Son also. Suppose you grant that, and say, "I love the Father and I love the Son, but nothing more: God the Father, and God the Son, our Lord Jesus Christ, who has ascended into heaven and sits on the right hand of the Father, the Word through whom all things were made, the Word that was made flesh and dwelt among us: I love nothing more." That is not true. If you love the Head, you love the members: if you do not love the members, neither do you love the Head. How can you not tremble at the voice of the Head, crying from heaven on the members' behalf: "Saul, Saul, why persecutest thou me"?[8] The persecutor of his members he called the persecutor of himself: that was to call the lover of his members the lover of himself. And who are his members, my brethren, you know—they are none other than the Church of God.

"Hereby we know that we love the sons of God, because we love God." How so? Are not the sons of God a different thing from God? Yes, but he who loves God, loves his commandments; and what are they? "A new commandment give I unto you, that ye love one another." None may make one love an excuse from another. Christian love is altogether of one piece, and as itself is compacted into a unity, so it makes into one all that are linked to it, like a flame fusing them together. The lump of gold is fused in the furnace, and a single object is made of it; but unless the fire of charity is kindled, there can be no fusing of the many into one.

4. We are told, then, how we may know that we love the sons of God. It is "because we love God, and keep his commandments." We are troubled and wearied by the difficulty of keeping God's commandment. But listen! Friend, you go through toil and labour, for the love of what? Of avarice. That love must bring toil to the lover: there is no toil in the love of God. Avarice will enjoin upon you the endurance of labours, dangers, wear and tear and troubles; and you will obey, but to what purpose? To gain the wherewithal to fill your purse, and to lose your peace of mind. Peace of mind, I dare say, you had more before you were rich than after you began to be wealthy. See what avarice has charged you with: a houseful of goods, and the fear of thieves; gain of money, and loss of sleep. There is what avarice bade you do, and you have done it. And what is God's charge? "Love me! You may love money and go after it, yet maybe not find it. Whoever seeks me, I am with him. You may love place and position: maybe you will never attain to

8 Acts 9:4.

them. No man has ever loved me and failed of my attaining. You would have a patron or a powerful friend, and you must go about to approach him by way of some inferior. Love me (God says to you); I have not to be approached through any go-between: love itself sets you in my presence." My brothers, there can be no sweetness greater than such love. Much to the point are the words of the Psalm you have just heard: "The unrighteous have spoken to me of delights; but not as thy law, O Lord."[9] The law of God is God's commandment, and God's commandment is that new commandment, called new because it gives renewal: "A new commandment give I unto you, that ye love one another." That this is indeed the law of God is confirmed by the apostle's saying: "Bear ye one another's burdens, and so shall ye fulfil the law of Christ."[10] That is the consummation of all our works—love. There is the end, for which and unto which we run our course: when we reach it we shall have rest.

7. "For this is the love of God, that we keep his commandments." You have heard the saying: "On these two commandments hang all the law and the prophets."[11]—You are spared the turning from one Scripture page to another. "On these two commandments": and they are: "Thou shalt love the Lord thy God with all thy heart and all thy soul and all thy mind," and "Thou shalt love thy neighbour as thyself." These are the commandments of which the whole of our Epistle speaks. Hold fast then to love, and set your minds at rest. You need not fear doing ill to anyone; for who can do any ill to the person whom he loves? Love, and you cannot but do well. You may rebuke, but that will be the act of love, not of harshness: you may use the rod, but it will only be for discipline; for the love of love itself will not suffer you to pass over the lack of discipline in another. Sometimes there is a kind of contrariness apparent in the products of hatred and of love: hatred may use fair words and love may sound harshly. A man may hate his enemy, and pretend friendship towards him: he may commend him when he sees him do wrong; for he welcomes his thoughtlessness, he is glad to see him rush headlong in pursuit of his desires, where he may fall beyond hope of recovery. He will, in the words of the Psalm, "commend the sinner in the desires of his soul";[12] he will smooth his going with the oil of flattery—hating, yet commending. Another, seeing his friend do the like, will call him

9 Ps. 119:85.   10 Gal. 6:2.
11 Matt. 22:37 ff.   12 Ps. 10:3.

back; and if the friend will not hear, he may use the language of
reproof, he may denounce, he may even prosecute; for sometimes
things may come to the point where there is no avoiding an
action at law.[13] Thus we may see hatred speaking softly, and
charity prosecuting; but neither soft speeches nor harsh re-
proofs are what you have to consider. Look for the spring,
search out the root from which they proceed. The fair words of
the one are designed for deceiving, the prosecution of the other
is aimed at reformation.

My brothers, it is not for my preaching to work the enlargement of your hearts. Ask God that you may love one another,
and he will grant it. You are to love all men, even your enemies
—not because they *are* your brothers, but in order that they may
be; so that brotherly love may ever burn within you, whether
for him who is already a brother, or for your enemy, that love
may turn him into one. Wherever you love a brother, you love
a friend. Perhaps he stands already with you, linked to you
already in the catholic unity of the Church: if his life accords
with it, he whom you love is already a brother and not an
enemy. Or if your love is given to one who has not yet believed
in Christ, or who has believed only as the devils believe, you
will reprove his folly: you will love him, and with a brotherly
love, for though he is not yet a brother, the aim of your love is
that he may be made one. Thus all our brotherly love is love
for Christian people, for all the members of Christ. The learning
of charity, my brothers, its vigour, its flowers, its fruit, its
beauty, its pleasantness, its sustenance, its drink, its food, its
loving embraces—all these can never cloy. And if God grants
us such delights upon our pilgrimage, what joys await us in our
homeland!

8. So, my brothers, let us make haste: let us make haste, and
love the Christ. That Christ is Jesus; and who is he? The Word
of God. The manner of his coming to our sick world is that "the
word was made flesh, and dwelt among us."[14] Thus has the
prophecy of Scripture been fulfilled: "it behoved Christ to
suffer, and to rise again the third day from the dead."[15] Where
is the place of his Body? Where do his members carry on their
labouring? and where must you be, to have over you the Head?
". . . and that repentance and remission of sins should be
preached in his name throughout all nations, beginning at
Jerusalem." There must your charity spread itself abroad. The

[13] Augustine has the Donatists in mind: see Introduction, p. 256 f.
[14] John 1:14.   [15] Luke 24:46 f.

word of Christ, the word of the Psalm, that is, of God's Spirit, proclaims: "Thy commandment is exceeding broad." And there are men who set the boundary of charity in Africa![16] If you would love Christ, stretch out your charity over all the world: for Christ's members are spread the world over. If your love is for a part only, you are sundered: if sundered, you are not in the Body: if not in the Body, you are not under the Head. There is no profit in the faith of a blasphemer: you would worship him in the Head and you blaspheme him in the Body. He loves his Body: you may sever yourself from the Body of Christ, but the Head cannot be severed from his own Body. "In vain do you honour me," cries the Head from above you, "in vain do you honour me." Imagine one that would kiss your head and trample on your feet—crushing your feet with nailed boots, yet seeking to embrace your head and kiss it. Would you not break through the speech of pretended honour with the cry, "What are you about, sir? You are trampling on me!" You would not say, "You trample on my head," for honour was being done to your head; but that head would make protest more for the trampled members, than acknowledge the honour done to itself. Would not the head itself cry out, "I want none of your honouring! cease to trample on me!" You may answer if you will, "Where is the trampling?": you may tell the head you sought to kiss it, to embrace it. But have you not sense to see that what you seek to embrace is all of a piece in structural unity with that on which you trample? You honour me above, you trample me below! and the pain of this exceeds the pleasure of that, for the honoured head suffers for the trampled feet. The tongue will exclaim, "That hurts me!"—not "That hurts my foot," but "That hurts me." No use to ask the tongue who touched it, who struck it, pricked it or stabbed it. The answer is, No one: but it is linked to those parts that suffer trampling, and how should it not suffer pain, when there is no separation between it and them?

9. Our Lord Jesus Christ, at his ascension into heaven on the fortieth day, commended his body to lie on the earth where he had worn it; and he did so, because he saw that many would pay him honour for his ascension, and that their honouring must be vain if they tread under foot his members upon earth. And to forestall the misprision of worshipping the Head in heaven while trampling the feet upon earth, he declared where his members should be found. Before his ascension he spoke his

[16] Donatists.

last words—the last he was to speak on earth. The Head, ready to ascend into heaven, commended his members upon earth, and then departed. From that time you will not find Christ speaking on earth: he will speak indeed, but it will be from heaven. And then, what will be the cause of his so speaking? It will be because his members were being trod down upon earth. To Saul the persecutor he spoke from on high: "Saul, Saul, why persecutest thou me?"[17] "I have ascended into heaven, but still I lie upon earth. Here I sit on the Father's right hand; but there still I hunger and thirst, and go a stranger."—In what way, then, did he before ascending commend his Body to us? When the disciples asked him: "Lord, wilt thou show thyself at this time, and when shall be the kingdom of Israel?",[18] he answered, on the point of his departure: "It is not yours to know the time which the Father hath set in his own power; but ye shall receive the virtue of the Holy Spirit, coming down upon you, and ye shall be my witnesses" . . . (see now the spreading abroad of his Body, the region wherein he will not have men trample on him) . . . "ye shall be my witnesses in Jerusalem, and into all Judaea, and Samaria, and to the ends of the whole earth:"—"This is where I who now ascend shall yet lie. I ascend because I am the Head: my Body yet lies here below. And where? Even through the whole earth."—Take heed, then, lest you strike that Body, lest you do despite to it, lest you trample upon it: for those are Christ's last words on the eve of his going into heaven. Have in your mind's eye a sick man, lying at home in his bed, wasted with illness, near to death, breathing hard, his soul at his very lips. Suppose it chances that the thought of something dear to him, greatly beloved, comes into his mind; and he calls for his heirs and says to them: "Do this, I pray you." He struggles to keep the soul within him until those words are clearly spoken and confirmed; and when he has so spoken his last, he breathes away his life, and his body is borne to the grave. Will not his heirs hold fast the memory of the dying man's last words? If any man should come and say to them, "Don't do it!"—what will they answer? "Not do that which my father charged me with his last breath—the thing that last sounded in my ears as my father left this world? However it be with any other words of his, those last words bind me in a special degree; for after them I never saw him or heard him speak again."

My brothers, think, as you have Christian hearts: if the words of a man on his way to the grave are so sweet, so welcome, of

[17] Acts 9:4.   [18] Acts 1:6 ff.

such weighty moment, to his heirs, what must be to the heirs of Christ the last words of him who was leaving them, not to return to the grave but to ascend into heaven! For the man who has lived and died, his soul is carried elsewhere while his body is laid in the earth: it matters not to him whether those last words of his are performed or not; quite other now are his doings, or his sufferings. Either he rejoices in Abraham's bosom, or in eternal fire he longs for a drop of water; and his dead body lies unfeeling in the grave. Yet his last dying words are faithfully observed. For what then can men look, who pay no observance to the last words of him who sits in heaven, looking from above to see whether they be contemned, or not contemned—the words of him who said: "Saul, Saul, why persecutest thou me?", who lays up for judgment all that he sees his members suffer?

10. And yet such men say, "What have we done? It is we who have suffered persecution, not inflicted it."[19] Unhappy men, you are the persecutors—persecutors above all because you have divided the Church! The sword of the tongue is more powerful than any blade of steel. Hagar, Sarah's maid, was proud; and because of her pride she was afflicted by her mistress. That was discipline, not punishment. And so when she had gone away from her mistress, what did the angel bid her? "Return unto thy mistress."[20] Even so you, carnal souls like that proud maid-servant, have no cause for your fury, though you may for discipline's sake have suffered some vexation. Return to your mistress, keep the Lord's peace. The Gospels are set out, we read of where the Church extends: you argue against us and call us "betrayers."[21] What then have we betrayed? Christ commends to you his Church, and you will not believe him: am I to believe your maligning of my forefathers? If you would have me believe your story of "betrayers," do you first believe the Christ. Which is the chiefer authority? Christ is God, you are men: which most deserves belief? Christ has spread his Church over the whole world: if it were I that said so, you might disregard it; but when the Gospel speaks, you should take heed. And what says the Gospel? "It behoved Christ to suffer and rise again the third day from the dead, and that repentance and forgiveness of sins should be preached in his name."[22] Where there is forgiveness of sins, there is the

---

19 See Introduction, p. 256.   20 Gen. 16:4ff.
21 The Donatist charge against the Catholics as all tainted with *traditio*, the surrendering of the Scriptures.
22 Luke 24:47.

Church. If you ask why, it was to the Church that the word was spoken: "I will give unto thee the keys of the kingdom of heaven; and whatsoever thou shalt loose on earth shall be loosed in heaven, and whatsoever thou shalt loose on earth shall be loosed in heaven, and whatsoever thou shalt bind on earth shall be bound in heaven." [23] Where then is this forgiveness of sins extended? "Throughout all nations, beginning at Jerusalem." There is Christ's word for you to believe. But you know well that if you believed Christ, you could have nothing to say about the "betrayers"; and so you would have me believe your slanderings of my fathers rather than yourself believe the promises of Christ. [24]

[23] Matt. 16:19.   [24] Here the *Homilies* end in all surviving MSS.

SELECT BIBLIOGRAPHY

A. *Histories*

Duchesne, L., *Histoire ancienne de l'Église*. Paris, Vol. II (4th ed.), 1910; Vol. III (5th ed.), 1928. (English Translation: London, John Murray, 1912, 1914.)

Fliche, A., and Martin, V., *Histoire de l'Église depuis les origines jusqu'à nos jours*. Paris, Vol. III, 1947; Vol. IV, 1948. (English Translation: London, Burns Oates, 1951-.)

Harnack, A., *Lehrbuch der Dogmengeschichte*. Tübingen, Vol. III (4th ed.), 1910. (English Translation: London, Williams and Norgate, Vol. V, 1898.)

Kidd, B. J., *A History of the Church to A.D. 461*. Oxford, Vols. II and III, 1922.

Monceaux, P., *Histoire Littéraire de l'Afrique chrétienne depuis les origines jusqu'à l'invasion arabe*. Paris, Vols. IV–VII, 1912–1923.

Tixeront, J., *Histoire des Dogmes*. Paris, Vol. II (9th ed.), 1931. (English Translation: B. Herder Book Co., U.S.A., 1930.)

B. *General*

Bardy, G., *Saint Augustin: l'homme et l'œuvre*. Paris (6th ed.), 1946.

Burnaby, J., *Amor Dei: a study of the religion of St. Augustine*. London, Hodder and Stoughton, 1938. Reprinted 1947.

Cayré, F., *Les Sources de l'Amour Divin: la divine présence d'après Saint Augustin*. Paris, 1933.

Cochrane, C. N., *Christianity and Classical Culture: a study of thought and action from Augustus to Augustine*. Oxford, 1940.

Gilson, E., *Introduction à l'étude de Saint Augustin*. Paris, 1929.

Loofs, F., art. "Augustinus," in *Realencyclopädie für protestantische Theologie und Kirche*. Leipzig, 1896.

Marrou, H. I., *Saint Augustin et la Fin de la Culture antique*. Paris, 1938; "Retractation," 1949.

A Monument to Saint Augustine—by various writers. London, Sheed & Ward, 1934.

349

350 AUGUSTINE: LATER WORKS

Pope, H., *Saint Augustine of Hippo*. London, Sands, 1937.
Portalié, E., art. "Saint Augustin," in *Dictionnaire de Theologie Catholique*. Paris, 1909.

C. *De Trinitate*

Barion, J., *Plotin und Augustinus: Untersuchungen zum Gottes-problem*. Berlin, 1935.
Cayré, F., *La Contemplation Augustinienne: principes de la Spiritualité de Saint Augustin*. Paris, 1927.
Chevalier, I., *Saint Augustin et la Pensée Grecque: les relations Trinitaires. La Théorie Augustinienne des relations Trinitaires*. Collectanea Friburgensia. Fribourg, 1940.
Dahl, A., *Augustin und Plotin: philosophische Untersuchungen zum Trinitätsproblem und zur Nuslehre*. Lund, 1945.
Gardeil, A., *La Structure de l'Âme et l'Expérience Mystique*. 2 vols. Paris, 1927.
Grabmann, M., *Die Grundgedanken des hl. Augustinus über Seele und Gott*. Köln, 1929.
Hodgson, L., *The Doctrine of the Trinity*. London, Nisbet, 1943.
Morgan, W., *The Psychological Teaching of St. Augustine*. London, Elliot Stock (n.d.).
Schmaus, M., *Die Psychologische Trinitätslehre des hl. Augustinus*. Münster, 1927.
St. Thomas Aquinas. *Summa Theologica*, I, qq. xxvii–xliii, xciii. (English Translation by Fathers of the English Dominican Province: London, Washbourne, 1911–.)
Webb, C. C. J., *God and Personality*. London, Allen & Unwin, 1918.

D. *De Spiritu et Littera*

de Plinval, G., *Pélage, ses Écrits, sa Vie, et sa Réforme*. Lausanne, 1943.
Dinkler, E., *Die Anthropologie Augustins*. Stuttgart, 1934.
Jonas, H., *Augustin und das Paulinische Freiheits-problem*. Göttingen, 1930.
Mausbach, J., *Die Ethik des hl. Augustinus*. Freiburg-im-Breisgau, Vol. II, 1929.
Oman, J., *Grace and Personality*. Cambridge (3rd ed.), 1925.
Rondet, H., *Gratia Christi: essai d'histoire du dogme et de théologie dogmatique*. Paris, 1948.
St. Thomas Aquinas. *Summa Theologica*, Ia IIae, qq. cvi–cxiv.
Whitley, W. T. (ed.), *The Doctrine of Grace*. London, S.C.M. Press, 1932.
Williams, N. P., *The Grace of God*. London, Longmans, 1930.

E. *Tractatus in Epistolam Johannis Decem*

Batiffol, P., *La Catholicisme de Saint Augustin*. Paris, 1920.
Combès, G., *La Charité d'après Saint Augustin*. Paris, 1934.

Frend, W. H. C., *The Donatist Church.* Oxford, 1952.

Greenslade, S. L., *Schism in the Early Church.* London, S.C.M. Press, 1953.

Hofmann, F., *Der Kirchenbegriff des hl. Augustinus.* München, 1933.

Le Landais, M., *Études Augustiniennes.* Paris, 1953.

Pontet, M., *L'Exégèse de Saint Augustin Prédicateur.* Paris, 1944.

Sparrow-Simpson, W. J., *Saint Augustine and African Church Divisions.* London, Longmans, 1910.

St. Thomas Aquinas. *Summa Theologica*, IIa IIae, qq. xxiii–xxxiii.

Willis, G. G., *Saint Augustine and the Donatist Controversy.* London, S.P.C.K., 1950.

INDEXES

GENERAL INDEX

Academy, the New, 124, 149 f.
Action and contemplation, 29, 93
Adam and Eve, 93 f.
Alexandria, 17, 48, 64, 100n
Allegory, 142 f., 198
Alypius, 288n
Ambrose, Bishop of Milan, 19, 184, 198n
Animus and *anima*, 128
Antichrist, meaning of, 279 ff.
"Appropriation," in Trinitarian doctrine, 159 f.
Aquinas, Thomas, 27 f.
Arianism, 17 f., 21, 166n, 176n
Aristotle, 27, 60n, 82n
Arles, Council of, 252, 254 f.
Athanasius, Bishop of Alexandria, 19, 166n, 167n, 176n
Augustine, references to other works of:
Contra Academicos, 150n
De Civitate Dei, 25, 66n, 86n, 231n, 232n
Confessiones, 24, 41n, 88n, 110n, 149n, 212n, 287n
De Decretis, 176n
De Diversis Quaestionibus LXXXIII, 276n
De Diversis Quaestionibus ad Simplicianum, 190
De Doctrina Christiana, 66n, 276n
Enchiridion de fide, spe, et caritate, 40n, 118n, 174n, 242n
Epistolae, 15, 288n
De Gestis Pelagii, 191
De Gratia Christi, 191
De Gratia et Libero Arbitrio, 192
In Joannis Evangelium Tractatus, 158n, 176n
De Libero Arbitrio, 86n
Contra Litteras Petiliani, 265n

Contra Maximinum Arium, 158n
De Natura et Gratia, 183, 190
De Peccatorum Meritis et Remissione, 186 f., 246n
De Peccato Originali, 186n
De Praedestinatione Sanctorum, 212n
Retractationes, 24 f., 150n, 192, 340n
Sermones, 288n
Soliloquia, 80n
De Vera Religione, 24, 86n
Aurelius, Bishop of Carthage, 13, 26

Baptism, as "enlightenment," 292; of infants, 183 ff., 293; validity of, 254
Biblical texts, Augustine's, 14

Caecilian, Bishop of Carthage, 251, 254
Caelestius, the Pelagian, 14, 185, 189
Cain and Abel, 299
Cappadocian Fathers, 18, 22, 32, 166n
Carthage, 48, 64 f.; Conference of, 251, 253; Council of, 232n
Changelessness, of God, 21
Charity, 35; "of God," 241; greatest of treasures, 317 f.; only mark of true Christian, 298, 315; perfection of, 296 f., 300 f.; and schism, 256; test of true faith, 310 ff.; and the Trinity, 33, 52, 54, 157 ff; welcomes demands, 329
Child observation, 104
Christ, and his Church, unity of, 261, 341; as *Magister interior*, 285; his Temptation, 277
Christology, 100n
Church, the Body of Christ, 163n, 341 f., 346; universality of, 266, 268 f., 271 f., 282, 344 ff.
Cicero, 49n, 80n, 99n, 110 f., 112, 124

353

BIBLICAL REFERENCES